To Anyone
Who Ever Asks

To Anyone
Who Ever Asks

THE LIFE, MUSIC, AND MYSTERY OF
CONNIE CONVERSE

Howard Fishman

DUTTON

DUTTON

An imprint of Penguin Random House LLC
penguinrandomhouse.com

LIBRARY OF CONGRESS CATALOGING-IN-PUBLICATION DATA
has been applied for.

ISBN 9780593187364 (hardcover)
ISBN 9780593187388 (ebook)

Printed in the United States of America
1st Printing

BOOK DESIGN BY LAURA K. CORLESS

For the ones who ask

CONTENTS

CODA

Walking in the Crystal Air

I am more or less pretty much entirely by myself, there being no one else here.

—Connie Converse[1]

A Star Has Burnt My Eye

It's not what happens to you,
it's how you *think* of it.

—CONNIE CONVERSE[1]

CHAPTER 1

Past All Dreaming

In December 2010, I was at a friend's holiday party. I didn't know many of the people there, and to ease my social anxiety, I was scanning the spines on the bookshelves when a song came up on the house speakers—one that sounded both entirely new to me and as familiar as my own skin. A woman was singing in a plaintive tone about "a place they call Lonesome," where she hears the voice of her absent love speaking to her in "everything I see"—from a bird to a brook, "a pig or two," to a "sort of a squirrel thing."

Contextually, I couldn't place the song. It possessed the openhearted, melodic feel of an old Carter Family recording, but there was also some gentle acoustic guitar fingerpicking that reminded me of Elizabeth Cotten, and harmonic movement that seemed to echo the songs of Hoagy Carmichael. The traditional elements seemed so finely stitched together, with such a sophisticated sensibility, that the whole sounded absolutely original—modern, even. The song swallowed me. The party froze. The room disappeared.

Eventually, I sought out the host, who smiled knowingly when I asked him what we were listening to. "Oh," my friend said. "This is Connie Converse. She made these recordings in her kitchen in the 1950s, but she never found an audience for her music, and then one day she drove away and was never heard from again." The name of the song was "Talkin' Like You."

On my way home that night, I stopped at a local record store that no longer exists and picked up a copy of *How Sad, How Lovely,* the recently released album of Converse's sixty-year-old recordings. Before going to bed, I cued up "Talkin' Like You," and listened to it a second time, now without any distraction.

Again, I heard the bluesy, spooky introduction, sung over an unusual series of seventh and diminished chords—placing it decidedly on the refined side of the popular music spectrum. The combination of the mysterious melody and complex harmony drew me back in, as did the song's lyrics.

> *In between two tall mountains there's a place they call Lonesome*
> *Don't see why they call it Lonesome*
> *I'm never lonesome when I go there.*

I listened as Converse's lilting, rolling guitar accompaniment followed, as the singer once again began her tale:

> *See that bird sittin' on my windowsill?*
> *Well he's sayin' whipoorwill all the night through.*

Surely, this was a nod to the 1949 Hank Williams classic "I'm So Lonesome I Could Cry."[1]

Like the protagonist of Williams's song, the whippoorwill keeps the narrator of "Talkin' Like You" company when others will not.

> *See that brook runnin' by my kitchen door?*
> *Well it couldn't talk no more if it was you.*

The dispatch of her lover's comeuppance begins, and then does not stop until the song finishes. The object of her affection will not talk to her? No matter; the water outside her door will.

> *Up that tree there's sort of a squirrel thing*
> *Sounds just like we did when we were quarreling.*

And there it was again. In a poetic leap, the singer identifies the curious sound she hears in a nearby tree as coming from "sort of a squirrel thing"—and sounds far more like a millennial than a young woman writing in the early 1950s.

> *In the yard I keep a pig or two*
> *They drop in for dinner like you used to do.*

Her ongoing traffic with nature continues. She keeps pigs, who join her for meals, the way her beloved does not or will not. The imagery could not be plainer: This person is no better than a pig, and she is perfectly happy to entertain other piglike comers if this one will not satisfy her needs.

> *I don't stand in the need of company*
> *With everything I see talkin' like you.*
> *Up that tree there's sort of a squirrel thing*
> *Sounds just like we did when we were quarreling*

You may think you left me all alone
But I can hear you talk without a telephone
I don't stand in the need of company
With everything I see talkin' like you.

It is a bravura bit of songwriting, a lyric both empowering and entrancing. She doesn't need anyone—neither their sympathy, nor their pity. We all want to be like this, all the time: self-assured, witty, happy, reliant on nobody and no one. Free. Listening to this song, I found it hard not to be captivated by this person, to want her as a friend, to know her.

～

Yet, as the rest of the album played, as I took in songs like "Playboy of the Western World," "Father Neptune," and "One by One," the suspicions that had been vaguely floating in my consciousness began to harden into the only obvious conclusion: This "Connie Converse" character had to be a hoax, a gimmick. The songs were too fresh, too modern, too anachronistic to have been recorded in the 1950s. And even if they *had* been recorded back then, someone surely would have discovered this person well before now. Music geeks like me would know about her, certainly, but more to the point: She was *so* good that we would *all* know about her.

These recordings didn't sound like the music of a forgotten someone who was essentially doing a lesser-known version of what other people had gotten famous for—a Big Mama Thornton to Elvis Presley, an Eddie Lang to Django Reinhardt, a Barbecue Bob to Robert Johnson. As far as I knew, there was no one from the early 1950s on the other side of the Connie Converse equation, not remotely—not in the wide margins of the years that came before her and not in those that immediately followed. This music, if I were willing to suspend my disbelief, would exist out of time, out of music history altogether.

And the liner notes confirmed what my friend had told me: that Converse had literally vanished. Not like a J. D. Salinger, who retired from the public eye but then had continued writing in isolation. Not like a Terrence Malick or a Lee Bontecou or a Henry Roth—artists who stayed out of sight for decades before finally releasing new work. And not like a Captain Beefheart or a Su Tissue, musicians who'd walked away from their careers to do entirely other things. No. Like a Jimmy Hoffa. Like an Amelia Earhart. Gone.

Online searches revealed spare facts, including images of a woman who looked and dressed like one I might see in my Williamsburg, Brooklyn, neighborhood on any afternoon. The cat's-eye granny glasses, the shirtwaist dresses, the librarian hairstyle, the parlor guitar—it all smacked of a certain twee Brooklyn aesthetic that back then had already become a fad. *No, no,* I thought. *No way.*

～

During my twenties and thirties, working as an independent musician, I'd come to know more than I'd ever wanted to about self-promotion. I was now forty, and only too familiar with the cleverness required to hook people's attention—the spin, the reinvention, the PR stunts. I'd played that game. I knew the P. T. Barnum touch when I saw it.

"Connie Converse" was clearly some canny hipster who'd come up with a clever marketing campaign for her music. Someone who—when not in character—had cultivated impeccable vocal fry and was devoted to the films of Wes Anderson. Her long vintage dress was likely hiding a series of inexpensive flash tattoos. She'd devised a name with a nice classic ring to it, like "Lois Lane" or "Marjorie Morningstar"; created a noirish backstory about a disappearance; photoshopped some images of herself posing in thrift store attire to make them look like 1950s-era snapshots; and tried to pass off her own music as some kind of "lost" recordings made by this imaginary woman.

John Lurie had done something like this in 1999, with his album *The Legendary Marvin Pontiac: Greatest Hits,* which was supposed to be the posthumously released lost recordings of a troubled musical genius who'd spent the last decades of his life in an insane asylum—though the album was actually Lurie and his pals having a bit of fun. "Connie Converse" was a Marvin Pontiac. She was not real. These were not old recordings newly discovered. She did not mysteriously disappear one day. There was no such person. She was a fiction. I was certain of it.

~

To satisfy my curiosity, I googled some more. Sure enough, I could find no news reports of a disappearance, no YouTube footage of Connie Converse performing, no reviews or accounts of her concerts, nothing at all related to her music that was contemporaneous with the time she was said to have been making it. All I could see was a handful of recent blog posts and articles related to the release of *How Sad, How Lovely*—at which point the internet came to a dead stop.

Then, rereading the album's liner notes, I noted a detail I'd overlooked—that Converse had served a stint as editor for something called the *Journal of Conflict Resolution.* I went back online and, much to my chagrin, there it was: a 1968 essay called "The War of All Against All," written by Elizabeth Converse, the journal's managing editor.

Pause.

~

Could it be true? Was she actually real, and had she indeed written these songs—little earworms that sound like absolutely no one else—in virtual obscurity in the early 1950s, a time in American music often associated with the safe, inoffensive sounds of performers like Rosemary Clooney and Perry Como?

The more I listened to her music, the more my curiosity grew. I felt the need to know the rest of Converse's story, the details that had driven her to make this particular music, at that particular time (if, indeed, she had). What had led to her tragic fate, to her simply vanishing (if that's what actually happened to her). Who she was or, even, potentially, could still be.

And I found that my experience was not unique. From what I could see online, Converse had already begun to attract a cult of followers who were freaking out about her on social media and chat boards. Because so little about her was known, she seemed more myth than person, and as Greil Marcus wrote in *Mystery Train*, "History without myth is surely a wasteland; but myths are compelling only when they are at odds with history."[2] This certainly seemed to be the case with Converse, someone upon whom we could project our own personal narratives and agendas, and no one could argue. She'd already been taken up as a cause by outsiders of many stripes—each of whom claimed her as one of their own.

I fell prey to this same tendency, the Rorschach inkblots of her recordings revealing characteristics I felt I had in common with her, for better or worse: outsize artistic ambition; vulnerability that lay protected beneath a hard veneer of willful self-reliance; a love of language; a disdain for conformity; a refusal to compromise; a desire to be understood; insatiable longing. Without knowing anything about Connie Converse other than what I heard in her music, I began to care about her. Extravagantly.

Had Converse's songs other than "Talkin' Like You" been mediocre or worse, had that song been the only real keeper she'd written and recorded, her story still would have been a fascinating one in the annals of American music, albeit a minor one. A young woman writing and recording her own songs in the 1950s, a DIY singer-songwriter back before such terms existed, might have interested scholars and music historians in a footnote sort of way.

But what I heard as I played these recordings again and again was far greater than that. The visionary, forward-looking quality of what Converse had been up to seemed to suggest the need to update the narrative of mid-twentieth-century American song altogether.

CHAPTER 2

"One by One"

If Converse's musical catalogue, taken as a whole, is like some metaphorical message in a bottle cast off from the shores of a dull, homogenous time of which she wanted no part (and that wanted no part of her), her song "One by One" may be its unifying message. The lyrics are direct enough:

> *We go walking in the dark*
> *We go walking out at night*
> *And it's not as lovers go*
> *Two by two,*
> *To and fro,*
> *But it's one by one—*
> *One by one,*
> *In the dark.*
>
> *We go walking out at night*
> *As we wander through the grass*

We can hear each other pass
But we're far apart—
Far apart,
In the dark.

We go walking out at night,
With the grass so dark and tall
We are lost past recall
If the moon is down—
And the moon is down.

We are walking in the dark
If I had your hand in mine
I could shine
I could shine
Like the morning sun,
Like the sun.

Converse crystallizes in song the feeling of disconnectedness of mid-century urban America, a trend that has exponentially increased to this day as the dominance of smartphones and social media has made us seem more than ever a nation of zombies cut off from one another and from ourselves (though it's also arguable that we're more connected than ever, only in worse ways).

According to the *How Sad, How Lovely* liner notes, Converse had written and self-recorded her songs while living in New York City in the mid-1950s, at a time when new fissures in the bedrock of American culture and society were beginning to have devastating impacts, creating the anomie to which Converse was responding. Urban populations were exploding, middle-class families were moving to the suburbs, and children in smaller towns and rural areas were becoming the first generation in their families to go off to college. Communities were in flux. In places like Manhattan, it had become a commonplace experience for a single person to feel, and to be, alone amid millions of other human beings. Modernity, which was bringing about medical and scientific miracles at a rapid pace, also caused its share of collateral damage.

Converse was expressing in song what Edward Hopper and Mark Rothko were in painting,[1] what Flannery O'Connor and Ralph Ellison were in fiction, what O'Neill and Wilder were in drama, what Bergman and De Sica were in film, and what Aaron Copland and Morton Feldman were in classical music. Unlike any of them, however, Converse was working in a vacuum. Her chosen medium of the pop song form was not one generally associated with existentialism. Few other known artists at that time were engaging in such weighty emotional investigations in popular music (let alone "folk music," a term that, back then, would not have included composers of original music). The closest analogue for what Converse was doing, and how and when she was doing it, may have been Molly Drake, another woman working in complete obscurity whose own home recordings from that era would not be commercially released until a few years after Converse's were.[2]

To our modern sensibility, themes of alienation and disconnection explored in song, with acoustic guitar accompaniment, are almost tropes. Not so in Converse's day. From what I could tell, Converse—unknown and working in isolation—was trailblazing, boldly pioneering emotional territory untraversed by her more mainstream musical peers.[3]

What songs from that era, or before, inhabit the same psychological universe as Converse's "One by One"? The only other examples come from what were then the fringes of popular recorded music. Converse, in this sense, might be said to have come from the same world that produced the early blues and hillbilly artists like Riley Puckett, Skip James, and Alberta Hunter, but her songs are far more urbane, more musically and lyrically sophisticated. Though these figures were mostly regional artists and not part of the general consciousness of the day, it is clear from Converse's self-taught guitar playing, and from the melodic characteristics of her songs, that she had not only been exposed to that music but had also deeply immersed herself in it in a way that allowed her to mine its raw immediacy and put it to use. And she did so in a more inventive, forward-looking way than any of her peers.

What seemed to be evidence of Converse's wide-ranging curiosity and an independent, investigative tendency was also part of her charm and her mystery. She had to have had access to hard-to-find recordings, recordings that would have existed well outside the realm of popular taste.

⌢

The halting, gravitational music against which Converse sets her quiet tale, combined with the sensitivity of her performance, engulfs the listener. It stops time. There is no rhythm to the song, no swing, no sway. This is not music to sing along to, or tap a foot to, or embellish. It sounds to me like the precise moment when things go wrong, the second before the impact of a terrible crash—like watching someone about to be electrocuted, or footage of the planes hitting the towers.

At its most basic, literal level, the "we" in "One by One" may have had as its basis some romantic interest of Converse's, either real or longed for. But as I was just then hearing her music, just scratching against the veneer of her story, it was all "mays."

For me, the lack of any specificity about her life did not diminish the song's impact. Not at all. We've all known this yearning for another, this desolate, hand-wringing aloneness. And at its core, Converse's vision has to be understood as one that gets at the root of the modern human condition. We all walk alone. We're all in the dark, hearing one another pass by, unable to *really* know anyone else. There is sometimes no moon to light the way; there is sometimes no light at all. In Converse's dystopian tale, we sense one another's presence, we hear one another pass by, just as others sense and hear us, but we are alone, without hope, "past recall"— that is, unless we can somehow, in some way, manage to join our soul to another's.[4]

Play the recording ten times. On the first listen, it is a stoic, personal confession. Somewhere around the fifth or sixth play, it becomes a diagnosis of a spiritual malaise—hers and ours. By the tenth listen, the song's true nature becomes clear: It is an indictment. It is a lullaby to a disintegrating culture, a quiet surrender to the yawning, infinite void. The song is frightening, full of naked despair, a piece that has no parallel in any recording of the day that I am aware of and certainly in none of the music that was commercially popular at the time of its writing, in 1954 (a year that included hits like "Little Things Mean a Lot," "Young at Heart," and "This Ole House").[5] Converse's rendering of "One by One" is one of intense vulnerability. It is a heartbreaking performance. It sounds as though she were singing to us—and by "us," I mean you, or me, or anyone who happens to have found themselves alone with her and this recording. It sounds like she is in the room. It sounds like she is here.

CHAPTER 3

A Ghost

Who was this woman? Why had this music been ignored? What happened to her?

The liner notes to her album had it that Converse had been born in New England and had come to New York City after college. She lived there during her years of music making, producing her own recordings of her compositions—songs that drew from varied strains of older American music, but that did not belong exclusively to any of them and did not fit into current trends. Though she briefly flirted with mainstream exposure, she didn't manage to break through, mostly (I presumed) because her music was neither fish nor fowl, and the music industry hadn't known what to do with her. She tried her luck in New York for about a decade, before giving up in despair of ever finding a larger audience. She never married, never had kids, and was never known to have had a significant other of any kind. And then, in middle age, she disappeared.

Like the old *Twilight Zone* episode about the shut-in actress who watches the same film over and over again by herself until, finally, she steps into the picture and becomes part of its plot, I couldn't stop listening to Connie Converse, couldn't not identify with her story or the issues I guessed might be part of it. I knew the fickle nature of the music business and what it felt like to be both courted and then pushed away. Like most professional artists, I knew the indignities involved in trying to sell unguarded personal expression to a marketplace and the attendant embarrassment when met with rejection or apathy. I, too, was crossing into middle age, unmarried, childless, living alone in a small apartment in New York City. I had also recently begun to wonder whether radical change was a viable option. I had not, yet, disappeared.

As I now sat in that dark, cramped apartment with *How Sad, How Lovely* on repeat, a strange thing began to happen. By the album's third track, "Roving Woman," a generally witty, lighthearted tune, I became gripped by the kind of overwhelming discomposure that can arrive when we hear, for example, a beloved song from our childhood, or one that reminds us of our first love or of some other pivotal moment in our lives. Music can have this power, to transport us back in time, reminding us of what it was like to feel extraordinarily happy, or hopeful, or cared for, or free, a phenomenon that is sometimes accompanied in our minds by a cinematic series of scenes, memories, and faces, all now gone for good.

Yet Converse's music was completely new to me. Why was it having this effect? Why did her songs, her words, the tone of her voice, leave me pacing the floor, wanting to know more about her, even—on more than one occasion—beset by episodes of unexplainable sobbing?

The confluence of hearing her songs, of reading about her tragic story, and of empathizing with her situation made for an emotional reckoning I hadn't seen coming. In Connie Converse, I heard the sound of every artist who has ever been ignored or rejected because their work was too personal, too idiosyncratic, too unmarketable. I heard Buddy Bolden's cornet, lost for all time but for a rumored Edison cylinder, the holy grail of jazz recordings. I heard arias from Scott Joplin's lost opera, *A Guest of Honor*; the voices of the people in Mike Disfarmer's photographs; and the unknown, other performances by Geeshie Wiley.[1] I heard the now-forgotten spirit of Susan Glaspell; and the unfinished plays of Eugene O'Neill, torn up and burned at the end of his life; and Barbara Loden's unmade adaptation of Charlotte Perkins Gilman's "The Yellow Wallpaper." I heard the dark American soul of Albert Pinkham Ryder, and Thelonious Monk, and Charles Burchfield, and Son House, and Vivian Maier. I heard the entirety of America's forgotten cultural history. In Connie Converse, I heard a woman reaching out across time and space to be understood, to locate her fellows—others who, perhaps like her, found mainstream American mores insulting and intolerable. And, like anyone who encounters these kinds of artistic expressions, who also knows what it feels to be apart, outside, alone, I heard myself—only better.

To say that I became obsessed would be imprecise. Obsession, I think, implies at least some degree of choice, and I didn't feel that I had any of that. Connie Converse seized me, the way that some are seized by unresolved mysteries like the JFK assassination, or the lost colony of Roanoke, or the life of Kaspar Hauser.

Like author A. J. A. Symons, who discovered the work of the obscure writer Frederick Rolfe and made it his mission to reconstruct Rolfe's life in *The Quest for Corvo*; like the pair of fans from South Africa whose mission to find Sixto Rodriguez became the basis for the documentary *Searching for Sugar Man*; like science writer Rebecca Skloot, who felt called to investigate the life and legacy of Henrietta Lacks—I experienced my life come to a screeching halt. Like those people, I felt my consciousness become infected by the energy of a flickery ghost, a figure about whom precious little was publicly known.

In short order, I stopped writing my own music and became devoted only to Connie Converse—to learning more about her; to piecing together her life; to spreading the gospel of her particular brand of genius everywhere and everyhow I could; to, eventually, inserting myself into the life she left behind to the point that—at times—I felt that I'd become part of the plot.

∽

The first pressing of *How Sad, How Lovely,* released in 2009, included seventeen Converse originals, each track featuring only her winsome vocals and acoustic guitar. Those liner notes consisted of three short essays: a brief biographical sketch of Converse's life and career; a remembrance by Converse's younger brother, Phil; and a few words from animator and audio enthusiast Gene Deitch, who met Converse in the 1950s and made amateur recordings of her back then, many of which were included on the album.

I read and reread these accounts, hoping that somehow the repetition would unlock the details that were missing: She was born Elizabeth Eaton Converse in 1924, in Laconia, New Hampshire, and grew up in Concord. She was the second of three children. A brilliant student, she attended her mother's and grandmother's alma mater, Mount Holyoke College, on a scholarship, but dropped out. According to Phil, her whereabouts were "sparse" for the next five years, until she eventually materialized in New York City.

Her musical activities included composing not only for guitar but also piano. She attracted the attention of Deitch in 1954. He tried to promote the recordings he made of her with the help of a friend of his named Bill Bernal. The pair was unsuccessful in their efforts, and in 1961, "Connie tired of New York and left for Ann Arbor, where her brother was a professor at the University of Michigan."

In Ann Arbor, Converse "implanted herself firmly in the academic community," which "left little time for music." The folk singer Susan Reed took an interest in Converse's songs and performed them in New York, but outside "a handful of scores for commercials and some work on a short film," Converse never came close to "the sort of widespread success she had hoped for her music."

By the 1970s, Converse had become "increasingly despondent." She requested a leave of absence from her job and took a six-month sabbatical in England, financed by "friends and colleagues." And then, in 1974, she disappeared.

Her brother's notes added some color: Converse's skills were not limited to academics and music; she was also a talented cartoonist, painter, sculptor, and poet. After she began composing songs in New York, she mailed him a new recording "every month for several years." Sometime around 1956, "she managed to wedge a piano into her tiny apartment" and composed a series of art songs "with a somewhat higher rate of music," settings for poems by Housman, cummings, and others.

One song a month for several years added up to more than the seventeen included on the 2009 album. What about the rest of those songs? Where were they? Every track on *How Sad, How Lovely* was a winner—not a dud among them. If there was an equal or so number of songs left off this release, what did they sound like? What about these piano songs—what did her brother mean when he wrote that they possessed "a somewhat higher rate of music"?

The questions multiplied and spread in my mind like a virus. Why had she abandoned her college scholarship? What did it mean that her whereabouts had been "sparse" for five years? How was she supporting herself when she lived in New York City? Was she performing regularly? And if so, why wasn't there any documentary evidence of it? If not, how had she found advocates for her music? Why had she "tired of New York" and given up on her music?

Deitch's contribution to the Connie Converse story recounted how he came to know of her and record her music, via Bill Bernal, who "brought me his latest discovery . . . a prim-looking school teacher–ish young woman with the euphonious name" who sang songs "the likes of which none of us had ever heard before." Deitch describes Converse as "emotionally repressed, whose every personal song seemed to be telling one or another aspect of her own inner life, which immediately struck me as one of mystery and magic."

Over the ensuing decades, Deitch continued to play his Converse recordings for anyone who would listen, until the "chance came when I was invited to play my favorite records on David Garland's WNYC *Spinning on Air* radio show. By the merest chance, an 'angel' [Dan Dzula, the album's producer] happened to hear the show," which resulted in this album, the long-delayed commercial debut of Converse's music.

All this seemed like a collection of pieces from a puzzle for which no representation of the whole existed, no picture on the front of the box as a guide, just "A Thousand Shapes and Shades"—the name, as I would later learn, of a Converse song of which no recording seems to exist.

Clearly, Converse had deserved better in her own time. The music she made in New York City in the 1950s should not have been ignored.

But she also deserved better now. Her newly discovered music revealed a tear in the fabric of our cultural history, one that required mending. Someone needed to call attention to the terrible injustice that this person had suffered.

This something-more-than-obsession with Connie Converse, this tractor beam I'd been caught in from the moment I first heard "Talkin' Like You," now began to expand. A door seemed to swing open before me, revealing an illuminated path forward and marching orders that rang in my head like a gong.

My mission couldn't have been more clear: to help lift Connie Converse up, to help shine a light on her legacy, to help tell her story. But even more: to help right a wrong. To help bring her back.

CHAPTER 4

Phil

Philip Converse wasn't just anybody. He was a renowned political scientist and an honored professor emeritus at the University of Michigan (where he'd served as a leader at both the Survey Research Center and the Institute for Social Research). He'd been awarded the Guggenheim, Russell Sage, and Fulbright fellowships, and had authored important books and papers, his work generally as well regarded and celebrated within his own sphere as his sister's had been ignored and obscure in hers.

Philip Converse would have an outsize role in her story and in what I came to know. His @umich.edu email address was easy enough to find, and I took a shot.

He replied within an hour. Yes, he was Connie Converse's brother; yes, he was happy to talk to me. How could he be of service?

Her brother! I begged the man's pardon for approaching him out of the blue and explained that I was contacting him with the hope of gaining wider exposure for his sister's extraordinary music. I didn't tell him that I had no real idea yet for what that might look like. I didn't tell him that I was proceeding on pure instinct. All that I could genuinely say about myself at that time was that I was a professional songwriter and performer and that I had taken a keen interest in his sister's work.

This, apparently, was enough. He told me that I should call him Phil and that he'd help in any way he could. "I have a question of you," he wrote to me. "Have you seen the 22-pager with a gaudy yellow cover labelled 'Connie's Guitar Songs'?? I put that together about the time I retired and was looking for some way to save Connie's legacy from final disappearance. If that's not familiar, give me a PO address and I will send you a copy."[1]

Thus began a correspondence, and a friendship, that lasted until Phil's death three and a half years later. I wasn't sure yet where any of this would lead. I didn't know that I was already stuck fast in the quicksand of Connie Converse Land, nor that my focus on her would come to define much of my life over the next decade and beyond. I didn't know that Phil would reveal things to me about his sister that I would struggle with, that were uncomfortable to hear about, and that continue to perplex me. I didn't know that I would be hit by tidal waves of mystery, delight, sadness, and intrigue over this time, nor that I would continue to be carried away by my self-assigned task with a certain terrible and irresistible force.

～

Phil told me that everything his sister had intentionally left behind was contained in an old five-drawer filing cabinet he kept stored in the garage of his house in Ann Arbor—something he hadn't been able to bring himself to open until after his retirement in the early 1990s. When that time came, he knew that his first and most important task was to find out what sort of shape her old tape reels were in and to have them digitized.

Relieved that they were not only still intact, but eminently playable, he had the most significant one—an "omnibus" collection of most of her songs she'd recorded herself in 1956—transferred to CD and then duplicated many times over, for anyone who'd ever expressed an interest in hearing her music.

Well before he was called upon to contribute his thoughts and memories to *How Sad, How Lovely,* Phil wrote and self-published another, more extensive set of liner notes to accompany this recording compilation and to memorialize his sister, assembling lyrics to all her songs; his own notes on the recordings, their history and provenance; a lengthy biographical sketch about her abbreviated life; and several 1950s-era photographs of her, including some I'd seen online. He called his book-and-record project "Connie's Guitar Songs": a spiral-bound folio produced and replicated at a local office supply store, bundled with an accompanying CD-R. This was what arrived in my mailbox a few days after I contacted Phil Converse.

Again, I had the sense of being in a waking dream. First, there was Converse herself, and her music, and her story—all of which I'd resisted believing. Now I'd been led to a surviving brother, who was not only open to talking to me but who'd already produced a homemade history of her and her songs. How many siblings would do such a thing? My own brother, three years younger than I, has always been an ardent fan of my music—maybe more dedicated than anyone. But it was hard for me to imagine even him engaging in the level of commitment it took for Phil Converse to produce and distribute "Connie's Guitar Songs."

I devoured its contents. The CD contained almost twice as many songs as the ones included on *How Sad, How Lovely.* But these were not B sides. The quality and richness of each song were on par with the ones that had already tattooed themselves on my consciousness. The final track on Phil's CD featured his sister performing a dirgelike, almost abrasive-sounding song called "Vanity of Vanities," featuring her playing piano, not guitar. On the recording, Converse sings at the bottom of her register about amnesia, salvation, and alchemy as she plunks out thorny chords on what sounds like an old upright in a haunted house. It scared the daylights out of me.

In his booklet, Phil wrote that while actively composing music in New York City in the 1950s, his sister invested in a Crestwood 404 reel-to-reel tape recorder, set it up in her tiny Greenwich Village apartment, and recorded herself singing and playing her songs there as she completed them.

Documenting ourselves has now become such a part of our everyday lives that it's easy to forget how relatively recent a phenomenon it actually is. Go back just a few decades, and we're in the world of cassette recorders, four-track devices, and camcorders. And a decade or two before that, home recording was unusual, and unusually difficult. The machine that Converse was using to make demos in the early fifties had been commercially available only since 1951, which means she was employing cutting-edge technology. It was a cumbersome, pricey device—and evidence not only that she was serious about music, but that her spearheading ways were not limited to songwriting. Some thirty years before Daniel Johnston made outsider home recordings a thing, Connie Converse had been there and done that.

There were additional tidbits. Their father had been a minister and was, for decades, head of the local temperance society. Their mother had been an accomplished pianist. Only religious and classical music were allowed in the house when they were growing up. Dancing, alcohol, and card playing were forbidden.

Phil described his sister as "a genius and a polymath," and he extolled her many precocious talents in his booklet in even greater detail here: her various artistic pursuits, the endlessly inventive original games she devised for them to play. As a child, she'd studied violin, but she "did not like the instrument and didn't practice. Later she picked up the piano and guitar largely on her own . . ."

He remembered his sister explaining to him that "the vast majority of Tin Pan Alley songs were pretty much like doggerel, musically as well as in their lyrics."

She was valedictorian of her high school class and awarded so many honors at the school's graduation ceremony that her name became a punch line that day, eliciting more jeers and groans with each mention, and embarrassing her parents.

Throughout his notes, Phil mentions their other, older sibling only in passing, briefly and never by name. I wouldn't learn about Paul Converse, or his complicated role in the family's dynamic, until later.

"Sis did not miss the Big Time by a whole lot," Phil wrote, noting that she once appeared as a performer on CBS's *The Morning Show*, hosted by Walter Cronkite, exposure that was almost the lucky break she needed. Almost.

∽

Converse's period of focused songwriting activity seemed to comprise a relatively short portion of her life. And though her life on either side of those years is filled, as I would come to learn, with other fascinating endeavors, encounters, achievements, and explorations, it was during that time, while living in New York City, that Elizabeth Eaton Converse transformed and briefly embodied the mysterious, beguiling character called Connie Converse—the one who should have been famous but wasn't.

Yet there had to be so much more to this woman—to her life, to her world, to her ambitions, and to the rest of her story—than Phil's adoring sketch provided. I knew this because of the richly layered brilliance I heard in her songs and because of the details Phil hinted at in the ulti-mately unsatisfying booklet I now held in my hands, concluding as they did with this provocative paragraph:

Sis composed because she had to for personal delight and expression. But in the long run her failure to attract large-scale attention left her depressed and defeated. She moved to Ann Arbor after she tired of New York, and for some years earned her keep as Editor of the Journal for [sic] Conflict Resolution . . . this period lasted about a decade, in which she did various kinds of writing, but no significant further musical composition. In the summer of 1974, discour-aged on a number of new fronts . . . she wrote fond letters to [my wife] Jean and me, as well as to numerous other Ann Arbor friends, saying she wanted to take one more shot at making a new life for herself somewhere else, although she was not optimistic about the likelihood. Then before the parting letters were delivered to reveal her secret plans, she packed her possessions in her Volkswa-gen Beetle, drove out of town and has not been heard from since.

CHAPTER 5

Pen Pals

I n "Connie's Guitar Songs," Phil wrote that his sister's decision to leave Mount Holyoke "shocked her new campus world" and was "a momentous kicking over of the traces, in many senses of the word. Our parents were devastated." But when I asked him to elaborate on the factors that led her to make such an unexpected move, he only reiterated what he'd written in his booklet: that he "vaguely knew that if Sis had decided it, it must have been the right thing to do." Despite laying claim to being her closest lifelong friend, Phil told me that the two of them had never discussed this issue in any detail. This seemed peculiar, but I was still getting to know this man and didn't press.

Instead, I peppered him with a gentle volley of simple, other questions. To his credit, Phil proved a dedicated, even eager correspondent, seemingly ready to reply to as many emails as I saw fit to write. At first, I tried to hew to topics that didn't seem too personal.

Converse's music was never commercially released during her years of activity, for instance, and she is not known to have ever made a single formal concert appearance, yet there she was, in photographs Phil had reproduced, appearing on television with Walter Cronkite, singing her songs. How had this come about?

Phil told me that he had no idea. He had not seen the appearance and didn't know much about it.

Having already scoured the internet and contacted both CBS Archives and the Paley Center for Media, I knew there appeared to be no surviving footage of Converse's performance on the Cronkite show. The only evidence of it seemed to be those few stills shown in Phil's booklet. Phil thought he remembered hearing that someone had taken photographs of the television as the program originally aired. This, too, seemed a bit strange. Who was that someone? How had they managed to successfully photograph a fuzzy 1954 television broadcast, using a camera from that era, a feat that would have required skilled knowledge of how to focus properly and set the correct shutter speed? Phil knew nothing about it.

I was encouraged by his willingness to at least entertain questions, and my email exchanges with Phil in that spring of 2011 grew in length, frequency, and intimacy. It wasn't long before we were corresponding almost every day. And as we did, our rapport deepened.

I began to probe Phil's memory for more details. What about his sister's romantic life? Phil confirmed that he never knew her to have one, that she never married, had a significant other, or even dated, as far as he was aware. Never? Never.

Had they ever discussed her feelings about this? No. Did she ever talk with him about her lack of a love life in any way? No. I don't know exactly when I became conscious that I was in fact in the early stages of doing research for a book about her, but it became clear soon enough, and Phil was immensely pleased by the prospect.

He began including details about himself in his replies, too—information about the books *he'd* written, the work he and his wife had spent their careers engaged in, the challenges of aging. We found common ground over a shared interest in literature and drama. As a means of better establishing my bona fides as a writer and researcher, I told him about my work as a research assistant for former *New York Times* managing editor Arthur Gelb, both on his memoirs and with him and his wife, Barbara, on their ongoing Eugene O'Neill biographical work. Phil revealed that he, too, loved O'Neill and that his sister, Connie, had as well. Once upon a time, he even considered pursuing a career in the theater, as an actor.

And after a while, I started to feel comfortable enough to broach the subject of his sister's disappearance. Because it was still 2011, there remained the tantalizing possibility that an eighty-six-year-old Connie Converse could be very much alive, somewhere. Given the rough physical, financial, and spiritual shape Phil said she'd been in when she vanished, the chances seemed slim, but biologically, it was eminently possible—an idea that gave my research added urgency. Perhaps if her life and music gained enough notoriety, I thought, word would reach her, somehow. Maybe she would end her reclusive self-imposed exile and emerge from her mountain shack, or from some remote Mexican villa, or from her cottage in the English countryside—wherever it was she'd been hiding away all these years—and the world's long-withheld love and attention could be bestowed upon her at last.

These scenarios began regularly populating my dreams, as did even less likely ones: She'd been taken in by a religious cult; a neighbor had been hiding her away in plain sight all these years, mere blocks from where she was last seen; Phil knew exactly where she was, but had been sworn to secrecy.

But then, there was also the very basic, practical issue of someone disappearing, an extraordinary event, the kind of thing that is typically the province of tabloid journalism and true crime TV. Surely, Phil had to have more to say than "she drove away one day and hasn't been heard from since."

It's an odd thing, dealing with someone whose family member has vanished. Where were the boundaries of good taste in this context? I wondered. Still, I had to ask. "The most painful parts of this happened almost 40 years ago," Phil had written in his first email to me, "so we as a family are long past the main grieving. So this is not real 'touchy' any more."

When I brought the subject up again, he now wrote: "There is much that we know we don't know," doing his best Donald Rumsfeld. "I think I have finally sorted out why she took the final steps when she did, although this was utterly opaque to us at the time it happened."

Genres

As Converse's songs played in my head on repeat, I could think of little else. A section of each of my own concerts I was giving at the time, as I continued to keep up my music career, was devoted to her—to playing her music and narrating the details of her life as I then understood them. I talked about being in touch with Phil and also made attempts to explain to audiences what encountering Converse's music had done to me—why I'd gotten stuck emotionally, intellectually, and artistically; why, when listening to her songs for the first time, I couldn't even understand what I was hearing, as though I were an astronomer and had been made aware of a previously unknown planet in our solar system that had been hiding behind the others all along.

But just as important, I tried to convey that in order to appreciate Converse's cultural significance—not only why the discovery of her music short-circuited my consciousness, but also why hers is such an important cautionary tale about our cultural habits and attitudes, about what we choose to celebrate and what ends up being ignored—it is crucial to meditate on the now-fading but once-omnipresent notion of "genre" in American popular music.

New acquaintances will sometimes ask about our favorite kind of music. Whenever I'm introduced to a stranger, the most common question I'm asked when they find out that I write and perform music professionally is: What kind of music do you play? But we don't realize, when we ask these questions about "kinds" of music, that we are participating in a century-old, outdated marketing system that was designed to make us bad, lazy listeners.

By "what kind," we mean: What style? What genre? Rock? Jazz? Blues? Country? A hundred years ago, such genres really did not exist, neither to describe recordings nor even in everyday conversation. Music was either formal (what we now call "classical") musical literature that had been composed for musicians and ensembles to re-create and interpret; or else it was informal, or "popular," vernacular music typically made by untrained players. Popular music would have included everything from sentimental parlor songs to religious hymns to songs that were sung while working, farming, praying, or when traveling by land or sea. The latter were often handed down orally within their respective communities, or passed on by itinerant musicians. Formal music relied upon the written instructions of a composer, but informal music could include extremes of variation and improvisation. The latter was what might be heard at a party, or at a dance, or on someone's front porch on a Saturday afternoon. (There were outliers, too—nineteenth-century composer/performers like Paganini and Gottschalk frequently incorporated extensive improvisation into their performances, but they were exceptions and not the rule.)

Beginning in the mid-nineteenth century, parlor songs, sentimental ballads, and minstrel ditties began to be popularized through the publication and sale of sheet music. These could be played by amateurs at home, and they included not only the Stephen Foster songs that so many children in the United States still learn ("Camptown Races," "Oh! Susanna"), but eventually the compositions of Scott Joplin (whose "Maple Leaf Rag" in 1899 is often apocryphally cited as the first song to sell a million copies).

But it wasn't until the recording industry began to boom in the 1920s that record companies started to see the benefit of distinguishing their product with more marketable language for consumers. Rather than advertising their entire inventory of popular artists by last name or ensemble or composer, record manufacturers and the stores that sold their products began coining categories within which they could group them. For the first time, genres like "hillbilly," "race," "jazz," and "blues" were introduced to the marketplace.

The first "country" music record to sell one million copies (eventually selling more than seven times that number) was released by the Victor Talking Machine Company in 1924, the year that Converse was born. It featured Vernon Dalhart, a singer of light opera and classical song.[1] On side A was his rendition of Grayson and Whitter's "Wreck of the Old '97," about an infamous 1903 train derailment in Virginia. Side B was Dalhart's take on "The Prisoner's Song," a traditional ballad of unknown origin.

Because of her parents' rules about the sort of music allowed in their house, Converse would not have heard this record as a child. But it was popular with a wide swath of American consumers, and made so much money for Victor, that the company enlisted talent scout Ralph Peer to go find more "rural" music. In 1927, Peer famously set up shop in an office in Bristol, Tennessee, sending out word far and wide that he was auditioning singers and musicians to make records. A yodeling brakeman named Jimmie Rodgers heeded the call, as did the Southern Virginia siblings Maybelle, Sara, and A. P. Carter, who would record their versions of old mountain folk songs under the name "the Carter Family." Rodgers and the Carters would go on to sell millions of records themselves and become country music royalty.

It's impossible to imagine the history of American music without the recordings of these four individuals, and their influence on Converse's musical sensibilities is hard to miss. Listen to Jimmie Rodgers singing "Treasures Untold" or "Old Love Letters." Listen to the Carters' recordings of "My Little Home in Tennessee" or "Bury Me Under the Weeping Willow." At some point, somehow, this New Hampshire girl from a strict Baptist family was exposed to what is now thought of as early country music.

But what makes some American roots music "country" as opposed to "blues" or "gospel" or "folk"? Rodgers and the Carters (along with many of their white contemporaries) recorded songs that, had the artists been Black, would have been labeled "blues" or "race" music. Both acts similarly recorded "gospel" and "spiritual" numbers that were also called "country" (or, sometimes, "hillbilly"), primarily because the performers were white southerners.[2] Early blues artists like the Mississippi Sheiks or Mississippi John Hurt recorded some of the same songs that Rodgers and the Carters did, often in a similar (what might be called a "country") musical manner, with nary a hint of blues hallmarks like twangy-sounding flat seventh notes (also known as "blue notes"), but these recordings were never marketed as country music. Judging by her guitar playing and early compositional style, Converse must also have heard a good deal of this music.

Jimmie Rodgers even recorded a track with Louis Armstrong, today universally known as one of the early fathers of jazz. What makes "Blue Yodel Number 9," the Rodgers-penned blues they recorded together, a "country" song and not a "blues" or "jazz" number? Had Rodgers instead appeared on Armstrong's label, would the record have been issued as a "jazz" (or "race," or "blues") record? Who decides whether a song belongs in one genre and not another, and why?

Answer: the recording industry. The industry codified and promoted the musical genre system to make it easier to sell records. Grouping artists into oversimplified categories that customers could easily understand turned them into flavors and brands, flattening and sterilizing much of the previously bold, idiosyncratic music that was made and recorded in the United States, especially in the mid- and latter half of the twentieth century. This kind of lowest-common-denominator approach to classifying music is as responsible as any of the other factors (like trends and gender) for barring the way for an uncategorizable artist like Connie Converse.

Soon enough, each of these manufactured styles began to possess its own set of unwritten rules, its dos and don'ts. What's astounding is that so many artists were (and even now, remain) willing to play along.[3] Consciously or not, musicians subscribed to the hallmarks of the styles they had been boxed into by the music industry, ensuring that they would be boxed in even further.

Country musicians were mostly white people with guitars who wore cowboy hats and boots and sang about heartbreak, money woes, and alcohol. Black musicians who sang about the same things that country singers sang about wore different kinds of costumes, and their music was called the blues. Before too long, blues got locked into the now-standard three-chord, twelve-bar AAB progression made famous by the likes of Robert Johnson and Muddy Waters and other early progenitors of the form, making its musical palette even more restricted than country. Both country and blues artists could feature instrumental improvisation in their recordings, but their music still wasn't considered jazz.

"Jazz" was a name used to designate the primarily instrumental dance music of the 1920s and '30s, but the term would subsequently come to be a catchall for the intellectual, exclusive music that still has as its figureheads today the moody, sharp-dressed bandleader/composers of the 1950s and '60s like Miles Davis and John Coltrane (both of whom composed and performed any number of blues compositions). The blues artist Clarence "Gatemouth" Brown and the country bandleader Bob Wills both fronted bands that played what *could* be considered jazz, though—perhaps because they both wore cowboy hats and played fiddle—almost no one called it that, then or now.

The song "Hesitation Blues" is a good example of why the definitions of genre in American music are mostly arbitrary. It's a song with no real known origin—what's known as a "traditional"—and one that Converse herself probably heard in one or more of its various iterations by the time she was living and writing in New York City. The lyrics are a series of interchangeable verses that have been given innumerable tweaks on scores of different recordings.

> *Hello, Central, what's the matter with this line?*
> *I've got to talk to that high brown of mine*
> *Tell me how long will I have to wait?*
> *Please give me 298, why do you hesitate?*

W. C. Handy's arrangement of the song (called "Hesitating Blues") is probably the standard-bearer; a classic rendition of it is featured on *Louis Armstrong Plays W. C. Handy,* a recording released in 1954, the same year Converse appeared on television. Armstrong and his band give the 1915 Handy arrangement a full traditional New Orleans greasing, setting it against a lazy, swaggering tempo, with a polyphony of horns (led by Armstrong's clarion trumpet). The sweet sound of a clarinet wafting high above the ensemble carries the tune. This style was the regional one Armstrong had come up in during his youth in the Crescent City, and it was enjoying a revival at the time of the album's release, sometimes in a watered-down, sanitized version that was being marketed as "Dixieland" (an idiom that counted among its fans, at the time, none other than Gene Deitch, the man who "discovered" Converse that same year).

But what genre is this recording? The cover art bears the proclamation that the album is the music of "'The Father of the Blues' interpreted by the master of jazz trumpet and jazz singing." Blues? What does a track like this have to do with the rough, hair-raising music of Bukka White, Charley Patton, or Blind Willie Johnson—other than the fact that all these men were Black and southern? Jazz trumpet, jazz singing? Does Armstrong's playing have any significant relationship to the hyperkinetic, experimental harmonic explorations of Clifford Brown or Dizzy Gillespie? And what makes what Armstrong is doing here "jazz singing"? Is it that much different from gospel blues legend Rev. Gary Davis's recording of "Hesitation Blues"?

Davis's take on the same song is more intimate, earthier, arguably unique. Jelly Roll Morton's is a time machine that transports the listener back to the era of whorehouse piano "professors" in New Orleans and to the moment when ragtime began to transform into jazz (or "jass"). Bluegrass legend Doc Watson, taking his cue from Uncle Dave Macon's 1924 version (entitled "Hillbilly Blues"), makes the song an Appalachian front porch flatpicking workout. The song has also been recorded by Janis Joplin (rock), Steely Dan (fusion), Jerry Garcia (jam band), Willie Nelson (country), and Old Crow Medicine Show (Americana).

What classifies these disparate versions of the song "Hesitation Blues" as being part of entirely different genres? The song has the same number of measures, the same melody, and, for the most part, the same harmony (allowing for the difference in the verses heard on the Davis and Watson versions, which are themselves more or less alike). In each version, there is musical improvisation, so there's no help there.

So maybe it's the instruments heard on the recordings that push the songs toward classifications like jazz, or country, or blues, or rock. Does the fact that we hear the blare of Armstrong's horn make this a jazz recording? Is it Doc Watson's dexterous acoustic guitar playing that identifies his recording of the song as "bluegrass"? Is this what our fidelity to our preferred genres is all about? Does it all come down to the types of instruments on which we prefer to hear our music played?

That doesn't seem right. There's something else going on, something in the delivery, or something about the culture from which these styles sprang, that has won our allegiance. When people say they hate country music, for example, they're not saying they hate guitars and fiddles. They may well *like* guitars and fiddles when they're played by people of other races, at other tempos, from other places. Are they perhaps saying (consciously or not) that they hate where this music has traditionally come from—white, rural, conservative America?[4]

If we profess to love "rock 'n' roll," maybe what we're really saying is that we identify with a spirit of rebellion, with giving the finger to authority. And perhaps the same can be said for the types of cultures surrounding hip-hop, techno, reggae, and folk. When we talk about these genres, and whether we like them, it seems possible that what we're really talking about is whether we're comfortable attaching our identities to the stereotypes we associate with them.[5]

As a working bandleader in New York City, I have performed in "genre" contexts throughout my career, making only the smallest requisite adjustments to ensure that the ensemble I'm leading on any given evening can be programmed in a jazz club, a country honky-tonk, a rock venue, or a blues joint. It's why canny professional musicians in any big American metropolis are able to eke out a living. One night, the band is attired in suits and ties, swinging the tunes for wealthy patrons. The next night, you're in flannel plaid shirts and jeans, playing the *same songs* in 2/4 cut time in a beer-soaked room with a floor covered by peanut shells. Same band, same instruments, same set list—the only things that change are the context and the presentation. In America, working, everyday musicians know how to play blues, country, jazz, rock, and so on because it's really all the same music.[6]

S o, what in the world is folk music? Armstrong is often credited with offering the famous quip, "All music is folk music. I ain't never heard no horse sing a song."[7] Yet, today, "folk" is generally thought of as quiet acoustic music written and performed by sensitive, primarily white, primarily lyric-focused types accompanying themselves with acoustic instruments—one reason some immediately assume that's how Converse's music should be categorized. But as it was understood and used as a term when she was getting started, "folk music" meant traditional songs featuring words with no known author and melodies with no known composer. Every nation has its own "folk" music. In the first half of the twentieth century, many of America's folk songs were collected by the likes of musicologists Carl Sandburg, John and Alan Lomax, and Pete Seeger—songs we all know, like "Down by the Riverside," "Turkey in the Straw," and "Li'l Liza Jane."

Until Bob Dylan came along, nobody *wrote* folk music. Musicologist Dick Weissman related a story to me about the late John Cohen of the New Lost City Ramblers, a group that earnestly offered faithful renditions of early rural American music, even going so far as to dress the part. Cohen, during the pre-Dylan era, once told Weissman, "You have no right to write songs!"

What Cohen meant was that traditional songs, and traditional-*sounding* songs, could be written only by people who grew up in the cultures from which they sprang. As far as Cohen and most of his folk-loving contemporaries were concerned, folk was, by its very definition, music created by and belonging to "the folk." There was an authenticity issue embedded in its definition, almost as if to say, "If you've been to college, you don't get to write folk songs."

Folk song collector, recording artist, and educator Ellen Stekert reinforced this idea: "John Jacob Niles, well before Dylan, was roundly criticized by the folkies for having written 'I Wonder as I Wander' and other songs or tunes he made up. It was better to the folkies in those days to have discovered the gem than to have written it. Today, if you sing folk songs, it is only a short time until someone asks you to sing something you wrote."

She continued: "In the fifties and early sixties, one could write political songs, but there could be no 'I' in them, unless the 'I' was a farmer, or a coal miner, or a sailor. Any song you wrote with the singer as an 'I' was thought to be an attempt to be a 'popularizer,' prizing the individual over the community. Popularizers were not 'authentic'; they were not 'ethnic.' However, 'ethnic' in those days meant *white* ethnic, generally.[8] Even Joan Baez never sang songs from her own ethnic background."[9]

The singer Ethel Raim, who was performing professionally by 1952, told me that when she started out, there was no significant trend toward songwriting in the folk world. The powerhouse singer and guitarist Odetta was on the scene the following year, but the songs she was delivering were spirituals and work songs.[10]

Songwriters like Earl Robinson and Lee Hays *were* writing and performing original "folk"-flavored popular songs like "Joe Hill," "If I Had a Hammer," and "The House I Live In" as early as the late 1930s and '40s, and Woody Guthrie and Pete Seeger were repurposing old songs (taking traditional melodies and slapping new lyrics on top of them to make them more topical) and recording them. But it took Dylan to stretch this practice to the breaking point in the early sixties, forcing new definitions of what folk was and wasn't. Songs like "Don't Think Twice, It's All Right," "One Too Many Mornings," and "It Ain't Me Babe" sure *sounded* like folk songs—they referenced the forms, structures, and even melodies of old folk songs—but Dylan's lyrics did more than just update those elements for the current moment; he mined their narrative and harmonic vocabularies, but then created something self-consciously new by inserting himself, the singer, into them.

Dylan was initially called a "folk singer"—this, despite the fact that his first album contains mostly traditional blues and country music. But Dylan was white, so it was hard to package him as a blues singer, and (despite his attempts to obfuscate his background) he was a middle-class Jewish kid from Minnesota, so he couldn't really be a country singer, either. His branding by the recording industry as a folk singer was a marketing decision, the campaign chosen to move his product along.

Within just a couple of years, wary of what he considered a stylistic straitjacket, and after he'd started composing more personal, introspective, and literary-leaning songs, Dylan famously began quarreling with journalists who called him a folk singer. At some point, the term *singer-songwriter* was coined. And if you asked a hundred random people today to tell you the difference between a folk singer and a singer-songwriter, my guess is that you'd be hard-pressed to get a single satisfying answer.

If, strictly speaking, a singer-songwriter is someone who sings songs that they themselves have written, this seems like a woefully inadequate term. What makes Jimmie Rodgers a country artist and not a singer-songwriter? Was Jelly Roll Morton a singer-songwriter? Was James Brown? What about Katy Perry? Is she a singer-songwriter? Is Beyoncé? Is Thom Yorke? Why *isn't* Lil Nas X a singer-songwriter?[11] These and countless other artists all sing (or sang) songs that they wrote.

But when we talk about singer-songwriters, there's a kind of unspoken understanding that this "genre" of music tends to imply introspective lyrics. If a genre *had* to be coined for this style of music, might not "sensitive" or even "autobiographical" be better and more accurate than "singer-songwriter"?

Since the 2009 release of her 1950s recordings, some have called Connie Converse "the first singer-songwriter." I think what is being referred to when this title is assigned to her has to do with the *way* she performed her songs. We feel taken into her most intimate confidence, a quality we generally think of as belonging to a later crop of popular artists, starting with Dylan.

Traditional American folk singers never strived to make the listener think the song was an expression of their, the singers', innermost feelings. These performers were mostly stoic as they sang, and used few dynamics or gestures, almost as though delivering a message from an oracle. But while Converse used elements of that style, she expressed her own emotions in both lyrics and performance.

∽

So, was Connie Converse the first singer-songwriter? Literally speaking, no. Human beings have been making up songs and singing them since human beings have been having feelings and singing. But was she imbuing her performances of her own poetic songs with a vulnerability that was unique for its time, in a way that would become commonplace within a couple of decades (and would come to be branded as "singer-songwriter" music)? Absolutely.

It's one of the reasons why even a casual exposure to Converse's recordings engenders a visceral curiosity about her. And it's also why her music failed to succeed in its day. There was no preexisting context for what she was doing, nowhere for her to find a snug fit. Her music was not folk, not pop, not blues, not country. It employed elements of all those forms, but in a way that hadn't been popularized yet.

This is the sad reality when businesspeople are tasked with the power to "break" a new artist, and one of the greatest obstacles that professional artists faced in the second half of the twentieth century.[12] The more original the art, and the less it sounded or looked like something already familiar, the greater the odds were that it would be passed over by the gatekeepers to success. And though today's technology has democratized this process to great extent, making it easier for artists to bypass the system altogether, the confining, outdated notions of genre have persisted.

If it's true that this paradigm is now undergoing a massive shift, so much the better.[13] As Kelefa Sanneh wrote in 2021, "Maybe, from now on, most musical consumers will be omnivores, to whom the notion of loyalty to a genre seems as foreign as the notion of 'owning' an album."[14]

Unfortunately for her (and for us), Converse was making music when loyalty to genres *was* practiced by listeners, by record labels and producers, and by musicians themselves.

What kind of music did she make? is a question I've been asked countless times during my research and writing about Converse. It is exactly the prevalence of this question, and the ignorance that underlies its premise, that doomed her to failure in her time.

CHAPTER 6

The Filing Cabinet

P hil continued to be encouraging. Because I'd taken up the book idea in earnest, he suggested that I really ought to think about paying him a visit "to go over the rather substantial materials here [in Ann Arbor] that bear on her states of mind in the final few years. I know that evidence well, and have in recent years put together what I think is the most likely understanding of the three or so MAIN pressures on her that led to her final decision. If you came out here I would lay all this out for you."

Yet, there was a caveat. "Suppose," he wrote, "some other totally different set of hypotheses had caught your eye, that you wanted to highlight as much more deserving of reader attention. How would this make Phil feel . . . ?"

It was more than odd that he was now referring to himself in the third person.

"Hopefully you would understand that I would be unhappy in the extreme if you did not vibrate in some fair degree to something like my 3-item solution."

I began looking into flights to Michigan.

P hil and his wife, Jean, lived in a modest suburban development home in Ann Arbor, not far from the University of Michigan. He was waiting at his front door when I arrived, and greeted me warmly.

There it was—the same sharp nose, the same jutting chin and high forehead that I'd been staring at for months in the few available photographs of his sister. As I shook his hand, it was, more than anything, overwhelming to think, again, *This is Connie Converse's brother. They grew up together, had the same parents, went to the same New Hampshire public schools, shared the same DNA.*

Along with Jean, we spent a little time making polite conversation over the little spread of cheese and crackers they'd laid out. Andrea Kannes, an NYU graduate student, was also there to work on a Connie Converse documentary with a local helper. We sat discussing our goals for what we each hoped to accomplish over the long weekend. But it was late in the day, and Phil knew full well that my time there was limited, so he quickly suggested that I follow him out to the garage. "I'll just show you where you'll find all of Connie's stuff, and you can have at it while we get out of your way!"

Andrea had already seen these things, so I followed Phil out through a side door, alone. He flipped on a light, and there, up against the wall directly to our right, was Connie Converse's five-drawer metal filing cabinet. It was old and dark, clunky and formidable in a 1950s industrial sort of way. Had the moment of discovery been illustrated in a comic book, R. Crumb style, the cabinet would have been emanating undulating squiggly bands of energy like the Holy Grail or the Ark of the Covenant. This, I knew, was everything she'd left behind, everything that was left of her. It was metal, it was creaky, its entire contents had her finger-prints all over it.

"You'll find everything in there, just as she left it," Phil said, pulling out one of the long sliding drawers to reveal its rows of carefully labeled folders.

As I began to thumb through, immediately aware of the breadth and depth of what had been there for decades, my heart began to race. Typi-cally, what constitutes a person's personal effects is a collection of ran-dom bric-a-brac, items haphazardly tossed into boxes and bins before being consigned to a musty attic or garage, their significance lost to all but immediate family and friends: a favorite hat, a stack of photos, an old yearbook, a meaningful letter or two, an address book, maybe a wallet, or some jewelry. In the rare case of someone like Henry Darger—another outsider artist who created in virtual obscurity during his life—what's left behind can be a messy, chaotic legacy of work carelessly scattered about for others to sift through and try to understand.

This was not that. This was an art installation, an immaculate archae-ological find. My mouth agape, I saw revealed a self-contained universe, the not-unproud distillation of one person's life of ideas, accomplishments, and unbridled creativity, all carefully curated and preserved.

There wasn't just a handful of letters here; there were *hundreds* of them, most written by Converse and organized by recipient. They were typed and inky, their pages dented by the heavy keys of a manual type-writer and clearly carbon copies she'd made for her own purposes, most single-spaced and running to several pages long.

Her 1950s-era recordings of her songs that Phil had digitized were there, but so were boxes containing other old tape reels: oral histories given by members of her family; radio broadcasts of classical concerts she'd recorded; an instructional piano tape she'd made for Phil to dem-onstrate a piece she'd written for him; a group of singers rehearsing her unproduced original opera(!). There was a handmade folio entitled

"Musicks," which contained her typewritten lyrics to all her songs, complete with her commentary and annotations.

There were what seemed like (at least, in those breathless moments of discovery) an endless number of photographs and slides spanning the course of her entire life, many of them organized by subject, date, and quality (yes, quality).[1]

And there was overwhelming evidence of what Phil's liner notes had hinted at: that Converse was much more than a great unknown songwriter. As Phil had claimed, she was a polymath—a talented illustrator, painter, thinker, published political cartoonist and essayist, poet, photographer, and aspiring novelist. She had published scholarly articles about international affairs in the Far East and about the science and study of conflict resolution and had also made deep dives into statistics, early computer analytics, and economics. She was a voracious reader, a writer of belles lettres, and a political activist. Even without the music she made, the sum of what she left behind in the cabinet revealed an important, richly layered life.

This doesn't belong here, I thought. *This should be relegated to a research library, or a museum, or to the Smithsonian Institution.* It was no wonder Phil had suggested I come for a visit so that I could see it for myself.

Like the mythological Cassandra (a character around whom, I didn't yet know, Converse had composed an entire song cycle), Connie Converse could see the future. The contents of the cabinet and the time she'd spent organizing it demonstrated as much. This was a time capsule, buried treasure just waiting to be discovered. Clearly, she'd left it behind with the hope that some future generation would eventually understand and appreciate what most of her contemporaries did not.

In her typed, meticulously detailed nine-page "Guide to Contents of Five-Drawer File" she'd prepared and left in the top drawer, Converse had indicated where and what everything was, which materials were included in which folder and in which drawer.

Phil explained to me that he had weeded some of this out at one point, and to my horror, I noted that the names of some of the materials Converse had inventoried had been crossed out. In pencil, the words "dumped" or "dumped in toto" had been written next to a number of items, including those described by Converse as "TRIES" (five folders containing "Miscellaneous fragments of my pre-1960 literary efforts") and "THOTS" (fifteen folders of various scholarly investigations and personal musings, all but two of which were gone).

⌒

By that first night, every square inch of Phil and Jean's dining room table was covered by stacks of letters, documents, photographs, and scrapbooks, laid out and organized as carefully as possible. "Just holler if there's anything you need," Phil had said as he and Jean went about their business and the film students disembarked to another part of the house to scan another pile of documents, leaving me alone at the table, head down, immersed. I began to triage, identifying what seemed the most important items first, reading as fast as I could and making copious notes.

At a certain point, I realized that there were no other visible lights on in the house save for the one overhead lamp directly above me, which seemed metaphorically appropriate. The entire world in that moment seemed to have been winnowed down to me, that table, and what felt like my feeble attempt to confront the immensity of everything that Connie Converse had left behind.

Suddenly, I became aware of another presence. Startled, I looked up to see Phil, silently standing opposite me, hands jammed into his front pockets. Because of his height—he towered above the lamp—his face was eerily lit from below, and he was looking down at me and smiling. Who knew how long he'd been there? It was an unnerving moment, something I chalked up to the intensity of my focus over many hours. Every moment I'd spent there so far had been about trying to get inside the lost world of Connie Converse. It felt as though I'd lost all sense of where, or even who, I was.

∾

The trip ended up being more successful than I had dared hope; I was returning home armed with enough primary research material to keep me occupied for many months, if not years. Every letter, every photograph, every receipt and bank register contained another clue, another lead to chase, another detail to add to the forensic reconstruction of Connie Converse's hidden, buried life I hoped to accomplish.

I began mapping a Converse family tree, sketching out a time line of her life, and, more important, making lists of the people I knew I would need to track down and talk to.

But, though I felt emboldened by what I'd been given access to in Ann Arbor and by Phil's having given me his absolute blessing to proceed with a biography, understanding the volume of Converse's carefully organized materials that were missing, likely for all time, was as difficult as it was upsetting.

I returned to Brooklyn surer than ever of the importance of my task, cognizant of its massive, intimidating scope, and aware that for every seeming answer I'd found, multiple questions had sprung up to take its place.

CHAPTER 7

We Have Never Seen Her Like

With their older brother, Paul, having died in 1993, and their parents long gone, I set aside further family outreach to focus on the area of my primary initial interest: the story of Converse's almost career as a musician in New York City in the 1950s. Phil suggested I contact Gene Deitch, the man who'd recorded Converse performing in his home in 1954 and whose 2004 appearance on a WNYC radio show led directly to the release of *How Sad, How Lovely* five years later.[1]

Deitch was easy enough to find. Despite his advanced age—he and Converse were born the same year, only five days apart—he was active on social media and regularly updated his website, which contained a section devoted to his role in the Converse story.[2]

But when I contacted him, his response was cold. The questions I had regarding the particulars of his history with Converse were met with the same answer: "It's all on my website."

It wasn't. As with Phil's recollections of his sister, there were essential details missing from Deitch's account, including specifics about how he came to meet and record Converse. Deitch claimed to know nothing about her other than that she was brought to his door one evening by his best friend, Bill Bernal.[3] Bernal had died in 1991, but his second wife, Barbara, to whom he was married in the 1950s, was then still around.[4] Deitch sent me her contact information and suggested that I reach out.

The former Barbara Jean Putney was as gracious and helpful as Deitch was recalcitrant. I began by asking for details about her former husband, the man Deitch told me was most responsible for anyone even knowing Converse's music today.

Barbara wrote that she met Bernal during her stint as an editor/reporter for *Women's Wear Daily* in the early 1950s. She was married at the time, but Bernal captivated her attention. "Bill was the kind of guy who immediately attracts attention when he walked into a room full of people," she wrote to me. He was a big man with a big presence (six foot one and well over two hundred pounds), a bon vivant, "charismatic" with "a booming voice. Heads would turn."[5]

But their connection was more than just physical. Bernal was a man-about-town, and she was drawn to his "expansive lifestyle," which was in marked contrast to the one she shared with a reclusive husband who "wanted to keep me in a box. I was outgoing, and spreading my wings, escaping into the wide cultural life of Manhattan, with Bill as my fascinating guide—to movies, nightclubs, the jazz scene."[6]

The two began having an affair, and soon after, she left her husband. She and Bernal became a fixture in a social circle that included a number of the illustrators and animators working at UPA studios in Manhattan, among them Deitch and artists like *New Yorker* cover artist R. O. Blechman, Shamus Culhane (lead animator on Disney's *Snow White and the Seven Dwarfs*), and Cliff Roberts (who would illustrate Langston Hughes's *The First Book of Jazz*).

Culhane's widow, Juana, told me that the Bernals were considered "the ideal couple. Bill was so charming, so enjoyed life . . . he could cook like a professional, was always engaged in some way, and just seemed to exude excitement and energy."[7]

According to Barbara, she and Bernal heard Converse for the first time together in 1954, at a listening party at Deitch's home. Such circumstances are common today to the point of being cliché; Converse was doing what any number of songwriters now do every single night, in every major city, all the time, and all over the world. But back then, salons like Deitch's were highly unusual, it being still a few years removed from the imminent rise of hootenannies and the coffeehouse scene. In 1954, a house concert featuring a singer performing original material—and a woman, no less—would have been considered audacious.

The atmosphere there, Barbara told me, was formal, even a bit stiff. "No drugs, no drinking, no reefer," she recalled. "Just squeaky-clean music lovers—not the groovy kind." She said that there were no more than a dozen or so people present the first time Converse showed up.[8] That night, most of the crowd had barely noticed the odd-looking young woman with the guitar. "She struck me as the type who might be a librarian, or a Catholic nun," Deitch later recalled.[9]

The singer appeared to Barbara hardly the vixen depicted in Converse's song "Roving Woman" (in which the narrator cheerily confesses to her habit of sleeping around), and what Barbara and Deitch recalled about her is commensurate with the ways most people subsequently described her to me: as a plain, unpretentious bookworm type. She didn't talk a lot, and when she did, it was with a formality and a self-consciousness that could be awkward and distancing.

Yet, at Deitch's house, an ironic dynamic was at play. Because of her demeanor, Converse was judged and even initially dismissed by this urbane, artsy clique as a boring nobody. But her songs would reveal her to be privately wilder than any of them.

The more I corresponded with Barbara, the more pointed her recollections of the introverted, then–twenty-nine-year-old singer became:

She didn't try to be sophisticated in the way she presented herself. She was boring to look at. She didn't try to be attractive. Connie came across as oblivious to "outer" trappings. Even thrift-shop clothes can be worn with special touches that give them style. She dressed rather shabbily, like she had just milked the cows, you know. She didn't wear makeup either. We live in a culture where a woman's looks have an impact, one way or the other.

Connie had a pretty face, her bone structure was classic . . . but she may have been unaware of her good looks—she was as far from a Lady Gaga show-off as you can get. She made no effort to be pretty, or to feel pretty. How did she wear her hair? Pulled back, plain, dull. And probably unwashed. She needed a makeover! I was Copy Chief for a time at Harper's Bazaar *magazine so, as you may imagine, my eye was perhaps too finely tuned to this woman's bland "look." It seems to me she was "in hiding." Never for a second did she call attention to herself—except, I guess, when she was performing her music. But, even then, it was her songs she wanted you to "look at," not her.*[10]

Converse's photographs from around that time verify what Barbara remembered. Converse had a full, even sensual mouth; her simultaneously penetrating and dreamy gaze, her high cheekbones and insouciant smile are attractive by almost any standard.

And yet her attire was unusual, to the point of eccentricity. The 1940s and '50s saw a revival of the "hourglass figure" of the 1890s in women's fashion, with tight belts and closely fitted tops and skirts designed to draw attention to a woman's shape. Women, and especially women performers, were culturally encouraged and even expected to trade on their physical appearance. During our talk about the New York scene of the fifties, Dick Weissman had told me, "Women musicians in that era, if they didn't have sex to sell, were pretty much worthless."[11] Some of the remarks Deitch would make to me also seemed to put forward this perspective. "Connie wasn't beautiful," he told me. "I wouldn't be surprised if she was deprived, sexually. Her personality was not the type that men seek out."[12]

But singer and folklorist Ellen Stekert, who began her career as a performer around that same time, disagreed. "I didn't wear makeup, either, and I dressed very plainly and tied my hair back, too, and I had no problem meeting people," she told me. "Of course, I was a lesbian."[13]

Barbara mentioned something else to me about Converse that she felt uneasy about divulging: "Truth is, Connie had very, very bad body odor," she wrote me. "I don't know why. I assume she bathed and wore clean clothes. So it must have been a natural sweat smell of hers. I'm sorry to say, Connie's 'odor' put me off. I didn't want to get close to her . . . I never ever hugged her! It bothered me that this delicate, fragile—but terribly gifted—woman could be so unaware of her unpleasant physical presence. I can't help but wonder whether her 'smell' was a way of keeping people from coming too close." (Bernal's daughter Victoria recalled her father telling her about a woman he knew "who did not use perfume, but would occasionally grind a little fresh nutmeg down her blouse," behavior that sounds eccentric enough to have been Converse's, though Barbara told me she didn't believe that could be so.)[14] This body odor issue was a detail she subsequently brought up again several times as something particularly telling about Converse.

Did it mean something more? The lack of care with which she presented herself in the world may have been an unconscious choice for Converse, or it may have been intentional. As she had already demonstrated by dropping out of college and moving to New York to pursue her artistic ambitions, and as she would continue to demonstrate for her entire known life (culminating in her decision to disappear), Converse cared little for conformity. She did what she wanted, when she wanted, with whom she wanted, and how she wanted, ever ready to jab a finger in the eye of what was expected (a tendency that's also displayed again and again in her lyrics, and in her music). The idea of there being a "right" way to dress, to talk, to act likely would have been absolute anathema to her. It wouldn't have surprised me if, for Converse, offending the principles of an unsuspecting "proper" foil like Barbara Bernal may even have secretly delighted her.

For whatever reason, during her years of making music in New York, Converse didn't seem inclined to play along with common expectations of how she should present herself. But unlike someone such as Katharine Hepburn, or even Converse's contemporary Carson McCullers, both of whom conspicuously clothed themselves in androgynous fashion as a form of rebellion, engendering their own sense of style and iconoclasm (and, in McCullers's case, telegraphing a coded message about her sexuality); or latter-day performers like Patti Smith, Billie Eilish, or Adrianne Lenker, whose anti-fashion fashion has garnered them points for authenticity, Converse—to hear Barbara Bernal tell it—just seemed sloppy and uncouth. She favored long plain dresses that were grossly out of style, and chose to keep company with her songs, unwilling to sacrifice her integrity for the sake of "the way things are done."

Slowly, the sketchy outlines of the woman Connie Converse actually was in her time were beginning to sharpen. Phil's remembrances to me—on the phone, over email, and in person—had humanized her, even through his particular lens of sibling worship. The contents of her filing cabinet, which I now had copies of (and which I felt I'd only begun to assimilate), illustrated the many ways she'd applied her creative talent and massive intelligence far, far beyond the scope of her songs.[15] Now Barbara

Bernal had revealed some chinks in the armor of what could be called the Hollywood version of Converse—that brave, unflappable twentysomething genius who blithely flitted through 1950s Greenwich Village with her guitar, the original sad girl.

And yet, Gene Deitch—the only person known to have recorded her (other than she herself), and whose memories I believed would add immeasurably to the picture that was emerging—remained an elusive get. It wasn't until I told Deitch that I was willing to travel to his home in the Czech Republic for an audience with him that he agreed to speak to me about Converse. My band had some dates in Europe shaping up, and I suggested that I fly to Prague at the tail end of our tour to meet him in person. Reluctantly, he agreed. "Just call me when you get here and we can meet," he wrote to me, unwilling to commit to anything more concrete than that.

Upon arrival, I checked into a quaint hotel in the city's Old Town, in what I knew to be the neighborhood Deitch had been living with his second wife, Zdenka, since his move there as an expat in the late 1950s. I contacted him as soon as I got to my room. "Can you meet me this afternoon?" he wanted to know. He gave me the name of a small café and told me to be there in a couple of hours.

I arrived ten or fifteen minutes early to assemble my notes, seating myself under an umbrella in the sunny courtyard—and sure enough, at the appointed hour, octogenarian Gene Deitch tentatively wove his way toward me, exuding an air of hesitancy and wariness, but otherwise in full command of his faculties and ready to talk. If he seemed suspicious of me, I couldn't blame him. To Deitch, I was just another of a growing number of Connie Converse obsessives, one who'd gone so far as to stalk him all the way to Prague.

And perhaps he'd already grown tired of talking about Converse in the wake of *How Sad, How Lovely*. Maybe he'd even become slightly resentful of the fact that his role in Converse's story had taken on an outsize importance in the arc of his own biography.

Whatever the reason, Deitch spent the better part of our three hours together relating minute details about how he got into animation, his brief military service during World War II, and his passion for New Orleans jazz. While most of the autobiographical details he relayed were entirely irrelevant to the purpose of my visit, his intense self-absorption was its own sort of reveal. When I was finally able to squeeze in my first question about Converse, he stated unequivocally that he knew nothing about her personally. "We were not friends!" he insisted.

Deitch told me that he and his young family were living in Hastings-on-Hudson, a sleepy upscale suburb twenty miles north of Manhattan, when Converse first showed up at his house. That accounts vary as to the circumstances that led to that moment may not be important, but it adds yet another layer to the mystery of her larger story. On what turned out to be one of the most significant nights of her musical life, there's little agreement as to how or why she happened to be there.

Deitch, for his part, stuck to his story: Bernal had been responsible. "Bill phoned ahead to tell me that he was bringing a sensational singer he'd discovered and that I should be set up to record her so that he would have a tape to play for a broadcaster or record company. Bill was intent on promoting her."[16]

The two men had been friends since 1946, when both were starting to make their respective ways in the film business in Los Angeles.[17] Bernal had gotten into film through his first wife, Marj Thorson, a rising star in the script department at MGM. Thorson was "tall, very attractive, poised, and stately," according to Barbara Bernal, and from a higher social class than Bernal and "more educated than he was." Though the Bernals were briefly thrust into the upper echelons of Hollywood society due to Marj's success, the marriage was a rocky one. "Bill suffered,"

Barbara wrote me. "Marj outclassed him, her salary was higher, and his masculinity was threatened. He became impotent with her, but began an affair with the wife of mutual friends."[18] They divorced, and Bernal moved to New York City.

Bernal and Deitch had met and bonded over their shared passion for old jazz 78s. Together, they organized gatherings for fellow enthusiasts for the purpose of spinning rare shellac, a practice they resumed after both of them had landed in New York City.

Sometimes, they invited musicians to join these get-togethers. When that happened, Deitch, an amateur audio engineer, would make recordings of the performances, later dubbing copies and distributing them to the attendees.

Deitch's hobby had already led to the first known recordings of a young John Lee Hooker in a Detroit garage while Deitch was living in that city between stints on the coasts.[19] Deitch subsequently made important informal recordings of other significant performers, including Pete Seeger and Eubie Blake.[20] Within the small pond of folk, blues, and jazz audio enthusiasts, Deitch was a big fish.

He told me that Bernal was the one who would often funnel new talent to the weekly gatherings. "Bill always knew things before anyone else," Deitch said. "Whether it was the latest film, or restaurant, or musician, Bill knew about it first."[21]

Deitch initially hesitated when Bernal told him he wanted to bring Converse to a salon to perform and be recorded. Deitch was really interested only in performers of traditional music, and—like the folk purists—the idea of someone singing original songs did not much appeal to him. But in the end, he deferred to his friend, whose tastes he knew to be unimpeachable.

When I told Deitch what Barbara Bernal had said about her and Bill hearing Converse for the first time together at Deitch's house, he disagreed, shaking his head. "She's wrong," he growled. "Bill Bernal introduced me to Connie Converse. I'm certain of that." He repeated the fact that Bernal wanted Deitch to record a good-sounding demo tape he could then use to get her music wider exposure.

Barbara and Bill's other daughter, Lindsay, said that Deitch's memory rang true as far as what she understood about her late father, with whom she'd had a complicated relationship. She described him as "a very social person," "a big personality," and "a good drinker." He drank every day, she told me, and would often stop off at a bar on his way home from work. But for what he lacked as a devoted parent, he compensated for in his service to others. "He was a super-connector," she said, ready to go out of his way to do everything in his power to help someone else, so it seemed entirely in character for Bernal to have been trying to further Converse's career.[22]

Between what Lindsay told me about her father and what Deitch now recalled, a picture emerged of this man who'd "discovered" Converse's talent: charismatic, confident, ebullient about his passions. Steeped in the arts and able to talk about them with intelligence and contagious enthusiasm.

Bernal, as Deitch described him, was "sandy-haired, virile, affable, and very sexual."[23] Juana Culhane had already told me that Bernal "adored women, and women loved his attention in turn. He always said just the right thing, and was so lyrical in his speech. Women would be shining, glowing under his attention."

Despite the fact that Bernal was newly re-married, "he came on to my younger sister and propositioned her," Culhane told me. She said she wouldn't have put it past Bernal to have been after more than just helping Converse's career.[24]

I'd tried to broach this subject several times with Deitch over email, but he'd conspicuously ignored it. What I was after was some explanation for how, if Deitch's memory was right, Bernal had come to connect with Converse in the first place. As far as I could tell, at the time of their meeting, Converse had no professional musical engagements or credits to her name. It wasn't as though she was out playing gigs. Given that Phil had already told me that it was his feeling that his sister "enjoyed being taken home by strangers" at this time in her life, could Bernal have been one of them, perhaps first meeting over drinks in the Village one night on his way home from work? Might he have suggested that they repair to her nearby apartment, and urged her to sing him some of the songs she told him she was writing? Was it Bernal's libido, rather than his musical radar, that had caused their paths to cross? Pure speculation, of course, but now that I was face-to-face with Deitch, I could finally confront him about this aspect of Bernal's personality.

Deitch dodged the subject. As close as the two of them were, he claimed, they did not discuss their private lives with each other. When I relayed the things that Culhane had told me, Deitch reluctantly offered that Bernal "may have had affairs" and that this may have been the result of his less-than-ideal domestic situation. "His marriage to Barbara was intense and stormy," Deitch said, "and often played out in public with screaming and fighting" (a far cry from the "ideal couple" Culhane had initially described).[25]

Finally, I asked him directly: Had Bernal been romantically involved with Converse? Deitch grimaced. "It's a distinct possibility," he said, looking down. "I don't know. It's not something that I would rule out."[26]

~

While it took some time to come to know, as best as I could, who introduced Connie Converse to whom, what was clear was that Bill Bernal's importance to the story of her music could not be overstated. Somehow, he discovered and became an advocate for her music, and she came to the session at Deitch's house when she was recorded by someone else for the first time. Deitch's son, Kim, then only ten years old, published his memories of that evening in *The Comics Journal* after the release of *How Sad, How Lovely*:

> No one paid any particular attention to her at first, as there were other performers on hand who my Father was busily taping. But at some point, whoever had brought Connie along urged her to sing something and with seeming reluctance she did. Well, it was one of those moments you often hear about but seldom witness . . . The tape machine was rolling as Connie launched into a humorous upbeat song called "Rambling Woman" [sic]. Even I quickly picked up on the fact that it was about being picked up in bars . . . One of our cats, Andrea, was in heat at the time and you can hear her howls of sexual longing in the background as Connie sings, and Connie makes an ironic aside about it when she finishes singing . . . She stopped the party cold in its tracks. From that point on the party was all about Connie![27]

The recording survives—complete with cat-in-heat yowling and Converse commenting, at the song's conclusion, "I think that makes a perfect background!" Though a degree of nervousness on Converse's part is evident—she flubs a lyric, and her guitar accompaniment lacks the steady confidence heard on her own recordings—the performance is a winning one, transforming her before the group's very eyes.

The various elements at play in her opening number that night—the gentle music; the subversive subject matter; the socially awkward, strangely dressed performer; the cat's cries—combined to create an appropriately weird, compelling, and entirely disquieting debut for this singular artistic voice. The moment displays all the trappings of a secret origin story—the mild-mannered nobody transfigured, suddenly endowed with dazzling, extraordinary powers.

Deitch's trust in his friend's taste was rewarded, in spades. "Connie transfixed us with her songs," Deitch recalled, "full of a unique mix of very personal sadness, joy, longing, frustration, and ironic humor. We were absolutely astounded!" He told me that she "played a couple of dozen songs" that first night, a testament to the extent to which she had them in her thrall.[28] Having a handful of tunes received well in such a setting would qualify as a success. When you're playing a couple dozen songs, there's something extraordinary going on.

~

Aside from Barbara Bernal, Deitch could not think of another surviving member of his music salon clique. But Barbara had suggested the name of a couple she remembered from back then, one with whom she had since lost touch: Julia and Fred Crippen. I found the Crippens not only alive and well, but immediately responsive to mention of the names Bernal, Deitch, and Connie Converse.

They hadn't thought about Converse for decades, they said, and were unaware of the existence of *How Sad, How Lovely.* Julia Crippen's impressions of Converse squared with Barbara's and Deitch's takes: She found the singer "almost librarian-like ... a gentle, quiet girl, but when she began to sing, she was so compelling and surprising, and sang with such pathos about lost love and hope."[29] She called Converse "a Village type ... not someone who would go and work in an office or something"—unaware that that's precisely what Converse had been doing back then to support herself, at a Manhattan print shop called Academy Photo-Offset.[30]

Crippen not only recalled the title of one of Converse's songs, "Playboy of the Western World," but then, to my astonishment, began to recite complete swaths of its lyrics to me over the phone, word for word.

"Playboy" was completed in 1953, the same year Patti Page's "(How Much Is) That Doggie in the Window" sold over two million copies—

exactly the sort of harmless, inane pap against which Converse was re-belling. Converse's song takes its name from the controversial 1907 play by Synge, which tells the story of a man in an Irish village who murders his father. But when news of the crime spreads, rather than ostracizing the killer, the locals become enamored of the audacity of his deed, and he becomes the object of infatuation for the women in town. The play caused riots in Dublin when it premiered, and again in New York when it played there four years later.

This sort of rakish protagonist—the irresistible bad boy, the unavail-able fantasy lover—appears in several of Converse's other songs, includ-ing "Man in the Sky," "Johnny's Brother," and "Father Neptune."

Her composition of "Playboy" is one of the most musically ambitious in her guitar song catalogue, though—like all of her songs—its struc-tural complexity is not what we register first. We just like it. As David Garland (whose radio show *Spinning on Air* had played a crucial role in the unearthing of Converse's music) told me: "It's the same thing that fasci-nates me about people like Brian Wilson. It's music that *communicates* first, without needing to get acclimatized as a listener. You get it, but then when you *want* to know how it works, you find that there are interesting twists and turns . . . that contribute to the fact that you got it right away. As opposed to someone who writes a song and your first thought is: 'Oh, that's really weird!'"[31]

"Playboy" features virtuosic wordplay to complement its inventive musical construction:

> *I knew a man*
> *Once, very long ago;*
> *They say that he was born in Buffalo*
> *But I don't believe it—*
> *Buffalo was never sufficiently gilded and pearled,*

And this man turned out to be
The Playboy of the Western World.

Oh, he was elegant
Past all dreaming,
He made seeming
Seem like the real McCoy;
All the sheiks of Araby,
All the Shahs of Persia
Couldn't hold a candle
To this boy.

Superficially, the song presents as a fairy tale, though Converse fixing its subject as a native of a specific industrial town like Buffalo immediately brings the story down to earth. The man is cultured, sophisticated, and also a magician—able to transform the mundane into glittering wonder. His Ford becomes a Mercedes, wildflowers picked in the park turn into beautiful bouquets, and everyday excursions taken with him seem like trips to luxurious destinations like "the Astor or the Sherry Netherland," with their ornate ballrooms, rooftop bandstands, and classy restaurants catering to society's elites.

To the working-class Converse, such places may have represented a reality from which she felt excluded. But by dint of being in this man's company, the singer becomes a Cinderella, and all doors open to her. He even makes it possible to "fall in love with everyone you'd meet when you walked with him down the street."

Alas, "playboys die young, this one did too"—another common theme in Converse's songs: the exit or absence (or both) of the object of her affection. And there is a final, unexpected twist, something that is a signature in so many of her guitar songs. When the singer attends the playboy's funeral, she presses into his hand a bunch of the same type of flowers that he, once upon a time, gave her.

After all the years passed, these were the lyrics that Julia Crippen recited to me over the phone. Virtually every single word of the first couple of verses was still strung through her memory. Delighted to know that she had such a connection to Converse's music, I asked her when she'd last heard the song.

"Oh, at the time of those parties. Maybe 1953 or 1954," she said.

Had she ever possessed a recording of it?

No.

How many times would she guess she heard Converse sing the song?

Two or three times.

Like Gene Deitch, Crippen was well into her eighties. How was it possible, I wanted to know, that she could recall the lyrics to a song she heard just two or three times more than six decades ago and get the words exactly right?

"It really made an impression on me," she said.

In time, I would track down another living member of this clique, an artist named Merle James (né Edelman), who told me he once hosted Converse at one of *his* parties. He'd been cautious when suggesting that she bring her guitar, he said, lest she feel obligated to perform without pay, but he hoped she would play some of her music for him and his friends.

She did. In his retelling of that evening, he, too, started reciting, and then singing, a song of hers, but this one was "Talkin' Like You." And I mean, word for word. Like the Crippens, Edelman also denied ever owning a recording of Converse's music. "I just loved that song," the eighty-six-year-old told me, adding that he hadn't heard or thought of it in over half a century.

This seemed like something out of an Oliver Sacks book, if not *Ripley's Believe It or Not!* When I brought the matter to a couple of memory specialists, I was made to understand that not only are such kinds of phenomena possible, but depending on how the event (in this case, the performance of a song) was initially encoded in the brain, this sort of recall can even be textbook.

And as unlikely as this seemed, when I thought about it, I realized that there are lyrics and melodies I heard in my childhood, many decades ago, that remain in my head to this day. Television jingles, some of my parents' favorite songs, the lyrics and melody to a song I sang with my class in school in first grade—one I haven't heard it since then but that I remember—mainly, I would assume, because it was the first song I ever performed in public, at a school assembly for family and friends. It had tremendous significance for me.

And Converse? "She must have been absolutely mesmerizing," Kelly Goedert, professor of psychology at Seton Hall University, told me, "to have impressed and impacted their memories that deeply."[32] Converse's house performances, for whatever reason, had burned themselves into these people's consciousness.

Neither the Crippens nor Merle Edelman knew anything about Converse's personal life, in keeping with what Deitch and Barbara Bernal had told me. "I loved Connie—but from afar," Barbara explained. "She seemed to enclose herself in her own private space, while, of course, revealing herself intimately through the poetry of her lyrics." They were not friends.

No. Connie seemed unapproachable. She was strange . . . there was something rather isolated and sad about her . . . a lonely, romantic spirit who was filled with longings that seemed doomed—or so her words told us. We were reverent. We

knelt at Connie's feet. I sat on a sofa across from where she was perched with her
guitar on her knees on an ordinary wooden kitchen chair, next to a table holding
Gene's tape recorder. Connie would take a short break between each song and
there would be chatter among the guests until the shy performer was encouraged
to sing another number. She smiled a lot and had a low, throaty, self-deprecating
laugh, and laughed easily once she began playing her songs. She was humble.

Deitch felt otherwise. He told me he had the feeling that "she looked down on all of us. She didn't think that we understood the meaning and depth of her lyrics."[33] And as a fellow artist, Deitch seemed offended by this. But Deitch was, first and foremost, a lover of "hot" jazz, music that historically expressed freedom and joyful exuberance. Seeger's music, too, was about connection, bringing people together through the shared activity of music making. Converse's songs, some of them, did have entertainment value, but built into most were subtleties of meaning and expression that deeply transcend these functions.

To his credit, Deitch had the sense to know that a unique talent had, quite literally, as he told it, been delivered to his door. He told me that he tried "for years and years" to interest people in Converse's music, to no avail. But after meeting and talking with him, I wondered if his sensibility and outlook were at least partially to blame. Given the maverick quality of her songs, Converse needed a different kind of champion than Deitch, who reduced her to superficialities. "All of her songs were sexual," he told me, an observation that misses the mark, by a lot.[34]

Some of Converse's songs explored sexuality, and loneliness, and matters of the heart. But all of them were vehicles to express her complex and well-guarded inner life. And her music, existing in an almost complete vacuum, managed to bridge disparate strands of American music and fuse them into a new style. What makes her so singularly compelling as a figure is that she somehow briefly managed to become a missing link among all these modes, her music an invisible glue that bound them all together in a way that—had it gained any sort of traction—may well have altered the course of American music since then.

Deitch and Barbara Bernal had conflicting thoughts on how Converse saw herself in the context of the music world at that moment. "We knew nothing of her hopes and aspirations," Barbara told me. "She didn't present herself as a person looking for recognition, or ambitious—you know, a person intent on 'selling' herself."[35] Deitch remembered it differently: "Connie believed in herself. She wanted to be known."[36]

It's possible that both things were true. Converse may have wanted a music career, but only on her own terms. I came to understand her as an idealist, a believer in the idea of meritocracy, as so many artists are. Her appearance on television soon after Deitch made his recordings of her seemed to bolster this hope, but Deitch told me that neither she nor Bernal was able to successfully use it as leverage for other opportunities.

And then there was Converse herself, the person creating these sounds. "Looking back, it just seems like Connie suddenly disappeared from our lives," Barbara told me. "We all just lost touch with her."[37] It was a virtual disappearance that would presage her actual one twenty years later. Deitch wrote on his website that "Bill Bernal exerted every effort to his dying day to get recognition for Connie, and I tried to carry on the quest,"[38] but after her final appearance at his house in 1954, Deitch told me he never had contact with her again.

I wanted to delve deeper into this disconnect, but it was late in the day, and Deitch said he was getting tired. Before ending the interview, I offered to play him a recording of "Incommunicado," a song that Converse composed for piano and voice but seems to have never recorded. Deitch was unaware of any of her later piano songs, he said, so on my phone I cued up a cover recently rendered by Charlotte Mundy and Christopher Goddard.

Shall I then expect a summer snow because you tell me so?
I might as well believe my absence made you grieve.
That tongue turns rain to snow and false to true;
What's grief to me is summer snow to you.
Shall I then leave you again?—la la la la

"It sounds like a Broadway song," Deitch marveled. "It isn't anything like Connie Converse's other music!"

From a strictly musical perspective, he was right. Converse's original manuscript identifies the song as a "baritone solo," so, although Mundy recorded it, Converse had composed it for a man's voice. The melody and accompanying piano part are flowing, lyrical, dramatic, and seem to anticipate the kinds of songs Stephen Sondheim would later write.

The words, however, maintain many of the same themes as the guitar music Deitch recorded Converse performing: A singer feels bad about a lover, seeing them as either too perfect or else bad and uncaring. One leaves the other (once this imperfection is understood) and the song becomes a web of love, abandonment, fear, and rage.

And, so often, a coded plea for help. Which may be another reason Converse has attracted such a fierce following. "I don't stand in the need of company," she tells us in "Talkin' Like You"—but what she really means is that, given a choice, she'd rather be alone than suffer fools. But also: She'd rather not be alone. Without her ever expressing it outright, what's built into so many of her songs is the idea that she *does* stand in the need of company—if only she could find the right kind. And so we flatter ourselves that maybe what she's longing for is us.

PART I

The End of My
New England Spine

My poor ancestors, who feed my sense of history
but sometimes starve my pride.

—CONNIE CONVERSE,
TRIES, undated

CHAPTER 8

Converses

I was looking forward to continuing my conversation with Gene Deitch the next day, hoping to shift his attention more sharply onto that fateful year of 1954, when Converse came so close to achieving success, but I was surprised that night by a terse message from him: "I have nothing more to say about Connie Converse. Good luck."

Stressing his importance to the greater story I was trying to piece together did no good; my appeals for him to reconsider elicited nothing but silence. Reluctantly, I returned to the States, knowing a lot more than I expected or needed to know about Gene Deitch, but precious little else about Converse—save for Deitch's tacit admission that she may have been having an affair with Bill Bernal, a possibility I could never confirm.

Now I shifted my attention back to Converse's family. Because she did not achieve even a sliver of fame during her lifetime, none of her surviving relatives (outside of Phil) had ever had the experience of outsiders knocking on their doors, asking for interviews, and probing for their recollections about Connie (or, as many of them referred to her,

Elizabeth). Most were unaware that she'd been serious about writing and performing music and knew nothing about the release of *How Sad, How Lovely*.

A number of her relatives were reluctant even to talk about Converse. Of those who would, some of them were willing to speak with me on the record, and others were not, or else were extremely hesitant about it.

The most helpful guide for understanding her father's side of the family history turned out to be a first cousin once removed named Joseph Thomas ("Tom") Converse, grandson of one of Converse's uncles.

A generation younger than Phil and Connie, and at least one world removed, Tom was born and raised in small-town Kentucky, far from the family seat in old New England. Tom, I soon learned, was a sort of unofficial family historian. His career as a U.S. consular officer, and a lifetime filled with global travel and its attendant variegated cultural experiences, may have given him a particularly unique perspective on the Converse family history. "People fascinate me, and I have always been pretty non-judgmental, which makes me easier to talk to for lots of people, not just family," he told me over the phone one night, delighted to be learning more about his parent's cousin from me, he said, than he'd ever known. I found him to be amiable and open-minded—wickedly smart, reflective, and self-aware, with a caustic wit and an unquenchable curiosity. I liked him immediately.

Although Tom met his father's first cousin only once, when he was very young, he had a nuanced understanding of the kind of family and background she'd grown up with.[1] He still had vivid recollections of his parents taking him on an annual pilgrimage to the Converse homestead in rural New Hampshire and of the special allure it always had for him. "The New England family," he told me, "was like watching a play which, even though it was in English, seemed to have another, semi-hidden murky meaning going on behind the spoken word."

After our first conversation, Tom took it upon himself to study up on cousin Elizabeth and her music. "I am deeply impressed and saddened that I didn't know her better," he subsequently wrote to me, a refrain I would come to hear again and again from people who'd known Converse only to realize they hadn't known her at all.[2]

What he *was* aware of was her end. At least, he'd heard apocryphal details about it.

To learn more about his family, Tom suggested I track down a copy of a two-volume vanity press genealogy of the Converses, warning me that reading it might make me cross-eyed. "Two brothers, Charles and Edward, arrived in 1630 on the good ship *Arbella*," Tom wrote to me. "Charles named his eldest son Edward, and Edward named his eldest son Charles, and these names criss-crossed through several generations until some Ebenezers and Luthers and Jacobs entered the family. Each brother had loads of children and each of their children had loads of children."[3]

That's actually about right. Local histories of the time paint the first two "Convers" patriarchs on New England soil—the terminal *e* was added to the last name much later[4]—as "staunch Puritans,"[5] a description that would continue to be part of the family's character through generations, even after numbers of them (including those on both sides of Converse's immediate family) became Baptists.[6] For hundreds of years, the Converses were a conservative, tough, and stubborn bunch.[7]

The history of the Converse family, like that of Connie's mother's, the Eatons, is intertwined with that of English settlement in North America. The Converses can trace their presence here to the arrival of Deacon Edward Convers (ca. 1590–August 10, 1663) and his family, who indeed landed in Salem, Massachusetts, in 1630, a mere decade after the first English Pilgrims arrived in Plymouth. (John Eaton arrived eight years later, in April 1638.)[8]

Edward Convers came with his wife, Sarah; their three children (Josiah, James, and Mary); and his brother, Charles, aboard Governor Winthrop's ship. Edward and Charles Convers were the great-grandsons of Richard (d. 1542) and Margaret Convers, of Navestock, Essex, England.

There is some dispute as to the earliest recorded traces of the Converse family in Europe. One long-held theory, recently debunked, had it that the lineage went back to Roger de Coignières of Navarre, France, known for his role in the Norman Conquests of the eleventh century, during the reign of William the Conqueror.[9] More recent studies suggest that the earliest known members of the family were working-class people from Essex, England, named Convers—likely derived from "le convers," the designation given to Jews who converted to Christianity in thirteenth-century England. "Convers" would only eventually become "Converse" in America. Even her name, by the time Connie was born, was contrary.[10]

Being among the earliest English settlers, ancestors of both the Converses and the Eatons helped establish the earliest towns and governments, and would come to serve in every significant American military conflict dating back to the War of Independence. A Convers survived the brutal winter at Valley Forge under George Washington; another fought in the Battle of Bunker Hill. Converses and Eatons fought in King Philip's War, the French and Indian War, the U.S. Civil War, and in both world wars. Branches of the Converses and Eatons lived in similar kinds of traditional New England communities, attended similar kinds of churches, and may even have fought side by side on the same battlefields.[11]

One of the Eatons played a homemade fife as a fife major in the musters, early evidence of the family's musical leanings; a century later, one Charles Crozat Converse (1832–1918) composed a cantata and a number of church hymns (including the evergreen "What a Friend We Have in Jesus") and also published *New Method for the Guitar*.[12]

Converse's ancestors were Pilgrims—those early strugglers, mythic in stature and aura; the hard-bitten Puritans who left their homes on perilous journeys, seeking a better life at any cost, stoically bearing life in the North American wilderness with the barest of necessities—without comfort, without safety, without ease; fighting hunger, pestilence, and extreme conditions that tested the limits of their endurance. They were part of a culture that exchanged food and goods with Native tribes, negotiating with them over land when those methods were effective; killing them when they weren't.

The first American Converses lived primarily around the Boston area, near what now is known as Woburn. From there, they multiplied and spread outward, becoming part of the firmament of Colonial New England—generally well-liked, respected pillars of their communities. And yes, there was an offshoot of the family that owned an early 1900s rubber plant that would eventually become the Converse shoe company, now owned by Nike. (At one point, the company lobbied to have one Howard Converse assume the role of titular spokesperson for the company—like an Orville Redenbacher or a Colonel Sanders—but the idea was ultimately too offensive to his Yankee sensibilities.)[13]

Converse's great-great-great-grandfather Robert settled in what is now Amherst, New Hampshire, around 1776, the same year that the colony became the first to establish a government and constitution independent of Great Britain's. He purchased a large farm there on which his son Charles would come to build a house.[14] To this day, it is known within the family and without as "the Converse Place," "the Old Converse Farm," or "the Old Home Place."[15] This is where Tom's family would make annual visits when he was young.

I made my way up there one warm summer day, to spend some time getting a feel for the land where Converse's father was raised, the quality of the air, the energy of the landscape. The stories and intrigue surrounding the Old Home Place had held Tom in their thrall all his life, and he'd urged me to go see it for myself.

On the day I drove there, the deep blue of a sun-drenched sky over-head cast a delirious glow over everything in view, all of it green (grasses and trees) and white (houses, fences, churches, people). Modern times have not encroached much on this out-of-the-way hamlet. I found the little village of Amherst to be still a little village. When I pulled up to the old general store on the main drag and purchased a coffee from an apple-cheeked teenager, her nervous glances from behind the counter made it clear she knew I was not from these parts.

At the library next door, I was made to understand that the Converse name still held real weight in the area. When I told the gracious librarian the reason for my visit, a quick search of her files revealed that Connie (listed as "Elizabeth") had, briefly, been a dues-paying member of the town's historical society. The librarian had no awareness whatsoever of any of Converse's musical accomplishments. She did, however, know exactly where the Old Home Place was, and offered me directions.

I drove the mile or two outside the town's center. The house still resides on a slow, winding country road with nary a streetlight or build-ing development in sight. There are tall trees, wide-open fields, and a sense of emptiness that feels both vast and confined. Amherst, New Hampshire, seems, as so many old American towns do, like a place of secrets, where so little happens that anything out of the ordinary is con-sidered news and might be remembered for generations.

Right next door to the Old Home Place, on what used to be the same parcel of land, is the small, original house that was already on the prop-erty when Robert Convers purchased it in the eighteenth century. This was where Connie Converse's great-grandfather Charles had been born and, after Charles built the home next door, where Converse's grand-father would move in and raise her father and his siblings. Given some of the things Tom told me, it was impossible not to get a sense of creepy,

Gothic, old New England here, the backdrop for the family history I was still learning about.

Young Elizabeth, too, would have heard these stories while growing up in nearby Concord and been privy to hush-hush Converse gossip. Her paternal grandfather, Luther Boutelle Converse, had a brother, Charles Jr., who died within the lowly confines of the New Hampshire State Hospital. His cause of death was listed, in part, as "psychosis," and he's rarely mentioned in any of the family histories—the stigma surrounding mental illness perhaps causing the Converses to sweep his story under the rug.[16] Through what seemed to be the Converses' generations-long habit of avoiding uncomfortable family narratives, young Connie may have internalized the idea early on that mental health was not something nice people talked about.

Converse's paternal grandmother, Nellie Tilden Conrey Converse,[17] had a brother who was killed while fighting for the Union in the Civil War.[18] Because he'd once sworn to her that he would return,[19] "she would always, always, set a place for him at the table for every single meal so that *when* he came home (not *if* he came home), he would know that she had kept her faith in his word,"[20] Tom told me.

I wondered whether Phil might still hold a sliver of hope that one day his sister might return. When I thought, hypothetically, about my own sibling vanishing, it was impossible to imagine the effect such a traumatic event would have on me—the sheer unknown of it, the lack of closure. Despite Phil's assurances to the contrary, did the shadow of such thoughts still regularly plague him, in a way similar to his paternal grandmother who had never stopped thinking about her own missing sibling?

Converse's father, Ernest,[21] one of six children, held forth about his parents in a tape-recorded oral history he gave eight years before his death.[22] Ernest's voice on the recording is stentorian and pure Pepperidge Farm, its tone taciturn and humorless. (It's worth noting that when I spoke to two of Converse's high school classmates, Jean Crowley and Dick Mullavey, both had the same heavy accent, which suggests that both Converse and Phil must have worked to shake off most traces of theirs after they left New Hampshire.)

In the recordings, Ernest is formal and seems to regard himself and the world with absolute grave seriousness. When he speaks about any subject, he does so in such certainties so as to seem almost angry, as though informing dolts about obvious truths, sans any kind of wry self-awareness that might make him simply a lovable curmudgeon. He sounds not unlike one of the sneering, suspicious men in Arthur Miller's *The Crucible,* or (despite his being a lifelong Baptist) the living embodiment of H. L. Mencken's definition of Puritanism: "the haunting fear that someone, somewhere, may be happy."

"People didn't travel in those days," Ernest declaims on the tape, detailing what he saw as his parents' admirably humble life. His father, Luther, farmed in the summer and worked timber in the winter; his mother, Nellie, took care of the home and children.[23] "In the main, a man found his wife within a couple of miles of where he lived, and where he would continue to live,"[24] Ernest said.

Mother Nellie was "devout, very stern. She wasn't one to joke. She almost *never* joked," Ernest said, with what sounds like real admiration.[25] Ernest had two sisters and three brothers, the eldest of whom, Grace, had epilepsy and birth defects.[26] "She was never normal. Never walked, never talked."

In Amherst, I experienced the sort of shiver I'd gotten meeting Phil and seeing the file cabinet for the first time. Converse had known this place well. These grounds, I knew from photos in her scrapbook, were where she and her brothers had played as children, on family outings to see her father's people. This stony, rugged landscape had been one she'd gazed out upon, knowing maybe even then that her destiny lay far away from here. And the house next to the larger, newer one next door was, undoubtedly, where her father Ernest's mind and character were forged.[27]

Tentatively, I knocked on the door. The man who answered identified himself as the house's current tenant. In contrast to the helpful librarian I'd just spoken with, the name Converse meant nothing to him. When I told him why I was there, and offered up a few facts about my mission, he shrugged and gamely offered to give me a quick tour.

Though the home's modest size would have made it practical to heat during the long New Hampshire winters, it was hard to conceive of a family of eight living in its cramped confines. The entire lot of them must have slept in the one upstairs room—about four hundred square feet of space and with a low ceiling. The downstairs had a small kitchen and living area. Below it was a dugout basement with secret passageways that had once been used to hide from Native Americans. The house still has what the Converses would have called "Indian shutters" (or pocket shutters) on its windows—solid wooden panels with holes bored into them that tucked into the walls. The panels would be slid out during skirmishes, offering protection from arrows, and the holes providing a good perch for the end of a rifle.

"The place is *definitely* haunted," the tenant told me matter-of-factly. He and his family, he said, often heard footsteps and women's voices inside the house at odd hours of the night.

Outside, between the small house and a woodshed, there had been an auxiliary structure, which Tom told me had "once served as either the county poor farm or the county madhouse," sometime before the Converses had taken up residence. "There were still chains attached to the walls up there when I was young, for 'the troublesome inmates,'" he said, quoting Converse's aunt Florence.

A barn had once housed the family's animals, and a large field of some many dozens of acres stretched far back beyond the house to the north, toward uninviting dark woods. To the house's east is a stone wall that serves as the dividing line between Amherst and neighboring Merrimack.

Converse's father, Ernest, would have known almost no privacy in this hardscrabble, claustrophobic living situation, though he must surely have felt a surfeit of physical and psychological tension. His sister Grace's grave disabilities (which, according to Tom, the family had done its best to pretend were nonexistent); his mother's insistence on setting a place at *every meal* for a brother who hadn't been seen in nearly half a century; and stories involving murderous Native Americans, chained-up miscreants, and lunatics inhabiting the grounds. It's almost no wonder Ernest grew up to be the humorless, teetotaling disciplinarian he did.

His siblings must have felt it, too. Tom's grandfather Henry, Ernest's brother, was a frightening rager. Tom recalls him being "cold . . . and unpredictable. I never knew when his furious temper would explode . . . My mother was always more than a little afraid of him."

Late in life, Tom told me, there was some significant drama involving Henry and his desire to move into the Old Home Place after his retirement in the 1940s, when he was living in Maryland. "My grandmother told him that the only way she would go back to Amherst was in a pine box. Those were almost her last words. She stood up from bending over a packing crate, said, 'Why is there blood running down the wall?' and collapsed with a massive stroke."

The Old Home Place had been Henry and Ernest's cousin Helen's home for all her life, and the plan was that Henry would buy her out, on the condition that she could continue to live there rent-free. But when Helen got cold feet at the closing, the deal fell through, and Henry refused to speak to her for the rest of his life, though "this didn't prevent him from visiting her there, nor having her in his home in later years," Tom said.

Henry Converse never mellowed. On the day he was moved to a

nursing home near Tom's parents, in Madisonville, Kentucky, he got into a heated philosophical debate with his new roommate. "They were assigned to the same room because they were both Baptists, but my grandfather was a Northern Baptist," Tom wrote me, "and this fellow was a Southern. Their argument escalated to a physical fight, resulting in the two old men wrestling around the room, knocking over a chair and a table and breaking the lamp, and one of them even landed a punch on an orderly trying to separate them. The upshot was that my grandfather had a stroke and died a few days later, never having spent even one night in the nursing home. He'd come down from New Hampshire first class on one Tuesday and returned to New Hampshire as freight the next—like his wife, in a box. The two are buried side by side in Amherst."[28]

Walter and Albert, Ernest's other brothers, lived their lives out as local men.[29] Albert's widow, Belle, late in life, "took all her family photos into the front yard and burned them, to prevent people from laughing at her relatives in their funny clothes and hairstyles," Tom told me. "I assume that fire also consumed any other papers she (or Bert) may have possessed."[30]

The epileptic Grace died of influenza and pneumonia five days shy of her twentieth birthday. Ernest's other sister, Florence, "became a practical nurse,"[31] taking care of the frail wife of a neighbor down the street and then marrying him when the woman died. "I think there must be [the makings of] several operas lurking in my family," Tom wrote to me.[32]

P hil hadn't mentioned a thing about these peculiarities of his family history, but Connie Converse apparently was well versed in them. "It occurs to me that the only difference between me and my ancestors is that I have learned to give in and disintegrate gracefully in moments of stress," she wrote to Phil and Jean in 1951.[33] A year earlier, writing just to Jean, who was about to become her sister-in-law, Converse sounds not unlike Dorothy Parker: "I trust . . . that you have been acquainted with the history of our ill-fated family. Great-aunt Flavia was burned as a witch; Cousin Charlie passed away in an Institution; and my brother and I are the last of a long long line of bats. (How well I remember our childhood in Carlsbad Caverns, rushing out at dusk to fill the air with thin, piercing shrieks!)"[34] As Phil would do in the short family treatment he authored for "Connie's Guitar Songs," she omits mention of their other brother, Paul.

Tom's attitude of bemused detachment toward their family's ancestry seems reflected in Converse's clever missive. In the letter to Jean, she writes that she's been advised to "have a few manhattans before setting pen to paper. But this sort of thing sets me back on the end of my New England spine, so after I have filled your tea-cup I shall retire behind my fan. (We pause now for the customary embarrassed silence which follows introductions.)"

Yet beneath such witticisms were serious implications for her. The history of the Converses seemed rife with stifling patriarchy and staunch conservatism, worthy of poking fun at in a superficial way, but in reality, a yoke from which she would spend most of her life trying to free herself. Her New England family—at least some of them—were a target for her scorn and resentment.[35]

By the time she began writing songs in her late twenties, Converse was ready to put some distance between herself and her vaunted heritage, to publicly out herself as an emancipated woman. And she would do so most explicitly in one of her most accessible compositions, "Roving Woman."

CHAPTER 9

People Say

A frequent topic at the Old Home Place, Tom told me, was the evils of drink. A Converse man who drowned in 1842 was still being talked about when Tom's family visited in the 1950s and '60s.[1] "Each time Great-uncle Eben was mentioned, someone would lean over to someone else and whisper, 'He drowned drunk in the Nashua River, you know.'"[2]

More significant, Converse's father, Ernest, was not only a teetotaler; he was a professional one. In his official capacity with the Anti-Saloon League of New Hampshire, he did his part to help steer the ultimately successful (if short-lived) drive to legally prohibit the manufacture, transport, and sale of alcohol in the United States. Even after Prohibition was repealed, Ernest continued to carry on the fight.

Yet, in "Roving Woman," written in 1952, here is Connie Converse, Ernest's only daughter, choosing to write and sing about one-night stands, gambling, and day drinking:

> *People say a roving woman*
> *Is likely not to be better than she ought to be*

What does this first line even mean? If what Converse means is "people say a roving woman is no good," she could have come up with a simpler way to say that. Somehow, though, it wouldn't have had quite the same ring. Instead, she draws us in, her lyric a little knot presented for our minds to untie.

> *So, when I stray away from where I've got to be,*
> *Someone always takes me home.*

Unlike most popular songwriters of that era—one not known for the depth of its lyrics—Converse never assumes that her audience is any less intelligent than she. She is in cahoots with us. We are her coconspirators as she leads us into the first verse of her narrative:

> *A lady never should habituate saloons,*
> *And that is where I find myself on many afternoons.*
> *But just as I begin to blow away the foam,*
> *Someone tips his hat to me and takes me home.*

Saloons? Foam? Men tipping hats? What century are we in here? It could be mid-century New York City, but it could also be her family's New England of decades earlier.

The collective unconscious of the New Hampshire Converses was riddled with the shame of kept secrets. There were crazy Uncle Charlie, epileptic Aunt Grace, furious Uncle Henry, and drowned drunk Great-great-uncle Eben. And then there was Converse's father's first cousin Helen—the same Helen who would decide not to sell the Old Home

Place. But decades before that situation, and just a few years before Converse was born, Helen had been run out of the Old Home Place, and out of town.

Helen's crime was conceiving out of wedlock.[3] After she returned, almost a year later, an "orphan" baby suddenly appeared on her parents' doorstep one morning and was adopted by the family. The people of Amherst were not fooled, and the story became an open secret. A favorite local topic of conversation included trying to guess who the father was.[4]

Helen spent the rest of her long life in Amherst living up to the reputation that all local Converse women had of being "strong-willed and independent."[5] She lived at the Old Home Place without electricity or indoor plumbing into the 1970s and died in the same bed in which her great-grandfather was born, shunned to the end (according to one of her neighbors and only surviving friend) by the community as an unmarried shamed spinster.

The bastard child whom the ostracized Helen gave birth to was Edith Converse Neff. Edie, as she was known, was close to Connie Converse when they were young. As to her parentage, Edie grew up thinking she was her mother's adopted baby sister and that her grandparents were her adoptive parents.

So, in "Roving Woman," when "people say," those people *might* be Converse's New York City neighbors, but probably not. The song is more likely a shot across the bow at the insular, backbiting New England world that gave birth to her father's morality fixations.

⌒

On its surface, the song is a musically pleasant ditty, its syncopated melody set on top of a simple harmonic structure that Converse appropriated from the most typical popular songs of that day: This is

Hoagy Carmichael's "Heart and Soul," Rodgers and Hart's "Blue Moon," the Gershwins' "I Got Rhythm," or any of the countless songs derived from these templates. Most every American child is familiar with the classic I-vi-IV-V chord progression, the bouncy "Heart and Soul" harmony that has been plunked out in homes and classrooms since 1938, when that song first became a hit. This harmonic movement is almost part of our culture's genetic structure, a musical cliché so common that jazz players soon came to coin the term *rhythm changes* as shorthand for communicating how to improvise over any one of the thousands of songs built on this foundation (meaning, the chord changes to "I Got Rhythm").

Converse, as was her wont as both songwriter and human, never met a convention she didn't try to topple, and "Heart and Soul" (and the multitude of songs that aped it) was as obvious a musical target for her as any. Frank Loesser's lyrics to Carmichael's melody read:

> *Heart and soul, I fell in love with you*
> *Heart and soul, the way a fool would do*
> *Madly*
> *Because you held me tight*
> *And stole a kiss in the night*

Lovely, romantic, wistful—a universal sentiment for a universal melody, lyrics customized for no particular sort of singer, of no particular age, gender, or class.

Lorenz Hart's "Blue Moon" lyric follows suit:

> *Blue moon*
> *You saw me standing alone*
> *Without a dream in my heart*
> *Without a love of my own*

Who can sing these words? Anyone. Ella Fitzgerald, Cyndi Lauper, Sam Cooke, Willie Nelson. The lyrics are nonspecific by design; almost any reading by any performer will do, whether the treatment be jazz, country, rock 'n' roll, or R'n'B. The term *standard* was coined to describe tunes exactly like this one: a song so well constructed, so unfastened to stylistic specificity, that it allows for an unlimited range of performative interpretation. It is a Ford wagon, a Stanley hammer, a turkey dinner.

"Blue Moon," "Heart and Soul," and their ilk are examples of the musically staid popular music Converse grew up listening to, and loathed. As Phil wrote later, "Both of us were devout followers, in the late 1930s and early 1940s, of Tin Pan Alley and the Hit Parade . . . After some years of such connoisseurship, Sis wanted to explain to me one night that nonetheless, the vast majority of Tin Pan Alley songs were pretty much doggerel, musically as well as in their lyrics."

Carmichael, Rodgers, and George Gershwin had fashioned a seemingly indestructible musical cookie cutter that, combined with Loesser, Hart, and Ira Gershwin's easy lyrics, produced whitewashed, soft-focus reveries of chaste romance. Here is Ira Gershwin's lyric for "I Got Rhythm":

> *I got rhythm, I got music, I got my man*
> *Who could ask for anything more?*
> *I've got daisies in green pastures, I've got my man*
> *Who could ask for anything more?*

Compare these bromides with Converse's tale:

> *Don't see why they always do it*
> *Can't be vanity; must be sheer humanity—*
> *When some kind soul remarks with great urbanity:*
> *"Lady, let me take you home."*

Converse appropriates the mold of the standard, a subtle but crafty ploy that allows her song to be framed in a superficially familiar way. It is a musical Trojan horse. Her music having "passed" for normal and acceptable, she can now further her agenda—and does so with the sadistic glee of a cat toying with its prey before pouncing. In the guise of innocuous, familiar musical motifs, the confection she creates bites. No moons in Junes here for her:

> *Of course, there's bound to be some little aftermath*
> *That makes a pleasant ending for the straight and narrow path*
> *And as I go to sleep, I cannot help but think*
> *How glad I am that I was saved from cards and drink.*

The not-so-subtle reveal in this last verse is that Converse's narrator is a woman at liberty who takes great pleasure in whatever goes on with the anonymous stranger whom she has allowed to seduce her—an activity that could be as innocent as a good-night kiss, though the wink in the lyric suggests it is something more substantial. "Roving Woman" jabs a finger in the eye of the traditional American culture in which Converse was raised. It is her Declaration of Independence.

How fanciful was the song's narrative, and how boundary-crossing its heroine? Phil told me on more than one occasion that he understood the lyrics to "Roving Woman" to be straight autobiography—his sister's brazen accounting of her nocturnal activities in New York.[6] If this is true, then Converse was leading a kind of dual existence: mild-mannered, introverted loner by day; liberated and unbuttoned free spirit by night.

Outside New York City, the Roving Woman's behaviors would have been shocking. The United States was still basking in the glow of post–World War II culture. Elvis hadn't happened yet. The Beats hadn't happened yet. The sexual and cultural convulsions of the 1960s were still far, far off on the horizon. Instead, a quaint, Norman Rockwell sort of American ideal was in effect in white America, at least in terms of appearances.

But when she wrote and began performing the song in 1952, Converse was living in Greenwich Village—a place that had acquired a reputation for being a wrecking ball when it came to being confronted with long-established social boundaries and norms. In her own way, she was contributing to the demolition.

Another possibility is that the song (and others of hers like it) was an exercise in wish fulfillment by fictional proxy, like a scene from Elmer Rice's popular 1945 drama *Dream Girl*—a play that had a long run in New York and that Converse was likely aware of (and may even have seen). Rice's protagonist is a young office girl who engages in waking daydreams that provide her with escape from a humdrum, unsatisfying reality.

Because Converse was so private, and because the few confidantes she did have during that period of her life have long since passed away, the truth may never come out. It doesn't matter. "Roving Woman," as performed by her on amateur recordings made in the 1950s, is a fascinating entry in her oeuvre. The X factor, as in most of her music, is to be found in Converse's performance of the song—the final, unexpected ingredient that lifts the composition past a merely tuneful, smart, and subversive poke at social mores and the small-town intolerant mindset of her family's New England.

Some of Converse's guitar songs, like this one, seem to have an almost built-in resistance to interpretation. Not that some haven't tried. In the 1950s and '60s, a small handful of established vocalists included her material in their performing repertoires. And since the release of *How*

Sad, How Lovely, others have covered her songs, both in commercially released recordings and in the scores of renditions to be found on You-Tube and social media. I've taken stabs myself, and have rarely been satisfied with the result.

Converse's material requires a unique combination of performative elements that's extremely difficult to attain. Not to mention that improvising instrumentally over many of them is really tricky. Compositions like "Father Neptune," "Playboy of the Western World," and even "Talkin' Like You" have harmonic structures that feel so wedded to their melodies that it becomes difficult to do anything but present them more or less as written. More than that is the tone of Converse's voice. It, too, feels somehow inextricable from the essence of many of her songs.

Gene Deitch had disparaged Converse's vocals to me. "It's too bad we could never find a real singer to do those songs better," he'd said. "Connie was a great songwriter, but not a very good singer."[7] Soprano Julia Bullock, today one of Converse's greatest contemporary interpreters, strongly disputes this. Bullock told me: "The sound of her voice is so alluring . . . She infuses all of her being into her sound. I don't have any tension listening to her sing. Channels start opening instead. There's a release that happens in my own body. She is a magnificently beautiful guide through her material."[8]

~

O n her own recordings, Converse delivers "Roving Woman" in a reflective, open, almost heartbreaking voice—seemingly in direct contrast to the humor and irreverence of the lyric. The tone of her vocal, shorn (as it is in all her recordings) of any trace of vibrato or affectation, suggests she is in a fragile state, possibly even in despair, yearning to be understood.

Forget, for a moment, what the words say. What I hear is: *I am so alone.*

I put on a brave face, but I secretly believe that I will always be alone. I am ashamed of myself. I am lost in a strange world, and I'm trying to keep my spirits up, but sometimes I know that time is rushing by and I don't understand how I'm supposed to use it. And: *I love someone. I just don't know who or where that person is.*

This is what I responded to most when I first heard the song. It makes absolutely no sense, and it's absolutely brilliant. Were someone who knew no English to listen to this song for the first time, it is impossible to believe they could guess its stated subject matter.

This interplay between the song's "standard" form, its coded lyrics, and the intimate delicacy with which it is performed creates a feat of uncommon artistry and expression. It is what drives the song straight into the fog of mystery, emotional connection, and bewilderment that many experience when listening to Connie Converse's music.

CHAPTER 10

Eatons, and Evelyn and Ernest

I t is time that we air one of the family skeletons," Converse wrote to
Phil and Jean in 1951, when she was twenty-seven and deeply enmeshed in her songwriting efforts in New York City. The subject was
her maternal grandfather, Daniel Emery Eaton, whom one of Converse's
cousins remembered once pounding out hymns on her family's piano
when he came to visit. She said he was not shy.[1]

This seems to have been true, and then some. But Converse's associations with Eaton (or "Emery" as many knew him) were not rosy: "You
inquire about . . . my grandgather—by George that was a typo but I think
I shall leave it just as it is," she wrote. "With all due reverence for his
ninety years, I do not LIKE my grandgather. In fact, he of all my relatives,
arouses in me the most positive emotions of distaste, simply because I find
him the epitome of a New England Yankee with emphasis on all those
historic traits which are better left unsung . . . I will add on his behalf that
my grandgather does not like ME, so we leave each other well alone."[2]

Like the Converses, the Eatons also have a long and tangled genealogy. Where the Converses had their Roberts and Charleses, the Eatons
favored Johns and Daniels. Though the first Eatons in America also set-

tled in Massachusetts, Converse's mother Evelyn's people eventually made their way to what is now Meredith, New Hampshire, led by Emery's father, Daniel Brown Eaton.

D. B. Eaton earned his living as "a typical old-time village schoolmaster" until 1866, when he bought a 110-acre farm in Meredith, off Old Center Harbor Road, for $3,500. Eaton lore has it that he led the family's sheep "all that ten miles or more" during the move. On the new farm, he cultivated and worked twenty-five acres, raising corn, oats, potatoes, and beans and cutting hay by the ton. He owned a dozen head of cattle and kept a blacksmith shop on the premises "for the benefit of the neighboring farmers." But where the Converses of Amherst had their hands in the soil, Eaton's head was in the sky. He was a self-educated Renaissance man with a passion for philosophy, astronomy, engineering, and law.[3]

Converse's "grandgather" Emery (1859–1952) got his start working for the Jordan Marsh department store in Boston before moving back to Meredith to take a post at Meredith Village Savings, the only bank in town, prominently located in the center of the village.[4] By the time he met and became smitten with Ella Alcesta Everett,[5] a thirty-one-year-old Mount Holyoke–educated teacher, he'd become treasurer,[6] known as "the one who made all the decisions."[7] They married and had three children, the middle of whom was Converse's mother, Evelyn.[8] The family eventually settled into a house overlooking Lake Winnipesaukee, on what is now Upper Terrace Avenue.[9]

Meredith Village today is mostly a destination for seasonal tourists who come to swim and boat on its large picturesqure lake and to take in the fresh New Hampshire air. The town's historical society was officially closed when I visited on a snowy February day, but a dedicated and knowledgeable board member named John Hopper graciously volunteered to meet with me there, and to show me around.

The building that now houses the society is the same one that Emery used to work in, when it was still a bank. As Converse does in Amherst, the name Eaton still means something in Meredith. Hopper impressed upon me the sense that Emery was a prominent figure in his day, described by the local newspaper as: "undoubtably one of the best known men in the country . . . His place in the community as a man of sterling worth and integrity has long been established. As a leader in church work, he has no peer locally, and in all circles he is recognized as a pillar of strength."[10]

Hopper showed me a number of items and papers related to Emery, walked me into the bank's still-extant old vault, and took me on a tour of local Eaton-related landmarks in town, including the houses where Evelyn was born and then raised.

Emery Eaton "did things his own way and in his own time," Converse's father, Ernest, recalled. "Some people used to think he was a bit odd, and I suspect that he was, but he was a man of a good deal of ability."[11]

Though the Meredith newspaper described him as a man of "intense vitality," the oddness that Ernest refers to here is probably about something else; before getting started with the bank, when Emery was working for Jordan Marsh, he developed his sense of fashion.[12] "He liked to dress in drag," Phil Converse recalled when I was in Ann Arbor. "I used to have fun asking people who saw [our] wall of photos to pick out my grandfather. Well, of course they couldn't, because he was in drag!" Jean Converse then chimed in: "There was some wonderment whether he was gay. We were thinking that if he was born in a different era, he might have been gay. That it was really suppressed in his contemporary life."[13]

So, while no drowned drunk or insane uncles, epileptic siblings, claustrophobic living arrangements, or neighboring lunatics informed Evelyn's childhood experience, her early life may not seem to have been entirely devoid of complexity.

One of Evelyn's great-nephews, Everett T. Eaton, added some of his own insights. He explained that, though he knows of Eatons all over New Hampshire, many branches of the family pretend they're not related to one another (a quirk I also found in evidence when I visited Deer Isle, Maine, where the name Eaton is one of the oldest and most common on the island). Everett T. told me about the Eatons of one New Hampshire town, near the seat of where the family first settled in America, where the family name has such a bad reputation around business ethics that when I mentioned that I might do some research there and wondered whether he could recommend a good place to start, he said, "You might try the local jail."[14]

⟳

Evelyn seems to have had a happy, active childhood.[15] She was spunky, just as her only daughter would turn out to be. As a teenager, Evelyn led a revolt against the local village school, a one-room red building in the woods that employed one teacher for the entire student population and was so rural and rudimentary that it did not even have state accreditation. Seeking a more robust education, she led a group of like-minded classmates by trolley to nearby Laconia every morning, to attend the public schools there.[16] It may have been Evelyn's thirst for learning, and her spark of idealistic stubbornness, that first endeared her to Ernest Converse.

Like Evelyn's hometown of Meredith, Ernest's home of Amherst, New Hampshire, at the turn of the twentieth century, was not exactly a seat of worldly sophistication. Higher education was frowned upon, thought of as "an expensive luxury, and a dangerous luxury," according to him. When Ernest made it known that he wanted to attend college, his father "was hostile to the idea," finally relenting only when Ernest's mother softened his opposition. Enrolling at the University of New Hampshire, Ernest was the first of his immediate family to be college educated.[17]

After graduation,[18] he spent a few years teaching in Virginia, got his divinity degree,[19] and then moved back to New Hampshire in the fall of 1912. "I took my first pastorate in Meredith, New Hampshire," he recalled later, "where I found my wife."[20]

⌒

Evelyn's family belonged to the congregation that Ernest inherited in Meredith, and her mother oversaw the church's Sunday school.[21] "Must be a pretty weak church if they can't find a *man* to be superintendent of the Sunday school," Ernest remembered thinking at the time.[22]

Evelyn was seventeen, completing her senior year of high school at Colby Academy, where she'd transferred after Laconia High.[23] When she came home for Christmas that December 1912, she met the new young pastor for the first time, in front of the old schoolhouse while out for a winter walk with a girlfriend.[24] "I didn't think much of anything" at the time, she would later recall. Ernest remembered it differently: "[We] were drawn together."[25]

After graduating that next spring, Evelyn took a job teaching at the same little school "way out in the country" at which she and her friends had turned their noses up years before. A contemporaneous photograph taken of her and her charges shows the rough-and-tumble rural nature of her post. At eighteen, Evelyn was not much older than her students.[26] She was petite, standing five foot two and weighing 118 pounds.[27]

By 1914, Ernest had begun moonlighting at the schoolhouse as a part-time teacher to help pad his small church income, and he and Evelyn began spending time together.[28] Over the course of the following year, they became close, walking and talking frequently, sharing confidences, and articulating visions for their respective futures.

Evelyn was intent on pursuing a college education for herself, as her mother had, an idea that drove Ernest to despair: "My dreams never would be fulfilled," he recalled. He was unambiguous about wanting to settle down, and soon, but Evelyn had "decided as a little girl that I would attend Mount Holyoke," and she was not about to let anyone change her mind.[29]

Off to Mount Holyoke she went, graduating in 1919.[30] When she came back home, she again took a job teaching, this time at Woodsville High School.[31] Ernest was still in town, still a bachelor, and still interested. Now thirty-six, he was also still handsome—dashing, even. An undated photograph from around that time offers a glimpse of how he may have presented to Evelyn: He has dark, masculine good looks and wears a three-piece suit and tie with a properly starched collar. His hair is neatly combed and parted, his eyes stare straight ahead almost pugnaciously, and he has a rakish-looking mustache that would not have been out of place above the lip of a baseball player or a boxer of the day.

Ernest was now actively campaigning for Evelyn's hand. As before, they were careful and private about the time they spent together. "We were both very anxious that nobody in town should know that we were keeping company," Evelyn later said, as it would have been unseemly for the pastor to be courting a member of his flock. Secretly, their bond was sealed that December 1919, in a horse-driven sleigh Ernest had borrowed to ensure their privacy. That night, he and Evelyn "came to an understanding" about their future together, Evelyn noting that she was "as much concealed as [she] could be," which would seem to suggest that there may have been more than mere polite conversation going on.

〜

The old photographs of her parents that Converse kept in her filing cabinet, and the stories that hovered around them, contained lessons she seems to have internalized: Courting went hand in hand with intrigue. Sex was scandalous and had to be hidden at all costs. In matters of love and romance, secrecy ruled over all.

Because Ernest had "decided to leave Meredith if I ever decided to marry within the town, to avoid any complications," he began applying for pastorates at other churches.[32] He took one in far-flung Pittsfield, Maine, where the couple would make their home for the next four years.

On August 11, 1920, the Amherst-born pastor returned to New Hampshire to marry his sweetheart, the college-educated schoolteacher from Meredith.[33] A photograph of the wedding party shows a severe-looking Ernest standing beside Evelyn, her eyes wide, almost frightened-looking. Neither of them touches the other; nor is either of them (or anyone else in the portrait) smiling.

E velyn was now free to join Ernest in Maine, and the newlyweds traveled there together by train.[34] Pittsfield was an inland mill town of 2,700 people in central Maine—small, but larger than either Amherst or Meredith. It had a railroad station, and some small industry (mainly wool). In August 1921, their first child, Paul, was born.[35]

Ernest had also established himself as a spokesperson for alcohol abstinence in upper New England.[36] He and his crusading brethren believed that alcohol lay at the root of society's ills, and that discouraging its consumption from pulpits and soapboxes was no longer sufficient; it needed to remain outlawed. Ernest's passion for hastening the cause grew during the couple's time in Maine; after only a few years there, he accepted a post with the Anti-Saloon League, at its New Hampshire headquarters in Concord, the state capital.[37]

"I had become uneasy in the pastorate" in Pittsfield, he later said, though, in true Conversian fashion, he did not elaborate on from what, exactly, this uneasiness stemmed.[38] What seems most likely is that Ernest wanted to be closer to the front lines of the battlefield on which he was now fighting. And with his new work with the League requiring him to travel more, Evelyn's desire to move back to New Hampshire, closer to her family, made sense—especially given that a new child was on the way.

CHAPTER 11

Sis

In 1924, as the young family started making plans to move back to New Hampshire, Evelyn was pregnant again. She was twenty-eight; Ernest, just shy of forty-one. Baby Paul was nearly three. On a summer vacation in Meredith, where they were visiting with Evelyn's family and with Ernest's erstwhile congregation, Evelyn's water broke. She was rushed to the nearest hospital, in Laconia, where, on Sunday, August 3, Elizabeth Eaton "Connie" Converse was born.[1]

Nineteen twenty-four was the year "Rhapsody in Blue" was first performed, Joseph Stalin rose to power, J. Edgar Hoover was appointed head of the FBI, and astronomer Edwin Hubble announced that the Milky Way was only one of many galaxies in the universe. Earl Scruggs, James Baldwin, Max Roach, Marlon Brando, George H. W. Bush, Shirley Chisholm, and Rod Serling were also born that year. Lenin, Puccini, Duse, and Kafka died. Calvin Coolidge was president of the United States.

Even as an infant, Elizabeth (named for her great-grandmother Elizabeth Fuller Converse)[2] got around. As the family moved from one locale to another, she made the more than three-hundred-mile round trip from New Hampshire to Pittsfield, Maine, at least twice during just her first couple of months. According to the "Baby Book" kept by Evelyn, the family took the train from Meredith back to Pittsfield in August, returning to Meredith in November—with Elizabeth ensconced "in a clothes basket on the rear seat of our Ford car. She slept most of the way, while the rest of us nearly froze, it was so extremely cold"—before returning once more to Pittsfield and then, finally, down to Concord, "our new home, on December 11 . . . Some travelling around before she was 5 months old!" Converse herself later wrote: "I trace my love of automobiles to an early journey of mine from Maine to New Hampshire, on a winter's day, reposing in a laundry basket on the back seat of a Model T. (Or was it a Model A?)"[3]

The Concord to which the Converses moved was, and remains, a classic small New England city. To better inform my understanding of Converse's first eighteen years, I spent some time there in between my trips to Amherst and Meredith.

Concord retains features that appear unchanged over the last century or more. It still has a double-wide main street, and narrow side streets that gently wind and roll into one another around the town's quiet center, many of them dotted by gracious houses with covered porches and widow's walks. There are any number of prominently situated churches and a stately village green.

Concord proper sits on the western banks of the Merrimack River. Today, after decades of urban blight, it once again seems the sort of place one might eye to raise a family, walk a dog, ride a bike, and pursue an unassuming existence. So must it have seemed to Ernest and Evelyn, who first situated themselves and their children in a small house I visited, just a few blocks west of the center of town.[4]

Life in Concord back then was not city life as it is thought of today. Unlike larger nearby metropolises like Boston (or even the far more modest Hartford, Connecticut), Concord was sleepy, surrounded by tiny rural villages and undulating hills. In the 1920 census, Boston had roughly 748,000 residents, Hartford 138,000. Concord, in contrast, had just 22,000, making it seem more like a town than a state capital.

This was a place that hewed to tradition. Its residents would have known quiet evenings spent strolling down lanes and sitting on rocking chairs or a swinging porch bench. It was a neighborly community; by city ordinance, wooden fences could not exceed a height of ten feet. And it was a strict one: No "musical performance or exhibition of singing or dancing or any other exhibition or amusement of any kind, with or without pay" could be given without a license or permit.[5]

The man who was now living with his wife and children in the house into which the Converses first moved, at 41 South Spring Street, was—like his counterpart in Amherst—completely unfamiliar with the name Connie Converse. He, too, was more than happy to show me around. As I toured the home, with its low ceilings, small rooms, and wide-planked wooden floors, I could imagine Ernest, Evelyn, and the two small children taking up residence there. South Spring Street is dotted with one house after another from that era, making for quite a change for the family from their more rural situation in Maine. They now had neighbors; there was foot traffic. In comparison to their time spent in Pittsfield, this reality must have seemed positively bustling.

As with my visits to Ernest's and Evelyn's hometowns, I looked for traces of the family here, visiting the city's historical society and the church where the family belonged, and also the venerable local music academy, where I thought perhaps there may be some record of the Converse children's studies (there wasn't). I talked to librarians, school secretaries, town clerks, and nursing home attendants (Evelyn spent her final years in Concord at Odd Fellows Home). No one I spoke with had ever heard of Connie Converse—nor of anyone from the Converse family, for that matter. Perhaps, in time, the city will memorialize its native daughter in some way—with a plaque, a day in her honor, maybe even a Connie

Converse Way. But to date, there is no glimmer of awareness, let alone civic pride, for her or her music.

The feeling seems to have been mutual. Reading Converse's letters and tracking her movements, I found that Concord was clearly not a place that took up residence in the warm, sentimental regions of her mind, the way childhood hometowns sometimes will. Though she would make obligatory returns for family visits as an adult, when Converse left, she did not look back. She didn't keep in touch with people there; nor did she attend her high school class's reunions. As Phil would tell me on several different occasions, from an early age, both of them began counting the days until they could get the hell out of there.

⌁

Young Elizabeth was a sickly child. During her first year, for a period of several months, she was bathed only in olive oil and given two daily feedings of malted milk, along with breast milk. By age three, she'd had bouts of eczema, measles, mumps, bronchitis, whooping cough, and chicken pox. Her parents often had her wear a mask. But though she struggled physically, her young mind developed by leaps and bounds. Evelyn noted that at only twenty months, Elizabeth had a vocabulary of nearly a hundred words.

At the age of two and a half, the toddler was participating in ceremonies at the Baptist church to which the family belonged, and by age four she had a basic understanding of issues around alcohol and national politics. "At election season, Fall 1928," Evelyn wrote, "Paul announced at supper table that Mr. W., a neighbor, was going to vote for Al Smith. Elizabeth looked up quickly and asked 'Going to be on the wet side?' Paul nodded and she exclaimed 'Huh!' With the greatest scorn and disgust."[6] (In the ongoing national debate over Prohibition, it was "dry" versus "wet.")[7]

Phil was born on November 17, 1928, completing the family unit. Evelyn wrote letters to four-year-old Elizabeth every day from the hospital following his birth, as a way to encourage her daughter's appetite for reading.[8]

Photographs of young Elizabeth suggest her to have been a happy if thoughtful blonde, with features that favored her father. In her first years attending the local public schools, she is recorded as being absent a full third of the time, though this did not impede her intellectual development. She learned and excelled at a high level and displayed an advanced early aptitude for drawing.[9]

By age eleven, Converse was formally studying piano and violin.[10] Though Phil remembered that she did not particularly care for the violin, she "took to all the rest of the seven lively arts as though they were second nature," drawing cartoons, sculpting, and writing poetry, short stories, and plays. Evelyn and Ernest even allowed her to paint murals on the walls of their home, including a scene of Robin Hood and Maid Marian in Sherwood Forest.

Converse took young Phil under her wing. In "Connie's Guitar Songs," Phil wrote: "In a very real sense, Sis raised me. I always wince at mentioning this truth because it sounds as though our mutual parents were on leave for that decade or two. In fact, they were very much there, and loving, as well as interesting fonts of intellectual stimulation . . . [They] would now and again spend an evening with the five of us reading a Shakespeare play." Still, he maintained, "I was blessed a million-fold with a sister who was not only brilliant but precociously doting as well."[11]

But Ernest and Evelyn were not very much there all the time. Letters, postcards, and newspaper articles suggest that Ernest's Anti-Saloon League responsibilities had him frequently on the road.[12] And Evelyn, following in her mother's footsteps, had a teaching position at the local church.[13]

The children seem to have been often left to their own devices, and Phil told me that what he most remembered was his sister watching over him. (Paul, a few years older, may have been off on his own.) Converse loved to create games for her and Phil to play, including one called Charps that "so overstimulated us that the parents could hardly get us to bed."[14] When he was old enough to read, the two used books about world history and famous figures to routinely quiz each other, "keeping score as in a school, I suspect," Phil wrote. "I learned more 'culture' at her knee than I ever learned in real school."

❧

Yet by the time she entered adolescence, it seems reasonable to believe that Connie Converse had begun experiencing the psychological effects of living in a challenging home environment. Ernest and Evelyn were loving parents, but judging by that oral history they gave a couple of decades later, they also seem to have been severe, and emotionally frozen. In a letter written in the 1950s, Converse wrote about her older brother's mental health issues, and the opinion of his psychotherapist, who'd concluded that "Paul's basic problem seems to have been a DOMINATING mother, from whom he felt he had somehow to escape or else be annihilated . . . Anyway, one may envision that somewhere inside himself he is still fleeing down a long dark corridor from that genteel, insistent, and horrendous Voice. Well, I'm reading in my own reactions—maybe it wasn't the Voice that got him; but as for me, I have long thought that if Mother had been stricken mute say, back in nineteen-ought-twenty, Harvard Street would have been a lovelier place to live in. (And maybe that's why I'm a notorious mute myself.)"[15]

The alcoholism of Ernest's infamous uncle Eben may have been a disease that coursed through the roots of the Converse family tree, a spiritual malaise that manifested in different members of the clan, in different ways, at different times.[16] There's little hard evidence as to what went on behind closed doors in the Converse household in Concord, but there are clues embedded in letters, in Converse's diary, and in the recollections of others. One letter in her cabinet, marked "Confidential," was written to Phil's wife, Jean. In it, Converse reveals, however opaquely, that there was at the very least dysfunction around the topic of sex during her childhood—which squares with the story of Ernest and Evelyn's courtship and its secret consummation.

Converse wrote the letter in 1971, while staying in a "bedsitter" in London—essentially, a furnished bedroom in a house shared with other tenants. Her letter tells of a young couple also staying there whose boisterous carnal activities can be heard at all hours:

> *Probably I am suffering from some hormone deficiency, so that if I were taking the proper pills I wouldn't wish more power to the couple upstairs, and envy them their pleasure, and look back over my own sexual life and feel extremely angry at the beginnings of it, when I was at the mercy of more knowledgeable but terribly constricted persons, and so that I wouldn't know now some things about sexuality that I could have profitably known as much as thirty years agone. It would be easier if I never learned them at all. Now that I know them it is much too late to profit from the understanding, and I can only unprofitably wish that my life had been different with regard to sex.*[17]

Converse was writing on the occasion of her forty-seventh birthday, three years before she disappeared.

~

How and when Converse learned the facts of life are not known, but whatever information was conveyed to her, it doesn't seem to have been of a helpful sort. Though she would indeed have sexual liaisons as an adult, those I learned about had been carried on in secret, with men who were unavailable in significant ways. And if she did engage in the kind of indiscriminateness described in "Roving Woman," that doesn't mean she enjoyed it. What Converse seems to be saying here is that she did not come to understand what healthy sexual pleasure was until, by her lights, it was too late.

The "more knowledgeable but terribly constricted persons" she mentions could have been either of her brothers, or may have included some unknown figures from her adolescence or early adulthood. The language she uses—"at the mercy of"—casts her as a victim, though whatever wrong had been perpetrated is unclear.

The most benign and least sensational possibility is that the people she is referring to are Ernest and Evelyn. Edie Converse Neff told me that they were "strict Yankees, as strict and straitlaced Baptists as could be. They wouldn't even mention the word *sex*." Such extreme primness seems to have been at the base of what I would come to understand as an unhealthy twist in the sexual sensibilities of all three Converse children.

It's something that turns up in Converse's song "Empty Pocket Waltz," written in 1955, the last of a series of guitar songs she composed before refocusing her ambitions on more formal music.

> *Shall we dine out, my dear, and dance the night away?*
> *Don't say you're tired, you know you haven't worked all day.*
> *We've paid the rent, finally, and we're free to be free*
> *Come now and waltz the Empty Pocket Waltz with me.*

Several of Converse's persistent themes are here. She chases the interest of a distracted other. She wants pleasure, but is thwarted. Fantasy stands in for reality. (As Ellen Stekert reflected, "Converse had an active daydreaming career.")[18] But then:

Let's close our door and make believe we're all alone
Grandma can't hear, and baby's sleeping like a stone.

Here is secrecy, passion that demands privacy, and an urgency for physical love amid the presence of family. Again, Converse's curious combination of a carefree, playful lyric with its opposite in melody and vocal delivery complicates our response as listeners. If it's a song about celebrating financial freedom by going out to eat and having fun (and maybe a little something else first, even though there are people around), why is the music so melancholy? If it's a ballad about a deadbeat, depressive partner who just wants to lie around all day, why all the joyful imagery in the lyrics?

If Converse was receiving mixed messages at home about what healthy intimate behavior looked like, she was about to meet someone with whom she could at least share these and other confidences as she began to experience the tectonic shifts of adolescence.

CHAPTER 12

The Life Under

Though Frannie Flint and Connie Converse sound like the names of comic book characters who may have gone steady with Archie and Jughead, the pair of Concord friends was nothing like the happy-go-lucky, carefree types who attended Riverdale High.[1] They were earnest and smart, more inclined to books and artistic pursuits than currying favor with quarterbacks, cheerleaders, and cool kids.

Frances Caroline Flint was born nine months after Converse, in May 1925. Though her family called her Keetah, friends knew her as Frannie. The Converses and the Flints lived a mile away from each other, on the opposite immediate outskirts of downtown Concord. The plot on which the Flints' home once stood is now occupied by a drive-through bank—no remnant of the house remains—but the home the Converses moved to when Elizabeth was nine still stands.

From the outside, 9 Harvard Street, a modest two-story white Colonial with a shady covered front porch, looks unchanged from how it must have appeared in 1933, when the Converses took up residence there.

It is situated on a relatively short, quiet block, with seven or eight houses on a side. I walked up and down the street, knocking on doors and talking to every neighbor I could. Like everyone else I spoke to in Concord, the name Converse meant nothing to them.

The street, too, had a small-town feel to it, and though it was mostly deserted on this hot summer afternoon, I could easily conjure scenes of small children laughing and running outdoors, playing hopscotch, throwing snowballs, and jumping into leaf piles, just as Converse and her siblings must have done in the 1930s. I could even imagine young Phil wringing a chicken's neck—one of his weekly chores, he'd told me.

Converse later wrote of having "an immensely detailed and cohesive memory" of 9 Harvard, "and whether or not one was happy there[,] one can always work up a kind of nostalgia about it, particularly if one is not likely to ever live in or even visit the house again."[2] She remembered the property having a barn, an apple tree she loved to climb, and elms that lined the sidewalk. All those things are still there.

Like Converse, Frannie Flint grew up in a college-educated household. Her father, William, was a Rhodes Scholar; had studied at Dartmouth, Princeton, and Oxford; and was a teacher of Greek and Latin. Flint's mother, Dolly, held a degree from Radcliffe and had spent parts of her youth summering in high-society Europe.[3] Unlike the Converses, the Flints were well-to-do, and had live-in help.[4]

The two young women differed temperamentally. Dick Mullavey, a nonagenarian high school classmate who remembered both of them distinctly, told me that Flint was relatively outgoing and sociable. Her aunt Carol recalled her as "brilliant, popular, a gifted pianist, promising, and intense." The teenage Converse was brilliant and intense, too, but quieter, shier, soft-spoken, and prickly. Mullavey described Converse to me as "something of a loner," "a nerd," and "a brain."[5]

Jean Crowley, another school classmate who remembered both girls well, used the same single word to describe Converse: "brain." Crowley told me that Converse "was off by herself all the time" and did not engage in social activities at school; she never knew her to have a boyfriend. "We were quite friendly," Crowley told me, but Converse "didn't talk that much." What Crowley remembers most of her is that she "knew the answer to everything."[6]

Converse and Flint had become especially close in junior high. They shared a small pocket-size notebook in which they wrote back and forth to each other, probably during class.[7] They also wrote each other letters, each offering the other feedback on the fruits of their respective artistic labors. Flint wrote of the day "when we [will] grow up and each go our respective ways, you to your literature, me to my music."[8]

Converse dreamed of becoming a writer. Whatever attempts she made at music, on the violin, were eclipsed by Flint's accomplishments as a concert pianist, though it's touching to imagine the two of them practicing together—Converse gamely contributing her fiddle skills if only to engage in a shared activity with her best friend.[9]

The girls had something else in common—both had an older brother who left for college as the girls entered their sophomore year of high school. Bob Flint enrolled at Harvard to study literature, and Paul Converse packed off to Denison University, in Granville, Ohio.[10] Both the girls' older siblings would come to play enormous roles in their lives in the years to come.[11]

As Converse began her freshman year at Concord High, she was already a working draft of herself. She was writing poetry, excelling academically, and beginning to kick against the repressive restrictions of her home life. Some two decades later, in a 1957 letter to Phil, she wrote, "I would like to know how, in your adolescence, you escaped . . . the parent troubles that I had."

Converse was earning the highest marks in every subject at school, so whatever conflicts she had on the home front could not have stemmed from a lack of achievement on her part. What is more likely is that she was rebelling against an unhappy home life by trying to escape it as often as possible—either through her writing and through books, or physically—by escaping the town's confines altogether.

The once frequently bedridden child had blossomed into a physically hearty, healthy young woman.[12] "She was always adventurous, very physically fit and in great shape," her cousin Edie told me.[13] Converse would frequently bike down alone to the Old Home Place in Amherst—a good sixty-mile round trip as the crow flies. In the 1930s, when many roads were still unpaved (and well before the establishment of state highways), such a journey on a one-speed bicycle, riding along winding, hilly New Hampshire dirt lanes, would have required no small amount of strength and pluck.

Mullavey, Crowley, and Edie all repeated a delicious rumor to me about the teenage Elizabeth, one impossible to authenticate but worth noting for its sheer audacity: "I heard she was mixed up with someone unlawful from outside of town," Mullavey recalled, "and that she may have mingled with the Mafia." Edie and Crowley confirmed that they'd each heard something along these lines, too. (I was never able to ask Phil Converse about this, sadly; by the time I tracked down Mullavey and Crowley, he had passed.)

The mere idea that this was the local gossip about the otherwise prim, brainy Converse is telling, and bizarre. Could she have been leading a double life even then, as a teenager? And even if she wasn't, people who knew her well thought she was, and it's fun to consider her as a prototype for a character like the hyperintelligent closet rebel Beth Harmon, protagonist of Walter Tevis's *The Queen's Gambit*.

But it's hard to imagine that anything about the Mafia story could have been true. What's known about the history of organized crime in Concord, New Hampshire, in the 1930s is that there doesn't seem to have been one. If some glimmer of reality was embedded in that particular story about her—if Converse was, perhaps, involved with someone she wasn't supposed to be—this would certainly fit into a larger pattern that would come to play out in her adult life, and in songs she would write like "Man in the Sky," "Incommunicado," "Johnny's Brother," and "Roving Woman."

What Phil did remember about those days was Frannie Flint. He couldn't emphasize enough the most significant fact about her: that she had died by suicide and that his sister had vigorously defended her friend's right to do so—to him, to their family, and to anyone else who would listen. But Phil remembered that Flint had killed herself while in high school; this was incorrect. In actuality, it would not happen until five and a half years later, and not in New Hampshire. The details of the event, I would come to find, were as unsettling and disquieting as its outcome.

$\backsim$

Flint's family sent Frannie away to finishing school at Abbot Academy in Andover, Massachusetts, when the girls were sixteen. "You needn't worry your little head about my going away," she wrote to Converse. "I only wish you could be in my place, for you could go out and show the world something wonderful, which is *you*. Here you have to stay cooped up in a stuffy little town, when the whole world is outside, and so receptive . . . You *must* get away, Elizabeth, and as soon as you can, and to the best place you can get. The world isn't this narrow-minded little hick-town."[14]

Converse had been overachieving in and out of school, but in her friend's absence, she became almost pathologically so. By her senior year, in addition to consistently scoring the highest academic honors in her class, Converse somehow found time to serve on the yearbook staff (as

editor and—uncredited—as writer/illustrator), on the school's newspaper staff, and as editor of its literary publication, *The Crimson Torch.* She
played violin in the orchestra, sang in the choir, belonged to both the
Debate Club and the National Honor Society, and acted in the school's
production of George M. Cohan's farcical 1913 melodrama *Seven Keys to
Baldpate,* an adaptation of Earl Derr Biggers's bestselling novel of the same
name (she was given the role of Mrs. Quimby, a woman not deemed person enough by Cohan even to be given a first name and so sexless that she
is repeatedly addressed by her husband with the antiquated pet name
"Mother"). Even so, Converse still found time for the hobbies she listed
in her yearbook profile, which included bowling, tennis, travel, writing,
drawing, and after-school nursing.[15]

In the spring of her senior year, Converse learned that she'd won
Mount Holyoke College's all-country regional scholarship to attend her
mother and grandmother's alma mater.[16] On her college application file
card, she is listed as standing 5'7.5", weighing 144.5 pounds, and having an
IQ of 138. She is described as having "a keen mind. Cheerful, cooperative,
adaptable, and possesses good common sense. Believe she will be out-
standing in college." She is noted for "standing highest in school work,
school spirit, and womanliness" and "as mature as they come."[17]

A t Converse's Concord High School graduation, she was valedictorian in her class of 195 students.[18] Phil did not stint in using the word
polymath when describing her, and chuckled when he related the story
he'd written about in "Connie's Guitar Songs" in which the repeated
mention of her name as the recipient of multiple honors became a source
of derision from the crowd. "She was the only true genius I ever knew,"
he told me.

But what was this whirling dervish of activity really like as she prepared to bid Concord adieu? The only real window into her psyche at

this crucial juncture is her ongoing correspondence with Flint that spring and summer.

It begins with a cryptic Western Union telegram sent by Flint from Andover, in April of their senior year:

```
Miss Elizabeth Converse =
Don't phone 9 Harvard St CR =
May there be no weeds between your mansion
and antiquity tonight =
MACFLINTY¹⁹
```

After graduation, in that summer of 1942, Converse took what she referred to as "my first real job," waitressing at Mountain View House, a historic resort hotel in Whitefield, New Hampshire, nestled in the bucolic White Mountains. Flint had held the job the summer prior and may have helped her friend secure the position. As the two young women prepared themselves for the life change that loomed for them in the fall (Flint had been accepted to Vassar), their epistles bristled with squirmy anxiety.

Flint implored Converse (whom she almost always addresses as "Prof" in her letters) to exploit her independence and not to get bogged down in the kind of depression she herself had experienced the summer before:

There is something wonderful in a summer like this, full of every emotion as despairing as any could be—checking off days for the release from bondage . . . I feel with you every time you get hard and bitter . . . Worthless, worthless, what is life? I see there is less in it all the time—I am grown and done—anything after now is just repetition—I have loved and hated, felt great and small, known glory and humiliation—I have had them all in their extremity—there is no life left, and last of all, I have done the worst—given up . . . The race we were running together you run alone—and I sit useless beside the track and breathe "well done!" as you pass on.²⁰

These hardly seem the musings of the sort of outgoing, unflappable teenager Dick Mullavey remembered to me, and they are only the beginning of the peculiarities that inhabit Flint's letters to Converse over the ensuing weeks.[21] In one, she seems to allude directly to whatever was the source of the local gossip about her friend:

> *I now know that what I thought and felt last summer was not in vain . . . I'm glad you admit that I understand you—I always flattered myself into thinking I did . . . especially this spring when your name was on so many lips. I just smiled quietly and said to myself that in Andover even I could reach into you and into your heart of hearts and know that you were more than any of them . . . even those who saw you every morning walking to school laden with lunch and books and violin . . . However, if I did understand you, perhaps I could have been of more help.[22]*

For her part, Converse felt a need for discretion, even when it came to sharing with her best friend. "Why the hell should I care if you smoke?" Flint writes at one point. "My god, you're old enough!" If Converse had even feared the moral condemnation of the edgy, irreverent Flint, it's worth considering the lengths to which she must have gone to hide from her family and the Concord community at large any hint of behaviors that might have been deemed improper.

"There's one thing worse than an adolescent, and that's someone who has just ceased to be one—think they know everything, and as a matter of fact, might well, if only their lives were not so conscious of sex," Flint wrote her friend. "Oh well, that's another subject."[23]

As the summer waned, with news of casualties and deaths from World War II dominating the country's consciousness, the correspondence continued. Flint wrote about being courted by "men, *nice* ones, and my own age too," and makes mention of when she herself "used to walk at night, as you do now (your life is the conventional waitress—a bit singular, but the same for everyone like you or me who seeks the life under . . .)" It's not difficult to hear strains of "One by One" here; perhaps Converse's habit of walking alone at night, as desolately depicted in that song, began here, in the White Mountains. A photograph she preserved in her scrapbook from this time bears the inscription: "First photo with new camera." An empty bed, in an empty room, suffused with bleak, empty light. All that's missing is a solitary figure to make it a setting for a Hopper canvas.

"The life under." Under the everyday, under the vapid, under the ordinary, under the status quo. "Oh Converse," Flint wrote at the end of July, "why does the fleeting mind have to be harnessed to cramped fingers and a leaky pen? Why do melodies, the work of the soul, have to be compelled to lie in little black dots with handles? Oh hell—why can we not be free—to write as fast as we can talk, to talk as fast as we can think, to think as fast as we can feel—to feel *every*thing—*every* thing, and never be numb to the world. Keep at your hellish work—your emotions will be sharp, your perceptions fast and bitter and all-inclusive—never live like me and find yourself growing into a stupor of contentedness—of physical comfort and mental laziness."[24]

If nothing else, the young women were bonded by a shared intolerance for superficiality. As Converse would write decades later in a letter to her friend and colleague Clint Fink:

> When I was a child sitting in church I used to look around at the solemnity of the faces and think that everyone must know some great thing that they had neglected to tell ME, even though I had been to Sunday school and day school and all that. Nothing that I had learned in those schools or at home could account—for me—for these reverent and ceremonious adult behaviors. The surface of these behaviors had such a uniform gloss to it . . . It took a long time for me to find out that the uniform gloss and the great secret, both of them

cherished by secret subcultures, tended to serve as lids on underlying conflicts and disagreements, and that people who publicly believe in God can still wither in private despair or suck the blood of their neighbors or sell their souls to the devil.[25]

Converse here sounds like fellow autodidact David Lynch discussing his work: "Just beneath the surface, there's another world, and still different worlds as you dig deeper. I knew it as a kid, but I couldn't find the proof. It was just a feeling. There is goodness in blue skies and flowers, but another force—a wild pain and decay—also accompanies everything."[26]

CHAPTER 13

Mount Holyoke

Mount Holyoke, situated in quiet South Hadley, Massachusetts, had already passed its one-hundred-year mark and was recognized as one of the most prestigious colleges for women when Converse enrolled as a freshman in the fall of 1942.[1] Though the war raged on, that reality may have seemed far removed from the genteel confines of the college, whose gates sheltered it from the outside world and where the primary focuses were on learning, sports, the arts, and high tea. "Am I disloyal to high New Hampshire peaks when I love a Massachusetts mountain?" Converse wrote for the college's newspaper. "New Hampshire is more rugged; all who live there are more rugged somehow, because their pleasures as well as their weather-spells are more rugged."[2]

She found college life liberating, rife with opportunities to continue to play out her hyperactive tendencies.[3] In addition to her studies and working part-time in the dining hall, in the library, and in the chapel, she sang in the choir, played in the orchestra, attended candlelit concerts of classical music, competed in sports, wrote for the school paper, went hiking, submitted to hazing rituals, pulled all-nighters, smoked cigarettes, and read Emily Dickinson.[4]

Whatever close relationship she'd had with Phil now became distant, likely due to circumstance. In what seems to be a rough draft for an autobiographical story she began in her diary, probably in 1950, Converse wrote about her changing relationship with her younger sibling, assigning Phil the name "Buddy":

> *I telephoned home from college and heard a strange bass voice saying "'This is Buddy,'" like an impostor, except that it was Buddy with his new fourteen-year-old voice. At the time, of course, I felt as if I had lost an old and dear playmate. After that I got used to it, and the life of Buddy and the life of me grew far apart . . . Because of this, I assumed that Buddy's progress through his early teens was somehow smoother and more rational than mine had been.*
>
> *Later still, I learned better.[5]*

Another puzzling set of thoughts about her brother. And then, again, there is no mention of Paul.

By most outside meansures, Paul had done well for himself. He'd graduated from Concord High as a member of the National Honor Society. Like his sister, he'd also distinguished himself by pursuing a number of extracurricular activities, including playing in both the band and orchestra (as a brass man), singing in the choir, running track, and serving in the class senate. By the time she'd enrolled at Mount Holyoke, Paul was on track to receive his degree from Denison. It seemed odd for there to be scarcely any indication, in any of her surviving papers, of what Phil's or Converse's relationship with their older brother was like when they were young.

The ex-wife of one of Paul's sons told me that he'd always been his mother's favorite.[6] Jean Converse told me that Paul was "a troubled soul" and she and Phil did not talk about him much. The more I learned about Paul from other family members, however, the more I came to sense what an impact he actually may have had on his sister and why references to him seemed scarce. This began with an unlikely source: Cousin Edie, who talked to me about him in the context of family get-togethers during her childhood in New Hampshire.

Converse's entire family would frequently visit nearby Amherst when the cousins were growing up. Edie and her sister/mother, Helen, were living in the Old Home Place at the time, and Ernest's siblings were nearby.

Edie told me that she remembered these visits well. When she was around ten, she, Converse, and their cousin Eleanor ("we called ourselves the three *E*s," she said) would go out to the barn and tell one another secrets, or else pass the time sitting atop a log pile "making up stories about each of us falling in love with the most handsome guy."

But sharpest in Edie's memories were the kinds of get-togethers that took place when she was what today we might call "a tween." She and Paul were about the same age, the two of them a few years older than Converse (to whom Edie was closest and whom she always referred to as "Sister").[7] The mere mention of Paul's name caused Edie to respond with revulsion.

"I never wanted to be alone with him," she told me in no uncertain terms. Even at a remove of almost eighty years since those visits, thinking about Paul made her uncomfortable. "He was strange," she said. "Very self-important. I think today people might call him gay. He was very much interested in men. And he was overly interested in sex. He wanted to know: *'How's your sex? How's your sex?,'* and this was always the emphasis in all of his conversations. I had an icky feeling about him."

What she saw as Paul's unhealthy obsession with sex was not limited to inappropriate conversation. "He would mess around with the farm animals when he would visit. I didn't like it. Funny business, you know."

Until I spoke to Edie, family members had mentioned Paul (when he was mentioned at all) only in bland, "nothing to see here" detail. But over the course of several phone conversations, Edie outed Paul as something else—a person who'd made sexual overtures to her, who had abused animals, and who'd made her feel unsafe.

That Edie, a tight-lipped Converse, as acutely aware as anyone of the damaging nature of gossip (given the scandal around her birth and upbringing by Helen), would air this sort of dirty laundry with me, a virtual stranger, seemed extraordinary.

"Paul was not a good person," his ex-daughter-in-law, Barbara Converse, told me. "He was very unkind. He pretended to be someone he was not."[8]

Had Paul's unhealthy obsession with sex manifested itself in how he interacted with his sister? "I don't know if he abused her," Edie Converse Neff told me. "It's possible."[9]

During her sophomore year at Mount Holyoke, away from home, Converse continued to thrive. "When I have ceased to wonder, at that moment I grow old," she wrote in an essay for her class's literary publication *Pegasus*. She also had her poetry and illustrations published by *Pangynaskean*, the college magazine; in the spring, she was nominated for the national Glascock Prize, a prestigious honor bestowed upon only eight undergraduates in the entire country, each of whom was invited to read from their work for the juried contest. (She didn't win the top prize, but her work received special mention.)[10] Converse chose seven short pieces, including this one:[11]

Reduction to Absurdity

One person out of ten acquires
The grace society desires

> *To justify advancing age;*
> *At seventy one is sweet and sage*
> *Or else lays claim to either.*
> *I am capable of neither.*
>
> *I think that I shall just regress*
> *From middle youth to childishness,*
> *From clover fields of infancy*
> *To restless prenatality,*
> *And then arrive where good souls go*
> *A cold and tired embryo.*[12]

The darkness of these lines notwithstanding, Converse seems to have been flourishing, her talents both recognized and celebrated. She was awarded the Foster prize in French, the Jessie Goodwin Spaulding Latin prize, and the English department's Louise Sproule prize, awarded to the student demonstrating the greatest promise as a writer.

And, in her position as "Song Leader," she is listed in her sophomore yearbook as "Connie Converse"—the first-known usage of the nickname she would use for the rest of her life.

But something happened that spring of 1944. Inexplicably, after completing her second year at Holyoke with honors, she informed the college that she was abandoning her studies and had no plans to finish her education there or anywhere else.[13]

Her decision came as a shock to her family (particularly to Evelyn, whose emotional ties to Mount Holyoke were so strong). "Our parents were devastated," Phil wrote. Again and again in conversation, Phil would return to this moment in his sister's history, judging her decision to drop out of college a critical mistake that he felt had led to lasting, damaging repercussions. But Phil Converse was proud to have spent his life in academia. His sister had other things on her mind.

CHAPTER 14

Fantastic City

Who knows what triggers a person to follow through on making the kinds of big, life-changing decisions many of us only dream about? How does "I could" sometimes become "I should" and then, more rarely, "I want to" and "I will"? Might the catalyst be some reminder of life's brevity—a newspaper obituary, a beautiful piece of music, or, as one of Converse's lyrics has it, simply "the fall of a leaf"? Is it an inner tug, a gut feeling (like the one I had when I heard Converse's music for the first time), some unknowable aspect of the universe pulling our strings? Perhaps, in some instances, it's not even possible to pinpoint any one reason, or one moment, that prompts us to choose a new, unexplored path leading away from the one we know.

There may be nothing terribly significant behind Converse's unexplained move to drop out of college. Certainly, the war made it less unusual than it might have been in the years leading up to or after that world-changing event. With so many young people eager to enlist, a number of colleges were compressing their calendar timelines and including summer semesters in an effort to graduate students early. Frannie

Flint had become part of Vassar's first accelerated class, graduating in three years rather than four.[1]

But Phil's repeated emphasis on this moment as a major turning point in his sister's life—one he couldn't explain and one that is not even mentioned anywhere in the filing cabinet carefully curated (by her) and carefully weeded (by him)—invites speculation.

Converse may have been bucking against her relatively conservative school, where the prevailing attitude—when the college was not hosting summertime summits for leading intellectuals—was to "blend and belong."[2] As one classmate remembered, "Mount Holyoke during World War II [had] very slight communication from the outside. We were told only what they wanted us to hear."[3]

She would not have been one to have her head in the sand. Converse would have known about the numbers of people being killed every day, about the jolting news regarding the surrender of European cities, and about the atrocities being perpetrated. Just as the Vietnam War and the political assassinations of the 1960s were soul killers that caused an exodus from college campuses, the constant death toll of World War II, and the evil personified by the Nazis, may have been enough to drive her to drop out and take her place in the real world.[4]

Yet, what amplifies this mystery is the fact that, for the nine months following her decision to leave Mount Holyoke, Converse seems to have pulled her first disappearing act. Her whereabouts during this time are completely undocumented. There's scant trace of her activities in any surviving letters, diaries, or photographs, either, and no documentary evidence of any employment, address, or phone number she had during this span. The entire chapter—from making the decision to leave school, to dropping out, to what happened for the remainder of that year—represents a sinkhole in Converse's biography.

The idea that she may simply have returned to Concord, living at home while working some small-time local job with the goal of saving up money for a relocation, is unlikely. Phil told me he had absolutely no recollections of her living back at home once she'd left for college.

So, given the absence of anything she wrote about this period, and her tendency toward secretiveness, it seems not inappropriate to consider more dramatic possibilities. Tom Converse wondered whether she had had a breakdown, one that presaged the one she had later in life, when she was in her late forties and living in Ann Arbor. Dick Aime, one of Converse's friends in New York, had a daughter, Adelaide, who became a social worker; she put this same hypothesis forward, especially after I told her about Converse's later struggles with depression.

"It certainly seems possible that she could have been committed to a psychiatric hospital like McLean's in Boston, which would account for her disappearing for a while. Back then," Aime told me, such a stay "would have been shameful, and she certainly wouldn't have been allowed back at a place like Mount Holyoke afterward."[5]

But then there is a 1971 letter—from a time when it's documented that she really *was* in the midst of a mental health crisis—in which Converse refers to "being a tramp once myself in Pennsylvania and we came to the back door of a farmhouse and asked for a glass of water and the lady drug us in her kitchen and sat us down at a big table and laid out platters [of food] . . ."[6]

Did Converse, whose lifelong wanderlust is well documented in her letters and diaries, take to the road in search of new, more authentic life experiences in the style of a Rimbaud or a Jack Kerouac? Perhaps she was encouraged to do so by Flint, who saw in her a version of herself that she was too timid (or too restricted by familial expectations) to pursue, a tendency that would soon have disastrous consequences?

❧

Somewhere toward the end of those lost nine months, Converse landed a job in New York City, working for the American Council of the

Institute for Pacific Relations, a private, independent research organization founded in 1925. Though the AIPR has largely been forgotten today, its goals and history continue to excite the mind of scholar Michael R. Anderson.

"The scholars, writers, and businesspeople who worked there were idealistic progressives who wanted to not just study but actually usher in a better world," Anderson told me with unabashed admiration. "They were trying to work out the biggest, thorniest issues of the day. The postwar world was being decided, and the IPR was part of that." It played a role in the formation of the United Nations, published articles and pamphlets that were read by millions of students, government people, and servicemen across the globe, and furthered a vision of the world that looked beyond colonialist and nationalist interests, he said.

"They were interested in everything," Anderson told me, "and asking the biggest questions in ways that we don't see today, because everything has become so specialized." He was not at all surprised that someone like Converse could find a place there, even without a college degree. "Anyone who demonstrated an open-mindedness was welcome in that community," he said.[7]

Because she was a New Englander with no known experience with big-city life, Manhattan had to have been a new universe for Converse. Skyscrapers, taxicabs, theaters, subways, and millions of people with their variations in speech, languages, backgrounds, and customs. This was a place that, to date, she'd likely known only from books, from movies, and from dreams. Now, less than a year after leaving Mount Holyoke, she was here, starting at the bottom but beholden to no one, ready to finally begin her life in earnest.

By the time Converse's first Manhattan address appears in the historical record, in 1945, the war was coming to an end, having left many of the great cities of the world scarred, if not ruined. Not New York City, which now rose up as the new center of global optimism and culture. "All signs were that it would be the supreme city of the Western world, or even the world as a whole," wrote historian Jan Morris. "New York in 1945 saw itself . . . as representing a people 'to whom nothing is impossible' . . . The Manhattan skyline shimmered in the world's imagination, and people around the globe cherished the ambition, however unlikely, of landing [there] one day."[8] To Converse, the idea was not unlikely; she lived there now.

"She was definitely in the right place!" historian Louis Menand chuckled when I told him about Converse's chosen new milieu.[9] The American IPR put her to work on the fortnightly journal it published called *Far Eastern Survey*.[10] She served first as an editorial assistant, then as an assistant editor, and eventually as a writer, at a time when Anderson told me the organization "was at the height of its influence with the government, doing unofficial diplomacy" in its attempt to help bridge the gaps between East and West.

Converse's first documented residence in New York City was at 62 Riverside Drive, near West Seventy-ninth Street on the Upper West Side of Manhattan, where she spent what spare time she had working on a novel.[11] And yet, she wasn't entirely alone. Converse had begun spending time with a young woman named Sarah Thompson, someone with whom she would remain close with until she left the city, fifteen years later.

They were the same age.[12] Thompson was from Westwood, New Jersey, described by Edwin Bock, her high school boyfriend (one hundred years old and entirely lucid when I tracked him down in 2022), as someone "who played touch football with us older boys in the '30s," and who was "never loud, never seeking star billing, but reasonable, friendly, stoic sense of humor, a truth-seeking, Thurber–*New Yorker* values appreciator."[13]

Like Converse, Thompson had eschewed attaining a college degree, choosing instead to volunteer for the Women's Army Corps (WAC) during the war, a newly formed auxiliary branch of the army. Bock recalled her confiding to him that she'd been assaulted by a medical officer during her service while stationed at Fort Hamilton, in Brooklyn.[14]

Bock met his girlfriend's friend Connie Converse in the mid-1940s when Thompson brought him on a date to a get-together at the old Lincoln Arcade building, located on Broadway between West Sixty-fifth and West Sixty-sixth, in what was then known as San Juan Hill.

The structure, built in 1903, had a reputation for being a haven for students, musicians, transients, and starving artist types. At various times, its residents included Robert Henri, Thomas Hart Benton, and onetime roommates Eugene O'Neill and George Bellows.[15] The rooms were large enough to function as both living spaces and artist studios and were used as such, often illegally.

Russian-born American realist artist Raphael Soyer lived there, too, and was known to sometimes help underwrite the rent payments of some of the young women artists in the building in exchange for their modeling services.[16] At least two of those women were Barbara ("Ming") and Adelaide Eby, two-thirds of a triumvirate of vivacious sisters with whom Converse was also hanging out (the third sister was Pat).[17] They were, like Sarah Thompson, also from New Jersey.

Ming Eby's daughter (Adelaide Aime) told me that these were artistically gifted, wild young ladies, prone to drinking and smoking and living the bohemian life, sometimes gallivanting from bar to bar with a song routine they practiced. Ming studied at the influential Art Students League of New York, and Ming's sister Adelaide modeled there. "It was a hip place to be," Adelaide Eby's son Jonathan related to me, "and my mother reminisced about seeing famous people such as Marlon Brando and others at the studio."[18] If Converse was hanging out with the Eby girls during this time, I was given to understand she was having an awful lot of fun.

They inspired one another. Converse served as inspiration for the Eby sisters. Ming, a skilled painter and line-drawer, made a contemporaneous pencil sketch of Converse, and Adelaide, a talented sculptress, made a bust of her, a photo of which was discovered by her son John, after he and I spoke for the first time.[19] Converse was also painting at the time, perhaps due to their influence.

The sons of Adelaide Eby made their own unwittingly provocative contribution to fleshing out this group of strong personalities and how they related to one another. Neither they, nor their cousins, nor Bock could say for certain how Converse and Sarah Thompson knew each other. But years after their mother's death, the three sons gathered to transcribe everything they were able to collectively remember their parents telling them about the timeline of their lives, including anecdotes their mother related over the years about those wild days of her young adulthood. One note, entered chronologically as something that happened in the 1940s, reads, "Mom meets Sarah Thompson and lesbian girlfriend Elizabeth Converse."

There were photos of Sarah Thompson, and at least one letter from her, in Converse's filing cabinet. Though Thompson was no longer alive, her niece Linda told me that her aunt had been a heavy drinker in the 1940s, that she'd gotten sober in the following decade, and that she'd met a woman in AA named Joan with whom she lived openly as partners until her death (one of Thompson's sisters, Joie, was also gay, Linda said).

But the note about Thompson and Converse is the only historical mention of the two of them being romantically involved, and the only one that suggests that Converse may have been bisexual (I already knew, by this time, that she later had heterosexual lovers).

Two decades after Adelaide Eby's sons had constructed their timeline, and with none of them able to verify where or when they'd heard this particular detail, they wouldn't stand by it as being accurate. There was certainly an understanding among their family, one of them told me, that Sarah Thompson was openly gay and that this was highly unusual at the time. But for all any of them knew, they may have merely conflated what they knew of Thompson's sexual orientation with some other of their mother's memories of Converse.

There was one more figure in this particular mix yet, one more person with whom Converse was spending time, in some now-ambiguous way: a lanky, wry-humored New Yorker named Richard "Dick" Aime (nephew of Harry Hopkins, liaison to the Soviet Union during World War II, and FDR's chief of staff).

Born in 1920, Aime had the dubious honor of being accepted to Yale twice; during his first stint, he had been expelled and then hitchhiked his way down the East Coast to Florida. A year later, he reapplied and returned to New Haven.[20]

Aime was a heartthrob. "He was always the life of the party. People were drawn to him," his daughter told me, sounding like she could have also been describing Bill Bernal.[21] All three Eby sisters, at various times, dated Aime before he finally married Ming in 1950. Ed Bock recalled once hearing all of them sing together "Once in Love with Amy," the Frank Loesser hit from the 1948 musical *Where's Charley?*

In one of Converse's photo albums from her filing cabinet, there are pictures of the three Ebys. And there are also numerous photographs of Aime, in military uniform, and a prominent one of him seated next to her at what looks like a ball game from that time. Though the two do not display any blatant signs of romance, her smile is blazing.

Aime died in 2013, before I was able to track him down, but his second wife, Lois, rummaged through his effects on my behalf and came up with gold: Aime's copy of that ballpark photo, some pictures of the two of them hanging out with the Ebys, and several shots of just Converse, the only known solo photographs of her in New York City in the 1940s. In one, she is taking a deep drag from her cigarette, staring at the photographer (presumably Aime) with an attitude that's almost punk-like. In another she again looks directly at the camera, but this time her demeanor is soft, open, smiling, both girlish and sophisticated. Aime had kept two copies of this one. One of them bears an inscription on the back that reads "Riverside Park." They were near her apartment.

Was Aime dating Converse, too? "It's entirely possible," his daughter told me. "People were not so exclusive back then," she said. "I mean, he dated both of my mother's sisters, so it's certainly within reason to think he could have been spending time with Connie, too, in a casual way."[22] One person familiar with the dynamics of this circle put it more plainly: "Everyone was sleeping with everyone."[23]

Aime's son, John, told me that his father had hitchhiked "everywhere" as a young man. When I told him about Converse's love for road adventures and asked if he thought there was any chance that his father was the one referred to when she once wrote about being young and tramping around with a fellow traveler from house to house, looking for food, he remembered that one of his dad's favorite stories involved hitchhiking in New England around that time.

"I don't know whether it's just the power of suggestion, hearing about Connie, or what, but it seemed to me that he would sort of smirk and kind of get a gleam in his eye when he talked about this—something I always understood to mean that he'd been traveling with a young woman"—someone who was not his mother, Ming.[24]

It's a leap to think that Converse and Aime were partners in crime—two college dropouts in their early twenties, hitching rides together and catching meals and rest where they could—and that this was how Converse came to know the Eby sisters in New York. But, as with so much involving Converse, it seems wrong to discount any possibility. Her story is consistently unusual enough to believe that almost anything about her could be true.

Take the following anecdote, prompted by another photo from Converse's scrapbook. In the picture, the Eby sisters appear in repose, along with Aime (the tableau almost looks like it could be the basis for a Raphael Soyer painting). Converse, seated in profile, her head down, plays an acoustic guitar—the first historical appearance of the instrument in her hands. She captioned the picture "The Old Songs," suggestive of the idea that it predates her writing her own material. What seems clear is that the Ebys and Aime were there for the embryonic state of a new persona she was forming.

When I shared this picture with Ed Bock, he immediately identified the room it depicts as the one in the old Lincoln Arcade building that Sarah Thompson had taken him to. And it triggered powerful and easy-to-access memories for him about those visits—memories that included Converse.

Bock told me that he was there on five or six occasions and remembered "abundant alcohol consumption." He said that the get-togethers often went well past bars' closing time of two A.M.

"I saw the room as an Eby girls territory that they maintained by adding relatively transient, congenial subtenants." The girls would sometimes shout down from their window at noisy passersby exiting the bar below.

Converse never participated in the general hubbub, he wrote. Instead, she would be at the typewriter, as though oblivious to what the group was doing. (As Converse recorded in her diary: "I suppose that if I were a more ardent and competent conversationalist I should not feel impelled to type up my witticisms, aphorisms, judgments, comments, reviews, arguments, metaphors, insights, and analogies.")[25]

Bock then mentioned something that stood out clearly in his

mind—something he found bizarre and alarming at the time, but that the Eby girls apparently took in stride:

> *Connie would keep typing while all the rest of us were in conversation. This was not seen as discourtesy. It fit into the prevailing "everyone does her own thing" culture. The high point of this separateness, after midnight, came when Connie walked slowly to the open front window and stood by it. What changed (and charged) the situation was when she began slowly climbing out the window onto the ledge. Saying nothing, not interrupting the general conversation, but gradually transforming the Chekhovian atmosphere, looking back in briefly, still silent.*
>
> *[The Ebys] seemed accustomed to this behavior, and continued the conversation. Connie then disappeared, heading—as I then thought—in a downtown-ward direction. After a while, she reappeared, quietly, from the inside rather than through the front door, to my relief and that of the other guests. This happened on two of my visits.*

Bock told me that he'd read an essay I'd written about Converse for *The New Yorker* with interest. "If, as she writes in one of the documents you have quoted, she felt she had difficulty getting noticed, her 'window-ledging' was a radical, silent solution."[26]

The Lincoln Arcade building was demolished in the late 1950s to make way for the new Lincoln Center, but archival photographs of it remain. There's no fire escape, nor any sort of landing, outside the windows at the front of the building—only what seems to be an extremely narrow lip protruding from each floor. The Ebys' windows faced east, looking out over Broadway, and above what was then the building's theater marquee, at least three or four stories up, Bock said.

Converse, he remembered, would be out there for "a long, long time."[27]

CHAPTER 15

A Death in the Woods

I f Converse corresponded with anyone during the period of her life just after she left college—be it peer, mentor, or lover—she did not preserve those letters the way she carefully archived the ones she'd received from Frannie Flint a few years earlier.[1] Had she and Flint kept up their friendship? Did they see each other in Concord during holiday visits, comparing notes about life and love? Or had the paths they were following diverged while Flint went on to complete her undergraduate studies and Converse decamped to New York? If they *had* continued to share epistolary intimacies, and *had* those letters survived, what they wrote might have shed some light on the even more dramatic events that would soon follow.

Flint achieved both academic and artistic success at Vassar.[2] She graduated in July 1945 and soon followed her Concord chum to Manhattan, arriving in early September, at the start of the fall season. A month later, she'd landed a job working as a proofreader at the American Research Institute.[3] For a brief moment, the two best friends seemed to be on similar footing: two smart, young, ambitious single women from New England trying to make it in New York.

Surely, this could have thrilled them, being at the beginning of their adult lives together, the entire world laid out before them. Flint may even have stayed with Converse for a time while looking for a place of her own, the two former New Hampshirites again spending time together, sharing their triumphs and disappointments.

Alas, this reality, if it played out at all, did not last long. Flint's father had a series of heart attacks and lapsed into a coma that fall. Only two months after arriving in New York, Flint left her job and rushed home to Concord, never to return.

Flint's father was only fifty-three, and his subsequent demise surprised and shattered his small family. Frannie stayed on in New Hampshire to help her mother, Dolly, put her affairs in order. Then, months later, instead of resuming her life in New York, Flint moved to Cambridge, Massachusetts, with Dolly. Frannie's brother, Bob, was now enrolled in Harvard graduate studies, and the three may have felt the need to be together after the elder Flint's death. Frannie and Dolly both got administrative jobs at Radcliffe, Dolly's alma mater, and Frannie enrolled there herself, to pursue an advanced degree.

This seems to have been the wrong move. Having just had the energizing experience of being alone and independent in New York City, Frannie was back to living under parental supervision while now also under the dark cloud of her father's untimely death.[4] This combination of circumstances weighed heavily on her, and by 1947, she began to become unstrung.

Dolly described her daughter at the time as "moody and downcast," and Frannie's roommate recalled that Flint was "terribly nervous."[5] She fell behind in her studies, was forced to drop some of her classes, and lived in fear that she might flunk out and embarrass her high-achieving family—especially brother Bob, who'd encouraged her to pursue a graduate degree rather than return to New York and who, according to family members I spoke with, pressured her to be more academically ambitious. "Several times," Flint's roommate remembered after her death, "she said to the other girls in the dormitory that she wished the world would come to an end." Halfway through her first semester in graduate school, Flint was put under the supervision of a mental health professional for treatment of "a hyper-nervous condition."[6]

~

Things got worse as the Radcliffe semester moved toward Thanksgiving break. She and Dolly may well have seen a young Marlon Brando in the pre-Broadway tryout of *A Streetcar Named Desire* when it played Boston that month. If so, Flint may have noted Blanche DuBois's account of her husband's suicide, a topic that suddenly seemed to be everywhere.[7]

A steady stream of suicides in the national and local news that October and November suggests something was in the air. Flint would have been confronted with the phenomenon on an almost daily basis when she read her morning newspaper, perhaps fixing the idea in her mind that this was something that regular people did.[8] She would have been acutely aware, especially, of notable New Hampshirite John Winant taking his own life.[9] Winant was a popular three-term governor of the state and a war hero. He'd also served as a teacher and as vice president of St. Paul's School in Concord when the Flint family was in residence there. Consciousness of a seeming epidemic of self-destruction, combined with Frannie's heavy school workload, may have wormed its way into her worsening emotional state.

Then, the week before Thanksgiving 1947, something seems to have shifted. Flint returned to Concord for a few days to visit with old friends. Converse was quite likely there, too, in town for the holiday. Did the best friends have a heart-to-heart that revived Flint's spirits (or, instead, strengthened her resolve)? When Flint returned to Cambridge, her room-mate recalled that she was suddenly "very happy." The Flint family later described her as having been seemingly "cured" of her psychological issues at around this same time.

But on Monday, November 24, 1947, Flint did not return home to Eliot Hall. Nor was she anywhere to be found the next day or evening. By the late afternoon of the twenty-sixth, Dolly, fearing the worst, phoned the police.

~

Today, the area around the spot where Glezen Lane and Concord Road meet in Wayland, Massachusetts, a quiet Boston suburb, is wooded, quaint, and mostly unexceptional. Houses built here over the last half century or so populate the quiet streets, and there is a sense that the town that sired Ted Williams, baseball's "Splendid Splinter," is prob-ably unaccustomed to much in the way of spectacle. It certainly doesn't feel today like the setting for the way Frannie Flint's life came to an end.

On Thanksgiving night 1947, at around eleven P.M., Flint's lifeless body was found face-upward in what were then deep woods near this intersection. She was naked and covered in blood. Her clothing, which included gray dungarees, a blouse, a sweater, and an overcoat, was found scattered along the trail and strewn on the branches of trees and bushes that led to the spot where she lay. Also found near her corpse were a pack of cigarettes and an envelope bearing a man's name and a Maine address (since lost). Flint had a bullet wound on the left side of her head.

A small-bore .22-caliber Winchester rifle was found nearby, some fifty to seventy-five yards away from her body (accounts vary). An auto-mobile with New Hampshire plates that Flint had been reported driving was parked off of Concord Road, some three hundred feet away. In the car was a rifle box and a bill of sale for the gun from the Sears, Roebuck and Co. branch on Massachusetts Avenue in Boston.

Flint's death, and its sensational nature, made the AP newswire, running in newspapers as far west as Pittsburgh, Pennsylvania, and as far south as Florence, Alabama. Articles proclaimed variations on the headline "Nude Frozen Girl Found Dead in Woods" and played up the fact that she'd been an honors student, and pretty.

Two days later, *The Harvard Crimson* reported that "State Police pathologists, specially summoned experts, and the District Attorney [were] unanimous" in ruling Flint's death a suicide. According to the doctors who performed the postmortem, "the .22 calibre bullet entered the left side of the brunette's head, and failed to penetrate the orbital region of the brain. Hence they concluded that the Vassar graduate would have been able to stagger 50 feet from the place where she actually discharged the weapon." *The New York Times* coverage indicated that the gunshot had blinded Flint, after which she walked or crawled some distance from the gun before collapsing and dying.

Police established that Flint had purchased both the weapon and a box of ammunition at the Sears in Boston that Tuesday, after a salesman there positively identified her from photographs. "Also indicative of self-slaying," the *Crimson* reported, was "a pool of blood over the area where the small bore gun was dropped."

None of this is run-of-the-mill. Depending on which news report is consulted, Flint was either shot through the left side of the head—was she left-handed?—or through the face, in the area of her nose. Either way, she shot herself with a .22 rifle, a difficult task. A dealer in vintage firearms whom I contacted confirmed that Winchester made a junior model that would have been easier for Flint to handle.[10] Even so, small-bore rifles require precision to be used effectively; trying to shoot oneself at close range would be challenging enough. Her aim would have to have been horizontal, intercepting the brain perpendicular to the spine.

Holding the gun with her arm extended and then applying enough force to pull the trigger would have required tremendous dexterity and strength, unless she'd sat on the ground with the gun between her knees.

If Flint wanted to kill herself, and wanted to do it with a gun, why wouldn't she have opted for a smaller one? The rifle would likely have been cheaper than a handgun, but such considerations would have hardly seemed important, given the circumstances.

Assuming that Flint did shoot herself, alone; that her aim was poor; and that the shot did not kill her, it's possible that the surge of adrenaline in her body afterward would have been enough for her to stagger the fifty to seventy-five feet away before collapsing in a state of semiconsciousness, likely in shock. Temperatures in the Boston area that week were in the upper thirties to forties Fahrenheit (and probably a few degrees colder in the shaded chill of the woods), so, in due time, she could have begun to suffer the effects of hypothermia (recorded in her autopsy as the cause of death). After getting very cold, her body, close to death, would suddenly have become tingly and hot, which could have led her to tear at and remove her clothes, perhaps flinging them about wildly. Because the bullet didn't reach the orbital lobe, which controls motor function, she may have behaved like an animal that has been struck but not killed by a fast-moving automobile—staggering raggedly, yelping, conscious but out of her mind.[11]

~

Flint's brother, Bob, three years her senior, never recovered from her death.[12] He felt responsible for having urged her to move to Cambridge and for what that led to. Although he would go on to have a successful career in letters, working at Harvard as a translator and librarian and corresponding with the likes of Saul Bellow and John Updike, he led a reclusive, private life. He never married, and he lived with Dolly until her death, and then alone after that. According to a close friend and colleague, even on his deathbed, in 2013, Bob Flint would not discuss his sister or what had happened to her.

What was it about these two overachieving, talented, brilliant best friends from Concord, New Hampshire? Was there something in their respective childhoods, some shared or similar trauma, that first drew them together and then eventually sent them reeling down into the depths of a despair that may have caused their respective dreadful ends separated by a quarter century? Converse appears to have turned away from her literary ambitions and moved toward music only after Flint's death. It seems plausible to consider this intentional, as a way to honor the spirit of her lost, musically gifted friend.[13]

Flint's violent end roiled the Concord community back home. Phil was still thinking about it more than fifty years later, in the context of his sister's disappearance following her own protracted period of depression. It's something he brought up repeatedly in our conversations and in interviews he gave to others.

"I remember when Frannie committed suicide," he told me. "The community was in an uproar" over what they considered to be "an antagonist act." They couldn't believe that Flint could do such a thing, leaving her family to process such an awful tragedy so soon after her father's untimely death.

If Converse had indeed been back home for Thanksgiving that year, this may be why Phil conflated the timing of Flint's suicide with an earlier period of their lives, when they were all in Concord together, attending high school. "Connie was angry at everyone for reacting the way they did, our parents included," Phil said. "I distinctly remember Connie saying, 'One of the main rights that every person has is the right to do away with themselves if they wish to.'"[14]

The statement had stuck with him. He'd known from a young age that his sister considered suicide a viable option if life did not go well, and he recalled a conversation that the two of them had had as children about what they each might do if they ever "needed to kill themselves." She told him, "I would go down to the sea and would get in a boat and row and row, out and out."[15]

CHAPTER 16

The Taking and the Keeping

Converse and Phil had their first Manhattan get-together in the late 1940s, after Phil had started college (like Paul, also at Denison University in Ohio) and stopped off to see his sister en route to a visit back home. "After the passage of years," she wrote in her diary, the two "met like strangers at Grand Central and fell to reminiscing over oysters."

What a scene for the siblings' reunion: the Grand Central Oyster Bar, a New York City institution. Opened in 1913, the restaurant resides on the lower level of one of the world's great transit hubs, its bustling, winding countertops offering patrons an immersive view of cooks ladling steaming bowls of its famous oyster pan roast; waiters clad in all white hurrying to drop platters of bivalves and crackers; customers conducting business lunches, enjoying dates, scribbling copy—the establishment was known as a hangout for newspapermen and writers—or just dining with a creased copy of the day's paper, lost in thought. A windowless subterranean world of its own thrumming along in concert with the heartbeat of the city.

Thinking of the two Converse siblings there brought to mind a moment that had baffled me on my visit to see Phil in Ann Arbor, the night I'd looked up to find him staring at me while I worked at his dining room table.

"How about a walk?" Phil had asked. "Might be nice to take a break from sitting for so long. And I remembered a funny little story I want to tell you."

Phil then exhibited a peculiar tic of his. During lulls in conversation like the one that happened now, as I paused my work to go outside, he would mindlessly whistle—if it could be called that. It was more like a wheezy sibilant rhythmically made through clenched teeth. No tune or notes per se, just joyless mouth noise. My maternal grandfather, who, racked by guilt at the end of his life, confessed to years of infidelity to my grandmother, used to do a similar thing.

Outside, without any preliminary windup or chitchat, Phil cut to the chase. He wanted a private audience with me to relate the following: Once or twice a year, while he was studying at Denison, he would hitchhike home to visit with "the folks" in Concord, often stopping off for a night to visit "Sis" in New York City.

I'd, in fact, just read a letter she wrote to him from around that time that backed this up. In it, Converse had asked her brother whether he might be passing through the city on his way to New Hampshire and invited him to stay with her there. "It doesn't really matter whether I know or not. It's OK if you turn up at my door at 5 A.M.," she wrote.[1]

Whether it was during that visit or another one like it, Phil related the following incident. "This is really humorous," he told me, "and probably not something you need for your book, but I just found myself remembering it and thought you might enjoy some brother-sister details."

According to Phil, Converse was briefly living in New Jersey at the time, just across the Hudson, and had a roommate.[2] Phil was still a virgin, he told me, and assumed the girls were, too. In his hopeful imagination, he'd concocted a scenario in which his sister might go out and leave him alone for a while with the roommate, or perhaps the three of them might explore their sexuality together. He was therefore disappointed to discover that they'd arranged for him to sleep on a cot in their kitchen.

What in the world was this? The details of a fantasy that included his sister were odd enough. But then, so too was the fact that he also wanted to share them with me, and that he was laughing about it all as he did.

Phil continued: The confines of the makeshift sleeping situation were such that he was unable to turn over in the night, instead forced to sleep on his back. That next morning, he told me, he awoke to the sounds of hushed giggling close by. Quickly, he surmised the situation: The girls were in the kitchen with him, taking stock of what, for all he knew, may well have been their first sight of a sexually aroused man.

Phil explained that his first instinct had been to cover up and make haste for the bathroom in shame, but he then thought better of it and hatched another plan. Pretending to still be asleep, he gave the girls "a little show."

This was a scene, he told me, that he and his sister would remember with great mirth into their adult lives—a story that came up often between them (and one he would bring up again with me over email and on the phone). His sister, he told me, had always expressed her "gratitude" for the exhibition.

It's not uncommon for relationships between siblings, especially brothers and sisters, to include at least some form of mutual sexual exploration at early stages of development,[3] but this episode had occurred when both of them were young adults. And of all the stories Phil could choose to tell me about his sister, this first time we'd met, why had he chosen this one? What was I supposed to make of this? I was absolutely nonplussed.

Though time seemed to have briefly halted while he related his tale, in reality we'd walked only about halfway down his short block—mere minutes. Phil now did an about-face and suggested we immediately go back inside so that I could get back to work.

∿

Encountering each other for the first time as young adults away from home, whatever initial awkwardness they might have felt, and talking of their shared experiences in Concord may have given way to matters of greater moment. Bringing her brother up to speed, Converse may have mentioned her literary efforts, or the fact that she'd been doing a fair amount of oil painting in her apartment, making moody portraits of men who resembled musicians like Frank Sinatra and Igor Oistrakh in a style that certainly seems indebted to painters like Raphael Soyer and Edward Hopper.

Phil also mentioned to me his feeling that his sister was probably a Red. In 1947, the State Department had begun investigating whether her employer, the IPR, might be harboring Communists[4]—activity that may have been one reason she planned to borrow their parents' car for three weeks, when her whereabouts would again be unknown.[5]

During his visit to New York City, the siblings may have talked about their father's decision to retire from his post as superintendent of the Anti-Saloon League[6] and to sell the house at 9 Harvard Street, the only home they'd ever known. (Ernest would subsequently take a pastorate in the tiny hamlet of Florida, Massachusetts, on Mount Greylock, just above North Adams.)[7]

Paul Converse was now living in New York, too, while studying at Yale Divinity School, but he wasn't present for the Oyster Bar get-together.[8] Instead, it was just Sis and Phil, surrounded by a teeming swirl of strangers, clattering dishes, and city energy. Phil may have continued on his journey home after this first visit, or he could have spent the night with his sister, an occasion that could have included the early-morning scene he shared with me on our walk in Ann Arbor.

U nlike Converse's collection of slides, which she'd carefully dated, annotated, and coded, the two heavy photo scrapbooks she'd left in her filing cabinet featured scenes from this period in her life (including photos of the Eby sisters) that were only in rough chronological order. People and places appear in them with the faintest of details—a nickname here, a last name there; sometimes, no identifying clues at all. One pair of photos, captioned "Dinner at the Changs'," showed an unidentified woman sitting at a table with Converse, the two of them eating with chopsticks.

The scene looked to be from the late 1940s, but it took me years to identify the woman in the photograph as Irene Conley Chang—someone who, I would come to learn, seems to have had a tremendous impact on the trajectory of Converse's life, spinning it off, yet again, in new, unpredictable directions.[9]

When I found Conley Chang's name listed in the employment rolls of the IPR, I was then able to determine that, though she was deceased, she had two living daughters. One of them, Rita, was living in nearby Massachusetts. I was able to track down a cell phone number for her and texted her a message, with a screenshot of one of the two photos. She replied immediately, "That's my mother."

C onley Chang was a new hire at IPR in 1949, a college-educated intellectual from Ohio, and Converse was hanging out with her and her husband, Kuo-ho, a Chinese-born translator who worked at the United Nations.[10] The Changs, Rita told me, were a high-spirited, well-traveled couple, interested in ideas and culture. Significantly, they were also "huge music fans." Irene played piano, Kuo-ho played ukulele, and they were "always encouraging friends to sing, dance, and make music."[11]

I visited Rita and her husband at their home outside Boston, not too far from where Frannie Flint had met her end. There, I spent time looking through Rita's parents' papers, which included photographs, letters, and her father's diary from the years when Converse and Chang worked side by side at the IPR. Rita welcomed me to look through everything she had.

And there it was, beginning in her father's 1949 diary, written in elegant black fountain pen ink: Among the daily accountings of their social activities in New York were multiple mentions of their friend Connie.

Because 1949 is the year Converse designated for her first composition for guitar, the Changs had to have seen at least some part of that transformation or that moment. Converse's relationship to the instrument, which seems to have begun during the time she was hanging out with the Ebys, had deepened.

"I've been looking up chords for guitar in the back of the People's Song book [*sic*]," she wrote in her diary.[12] "I find I had figured most of them out by myself, without thinking about their names. I used to think a guitar was a vulgar and unpleasing instrument. But if treated properly, it rises above the realm of the musical cliche. And with a good song[,] even cliches sound good."[13]

Rita felt sure that Converse and her parents would have had musical evenings together. Her sister, Nadya, agreed. "I think my parents would have been drawn to her music and artistry as well as her intellect and independence," Nadya wrote to me. "I'm certain that my father especially would have wanted to know about her music. Though my mother was bookish and a bit inward, he was curious and gregarious and liked to engage with people about their interests. He really enjoyed the company of artists and musicians, always wanting to talk to them about their craft and to try and persuade them to show him their work or perform for him."[14] Whatever sparks had helped to ignite Converse's interest in performing and songwriting, it seems likely that the Changs had helped to fan the flame.

∽

Five years later, on a tape reel that Gene Deitch made of her performing in his home in Westchester, she can be heard trying to explain how she came to start writing songs:

> *CONVERSE: As I told you, I sort of, half, I uh . . . I sort of hum things until I got to the point where I thought, "Well, that's a tune that I made up and was never polished off," or words that . . .*
>
> *DEITCH: So, you were just humming tunes, and then you realized that you had written something . . .*
>
> *CONVERSE: (Laughs) Yes, or uh . . .*

Alongside her new musical activities, Converse's social circle expanded as well. The Changs introduced her to Johnny Hsing, a close friend of theirs with whom she at times paired off in their presence. In one diary entry from the summer of 1949, Kuo-ho recounts a picnic outing that included him and Irene along with "Tony and Marilyn, Gladys and Frank, Ruby and Jo, Johnny and Connie, and Allen."[15] Given that Allen's is the only name listed on its own, the implication here is that the others were couples.[16] A week later, another of Kuo-ho's entries includes "Lunch at Miyako with Irene, Connie, and Johnny."[17]

Rita related that Hsing was from Taiwan, "full of life, happy, fluent in English, adventurous soul, out there, singer."[18] Photos of him from that time show a handsome, fit young man with a boyish smile and an air of confidence.

On one group outing to Morgan Memorial Park in Glen Cove, Long Island, Chang recorded that on "a beautiful day, crisp and dry," the group of UN/IPR friends ate sandwiches for lunch and then all took a boat ride, "speeding in the Sound." When they returned, Chang and Irene played softball with Johnny and Connie, before they all packed up and drove in two cars to a "semi-private beach," where Chang swam in his underwear and where the group engaged in "a lot of horseplay among ourselves."[19]

These small but tactile bits of evidence were accumulating and—like Ed Bock's memories of Converse's unusual behaviors at the Ebys' Lincoln Arcade studio—pinned Converse to a particular time and place at this moment in her life in a way that Phil could not. She had a diverse group of cool friends. She went on outings, in couples. She was a person, in a world.

⌒

Rita Chang enjoyed reading these entries, too, learning more about her parents and their role in Converse's story. After we'd spent a long day together thoroughly exhuming every scrap and photo belonging to her parents from this era, she and her husband prepared a delicious meal in my honor, and insisted I spend the night in their guest room rather than follow through on my plan to find lodging nearby. Taken by their warmth and gracious hospitality, I accepted.

Rita's husband then excused himself to do some work, and Rita asked if it might be possible to hear some of Converse's music. Always happy to provide new listeners with their first exposure to her songs, I plugged my phone into a speaker in their kitchen and pressed play on *How Sad, How Lovely.*

As the two of us sat listening to the album together, Rita wondered aloud whether the song "Johnny's Brother" could refer to Johnny Hsing. The tune, written in 1952, borrows directly from the old nursery rhyme:

> *I'll tell you a story about old Mother Morey,*
> *And now my story's begun*
> *I'll tell you another about her brother,*
> *And now my story is done.*[20]

But, as with several of Converse's songs that also present as children's ditties (including "Down This Road" and "The Clover Saloon"), Converse uses a naïve form to disguise a more complicated, winking foray into more adult themes. This time, it's familial and marital infidelity:

> *I'll tell you a story, about Johnny McClory*
> *That's how my story was begun*
> *I'll tell you another, about Johnny's brother*
> *And now you may think my story is done.*
>
> *The first time I met Johnny I could see he was bonnie*
> *And when he looked at me how he did glow*
> *But just as we were gazing at each other*
> *Johnny's brother*
> > *Was down in Mexico.*
>
> *I went to a party, with Johnny, my Hearty*
> *I never felt so happy and so gay,*
> *But just as we were drinking to each other,*
> *Johnny's brother*
> > *Was down in Santa Fe.*

And down in the garden, my heart would not harden
How well I can recall those tender scenes,
But just as we were kissing one another,
Johnny's brother
    Was down in New Orleans.

I didn't want to tarry, my Johnny to marry,
And so I got myself a wedding gown,
But just as we were wedded to each other
Johnny's brother
    Came riding into town.

The years have been merry, oh very, very, very,
I love my Johnny well and he loves me,
But all the while we're loving up each other
Johnny's brother
    Holds the baby on his knee.

I've told you a story, about Johnny McClory
That's how my story was begun
I've told you another, about Johnny's brother
And now my story is done.

Narratively, the singer is telling two stories at once: The beginning of each verse reports on her developing courtship and relationship with a man (Johnny) who falls in love with her and whose attentions she cannot ignore (or, at least, chooses not to). The end of each verse, however, is a kicker, revealing the status of Johnny's unnamed brother, the man she's really thinking of. He's moving from place to place, from Mexico to Santa Fe to New Orleans, until he finally arrives on the scene just in time for her nuptials to Johnny. The last time we see the brother, after the loving couple has been together for many "merry" years, he is holding an infant.

The upshot of the tale is unclear. Has the singer been carrying on a secret long-distance affair with the brother of her betrothed, or does she just desire him? Has she in fact carried his child, whose true paternity she hides? Did the tangle of relationships between her, Sarah Thompson, the Eby sisters, and Dick Aime offer some inspiration for the tune?

There are at least a few autobiographical hooks to grab on to in the lyric. Mexico, Santa Fe, and New Orleans were all places Converse visited on an epic cross-country trip she undertook in June 1949.

C onverse summarized this adventure in a short unpublished manuscript called "Notes on a Journey." The westward portion of the trip was undertaken by car, with a couple named Per and Ruth, whose names never appear again in any of Converse's effects, and whose identities remain a mystery.[21] It was June, and the trio routed along the northern parts of the country, moving through upper Michigan, Wisconsin, Minnesota, North Dakota, and Montana. In Washington, they visited with one of Converse's IPR colleagues, Ben Kizer (in Spokane), and his daughter, the poet Carolyn Kizer (in Seattle).[22] Converse still had literary ambitions, so the two young women may have compared notes about the writing life.

From there, Converse and her two road companions headed south, through Portland and Northern California, before landing in the Bay Area and parting ways. She visited briefly with the family of another IPR colleague—Phil Lilienthal, who'd moved out there in the late 1940s—before beginning the second, solo half of her trip, by Greyhound.[23]

From San Francisco, Converse traveled south to Los Angeles, over to Arizona and New Mexico, and then down to Texas. A quick sojourn over the border had her drinking "tequila with the schoolteachers," before heading over to New Orleans. Then it was up through the Deep South, where she was dismayed to see the segregated water fountains and bathrooms and by the ugly, racist attitudes on display.

Converse made temporary friends among the strangers she met on the bus—a couple of jokers from the military ("a laugh every half mile"), a woman who took her to lunch and sent her to have a filling replaced at her dentist, and a bricklayer who unabashedly used her shoulder to sleep on for most of a night. In D.C., she boarded an airplane for the first time, for the short hop back to New York, "which looked like a hundred million sooty freight-cars dumped into a freight-yard after their last trip."[24]

Ever since *The New York Times* heralded the publication of Kerouac's *On the Road* as "a historic occasion," young Americans have used his cross-country exploits as a template for liberated exploration. Getting in a car and zooming across America, with no goal in mind other than having fun, might include sleeping outdoors or in the car or crashing on people's couches; stopping wherever and whenever the inspiration struck; driving all night for the hell of it; avoiding run-ins with the law; drinking wine or smoking weed or popping pills; making fast romantic connections and leaving them faster, throwing logic and custom to the wind. Sunsets and sunrises, mountains and valleys and huge expanses of nature; nothing to think about but the wide swath of years that lay ahead, one's entire life, nowhere to be, no one to tell us what to do, every day filled with the energy of knowing that life is really being lived. Millions have done it, in their teens and twenties, young and carefree, following in Kerouac's frenzied, half-baked, and wondrous footsteps. I'm one of them.

But *On the Road* would not be published until 1957. Mad dashes across the country were not yet a cultural phenomenon. Few were doing this, other than truly adventurous souls (including Converse's fellow, more professionally successful songwriter Earl Robinson). And young women were *really* not doing this—taking these sorts of chances, going off on whims, and then writing stream-of-consciousness accounts of their odysseys, as Converse did:

> *Night ride across Michigan, a deer dashing in front of the car . . . moon nearly full . . . pulling into Ludington at dawn and having breakfast at an all-night cafe with a jukebox going full blast, as if it were the shank of the evening . . . the car ferry: off in a blaze of sunlight across Lake Michigan; then fog closing in, thicker and thicker . . . the terrible fog horn, the gentle replies of others . . . white breakwater tower coming out of the fog like a ghost . . . we, having found our harbor blind-folded.*

Her breathless account of the journey reads like notes from one of Kerouac's books—years before they were published. She was tapped into the zeitgeist, even a step ahead of it. Her prose about the natural beauty of the country's landscape as she crosses it, and her colorful descriptions of the people she meets along the way, suggests that this was meant as a jumping-off point for a literary treatment of some kind, perhaps even the sort of "autofiction" soon to be made popular by the Beats.

> *New Orleans at noon, hot, dazed, and weary; Shower and sleep at the Chalmette Hotel on Carondelet Street . . . The big end of the Mississippi, the color of coffee with cream in it . . . the man on the bus calling us Damyankees as if we ought to be pleased to be insulted by a Southerner . . . Canal Street . . . the monument to the men who died for white supremacy . . . The French quarter, carefully preserved on the verge of collapse . . . Huey Long's hospitals and bridges displayed with tremendous pride . . . A man walking down Carondelet Street in a white suit with a gleaming sword in his hand . . .*

If, to some, Converse was almost Bob Dylan, it seems as though she were almost Jack Kerouac, too.[25]

∽

When I go traveling
I take along with me
Something to tell me why i went away,
Something to tell me why I'm coming back someday.

Take along my white satin,
That's what I wear to dine and dance.
When I sail from Manhattan,
To the South of France.

This is Converse's song "When I Go Traveling," from 1952. Its melody borrows from Richard Rodgers's "I'm Just a Girl Who Can't Say No," from *Oklahoma!*, a song that may have influenced her in more ways than one. Oscar Hammerstein's lyric to it also seems to have helped pave the way for her "Roving Woman."

Like so many of Converse's narrators, the one in "Traveling" is dreaming, and spinning a glamorous fairy tale. By the time she wrote it, Converse had been all over the country, with brief sojourns over the borders to Canada and Mexico, but the beauty of the South of France was something she could then only imagine.

If the lyric is fairly simple, the musical composition is anything but. "Traveling" is among Converse's most complex guitar songs, ranking up there (along with her "Playboy of the Western World") with the best of Cole Porter and Jimmy Van Heusen for harmonic inventiveness. As with

"One by One," it's fair to say that few artists were releasing songs like this at the time, though this one is unique in its own way.

The guitar part in the song's chorus that begins at the top and is then repeated throughout is rhythmically ambitious in the right hand, and the voicings Converse gives to the chords in her left are wildly unusual. The second and third sections of the song contain a sort of "stop-time" rhythm that may have its roots in early New Orleans jazz as a technique, but is here put into service in a way that is more of a wave to that idiom from afar. And the harmonic construction of those sections is brazenly eccentric. The effect achieved—a combination of simple story, jagged rhythm, and harmonic and structural idiosyncrasies—makes this song a musical triumph.

⁓

Traveling" was not included on *How Sad, How Lovely*, so it wasn't one that Rita Chang heard as we sat in her kitchen listening to Converse's songs. We mostly remained in complete silence, letting the music, with its waves of different but still-charged significance for both our lives, wash over us. For Rita, encountering these songs made by a close friend of her parents, and recorded at a time when they'd been so young, had its own palpable emotional density.

By the time we got to the album's title track, Rita's eyes had begun to well up, as had mine. Staring at me from across the table, she said to me quietly, "I understand now. I completely understand why you've undertaken this quest. This music—she's reaching out to someone she can't touch." I nodded. "Maybe you are, too."

Yes, I admitted. I'd had a feeling like that often when listening to these songs. "But, really," Rita said, "I'm intuitive about these things. I feel like it's almost as if she's singing to *you*, as though you're connected, somehow, across time. You need each other."

Rita was right, to an extent. My sense of connection with Converse had naturally grown during this process of hunting down details of her life. But what I also knew was that this sense of codependency with her was not at all unique. Yes, I felt that she was singing across time to me, but I also knew that she was singing to all of us, to an audience that did not yet exist.

That night, I retired to my room tweaked by the intensity of the encounter. By the time two A.M. rolled around, I knew it was hopeless to think I would get any sleep. As quietly as I could, I got dressed, packed my things, and left a note for the Changs, thanking them and begging forgiveness for my unplanned departure. I had a bad case of insomnia, I wrote, and thought it best simply to get in the car and make for home.

Driving south along the empty interstate that night, I couldn't shake a feeling of being absolutely haunted.

CHAPTER 17

She Emerges

Rita Chang told me that her parents were living in Greenwich Village during the time that Converse was hanging out with them, and Converse's visits to their apartment there placed her smack in the middle of what was then one of the most exciting neighborhoods in the world. Rents were cheap, attitudes were permissive, and the streets were steaming with the energy of the most cutting-edge music, art, theater, dance, and literature in America.

Carson McCullers, William S. Burroughs, Margaret Mead, and John Cheever lived there. So did Patricia Highsmith and Anaïs Nin. Also, e. e. cummings, one of Converse's favorite writers, and Djuna Barnes, African American and openly bisexual. It was the Bushwick, Brooklyn, of its day—a vibrant "anything goes" sort of scene, full of young dreamers and far removed from the touristy, high-end enclave of boutique shops and expensive coffee bars it has since become.

"The Village was the Left Bank of Manhattan," the writer Gay Talese told me. Talese lived there briefly during this era, himself no stranger to liberal mores. He recalled the scene vividly: "There was a sense of freedom there that was not present uptown. Interracial couples were common—you wouldn't see that anywhere else. Poets and musicians and bookshops were everywhere. The Village had whiffs of the future in it."[1]

For Converse, the neighborhood's allure may have been too great to resist; after a brief stay at 33 West Seventy-fourth Street,[2] she moved to the Village the following year.[3] She took a tiny studio in a nondescript twenty-five-unit apartment house at 23 Grove Street.

Grove between Bleecker and Bedford was a relatively quiet block then—and is even today—and mostly residential. But it was also merely a block and a half away from the busy Christopher Street IRT stop. Her building, constructed in 1888, was a few doors down from where Hart Crane lived when he killed himself and just a block away from the new upstart Grove Press. There was a strip club near her apartment called the Nut Club, where now-legendary jazz players gigged, and in 1947, Anthony Hintz, hiring boss for Pier 51, was shot outside *his* Grove Street apartment, part of the story that would inspire Budd Schulberg's screenplay for *On the Waterfront*.[4]

Converse's apartment building is still there and looks today much as it probably did back then. The interior hallways and stairwells are still narrow and a bit homely. Her photographs of her flat's interior reveal a small room containing a single twin bed near a window, a nightstand for her typewriter, several lamps and chairs, and a few shelves of books. In a recording Converse made of her family's visit to the apartment a few years later, her mother is heard to remark on the absence of what had been a second bed, which suggests that Converse may have indeed had a roommate at one point, supporting Phil's claims.[5]

Yet it's hard to understand how two single people could have shared what is only about four hundred square feet of space. (It's also hard to believe that Converse could have recorded her songs in what she called in her diary "an afterthought kitchen.") The apartment gets good light from two exposures, and has hardwood floors and a fireplace, but if it sounds romantic, her description of it includes: "a high-vaulted room . . . and nothing that feels like home."[6]

Young single women living alone at the time might have been unusual, but not in Greenwich Village.[7] Not that there wouldn't have been a stigma, in the eyes of a certain kind of person. As Norman Mailer once chauvinistically put it, "If a girl lived in Greenwich Village, she could be had."[8]

But longtime Village residents I spoke to derided such ideas. The puppeteer Penny Jones, who lived there in the early 1950s, told me "it would not have been an issue. Not at all. I'd turn up my nose to someone who said that. I think [Converse] would have, too."[9] Poet Edward Field agreed. "The Village was the one place you could move to be who you are, and no one would bother you," he told me. When I mentioned Converse's politics, and her work with the AIPR, he added, "Everyone I knew in the Village was a lefty."[10]

While her brothers would both earn master's degrees (Phil's in English literature from the University of Iowa, Paul's in sacred theology from Andover Newton Theological and a degree from Yale Divinity), Converse was busy making impressive scholarly strides of her own. After a few years spent researching and editing pieces for the AIPR, in the June 1, 1949, issue of *Far Eastern Survey,* writing as Elizabeth Converse, she was published for the first time, with a short essay on Papua and New Guinea. Other, longer pieces about India, Formosa, Micronesia, and other topics followed.[11]

"I am struck by the breadth of the topics she covered," scholar Michael R. Anderson told me. "[Each of them] represent a vastly different set of problems, and she addresses them . . . with the verve of a seasoned academic summarizing findings for a more generalized readership. Most striking for me was the fact that the AIPR would put Converse onto an article on Formosa ... at the very moment that Mao was inaugurating his Communist state. Her authorship of this article is remarkable, and must reflect the trust and esteem they placed in her, given the number of seasoned China specialists on hand who might have been commissioned for such a piece."[12]

Converse was as productive as she'd ever been, her professional and creative impulses spilling out in all directions. She continued work on her novel, the remnants of which were among the items Phil threw out when he went through her cabinet.[13] Thankfully, he at least left intact parts of the diary she'd begun keeping:[14]

> *Today I saw the second and final section of my Micronesia article in print. A year ago today I didn't even know where Micronesia was. No one need be denied the pleasure of a voyage of discovery. I suppose one reason why I plunged so thoroughly into Micronesia was because it helped me with the Flapdragons. Or maybe it sank the Flapdragons with the sheer weight of details and complications. My own islands keep submerging and reappearing, looking more formidable each time.*

The "Flapdragons" reference is to a literary project Converse was working on, the remnants of which were also preserved in her filing cabinet until Phil tossed them, too, after she was gone.[15]

That fall—as if her recent status as a published writer were not enough—Converse's cartoons saw print in *The Saturday Review of Literature*.[16] These collaborations with Larry Rosinger (one of her editors at the *Far Eastern Survey*; he seems to have supplied text for her drawings) show her nimble pen-and-ink work and a fluid, graceful sense of line and form.[17]

The cartoons are in the now-classic *New Yorker* mold—one-panel illustrations with a punch line caption underneath. When I asked Bob Mankoff, one of the magazine's longtime cartoon editors and artists, to weigh in on her efforts, he told me, "This was the golden age of magazine cartooning, where publications such as the *New Yorker, Esquire, Colliers,* and *The Saturday Evening Post* would be getting thousands of submissions. Breaking in would not only require talent but dogged persistence."[18] Had this been Converse's primary ambition, she may have stuck with it and maybe even found some success. But cartooning was only a small offshoot of the myriad activities she was now engaged in.

Converse was blossoming. She'd become closely associated with a group of young international friends, she'd dated Johnny Hsing, she'd undertaken an ambitious cross-country trip, and she'd been published for the first time, as both a journalist and a cartoonist. She'd also moved to Greenwich Village and begun a practice of setting down her thoughts for posterity.

And yet the most significant thing to happen to Converse at this time was greater than any of these other developments. It was her decision to try her hand at an entirely new art form: songwriting. Likely encouraged by the Changs, and surely inspired by her new neighborhood's aura, she composed her first song, the start of a bold new chapter, the ripples of which have only now begun to be felt.[19]

And then there was another diary entry, in which she seems to foresee the interest that her work would one day attract: "I see that F. Scott Fitzgerald has given me a license for this kind of fragmentary exercise. To Whom It May Concern: These notes, copied periodically from scraps and scrawls, may someday net you a tidy sum for post-mortem publication. If it turns out otherwise, please consider that the best ones died with me. Of the dead, nothing unless good."[20]

~

The first track on the CD-R Phil sent me is her earliest-dated com-position, from 1949—a setting for a poem by the renowned scholar and classicist A. E. Housman, from his most well-known collection, *A Shropshire Lad* (first published in 1896), entitled "With Rue My Heart Is Laden":

> *With rue my heart is laden*
> *For golden friends I had,*
> *For many a rose-lipt maiden*
> *And many a lightfoot lad.*
>
> *By brooks too broad for leaping*
> *The lightfoot boys are laid;*
> *The rose-lipt girls are sleeping*
> *In fields where roses fade.*

Converse, having only recently come to an awareness of her potential significance as an artist (as evidenced by the note about Fitzgerald), intro-duces her sound to posterity with understated, straightforward elegance. She strikes a bass note on her guitar, strums a single chord, and pauses.

And then we hear her voice for the first time—wistful, openhearted, humble, without a trace of pretension or guile. There is no grasping here, no attempts to ingratiate herself to her audience, to win anything. Rather, we hear introspection, simplicity, stateliness. The song lasts for all of forty-two seconds, and in that space of time, Connie Converse is born.

Converse the songwriter and musician quietly comes into existence the product of an already convoluted life—a childhood marked by judg-mental, old-fashioned New England; by the uncomfortable attitudes toward sex exhibited within her family; by whatever scandal she was rumored to be involved with in high school; by her decision to abandon her college education; by whatever prompted her to spend time out on the ledge of the Lincoln Arcade for hours at a time; by the gruesome suicide of her closest childhood friend.

Converse's first song has her singing about rue, about bitter regret weighing down her heart. She is twenty-five years old, living alone in New York City, smack in the middle of her known life, and part of a culture beginning to process the horrific impact of World War II. As Anatole Broyard wrote, "Looking back at the late 1940s, it seems to me now that . . . the war had broken the rhythm of American life, and when we tried to pick it up again, we couldn't find it—it wasn't there. It was as if a great bomb, an explosion of consciousness, had gone off in American life, shattering everything. Before that we had been too busy just getting along, too conventional to be lonely. The world had been smaller and we had filled it."[21]

Converse had chosen, for her songwriting debut, verses that had already been set to music by a number of composers in the first half of the twentieth century, including Vaughan Williams, Graham Peel, and (most notably) Samuel Barber. Barber's setting of "With Rue," one of his earliest compositions, was published in 1936, when he was twenty-six, only a year older than she was now.[22]

In her version, Converse's musical language is markedly different from Barber's. His setting is lush, romantic, modern. Converse, for her part, makes of the poem a tune that seems to exist somewhere between a Shaker hymn and something Sara and Maybelle Carter might have sung.[23] There is a descending bass pattern on the guitar, similar to the one Converse would soon use in her song "Down This Road." The harmonic structure of the tune is simple, based on the classic I-IV-V chord structure to be found in an infinite number of Anglo folk songs, imbuing the deep feeling of the poem with a particularly American flavor, wide-open and plain.

In her recording of the song, Converse's execution is confident and direct. There are short fermatas, or "breaths," at the end of each line, where time stops for the briefest of moments while the stated sentiment is given room to breathe. Though the words are not hers, she owns them, easily slipping into the role of the lachrymose protagonist, a character she will portray again and again in subsequent compositions like "One by One" and "There Is a Vine."

Some other considerations of why Converse may have chosen these particular lines to work on first, and why they may have meant something to her: These poems of Housman's were commonly thought of as paeans to soldiers killed in battle. Converse surely would have had peers who'd lost their lives in World War II—either people she'd grown up and gone to school with in Concord or else those she'd met during her two years in college, from 1942 to 1944.

Housman was also a closeted homosexual (or, at least, bisexual), and his poem refers to both maidens and lads. Though his private life and orientation would not be revealed until after his death, Converse was intuitive enough to make such subtle inferences. The question of what her own sexual orientation was is complicated and, at times, hovers ambiguously over her life and work. Aside from the one note from Adelaide Eby's sons, there are no other references to her being a lesbian; nor was she completely asexual (though both hypotheses were put forth to me by some who knew her). If she *was* bisexual, this would be another reason this poem may have resonated with her.

The quiet intensity of the music, and of its performance, in Converse's recording must have had something to do with these various layers. She might have been memorializing friends. She may also have been gazing backward to her lost youth and innocence. Twenty-five was still young, but she'd now been living in New York City for almost five years. The experience had liberated her in ways that stood in contrast to her upbringing, but that had also, perhaps, hardened her spirit. I hear this in the recording, too. And then, also, there may be her subtle outing of herself as someone who has known deep love, even if platonic, for both women and men.

All these elements may be present, but my hunch is that when she decided to set to music and record Housman's poem, she was thinking mostly about Frannie Flint, the aspiring young musician whose torch Converse perhaps decided to accept as a way to honor her lost best friend.

The following short poem was in Converse's filing cabinet, too. Though it's undated, it looks to have been typed on the same machine she was using around this time. Something tells me that this, too, may have been inspired by her friendship with Frannie Flint:

> *You found your me; I found my you,*
> *And thus*
> *Did us*
> *Take birth:*
> *As grass finds green, and sky finds blue*
> *And meets to form the earth.*
>
> *But now your me is left alone;*
> *I rue*
> *My you*
> *Who parted.*
> *Our came was quickly turned to gone,*
> *And just when us had started.*
>
> *I heard a was the other day:*
> *Hush—a footstep fell;*
> *And though I looked it passed away,*

And whither—who can tell?
Can how? or why?
Can you? or I?

All is nothing; no one knows,
And yesterday won't let him say,
That's why my was is goes.

PART II

"Connie's Guitar Songs"

While writing codes for happiness,
include health, creation, recognition, and love.
Insert a footnote to the effect that happiness can be
obtained without taking it away from someone else.

—CONNIE CONVERSE,
TRIES, undated (ca. 1950)

Dizzy from the Spell

A s the twentieth century hit its midway point, Connie Converse, still working for the AIPR, "would have felt like she was at the center of things," IPR scholar Michael R. Anderson told me. "For someone of her level of intellect and curiosity, it would have been an incredibly exciting world"—no less so for the political controversy that now swirled around it.[1] Combined with her new songwriting practice and artistic ambitions, Converse's life now seemed to be at full boil.

I sit here in this invulnerable silence and the whole world creeps into my apartment, my floor is not clean of sweat and blood; my mind is riddled with the megalomania, the delirium, the paranoia, the hebephrenia that rides the land; my body encloses the germs of the nation; my fate is tinged with the fate of the Bowery bum, the Chrysler worker, and the Georgia cracker; they come in, they creep in, this is their apartment too, they are like gravitation, I cannot evade them.[2]

This is Whitman, and Dos Passos, and Steinbeck, and Thoreau.

Converse's voice—vibrant, epic—is the voice of America, articulating a deep empathy with the country's people and its rich history of literature and thought. Her words smolder with a feeling of being completely alive in the moment, and to the moment, her pulse aligned with the beat of the world she inhabited.

Anyone who's lived in New York City and been possessed by the fever of creative ambition knows what this is like. Few experiences can match the feeling of simply walking the streets of Manhattan (especially in a neighborhood like Greenwich Village), knowing that one's heroes, living and dead, have walked them, too. There's something about feeling called to do something great, and also being surrounded by the spirits of those who already have or are, that spikes our confidence and makes us giddy.

Converse absorbed all of it—its immensity, its history, its structures, its art, its language, its personality—becoming the character she'd played in her dreams as a hemmed-in teenager in Concord. Here she was, actually doing it, living it. Reading through her occasional diary from this time, it's easy, and delightful, to imagine her reading *The New York Times* every morning, following her beloved Yankees, applying her reason and convictions to global problem-solving by day and then staying out as late as she pleased. Leaning out her window or perched on her fire escape at night with a lit cigarette while all the creative energy of New York hummed beneath her—and then jumping back into her apartment to type out some fresh, new inspiration in the wee hours of the morning, trying to give some voice and shape to the overwhelming feeling of limitless possibility that ran through her like an electric charge. I envision her feeling at home in the world, part of it, happy, exactly where and how she'd always imagined she would be.

Even so, few of us are who we think we are. We move through the world with narratives in our heads about our station in life, about what role or roles we have in the greater drama of reality. And sometimes those stories can exist in marked contrast to what's actually going on. Later in Converse's life, her view of her identity became distorted to the extent that she felt the need to escape from it entirely.

What some of the world might have seen now—what her family and maybe her old hometown community saw from afar—was not the image Converse saw reflected in the mirror of her consciousness, the role she assumed when writing in her diary. To those back home she'd once impressed with her manifold achievements, she was a college dropout who'd moved to New York and was working in the office of some organization that, if they knew anything at all about it, had something to do with Asia. As far as they knew, she lived alone, had no suitors, and kept to herself. She was, more or less, invisible.

But that's not the story Converse was telling herself in her journal, and it's probably not what her New York friends and co-workers saw, either. She'd broken the tie to her provincial background, a past she was neither proud of nor to which she ever intended to return. In her letters, in her articles, and now in her songs, she was moving toward her destiny. She was a New Yorker now, an up-and-coming artist and thinker bound to join the ranks of her cultural heroes, a citizen of the world. That world did not know her yet, but she was determined to change that.

I remembered what Phil had written in "Connie's Guitar Songs": "Sis composed because she had to." Now, having loosed the gate, a rush of brilliant music was about to follow.

Converse's decade and a half in New York City can be neatly divided up into three even and discrete sections, each lasting roughly five years, boundaried by the neighborhoods she lived in.

From 1945 to 1950, Converse worked toward establishing her intellectual and professional credentials. While living on the Upper West Side, she wrote and edited for the AIPR, worked on a novel, drew illustrations, and hobnobbed with an idealistic, international crowd of scholars and activists.

Later, from 1955 to 1960, she would live uptown again—first in Harlem, and then back on the Upper West Side—while writing more formal music and working on her piano and compositional skills.

But this, now, seems to have been the most wide-open time of her life in New York City: her middle years there, from 1950 to 1955, when she was living alone in Greenwich Village and composing and self-recording her guitar songs.

The Eby sisters had gotten married (one of them to Dick Aime). Sarah Thompson was getting sober in AA. Johnny Hsing was no longer in her orbit, and the Changs moved to Queens to start a family. Converse's job at the AIPR had shrunk to almost nothing.

It was against this backdrop of change that Connie Converse seems to have made a conscious shift from aspiring novelist to active songwriter. Divining her music from this distance, her dreams, such as they can be guessed at, seemed within reach. She was about to come closest to achieving the sort of success that might have made the difference between drifting into painful anonymity and becoming a household name.

CHAPTER 18

Musicks

Unlike in her attempts to write a novel, which frustrated her, Converse found flow in her songwriting, the best outlet yet for her particular creative talents. She was prolific, and then some.

Spending a period of one's creative development hungry is not a prerequisite for success, but it can help. When I started out as a young musician, subsisting on vacuum-packed bricks of cheap Mexican coffee and dining in every night on lavish meals of peas, beans, and rice, my lack of creature comforts fueled a motivation to work and to work hard. I learned the ins and outs of my musical craft. I practiced. I learned new chords. I recorded myself and then listened back, sometimes proud to hear my progress, other times wincing at mistakes and gaffes. I took home stacks of songbooks from libraries and taught myself a repertoire of hundreds of songs—a practice that, in turn, taught me about what *makes* a good song, what good songs have in common, how certain chords relate to one another, and how composers employ signature gestures and create their unique vocabularies. Over the course of innumerable hours, I began to understand how songs were built.

This is what I imagine Converse doing then—and what she certainly *would* do eventually, in stringent, scientific form. Stay tuned.

By all accounts, Converse was self-taught, both as a songwriter and a guitarist. And she was not kidding around. Her mastery of the instrument and her nuanced understanding of songcraft reveal her to be someone who engaged in rigorous, self-directed study. If there is scant evidence of a robust social life during this next period of her life, it may be because she was cloistered away in her apartment, practicing, experimenting, learning.

In fact, the AIPR's now-precarious existence (made so by further investigations of members of its staff by the House Un-American Activities Committee, or HUAC) may have been the very situation needed to set Converse on a path to writing songs with real intentionality. This process began with "Down This Road," her first composition to feature both original music and lyrics (with its clever subtitle "Monday Morning Dream of a Clerk-Typist").[1]

Having dipped her toe into the writing and self-recording of music with "With Rue My Heart Is Laden," Converse now enters the songwriting fray with assurance and brio. First comes the "hook," the descending bass line on the guitar's lowest string, giving the song a happy, steady rhythm that immediately pulls us in. It has something of what some might call a country or western (or country-western) flavor to it, a gentle 2/4 trot that could lend itself to an American folk dance. A simple melody follows in the first section of the song—gracious, easy, humble— combined with those same qualities heard in the timbre of the singer's voice. A story is being laid out, a journey with the singer. She invites us along:

> *Down this road on a Monday morning*
> *Came a-riding three strangers*

That the strangers number three could be a biblical allusion, or a reference to Thomas Hardy's short story of the same name.

Converse's narrative has a lighthearted, childlike cast. She may have even subconsciously taken her cue from one of the most popular songs of that year: Johnny Marks's "Rudolph the Red-Nosed Reindeer," a number-one hit for Gene Autry in 1949 and a song that would have been constantly on the radio. The holiday song *also* tells the story of a put-upon protagonist whose spirits are lifted by the entrance of a kindly interloper (in that case, Santa Claus, who rescues Rudolph from his bullying fellows). But though "Down This Road" begins with a similar sort of gentle openness, Converse's song quickly reveals layers of complexity and ambiguity not to be found in the Christmas ditty.

An unusual key change happens after the eighth bar of the song:

> *There was one wearing green, and one a peacock feather,*
> *and one wearing overshoes against the wintry weather.*

Where had she acquired the sort of musical sophistication that would allow for this sort of compositional feature? Phil had written in "Connie's Guitar Songs" that, though his sister had little patience for most of the pop music they'd grown up hearing on the radio, she felt that Kern and Hammerstein's "All the Things You Are," a song popular when the Converses were in high school, was "a cut or two above the stereotypic mean."[2]

That tune has since become a jazz standard, noted for its unusual number of bars, eccentric structure, and its obstacle course–like harmonic modulations, in which the key (or tonal center) of the song continues to change. Using the logic of what's called a "circle of fifths," the last chord of each section becomes the fifth (or "turnaround") of the next, ever propelling the harmony mathematically into the next sequence of chords.

It's easy to see why Converse, who loved logic and saw beauty in formulas, would have been drawn to this sort of composition. She may have spent time pursuing her own analysis of it, breaking it down to see how it worked, and then transmuted her understanding of it to songs like this one.

> *And they gave me six white horses for to carry my load*
> *And they beckoned me to follow and they took me*
> *Down this road.*

As the song changes key, the imagery in the lyric expands. One stranger wears green, another a peacock feather (a symbol of both immortality and prosperity and one she would return to later in the decade, when she composed a setting for Yeats's "The Peacock"). The third wears galoshes. Whimsy, perhaps, but evocative whimsy.

The image of the white horse stretches back to the oldest mythologies—to winged Pegasus, to Zoroastrian texts, to Hinduism, and to the Book of Revelation. The horse sometimes carries an important messenger, or symbolizes spirituality, or death. Sometimes, it arrives to bear a person away to spiritual or literal salvation. It's a symbol that has been used over and over again in song, as in "She'll Be Coming 'Round the Mountain," a lyric that also features six white horses.[3]

What is this load they're helping her with? It's unclear. But in this, labeled as her first wholly original song, she's already establishing a theme that will carry over into so many of her lyrics: She is someone who needs to be helped, or rescued.

In this song, we never do find out why. The strangers gesture to the singer: *Follow us.*

Great, let's go! Where to? But instead of an answer, an entirely unpredictable element is introduced: A second voice is heard, singing a wholly different melody over the same harmonic structure.

The first singer is now going back to repeat the first verse, telling us again about its being a Monday morning, but we're not listening to that voice any longer. We've heard that information. What is this second voice—who is it, and what is she telling us? Is this an entirely new character singing, or is it rather another facet of the narrator's mind, singing in interior monologue?

Almost any day when I'm weary, almost any day when I'm blue

This second voice is in direct contrast to the first, the one who seems happy with the interruption of her Monday morning routine. This one is downcast and wants to disappear. The quality of Converse's delivery here is strong, even defiant.

I want to take a train and ride it,
Or dig a hole and crawl inside it.

It's surprising, realizing,
What a little bit of dreaming will do.

Through the combination of the two narratives, the two melodies, and the two decidedly different voices and tones, the songwriter/performer achieves a recondite sketch of herself as a young workaday employee. There's Converse, humming the tune on her way to work, heading uptown from Grove Street, commuting with the masses, part of the humanity around her. She's inspired by her independence, her surroundings, the brightness of her future.[4]

Then, partway through her morning, something sours. She reflects on the precariousness of her work situation and is confronted once again with the reality that she may well soon be unemployed. Pessimistically, she considers: If she is unable to continue with the AIPR, and if its reputation is stained to the extent that it—her only work to this point—will be a black mark on her résumé, what then? More important, what of the grand ideals to which she'd devoted so much of her time in New York? The singer longs for an escape from it all but doesn't see one—a situation that suffocates her, making her long to get far, far away.

⁓

The song is a trick, a sleight of hand, both as emotionally access-ible and structurally unusual as anything else being written at the time.

What's also surprising about "Down This Road" and the songs that followed it in rapid succession is that Converse did not infuse her music with more topicality. With the political turmoil happening all around her, why wasn't she joining the likes of Seeger, Guthrie, and Earl Robinson in writing sociopolitical protest music? Aside from the anti-Communist mania that had engulfed the AIPR, she would surely have been upset by events like the Peekskill Riots in August and September 1949 involving singer and suspected Communist Paul Robeson, and the arrests of Julius and Ethel Rosenberg in 1950. It seems noteworthy that she was not using her newfound songwriting talents as a way to contrib-ute her voice to the national conversation, but instead chose to keep her politics and her art separate.

Because she sounds so mature and self-assured in her songs and re-cordings, it's easy to forget how young Converse still was when she was writing them. They seem to have been—at least, in part—vehicles for processing her youthful angst.

As she crossed the line into the second half of her twenties, Converse lamented her lack of good success in the realm of romance. The court-ship with Hsing seems to have petered out within just a few months of their meeting, and nothing substantial had replaced it.[5]

"My state of single cussedness grows less welcome to me in geometrical progression with the passage of days," she wrote in her diary after getting together with a couple of her former Mount Holyoke classmates, both of them now married. "Then I . . . figure at least I'm better off than unhappily married . . . We will make do," she wrote, "with an eye out for the main chance."[6]

The men she worked with were mostly older, but that may not have mattered—especially back then.[7] If American culture was increasingly taking cues from Hollywood, there was no shortage of cinematic examples that sanctioned older men romancing much younger women (a model that, even today, has not entirely disappeared).

Converse was spending time outside the office with one of her bosses, Laurence "Larry" Salisbury,[8] a man over thirty years her senior, someone with whom she would remain in close contact for the next two decades and with whom, I would learn, she may have had a romantic relationship.

Friends described Salisbury as "delightful. He had a dry sense of humor, was charming and elegant, and discreet—a typical New Englander," maybe even reminiscent of an emotional type that Converse grew up around in New Hampshire.[9] He was an impressive figure, having served in the British Army in China during the First World War,[10] hung out with members of the Bloomsbury Group in London,[11] and been appointed to State Department posts in Japan, Paris, and the Philippines.[12] And Salisbury played the piano. On balance, it sounds as though he could even have served as a model for Converse's "Playboy of the Western World"—someone whose maturity, worldliness, and reserve may have been the sort of anchor that Converse, in this still-ascendent phase of her life, found helpful, and attractive.

But Converse's relationship with Salisbury, such as it was, did not transform wildflowers into roses—at least, not as her lyric had it. At this moment in their lives, he may simply have been her platonic gateway to the city's nightlife, her ticket to the many theater, opera, music, and dance performances her diary records her taking in with him.[13]

Jean Converse thought that what she understood to be her sister-in-law's perpetual bachelorette status must have been due to her being so intellectually intimidating. To others, it was her shy and inward-looking nature that must have prevented her from having a known romantic or sexual life.

Neither theory holds much water. A young woman with the temerity to drop out of college and move, alone, to Manhattan; who was comfortable taking long, far-flung out-of-town trips by herself, even across the entire country; and who could hold her own with some of the top internationalist thinkers of her time, was not lacking in boldness—at least not the kind that comes from self-reliance. She lived in the Village. She liked to drink and hang out with colorful personalities. Of course she was meeting potential partners—if for no other reason than the fact that the city's noise ordinance meant she had to stop typing or playing music by eleven o'clock each night, a fact she noted with some irritation in her diary.

She was a night owl, and given the constant churning of her overactive brain, it seems right to imagine her walking out her Grove Street door on any given night in search of nocturnal company—or, at least, experience. "Worry must damage the mind as much as alcohol; its effect is less observable, slower, more insidious," she wrote, perhaps in reference to her father's lifelong temperance campaign. "I can't get gravitation off my mind (sing to the tune of 'Can't Get Indiana off My Mind')."[14]

Her neighborhood offered myriad options, many of them featuring the latest jazz, blues, and folk every night. She could walk down to Arthur's Tavern to hear Charlie Parker; to Café Society to hear Josh White; to the Village Vanguard to hear Pete Seeger's popular group, the Weavers, or a jazz ensemble featuring the musically ferocious Charles Mingus on bass.

And she was only blocks away from the White Horse Tavern, stomping grounds for Dylan Thomas, another of her literary idols.

Writer and producer Nick Pileggi recalled the scene in those days. "Single people would hang out at their neighborhood bar the way that people today congregate at Starbucks," he said. "Bars were not the loud, crowded pickup joints that they are today. They didn't have TVs or loud music. Places like Louie's, or Julius', for example, were operated on the English pub model, where people went after work to socialize. Single women were known in the bars they would frequent. They would have their neighborhood spot." Photographer Maggie Berkvist told me that hers was Louie's. "I went there by myself all the time," she said.[15]

When I told Pileggi that Converse was a writer living on Grove, he said, "Then she probably hung out at Chumley's, on Bedford between Grove and Barrow. It had a fireplace, terrific food at reasonable prices, [and] people would go there to talk, or play chess, or read a book." It's not hard to picture the twentysomething Converse seated at one of the former speakeasy's cozy, dark leather banquets, a paperback or a notebook and a drink (or all three) on the small table in front of her, a cigarette between her fingers, a self-possessed smile on her lips. Maybe this was even how Bill Bernal had first encountered her.

What might those mocking classmates back home in Concord say if they could see her now? Between her avant-garde artistic efforts, her job working for an organization suspected of harboring Communists, and her residence in the Village, she'd have been scarcely recognizable to any of them.

Another of the Eby sons' written recollections of things their mother had once said identified Converse as a "card-carrying Communist," and Phil had told me he felt that this may have been true. No less than Joseph McCarthy himself, the crusading demagogue at the center of the anti-Communist hysteria that was now infecting the American political conversation, had accused Converse's editor, Owen Lattimore, of being "the top Soviet agent in North America."[16]

Converse was not called to testify, but a number of her colleagues were, including Salisbury, Lattimore, and her cartooning collaborator Rosinger. Writing in her journal, Converse reported her thoughts. She did not like what she was seeing:

> *Troubled and hectic times, capped by the feature bout of Lattimore versus McCarthy. If McCarthy wins, it will establish the prevalence of witches; if Lattimore wins, it will show his innocence of sorcery, but not the nature of witches . . .*
>
> *So we plunge from the bright if bloody history into a dark and bloody future. I cannot help this private pessimism. The sun shines in many places, but this continent seems to be declining into a long winter, and all our strength, all our warm tradition may not be enough to hold it back. We have become a nation of awful paradox: hysteria inlaid with unconcern, literacy woven with misconception, democracy wrapped up in tyranny, boldness nailed down by fear. I have no doubt of the outcome, but I dread the interval.*[17]

If this sounds like it could have been written today, in this moment of the "alternative facts" culture of the MAGA movement, it gets better (or worse):

> *The terrible thing about it is that you get used to anything. A lot of German people discovered that you can live under fascism . . . After a little struggle, they find it possible to cut the living thread that connects them with other people, with the Jews, with the anti-fascists, with the expendables. If I ever cease to recall that my destiny is bound with a living cord to the destiny of the Jews, the Negroes, the anti-fascists, the expendables, I shall indeed be half dead.*[18]

This is Converse, talking about antifa. In 1950.

Unsurprisingly, she did not cut and run. Converse stayed put, as best she could, on the periphery of the moment's greatest political controversy, keeping an active eye on the hearings and sometimes attending them in person—including the trial of IPR trustee Alger Hiss, held on Seventh Avenue.[19]

But as the AIPR's budget shrank, her already meager income dwindled further. "Let me share with you my latest trick of economy," she wrote in her diary. "Whenever I feel like relaxing at a good movie, I trick myself into going to a drugstore for a whodunit, which is cheaper; then, once in the drugstore and feeling intellectual, I trick myself into buying a Penguin, which is more expensive than a movie."[20]

More time on her hands and little disposable income also meant more songs issuing from her guitar. One of these is "The Moon Has No Heart," a tune with a crisp, concise lyric:

> *The moon has no heart*
> *Else why did she fly down the west of the sky*
> *When my lover and I had to part?*
> *The moon has no heart.*

> *How sly was her art*
> *To light up the night when our love was still bright*
> *But when from my side he did start*
> *The moon had no heart.*

On her original sheet music, Converse indicates that the composition should be performed "moodily" and, in her own recording, it is. Yet in the bridge, a modulation to the song's relative minor key and a delightfully ornate guitar fingerpicking pattern allow the song to break free briefly from its funereal, baroque-sounding beginning:

> *He is gone and I weep, and I never shall sleep*
> *But still in the west, with her hand on her breast*
> *Not a tear in her eye, she stares from the sky*
> *And I cry.*

Even so, the gloom does not lift; the tune is dashed back to earth again with a restatement of the opening line and melody, and an uncharacteristic (for Converse) "woe is me" feeling persists.

No such trouble exists for "Trouble" (or "Ever Since We Met"). Like "Down This Road," it is delectable and beguiling, filled with joie de vivre, lyrical depth, and unexpected musical twists.

> *Ever since we met, the world's been upside down,*
> *And if you don't stop troubling me, you'll drive me out of town.*
> *But if you go away, as trouble ought to do,*
> *Where will I find another soul to tell my trouble to?*

In songs like "Down This Road," Converse is singing to her audience, telling us a story. In others, such as "When I Go Traveling," she is the intrepid heroine, musing to herself, imagining another reality. But in "Trouble," she takes up a new approach, singing to an abstract concept— trouble itself, a device used in blues standards of the day like "Blues Stay Away from Me" and "Trouble in Mind."

The song starts with a simple statement of theme and purpose. The singer sketches an emotional landscape. At first, we assume that she is talking to a lover ("Ever since we met, the world's been upside down"), but then, after a sly fermata that serves as the dramatic launch to the next section of the song, it is revealed that she could be playfully addressing trouble itself, telling it to get lost.

At the end of each verse, she asks rhetorically, "But if you go away, as trouble ought to do, / Where will I find another soul to tell my trouble to?" For all the difficulty that trouble affords her, it is, in the end at least, some form of company and better than being alone—an example of Converse's penchant for upending our expectations. This is then followed by a neat, dance-like guitar motif, interludes that end with yet more dramatic pauses before she begins the next verse.

Verse two contains more lyrical treats—indeed, some of the most satisfying in her guitar song canon:

> *My bed is made of stone, a star has burnt my eye,*
> *I'm going down to the willow tree and teach her how to cry.*

How evocative, how intimate. We now know so much more about the singer than we did in verse one. She cannot rest. Her bed, the place where she can most be alone and safe with her own counsel, is inhospitable.

This is not a new image for Converse; in a poem she submitted for the Glascock Prize in 1944, she wrote, using the voice of a beggar in the street:

> *"I sleep well in an unyielding bed;*
> *Stone and the night equally hard and cool . . ."*[21]

And then, in "Trouble": "a star has burnt my eye," one of her most powerful images. Stargazing, that activity so associated with dreaming, with forward thinking, with wonder, has punished her. She has turned her gaze to the heavens only to be dramatically rebuked, her eye scorched, injured by the effort. The things she is most attracted to damage her.

She goes down to the weeping willow tree to "teach her how to cry." This, a full eight years before Johnny Cash would record "Big River" (which begins with the immortal line "Now I taught the weeping willow how to cry"). Did Johnny Cash somehow hear a recording of Converse's "Trouble" on a visit to New York? Did one of her tapes make it into his hands?

> *They bid me wear my hat, put on a nice new gown,*
> *I've tossed my bonnet over the roof*
> *And I guess it won't come down.*

Converse the rebel, Converse the converse, revealed again in song—the nonconformist, the independent woman, heedless of convention. She is told how to dress and what to wear, but she throws what is expected of her away, so high that it disappears, never to be seen again. No hats for her. No gowns or bonnets, either, thank you very much. She is done with that bullshit.

In the song's last twist, after repeating the refrain, she finishes with a flourish, landing on a final, unresolved major third chord. It is at once a wonderful last statement of pugnaciousness (why end the song traditionally, either?) and also a suggestion that the tale's narrative is not finished—a cliff-hanger. Like so many of her songs, "Trouble" is concerned with transformation.

A s Converse was writing these songs, the New York City art scene was animated by the ideas of a new group of artistic upstarts. John Cage's *4'33"*, a composition written "for any instrument or combination of instruments" contained no music.[22] Cage was part of a coterie that included performance artist Rachel Rosenthal, painters Jasper Johns and Robert Rauschenberg, and Cage's partner and frequent collaborator, the choreographer Merce Cunningham. (Cunningham believed that dance and music should work independently of each other; his ensemble typically did not hear the music for his dances until it was time for them to be performed.[23])

In any era, at any given time, it is impossible to distinguish between the passing trend and the epochal. We can't look around us and know, with any degree of certainty, what will survive and what won't. History decides those things, not us.

Converse was making work in the midst of paradigm-shifting artists, but—back then—she was invisible, writing song after song with little to fuel her other than a belief that her efforts were worthwhile. But sometimes, that's enough. Sometimes, we believe: *This will survive me*, and *It doesn't matter whether it's successful now; it will find its audience someday.*

A new composition, "Honeybee," represents another development for her, both as composer and guitarist. The guitar motif she uses in the main theme seems a subtle nod to the Ink Spots, and her chord voicings include both diminished and major seventh chords, hallmarks of a jazz vocabulary. The two key changes that occur during the bridge also move the song away from what today would be called folk or singer-songwriter music. Instead, "Honeybee" lives in the realm of the standard, far more open to interpretation and embellishment than many of her other songs to date.

The narrator of "Honeybee" is, once again, lonely and yearning for a lover. What's different this time is that it's not a dream lover; this is someone with whom she is in an active relationship. The story, such as it is, is simple: After a quarrel, the singer regrets her part in the drama, though pride prevents her from admitting as much. Instead, she tells a bee to tell a bird to apologize on her behalf.

Converse would revisit this dynamic, with greater maturity and nuance, in her piano song "Incommunicado," the one I had played for Gene Deitch in a Prague courtyard. "Fare You Well" (or "Walkin' Shoes"), another new song from this time, also finds her exploring new stylistic ground. It features the sort of upbeat swagger of Western swing music, a style that had reached its apex of popularity at the time. Surely Tommy Duncan, fronting Bob Wills and His Texas Playboys, could have had a ball with this one.

Then, too, it's another "goodbye and good riddance" sort of number, the kind of kiss-off out of which Bob Dylan would come to make an art form a little over a decade later with songs like "It Ain't Me Babe," "Don't Think Twice, It's All Right," and "Positively 4th Street."

⌒

P roud of the work she was producing, Converse was recording tape reels of these songs and mailing them to Phil and Jean, who'd become, according to them, her biggest fans.[24] Phil later told her that the songs served as a litmus test for any acquaintances they invited to their home for dinner and cocktail parties: If the guests didn't take to her music, they were not asked back. And she was likely playing them in person for friends in addition to the Changs, gaining in confidence in her new vocation as composer, singer, guitarist, and performer as she did.

But the beginning of these prolific years of music making now coincided with the suspended animation of the other career track she seems to have been on. If Converse's activities as editor and reporter with the AIPR had been the first steps toward a life she envisioned as a public intellectual, they'd now come to an abrupt end as her job there dissipated completely under the weight of the HUAC hearings. On balance, while the writing she did for *Far Eastern Survey* is not quite enough on which to base a prediction that she might have become another Hannah Arendt, or a Susan Sontag, the insights on world affairs and human behavior contained in her letters and in her work years later as editor for *The Jour-nal of Conflict Resolution* suggest that this could have been an avenue she'd envisioned herself following.

For now, she chose music.

~

Courting and marriage were at the heart of a number of songs Con-verse wrote in 1951, and no wonder. That August, the Converse family convened in Chicago for Phil and Jean's wedding (Paul presided over the ceremony);[25] two months later, Paul married Hyla Clark Stuntz, in Washington Square, a short walk from Grove Street.[26]

For Phil and Jean's wedding, Converse wrote and recorded "Where Are the Roses?" a puzzling composition. She'd hoped to bring the finished piece to Chicago, Phil remembered, "but it was far from ready, and we only received it some weeks later. This accounts for the less than tri-umphal lyrics."[27]

Those lyrics mostly match the melody—mournful and sad. While a descant part written for a second voice adds real musical beauty to the composition, at its heart, this seems to be another example of Converse turning expectation upside down. Rather than fashioning a sentimental ode to love for her younger brother, to enshrine the moment in musical amber, she instead has the couple talking to each other in song and in some confusion. Where are the roses that people had brought them? They are faded or gone. Where are the presents they'd received? These, too, are gone or broken. And where are all the cherished family and friends who'd come to celebrate with them? They've left and are return-ing home, leaving the newlyweds alone with nothing but each other—who will, at least, "stay together, tried and true, as lovers do."

Not exactly a blissful picture, but perhaps a realistic one. Phil and Jean told me they absolutely loved the song, and they wrote to Converse telling her as much. "Connie, it is so good . . . completely the nicest wedding present ever . . . Long after the happy checks are dead and gone, the alto and baritone will be checking on the roses."[28]

This sort of feedback bolstered Converse's confidence and spurred her forward. Such was the case in the summer of 1952, when she set some of Chaucer's verse to music. "Your Chaucer masterpiece sounds fascinating," Phil wrote in response. "Modal as hell, that's what we like to hear."[29] With the launch of the Korean War, Phil had been drafted into the service, landing a relatively cushy post as an army newspaper editor in Battle Creek, Michigan, where he was able to stay close to Jean.

There are no known recordings of Converse performing "Chaucer: Introduction to 'The Canterbury Tales,'" but her intricately notated sheet music for guitar and voice is extant. It's felicitous, with an appropriately traditional English folk music feel to it—almost the sort of thing that Cat Stevens would record twenty years later at the height of his early 1970s popularity, but more structurally original. Converse did not translate the lyrics; the song is meant to be sung in Old English.

These Converses. They loved language. Phil was studying Russian for fun, and on a couple of occasions practiced his new skills by writing portions of his letters to his sister in Cyrillic script. Converse had no problem translating and even correcting his Russian grammar; somehow, she already knew the language. Phil had also gotten himself a guitar and had begun learning her songs from the manuscript pages she was sending him. "I can play 'Down This Road' with some aplomb," he wrote, "and lust after more private art songs."[30]

One of those he requested was a transcription of "Chanson Innocent" (or "Innocent Song"). A setting for the first poem in e. e. cummings's "Chansons Innocentes," it begins—in Converse's recording of it—with a long, bluesy guitar introduction that would not have sounded out of place as rendered by Rev. Gary Davis. When the vocal arrives, however, the melody reveals itself as angular and through-composed—evidence (along with the Chaucer piece) that the art-song form she would begin to focus on exclusively just a few years later was already a part of her musical vision.

"Chanson" is a short composition, but an adventurous one, displaying not only Converse's continually impressive guitar skills, but also her developing sense of an expanding, and modern, compositional vocabulary. Phil loved the result. "Your accompaniment to the Cummings [*sic*] just-spring piece I dearly hope you will preserve," Phil wrote. "I say this as it is perchance the sort of thing you would not keep well oiled."[31]

This kind of correspondence with Phil (and Jean) was now frequent, and she began soliciting their input on all her freshly composed songs. These letters also constitute the most significant documentary evidence and record of her daily life in New York during this period, outside of her diary. At times, they are richly detailed, and virtuosic in their prose. At others, they're tantalizingly, woefully incomplete. There is little in the way of where she was in her emotional life, and never a mention of a romantic or sexual life of any kind. (This is no knock against her; many of us are less open with our families than we are with our close friends on the topics of love and romance.) If there were other letters from this time that may have offered such insights, I did not find them in her cabinet.

Instead, she sticks to topics like her musical activities, her monetary struggles, her plans for and reports of what seemed to be a constant stream of out-of-town road jaunts, and boastful accounts of her nicotine and alcohol intake vices, already in evidence as far back as her teenage correspondence with Frannie Flint—habits that would continue for the rest of her life. "I write with a glass of reminiscence tinkling merrily in one hand," she wrote one night. "Alcoholics Anonymous is sending down a representative."[32]

This may have been one of Converse's self-deprecating witticisms, or it could have been rooted in truth. Sarah Thompson was now an active member of AA. Thompson met Joan Cooper there, who would become her life partner, befriended Bill W., and began working for *The Grapevine*, the organization's magazine.[33] But if Converse ever accompanied Thompson to a 12-step meeting, there is no evidence of it.

Converse's epistolary relationship with Phil—one that has echoes of the Van Gogh brothers' in terms of its dedication, enthusiasm, and the dynamic of one sibling serving as a booster for the other's unrecognized talents—would continue throughout the remainder of her time in New York. Phil was dazzled by her songs and validated his sister's view of herself as a working artist. Privately, though, he seemed to harbor a conviction that she ought to be doing something different with her life.[34]

CHAPTER 19

A Family Visit

Perhaps fortified by the encouragement she was getting from Phil, Converse outed her songs to their parents when Evelyn and Ernest visited New York for Thanksgiving 1952.[1] There, they joined Paul and his wife, Hyla, for a visit to her Grove Street apartment.

Converse deemed the occasion momentous enough to preserve it on tape—and not just the music, though this informal performance for her family constitutes the earliest-known recording of Converse playing her songs anywhere, for anyone other than herself.[2]

The tape begins with Converse blowing into the microphone to test it, followed by random chatter. Evelyn asks her daughter if she works at "the little coffee table, on that stool?" to which Converse, almost curtly, replies yes.

Evelyn marvels that Connie doesn't have an alarm clock.

Converse: "The alarm doesn't wind anymore."

Not much happens on the recording until around the nine-minute mark. Then, without any preamble, Converse is heard strumming random chords on her guitar. It sounds as though she has been coaxed into playing some of her songs and is perhaps trying to rise to the occasion.

That she would elect to perform for them at all is surprising, given Phil's memory of secular music being forbidden in their childhood home. From the interstitial chatter on the tape, it seems that one of her brothers must have forced her hand by sending Ernest and Evelyn a tape reel of her playing her songs in advance of this visit.

Outside of that recording (whatever it was), this may have been the first time that her parents had ever heard her perform in this way. In school, she'd sung in the choir and played in the orchestra, and the family had also sung hymns and carols together in church and at home, but Converse's original song compositions are an entirely different animal and had to have at the very least challenged Evelyn's and Ernest's sensibilities. Her daring to reveal her craft on this occasion—in spite of familial tensions that remained just under the surface—said something about the level of faith in herself she'd achieved in the three years since she began her songwriting practice.

But then, on the tape, her confidence seems to wilt almost as soon as she begins. As any introvert who's been called upon to perform in such informal gatherings knows, a certain amount of mortification accompanies these kinds of experiences. It's not difficult to imagine her singing to the floor, unable to make eye contact with anyone.

She opens with "Man in the Sky," sounding tentative, nervous, and scared. Imagining her exposing this level of vulnerability before the strict, disapproving eyes and ears of Ernest and Evelyn makes this portion of the recording uncomfortable to listen to.

"Man in the Sky" contains themes close to Converse's heart. She's fantasizing again, dreaming again, chasing again. As with "The Moon Has No Heart," she's looking to the heavens for help with her melancholy mood. As in "Trouble," "Talkin' Like You," and "Honeybee," she communicates with things that are not human—in this case, the constellation

Orion. It is, in fact, the mythical Orion who becomes the object of the narrator's affection when she tires of fickle, feckless mortal men.

She calls out to her chosen savior in the dead of night, imploring him to come down, lest she "pine and die." And though he continues his walk through the night sky, she succeeds in snagging his attention, at least; he now has "a gleam for her in his golden eye."

Since he will not come to her, she will go to him, "to the place where the planets are," where she jumps "from there to the nearest star" and plays with the creatures who make up the various constellations, eventually laying her head on the shoulder of her love at last.

Yet even as she does so, she sees that his gaze is "a million miles away" and that he is "just like other men"—which leads to the story's upshot: Her love remains unrequited, she dies forgotten, while the man continues his roving ways. Consistent with so many of her other songs, this one, too, has a kicker: Orion remains a perpetual bachelor, unwilling (or unable) to accept the love of another.

Musically, the song is Converse at her most strophic. It's also one of her *longest* guitar song lyrics, and the song suffers somewhat for its monotonous, repetitive verse-chorus structure. Still, her compositional inventiveness is ever on display, especially in the interplay between the minor and major tonalities she employs throughout.

"Oh, I really like that one!" Evelyn cries at the song's conclusion, a reaction that is perhaps more than the singer was prepared for.

Converse relaxes. When she then launches into "Talkin' Like You," we hear the arrival of the Connie Converse we know from other recordings: secure and sly, singing with that rare combination of pride and softness.

"Talkin' Like You"—also known as "Two Tall Mountains" and, as she originally titled it on the lead sheet she sent to be copyrighted (and then crossed out), "Lonesome Gap"—may be Converse's most iconic song, her greatest hit. It's the first song on *How Sad, How Lovely,* the one that pops up first in online searches for her music; the song with which, Phil told me, the few fans she did have most associated her. After the hesitant, wobbly "Man in the Sky," Converse throws down her ace.

While her notes place the composition of this song in 1951, the inspiration for it almost certainly comes from the White Mountains of New Hampshire, where she had spent time as a young girl, where she had gone to work during the summer before beginning her studies at Mount Holyoke, and where, between a couple of high peaks, there is indeed a lake called Lonesome.[3] Converse may even have once stayed in one of its rustic guest cabins at some point, little scenic getaways that remain available to hikers and explorers to this day.

Though the intro and coda of the song look toward Tin Pan Alley and jazz, the main body of it seems to draw musical inspiration from the rural America of the 1920s and '30s and anticipates the swell of interest in the scratchy recordings from that era that rose up around the 1952 release of Harry Smith's epochal *Anthology of American Folk Music.*[4]

Smith's curatorial feat was inspiring scores of new young listeners to turn their attention to a forgotten, secret-sounding musical universe. Earnest, college-educated, mostly white young men and women began attempting to imitate these regional, unusual styles as "authentically" as possible, picking up guitars and banjos and forming groups like the New Lost City Ramblers, some going so far as to dress like the 1920s and '30s musicians they were emulating.[5] Dave Van Ronk, one of Bob Dylan's mentors and present at the dawn of what would become the new New York City folk scene, called the records "our bible," and wrote "without Harry Smith's *Anthology* we could not have existed."[6]

Happy Traum, who as a young man was also part of this nascent movement, joined the chorus of people who confirmed for me that Converse's writing and performing personal music rooted in these older styles would have been highly unusual at that time.[7] Ellen Stekert put this idea even more bluntly when she told me: "In those days, people were *accused* of writing their own songs!"[8]

Smith's *Anthology* struck a cultural nerve, but Converse was a step ahead of the explosion of interest in older American music it caused. Because even if she was as well versed in these idioms as any of them, Converse wasn't a revivalist. She had no interest in nostalgia. Instead, she was concocting brand-new music inspired by Smith's magical ingredients. And it was more original, more personal, and arguably more artistically worthwhile than the sometimes ersatz-sounding anthems being penned by the likes of Seeger and the Weavers—many of whom disdained songs that lacked a political or social function. "Seeger wasn't introspective," Stekert told me, one reason she felt that he lost faith in Dylan when the latter's songwriting became more personal. "Pete was all about his causes."[9]

Van Ronk reiterated this point, recalling that songwriters from the pre-Dylan era of topical "folk music" in the United States despised music that could be said to have primarily entertainment value.[10] Seeger and company were inhabiting the idealized dream of a movement, while Converse was busy breaking the rules, wide awake.

⌒

As Converse's Grove Street performance of "Talkin' Like You" concludes, Evelyn's voice emerges again on the tape; she offers a backhanded compliment: "Your singing has improved *very* much," she says, and it's hard not to hear the condescension in her tone.

Ernest wants clarity: Was it "pigs" that his daughter was singing about? Yes, their daughter responds. It certainly was.

"Let's do 'Down This Road,'" Converse then says, and Paul and Hyla add their vocals to hers, freeing her to sing the descant in a rendition that suggests this was something the three had rehearsed. It's the only evidence that Paul was in any way invested in his sister's musical pursuits. (Hyla was a devotee of traditional music and adored her sister-in-law's songs, so this little trio may have been her influence.)[11]

"That's cute," Evelyn says when they finish.

Evelyn then requests "Father Neptune," prompting giggles from Hyla and Paul, and Converse demurs, likely embarrassed to learn that her parents are even aware of the existence of a song she'd written in which the narrator reveals her ardor for a romantically brooding "man with a beard and a tan."

It's a song onto which she'd only recently put the finishing touches, and another quiet gem.

> *When my man goes to sea*
> *He steps so high and free*
> *I think I know as I watch him go*
> *That he has no need for me, for me.*

> *And when my man comes home*
> *And waits a while to roam*
> *I think I see when he smiles at me*
> *That he's dreaming of the foam, the foam.*

While singer Jo Stafford was imagining silver planes and tropic isles in the gauzy "You Belong to Me," one of that fall's biggest pop hits, Converse was reaching back to the strange English "folk music" of her ancestors, songs sometimes referred to as Child Ballads.[12] This is a weird collection of songs, their lyrics frequently dealing with themes of jealousy, infidelity, murder, death, deception, and fate—and often with an appearance by the supernatural and the fantastic.[13]

I hear this influence not only in "Father Neptune," but in other

Converse songs like "The Witch and the Wizard," "Here Is the Door," and "Man in the Sky." These are latter-day stepchildren of old warhorses like "Barbara Allen," "Love Henry," and "The Golden Vanity"—songs that the British Converses and Eatons may even have sung, or listened to others sing, during their passage to the New World.

"Father Neptune" is another adult fairy tale, cousin to both "Man in the Sky" and "Playboy of the Western World." But more damning than the lascivious undertones of the "beard and a tan" line is Converse's blatant rejection, in the lyric, of the moral, religious foundation on which Ernest and Evelyn had built their lives. If such is implicit in "Roving Woman," here she makes it plain:

> *I'm not a pious Christian*
> *And I do not go to mass*
> *But I pray to Father Neptune*
> *To let him safely pass.*
>
> *I sing to the God with the three-pronged rod*
> *And the whiskers wild and free*
> *That I've got a man with a beard and a tan*
> *And a passion for the sea.*
>
> *He rides through the storm*
> *And the cold and the warm*
> *And he loves to risk his neck*
> *And I like to know when he goes below*
> *That it's just below the deck*
>
> *Oh Neptune! Father Neptune!*
> *I tell you fair and true*

That if you should lose my sailor
I'll sing no more to you!

When he's home from the sea he's half with me
And he's gone when I close the door
And it's still his creed that he has no need
Of a wife except on shore.

I know it's the boat
That keeps him afloat
But I like to think it's me.

And if it were not for this
I would sink to the depths of the sea.

These final lines, though humorous in their agile wordplay, also contain real despair, as the singer considers the possibility of suicide.

C onverse declines to perform this song for her parents, instead answering in the affirmative Evelyn's question about whether she has taught herself how to play the guitar. Converse then offers the cummings treatment "Chanson Innocent," followed by "When I Go Traveling" and then "Sorrow Is My Name."

The latter is similar to "The Moon Has No Heart," but more successful—mainly for its adventurous musical language, and also for some poetic tricks the narrator again has up her sleeve. Here, Converse conceives of an effective, unusual rhythmic pattern in her right hand that serves as a sort of tolling-bell counterpoint to the woebegone lyric. The melody—mostly plaintive, but in moments, angular—helps carry along the story of Sorrow, who offers advice and pronouncements:

Oh, keep on sleeping, when I pass your door,
And keep on hoping I will come no more.
Oh keep on singing, when you hear my feet,
And keep on dreaming, if your dream is sweet.

Then, in the bridge, come the mystical, paradoxical rules:

And if you fear me, I will come in haste;
And if you love me, I will go away;
And if you scorn me, I will lay you waste;
And if you know me I will come to stay.

On the surface, Sorrow is instructing her listeners in ways to attract and repel its attention. By fearing sorrow, sorrow will come; by loving sorrow, sorrow will fade. Just as revealing is the implication that the singer may be singing to a lover, addressing the confusion and messiness involved in courting someone like her.

Maybe the most intriguing thing about the song is the possibility that it may have been inspired by Aeschylus's *Agamemnon*, in which the cursed prophetess Cassandra cries out: "O Sorrow, sorrow of my city dragged to utmost death."[14] Cassandra would become a figure around whom Converse would eventually compose an entire set of songs—words and music with a vastly different cast from the ones she was writing now.

There Is a Vine" follows on the Grove Street tape—or, at least part of it. This is one of Converse's most perfect songs—elegant, classic in structure, beautiful in her stoic recordings of it, and profound in how it manages to reveal, intimately, its narrator's pure, romantic essence.

In three compact verses, the singer of "There Is a Vine" details the unrequited love she feels for an unnamed other, subordinating herself and even her self-worth as she waits alone for that one who can complete her. The song has the same kind of stately, inevitable, hymnlike melody heard in some of the songs written by the songwriter's collateral relative Charles Crozat Converse.

In the first verse, the singer compares her self (or her feeling of love) to a vine—wilted in autumn, but bursting with passion in the spring. In verse two, she describes a gate by her garden that she locks up at night before stealing herself away. In the daylight, though, she opens the gate wide "for all who would come through"—perhaps a not-so-veiled depiction of what may be the real-life promiscuity Phil thought that Converse was engaging in in New York City. This verse is omitted when she peforms the song for her parents. The narrator's beloved, the one who holds the key to her most private self, however, always has access. For that person, the gate is open night or day.

But in the third verse we hit the song's emotional pay dirt. We learn that a tree grows near the gate, behind the wall. There it stands, waiting, year after year, alone. A big reveal, Converse's signature, concludes the lyric: The singer herself appears, standing beneath the tree, no longer hidden behind metaphor, exposed now for the lonely, gentle, shy soul she is—waiting, patiently, for the love she yearns for above all else:

> *There is a tree*
> *Growing by my garden gate*
> *And year by year*
>   *it seems to stand and wait*
> *And here am I*
>   *beneath the tree*
>   *for I am waiting too*
> *And oh my love*
>   *I will always wait for you*

It is one of Converse's most undefended images, and with it, we see in song the songwriter shorn of any cleverness, linguistic or musical tricks that might throw a listener off her trail. There she stands, wanting nothing more than to be able to express and share love, a feeling she is able to communicate through song in ways that she perhaps could not in everyday life.

And then, as in "One By One," there is the sense that the only way to navigate darkness is through connection. This is something at the root of many of Converse's lyrics, even at their most impassive. We know what this is like on a more universal level; it's the emotional baggage we all carry with us—the pain, confusion, sadness, and hurt that accumulate with age; the darkness that can make life challenging at the bare minimum and unbearable at the worst. We require connection to one another to survive this, maybe now more than ever. In today's world lit by glowing screens, many of us have lost touch with, or were never given, some of the tools with which these bonds can be formed and strengthened: having conversations with one another, in real time; making music or art with one another; taking walks, cooking meals, playing games, holding hands.

It's a cliché, but also true, that creatives are often working out the emotional damage they endured at some formative time in their lives. Art making is one way to deal with that trauma—a survival mechanism, a way to form those connections we require to inhabit a meaningful life.

Converse's lyrics, music, and recordings express this: a yearning attempt to make herself known. She had her self, and then she had this art as a means of effectively expressing that self. But the third part of the artist's triangle, the audience, was missing for her—at least, in her own time.

I think this is what Rita Chang intuited in me—this visceral sense that others feel of being called to be that side of the triangle for her, the one she could not find when she was composing. What she was doing then was so unusual that audiences outside her immediate circle (and maybe even some of those inside it) couldn't "hear" her. It was as though she were speaking another tongue.

Today, we've grown so accustomed to the prevalence of self-revealing, genre-defying music that—for us—there are no obstacles. Of course we hear her. Of course we want to be her audience. Of course we understand how painful it must have been for her to be so vulnerable in her music only to have it answered by an earsplitting shrug. Of course we want to help her.

This is why listening to Converse's recordings of songs like "There Is a Vine," "One by One," and "How Sad, How Lovely" can provoke a feeling not unlike the one that rises up from reading the goodbye letters she wrote just prior to her disappearance, from thinking of her driving away for good. The evangelism that first compelled me to tell the world about Converse has something to do with empathy for so *many* artists whose work, or whose lives, have been met by the cruelties of misunderstanding or apathy. Which is more shocking—the incontestable beauty of Van Gogh's paintings, or the fact that his contemporaries were unable to see it? For me, the same question hangs over the music of Connie Converse.

～

Paul was now visiting Ernest and Evelyn in New England practically every weekend.[15] The week after the Converse family's Thanksgiving visit to Grove Street, he brought with him another tape of his sister's original songs—one that included "Roving Woman."[16]

Converse was furious. Paul would have to have known that exposing his sister through these lyrics in particular would shock and mortify their parents. Phil suggested to me that Paul's motives may even have been "malevolent"—that he was mischievously seeking to sow discord and scandal. It wouldn't be the last time he crossed a line with his family.

Yet the dustup, such as it was, didn't last. Ernest had taken another new post, this one in Woodville, Massachusetts, and Converse drove up there with Paul and Hyla just a few weeks later, for Christmas. She brought her bulky recording machine with her and made more home-recorded tapes there—one of the family taking turns reading from *Winnie-the-Pooh* and another of all of them singing Christmas carols and hymns together a cappella.

The group singing is lovely and affecting. It sounds like this was one way the family was able to genuinely come together. There is a shared focus to their harmonies and what seems to be real reverence for the material (or, at least, for the shared activity). The mood of the performances—if it's fair to even label them as such—on songs like "Go Tell It on the Mountain" and "Gloria" seems solemn and deeply felt. I imagine them in a room staring at one another to get their cues right, stern, stiff, and uncomfortable, but also bound together.

The holidays in New England this year also featured some news to share about doings back in New York: Sis had found a new line of work.

CHAPTER 20

Free to Be Free

A fter gathering with her family for the holidays, Converse returned to Manhattan and began a full-time position with a small printing and publishing concern called Academy Photo Offset, Inc.[1] She had spent the time after her departure from the AIPR bouncing around in the employment wilderness with a temp agency while also seeking out odd freelance editing and writing jobs where she could find them.[2] Academy Photo Offset, half a block away from the iconic Flatiron Building, now became her place of employement for the remainder of her time in New York.[3]

Printing was the second-biggest industry in the city (after textiles). Ron Gordon, founder of the New York City–based Oliphant Press and a self-described print obsessive, told me that Converse working at Academy at that time would have been unique in a number of respects.

"She would have been one of very few women doing this kind of work," which often involved handling big, heavy machinery. "I bet she was the only woman there," Gordon said. "If there were others, they would have been secretaries. That was a man's world. It was 'roll up your sleeves and get dirty' work you did while cursing and talking about the Yankees. And after work, you go out for beers. She had to have been pretty tough to work in an environment like that."

The son of one of Converse's co-workers at Academy remembered visiting the shop as a child, and his memories squared with this image. He told me that the atmosphere at Academy was casual and convivial. Though he didn't recall ever meeting or hearing about Converse, he remembered the staff of half a dozen or so employees being close, and that they spent off-hours together at a local bar and getting together on weekends, too.

The work Academy specialized in was considered cutting-edge for its day.[4] Offset printing, unlike the more old-fashioned letterpress technique, involved the new process of setting type without metal. "There were not a lot of places like this back then," Ron Gordon told me, "so in that sense, she was ahead of her time, using skills that were brand-new. You could think about it this way: If she were alive today, she'd be designing apps."[5]

Converse may have hung around with her male colleagues after work, but a letter to Phil that spring reveals her real attention was elsewhere: "Business has slumped in the offset line . . . and I find myself filling in in the office. Not so exciting as production, but . . . I am resolutely hewing to my newfound trade. Meanwhile I am furtively exploring the concrete commercial alleys of the song-writing racket, just in case there might be a buck in it for me."[6]

She wrote a new song that fits this bill, "Love in the Afternoon," for which no recording has surfaced and which seems as commercial-ready as any Converse ever wrote (perhaps one reason she opted to omit it from her "Lyrics for Tapes" collection of typewritten original lyrics).

> *We're a little too young to sit and play chess*
> *And a bit too old for hayrides I guess*
> *Tho' for some it's right to wait for the night and the moon*
> *We can live and have our love in the afternoon.*[7]

These are not the kinds of wily, erudite lyrics found in most of Converse's other songs (there's even a June to match this moon later in the song), but "Love in the Afternoon" still succeeds on the strength of its melody, which—when paired with the words—makes for a tender love song that could easily have become a medium-swing standard. Rare for her, too, is the fact that it's a song about being in love, together, knowing that nothing lasts, but also that the happiness felt as the couple is "taking our ease" somehow exists beyond time.

"A good song must imply its own harmony," Converse wrote in her diary. "To test, whistle it a capella."[8] Like with a few other of her guitar songs (including "Roving Woman," "Johnny's Brother," and "Honeybee"), when Converse registered this one with the Library of Congress, her manuscript sheet music included only the melody line.

If "Love in the Afternoon" was an experiment in consciously trying to be commercial, then "Thunder Mountain"—also from this year, also never to show up on any known recordings—is a study of another kind. It is intensely dramatic, driving, and unlike any other known Converse song. Composed for guitar and voice, Converse's written instruction to the performer (on her manuscript score) reads: "almost savagely."

The lyric describes a stormy night on a mountain, complete with driving wind and rain and a desolate narrator:

> *This is no summer shower with a clearing in sight*
> *Show me a single flower that will live through the night*
> *Living through the night won't be an easy story*

When I have lost the glory
Of Thunder Mountain.[9]

Of all of Converse's known guitar songs, "Thunder Mountain" is the only one written in a minor key. Though she does segue to the relative major in the bridge, the tonality of the whole gives her compositional voice here surprising flavor—dark, muscular, and almost operatic.

Had today's technology and habits existed in the 1950s, we'd have video clips of Converse in performance at our fingertips, recorded and uploaded by people who were seeing her live. Though there is no documentary evidence of her ever giving a formal concert, as Gene Deitch, Barbara Bernal, the Crippens, and Merle Edelman told me, she was performing within the confines of private homes. And if she had indeed made music with the Changs, perhaps playing her freshly minted songs for them, this has to have been the context in which she was introduced to their close friends, a couple named Chris and Ada Ishii.

The Ishiis' daughter, Naka, remembers hearing recordings of Converse's songs throughout her childhood, from the time she was very young. Her father, Chris, was an amateur musician, she said—a guitar player and a hipster. He'd achieved success as an animator, working with Walt Disney Studios in California on films like *Fantasia* and *Dumbo*.[10]

Like the Changs, the Ishiis held effervescent dinner parties that typically evolved into informal music-making sessions. Chris had a fondness for singing and playing Mexican folk songs like "El Rancho Grande" and "Calisto,"[11] and the Ishiis were part of a social circle that included others from the animation world, like Gene Deitch. I can't prove it, but I'd place a confident bet on the notion that this was how Converse was introduced to that world, and how she met others who would change her life, ever so briefly.

———

If displays of the outward joys of family life and matrimony were rubbing off on Converse in any way due to her exposure to the Changs and now the Ishiis, or to the fact that her brothers were both now husbands, most of her songs didn't reflect it. Two more of them, "John Brady" and "Sweet Amelia," blatantly mock romance. Both deal, too, with protagonists who lose the affections of a lover to more well-positioned rivals.

"Amelia" finds Converse in high dudgeon mode, the song's sarcastic tone and lack of seriousness foretold in its subtitle: "Inspired by Falling over Something in the Dark."[12] The stately strut of the music is subverted by the lyric, in which a facetious narrator skewers the song's eponymous ingénue, "lovely far beyond comparison" and with any number of suitors vying for her affections—among them, Henry Clay, Ebenezer Jones, and Dick Van Dyke.[13]

"Amelia" has an innovative structure, employing a device in which the singer makes parenthetical commentary on her own story as she tells it—something she may have borrowed from popular German folk music.[14] Here, Converse essentially enacts two roles, the telling of a story at face value and then the making of asides to her audience.

While her gift for social satire in "Amelia" does not pay the kinds of emotional dividends associated with her more personal, introspective songs, the composer is nonetheless on sure, even expert ground here. "Amelia" has moments of laugh-out-loud hilarity in its dry send-up of a certain kind of society debutante, one whom Converse undoubtedly encountered more than once at Mount Holyoke (and that she clearly loathed).[15]

"John Brady" is more complicated. It again shows Converse's familiarity with Child Ballads, especially "The House Carpenter" (sometimes called "The Daemon Lover"), in which a woman is lured away from her love by the promise of another's riches. Musically, "Brady" suggests another attempt to make her songs more commercially appealing. The tune is melodically light and pleasant, even if the subject matter is less so, with a chord progression that—like "Love in the Afternoon"— would not be out of place in the repertoire of a pop-jazz singer of the era.

But, lyrically, Converse is again dispensing some of her patented graveyard humor (this time, literally so): As the song concludes, we're told that the protagonist is "six foot under, where it's shady," joining the song in spirit to another new Converse composition, "The Clover Saloon," a happy/angry genre experiment (or, as her annotation reads, "I set out to write a western").

The tune anticipates the clever cowboy numbers that would be recorded just a few years later by Katie Lee (like "Johnny Ringo"). Converse here puts a distinctive mark on her effort, imbuing the song with eccentricities that belie the typical standards of the form. The narrative is simple enough: A "dusty cowhand" is sitting in a bar with no ambition other than to "drink a glass of pleasure, full measure, bulgin' out and brimmin' over." She is minding her own business when she is rudely insulted by a stranger. (After listening to Converse's recording of it, then-eighty-seven-year-old Ellen Stekert wrote to me, "He probably called her a cunt."[16])

Furious, she hurls a bottle at him. He ducks, and it shatters a mirror. Undeterred, she draws a pistol and kills him. And though she is to hang for the murder the following day, she blithely reports that the broken mirror and the dead man have led to the real tragedy of the situation: She has lost her credit at the bar.

It's not, on the face of it, a charming tale, but recordings made of her performing the song show her delivering it with such gusto and with such ironic, bone-dry humor that the story of an outlaw who would rather kill and be hanged than be disturbed while engaged in her "one ambition" in life, drinking alone in a bar, somehow makes it seem not dark at all. Instead, she makes a point of extolling the pleasures of alcohol, and damn the consequences.

Westerns had already been a fixture in American culture since the late nineteenth century, dating back to cultural phenomena like the Wild West shows made famous by "Buffalo Bill" Cody, the pioneering short film *The Great Train Robbery,* and more contemporary popular figures like the Lone Ranger and "Singing Cowboy" Gene Autry.

Converse makes her hard-drinking, homicidal cowboy a woman—a figure entirely acceptable in our post–*Thelma and Louise* world—but like the protagonist's proclivities in "Roving Woman," decidedly out of step with what a woman's priorities were expected to be in the 1950s.

The tune has the feeling of a children's ditty, kin to songs like "Ring Around the Rosie" and "London Bridge Is Falling Down," where a singsong melody belies graver subject matter. Its setting may have been inspired by Patsy Montana's 1949 song "I Didn't Know the Gun Was Loaded," or Converse may have been thinking about the protagonist of Irving Berlin's hit musical *Annie Get Your Gun* when she wrote it. But her portrayal of a female antihero, coupled with the nursery rhyme feel of the melody, makes for a song that shows its composer to be keenly aware of social norms, eager to flout them, and fully cognizant of the horrors of "normal" life, for which she feels herself to be entirely unsuited. Her ability to mix darkness with charming melodic writing shows her mastery of the short song form at this point in her still-hopeful career as she moved into what would be the most significant year of her life as a would-be professional singer and songwriter.

CHAPTER 21

Bloom by Night

Nineteen fifty-four was a turning point for Converse. She would turn thirty. Her music was about to be discovered by the Bernal-Deitch crowd. She'd built up an impressive catalogue of original songs. She would have a brush with mainstream exposure as a performing songwriter. And she would commit herself to moving beyond the guitar song world and into more serious musical realms. The year was the fulcrum of her time in New York: Everything before it seems to build steadily toward this moment, and everything afterward, until she left the city, seems more like a bumpy decrescendo.

As she approached the three-decade milestone, Paul and Hyla were pregnant with Paul Bruce (or, "P. Bruce," as he would be known as a child),[1] and Converse was about to become "Aunt Connie" for the first time, a fact that may have again triggered further frustration about her place in the world, a reminder of the creep of time.

In the 1950s United States, single adults were considered outsiders by their communities. Americans then married younger and had children quicker than in any other twentieth-century decade, with an astounding 95 percent of the population who came of age in the '50s tying the knot (and half of all American women doing so by the age of twenty).[2]

Converse's residence in the Village would have immunized her somewhat from this phenomenon, to the extent that her chosen community was hardly in step with national trends or social norms. As Mary McCarthy wrote in 1950, "The Village . . . is a sort of clearing-house for all those curiosities, sexual, artistic, or merely decorative, that are thought of as un-American."[3]

Still, she wasn't able to ignore it entirely. Converse seems to have at least absorbed the notion, if not the practice, that to be complete, a person had to have a partner. For every "Talkin' Like You" and "Fare You Well" celebrating the joys of being alone, there is a "Father Neptune," a "There Is a Vine," and even a "We Lived Alone," in which the singer wonders whether she can successfully persist in life without the affection of another.

As Anne Bernays wrote in *Back Then,* a memoir of living in Manhattan in the 1950s, "All my female friends, intellectual, artistic and/or professionally ambitious, were . . . looking for mates. That's what you were expected to do and that's what you did. You got educated, you married, you had children. To reach your late twenties without being at least engaged was to face a future as a 'spinster.'"[4] Bernays was not a Village denizen, and may not have adopted a Bohemian lifestyle, but she was a writer, so there clearly was some of this kind of pressure even among artistically ambitious city women.

This was, after all, the family-centric Eisenhower era, when the postwar glow of American affluence engendered the popularity of phenomena like *Ozzie and Harriet,* manicured lawns, and frozen TV dinners—what cartoonist Barbara Smaller, when thinking about the challenges Converse must have faced as an artist, described to me as "an aggressively conventional time."[5] Though the controversial Kinsey Reports had recently exposed the private habits of everyday Americans, such topics were not discussed in polite conversation. Fredric Wertham's book *Seduction of the Innocent* convinced parents that comic books turned kids into juvenile delinquents and should be sanitized or banned, crippling the industry until Stan Lee and Jack Kirby revolutionized it with their rollout of a roster of sensitive superheroes. This was still around the corner, and would coincide with a new political era, the mainstreaming of what became known as the counterculture, broad support for enacting new civil rights legislation, and the explosion of the folk music craze centered in Greenwich Village.

But all that was still half a dozen years and a different America away. For now, marriages and babies were booming all around Converse. Whether out of rebellion, exasperation, or a mixture of the two, she leaned even harder into her music.

Her letters indicate that she was burning the midnight oil, trying to get just right the new songs that were coming at a faster and faster clip (including the compositions "O Mistress Mine" and "Sad Lady"). She seems to have sacrificed comfort and self-care as she did, maybe even her social life, such as it was. But she believed that she could make it and could do so on her own terms. And as her songwriting now reached new peaks of productivity, she met a small group of people who helped to almost make that happen.

In 1953, Bill and Barbara Bernal moved to Astoria, Queens, to the same apartment building that Chris and Ada Ishii lived in. (They took the unit right next door.)[6] And the Ishiis were best friends with Converse's pals the Changs. What seems most likely is that the Bernals heard

Converse perform for the first time *not* at Deitch's house, but at the Ishiis', at one of their musical dinner parties.[7] (This would explain why Barbara remembers hearing Converse for the first time with her husband and why Deitch told me that it was Bernal who brought Converse to his house. Both could be true.) Then Bill Bernal, knocked out by Converse's music, rang up Deitch and told him to get ready to record his newest discovery.

On January 23, 1954, either chaperoned by Bernal or traveling under her own steam via the New York Central, Converse made her debut at Deitch's bungalow at 9 Ronny Circle in Hastings-on-Hudson.

These last few years of diligently honing her craft, perfecting her skills, making tape reel recordings for Phil, and giving outings of her songs in informal settings had brought her to this moment.

Whether she knew it or not, these were people with connections, and when the spotlight found her here, she did not shy from it. The unanticipated reveal of the bookish wallflower transforming herself into a "Roving Woman," the cries of the cat in heat, the immediate enraptured response from everyone present—it all happened that January night. And it seemed as though Converse had, at last, gotten the break she needed.

Plans were immediately hatched to bring her back for an encore performance. As Kim Deitch recalled, "My parents' crowd and my parents themselves were, from that moment on, rabid Connie Converse fans."[8]

Gene Deitch dubbed copies of the recording he made of Converse that night for his friends, and they then played these proto-bootleg reels for *their* friends. Again, this was still well before the advent of the cassette tape, making the ease of making, playing, and spreading this music more difficult than it would become a couple of decades later. Their dedication to listening to (and even learning) Converse's songs using this early technology is a testament to how greatly her music affected them.

Converse had found an audience. It was a small but enthusiastic one, and Deitch told me that Converse came back to Hastings-on-Hudson at least two or three more times over the next few months.[9] When she did, she discovered that his crowd had learned her songs. On some of Deitch's subsequent recordings, she even performs vocal duets with one of them, the voice actor Allen Swift.[10]

According to Deitch, it is Swift heard taking the lead vocal on takes of "Talkin' Like You" and "Down This Road." Converse improvises vocal harmonies, accompanying them both on her guitar.[11] It sounds a bit thrown together, but it's also an indication that Converse was in no way a diva when it came to the presentation of her music. She even sounds positively tickled to have a roomful of people sing along to her "Clover Saloon," making a happy mess of it.

None of these somewhat cloying efforts by the Deitch gang predict the kind of real choral beauty they were capable of contributing, heard when Converse turns to one of the few non-originals in her known repertoire, "The Ash Grove."

The song's provenance and pedigree shed some light on the musical world into which Converse may have seen at least some of her guitar songs fitting. Its melody comes from the eighteenth-century play *The Beggar's Opera* (adapted by Bertolt Brecht in 1928 as *The Threepenny Opera*) The tune was also arranged by Beethoven in his *Twelve Scottish Songs,* and more recently by Benjamin Britten, in 1943. In choosing it, Converse was signaling what she considered some of her artistic brethren, her knowledge of classical and art music, and her own aspirations.

But all this is secondary to the recorded performance of the song itself, which is positively arresting. There is such a fierceness to the image of this woman singing this song in this way at this moment to these people. Converse has been described as being, at this time, unwashed, dressed and smelling poorly, with bad teeth and probably bad breath—a vision of the Noble Savage (à la Woody Guthrie) adopted by the lefty folk music crowd of the day who loved such people for their "realness"— and existing and operating separately from them on every other level save a musical one.[12]

And yet, Converse is not singing "Pastures of Plenty," nor "John Henry," nor any one of the innumerable labor/union/rural songs, with their plainspoken lyrics and rough-hewn melodies, for which those Noble Savages were so embraced. Instead, she sings "The Ash Grove," quietly, introspectively, giving it the spare humility of an inward-looking hymn.

Hold your breath: Two verses in, Converse is suddenly joined in song by a chorus of voices. She, the outcast, the misfit, the person doing it all wrong, now becomes leader of the flock, the one behind whom those more accepted members of society arrange themselves and follow. It is such a painfully beautiful moment, the sound of a thousand angels, the murmuring of generations of departed ringing from beyond eternity, like the dead who gather in Francis Phelan's mind in William Kennedy's *Ironweed*. As Converse begins to sing harmony and the group enters, their contribution becomes a shimmering glow surrounding hers.

⌒

The Bernals hosted Converse, too, at their apartment in Queens. Julia Crippen, who recited the lyrics to "Playboy of the Western World" to me over the phone, first heard her there when Crippen and her husband, Fred, went for dinner parties; she confirmed that the Ishiis from next door would have been there, and the Deitches; and that Pete Seeger would even come by on occasion. (Whether Seeger ever heard Converse perform, they couldn't say.) Bernal often cooked up Mexican food for the occasions, a fitting complement to Chris Ishii's fondness for playing folk songs from south of the border.[13]

Was another brand-new composition, called "Fortune's Child," among those Converse broke out in Astoria? If so, it's tempting to wonder whether the lyric may contain a veiled reference to whatever may have been happening in Converse's love life. Of particular interest is the stanza:

> *You may recall, my heart was wild,*
> *And to your love I paid no mind.*
> *We never could go hand in hand,*
> *Though to your love I only smiled.*

Again, there is the suggestion of a relationship that is socially unacceptable, one she had to keep hidden.[14]

"Here Is the Door," another 1954 composition, essays the theme of forbidden love as well. Converse gave the song the subtitle "An Oblique Ballad"—and oblique it is. The lyric is her take on a tale common in the world of folk music (perhaps most famously the Child Ballad "Young Hunting," also known as "Henry Lee" and "Love Henry"): of a jealous woman who kills her unfaithful husband.

In Converse's song, the narrator ventures to the door of a woman who's been widowed "just an hour ago / By the well in the meadow." The narrator wonders: "Who will ring the bell? What shall we say?" (It is never revealed who the "we" in the song refers to.) Most of the lyric trucks in the narrator's cynical views on romantic love, including warnings she has either already made to her friend or would like to:

> *. . . A loving is a losing—*
> *Why must we be choosing*
> *To love what we must part with?*

Then:

> *When her lover is a stranger,*
> *Loving is a danger*
> *Because his heart is hidden.*

And the narrator reminds her friend that:

> *He was living fancy—*
> *Every Jane and Nancy*
> *Found a place beside him.*

Why love at all? is the question implied here. Why give of ourselves to someone else when we know we will inevitably be alone again? A modern, decidedly unromantic philosophy, one out of step with the sentiment expressed in "There Is a Vine," but one consistent with other of Converse's darker songs and certainly in line with the worldview expressed by some of her favorite authors, if her reading lists at the time are any indication.[15] Perhaps more telling is the suggestion that even if the man in question does cheat on the woman, "that was something human."

True to form, a twist appears in the last verse. The narrator reveals that "I heard her by the well," where he was murdered. "Talking with him, she was raging, she was weeping." The singer wonders, "What shall we say if she swears that she was sleeping?" The woman behind the door is revealed as her lover's killer, leaving the singer wondering whether to bear false witness against her, or to remain silent.

"Here Is the Door," like "Fortune's Child," is minor Converse, but also unmistakably Converse. As with "Man in the Sky" and "Father Neptune," we are made to understand that a man's nature is to be noncommittal. Mortality crops up yet again; as in "The Clover Saloon," "Playboy of the Western World," and "John Brady," a man dies. And as in so many of the songs she had written up until this time, love breeds mainly aloneness, confusion, tragedy, and despair.[16]

~

Outside her trenchant letters to Phil and Jean, and the recollections of people who heard her perform in private settings but did not know her personally, Converse during this heady period in New York is a ghostlike figure, appearing suddenly in the record, here and there, and then vanishing from it just as quickly.

Though she certainly seems to have been in demand among the Deitch clique, in Westchester and in Queens, she did not become part of any of the established Village "scenes" where she actually lived—not among the remnants of the literary/artistic bohemian Village days of the 1920s and '30s (made famous by the likes of O'Neill, Edna St. Vincent Millay, and Djuna Barnes), the new music/art crowd of Cage, Feldman, Cunningham et al, or the emerging Beats, who coalesced around Kerouac, Ginsberg, and Burroughs.

Clearly she was aware of the lefty "folk" crowd surrounding Seeger and Guthrie, but she wasn't part of it. Nor did she find a place in the folk-music-as-art-song circle that included singers like Richard Dyer-Bennet and Cynthia Gooding. Converse was making music in the margins of these churning creative movements and yet was not part of any one of them.

Instead, it was only the Deitch clutch of music-loving animators and cartoonists whom Converse impressed, who understood that she was doing something special. This is apparent during what was probably her final appearance at Deitch's home, on May 29, 1954, the recording of which, fifty-five years later, would be mined to produce the bulk of *How Sad, How Lovely.*[17]

T he U.S. Supreme Court had just ruled on *Brown v. Board of Education,* declaring segregated schools unconstitutional. The turning point in Joseph McCarthy's long-running witch hunt was only two weeks away, when Joseph Welch, an attorney for the U.S. Army, famously questioned the Wisconsin senator's sense of decency. And Bill Haley and His Comets released "Rock Around the Clock," originally a B-side, just nine days before Converse's final recording for Deitch.

Likely due to the holiday weekend, this session at Deitch's was sparsely attended. Only the Bernals, the Deitches (including Gene's younger brother, Don), and one other couple were there.[18] But because Converse was now a cause célèbre among this set, and because there had been a major development in her professional prospects, there seemed to have been a sense of occasion about the proceedings.

This was because Bill Bernal had succeeded in his mission. He'd taken demos culled from Deitch's home recordings of her, and gotten them into the right hands. As a result, Converse had been booked on television. She was to be a featured guest on CBS's new *Morning Show.* This was a big deal, and everyone at Deitch's house that day knew it.

Today, when we live in a culture in which people broadcast themselves all the time, every moment of the day, for every reason, it can be hard to imagine just how momentous the occasion of appearing on the then-new medium of television actually would have been. The session at Deitch's may even have served as a warm-up, arranged with the idea of getting Converse accustomed to fielding the sorts of questions she might be asked by host Walter Cronkite.

The recording from that day begins with him interviewing Converse about her process:

DEITCH: Well, how did you get started writing songs?

CONVERSE: Well, I, I, uh . . . pffft! I always did, uh, sing-hum things to myself and when I started . . . when I got the guitar . . . I was picking up folk songs and then started to, to . . . uh, make my own little tunes, and words . . .

DEITCH: How long ago was that?

CONVERSE: Oh, about four, five years ago.

DEITCH: And how many songs have you written?

CONVERSE: Oh, about twenty-five or so.

DEITCH: Well, why don't you sing some of the ones you like the best and then sing some of the new ones you were telling us about?

CONVERSE: Well, what . . . which of the old ones do you want?

DEITCH: How about "Two Tall Mountains"?

Converse sings it. "Talkin' Like You," the song Deitch is referring to, is followed by more of his awkward questions and her even more awkward answers.

As Barbara Bernal told me, "Everyone was extremely happy to just bask in the glory of her songs—and she must have felt that love flowing across the imaginary stage lights. Connie was given the honor she was due. But, except for her singing, she didn't court us with her charm. Nope!"[19]

DEITCH: When did you write that? How did you happen to, uh . . . get that idea? How'd it develop?

CONVERSE: I . . . I honestly don't remember. It's awfully hard to remember . . .

DEITCH: Was that one of the first ones . . . ?

CONVERSE: Uh . . . no . . . uh . . . 'bout the first really complete thing I did was "Down This Road."

What can be heard in her tone, and what Deitch confirmed when I spoke to him in Prague, is that, for whatever reason, he put her off. Deitch's questions are respectful enough, the sort of softball prompts that could be expected to soon be lobbed her way on TV. If Converse evinced a haughty disdain for what she felt was a lack of sophistication in his queries, it places her in the vanguard of artists who held interviewers in contempt. What's remarkable and poignant is that, unlike (for example) Dylan or the Beatles, who would later make sport of being vague or even intentionally misleading in response to the banal questions they were asked in public, Converse had not been lionized outside a few New York–area living rooms.

Entertainers at that time (unlike, say, writers or visual artists) were generally expected to be polite and compliant. While she may not have been willing, when discussing her work, to engage in the more pugnacious deflections articulated by her peers in other disciplines (i.e., Flannery O'Connor and Jackson Pollock), she, at least in this moment, made no extra effort to explain herself or her work.

DEITCH: You said that you had some new songs.

CONVERSE: Uh, this one is called "One by One."

DEITCH: When'd you . . . When did you do this?

CONVERSE: This I did about . . . uh, three o'clock one morning about . . . uh, about a month ago, or six weeks ago.

She plays the song. And, like her own home recording of it, her performance of "One by One" at Deitch's house is suffused with incredible intimacy. When the song finishes, there is something like a collective gasp in the room.

What must those at the Hastings-on-Hudson gathering have thought and felt about what they'd just heard? Deitch can only say, quietly, "Beautiful," and then he repeats his question: "And when did you write this?" To which Converse says, again, "I dunno . . . about a month ago or six weeks. I don't remember."

My hunch is that Converse was not being intentionally contrary or aloof in her responses. As any performer who has made themselves vulnerable knows, to be asked in the midst of a performance, or immediately following one, to engage in small talk about one's creative process or, worse, to be asked to "explain" one's art can be uncomfortable to the point of being destabilizing (a dynamic also in evidence in the 1952 Grove Street performance for her family).

Creative expression in a live setting is enervating enough for a reluctant performer who must essentially become an empathic proxy for the audience—a function that stretches back to classical Greek tragedy. The performer is physically separate from the audience, a fish in a tank (the "immersive theater" trend of the twenty-first century notwithstanding). But the task of that artist is to be the seer, not the seen, to facilitate an experience, to take an audience on a journey along unknown or unfrequented paths, as Converse was doing.

If the performer's goal is to create something more than simple entertainment, their ego must disappear, along with any other symbolic or psychological safeguards. Like high-achieving athletes, performers sometimes refer to this as getting into a zone, beyond conscious thought, "forgetting"—temporarily—everything but what's needed to be of service to the task at hand.

Still, as exhilarating as these kinds of experiences can be, with their accompanying rushes of adrenaline, dopamine, and oxytocin, the reentry into everyday interaction and conversation afterward can be rough. It's one of the reasons so many performers reach for alcohol, tobacco, or drugs to soothe and calm themselves during the comedown after an intense performance—buffers employed in the transition back into "normal" life. In the moments immediately following a performance of a song like "One by One," it's hard to imagine Converse wanting to hold forth about anything.

The tape then cuts off. When it resumes, Converse delivers "We Lived Alone," another song debuted for the occasion that day. A sort of sequel to "Talkin' Like You," the song begins with a statement that the singer is content with being a loner and then a catalogue of the pleasures of the single life:

> *We lived alone, my house and I*
> *We had the earth, we had the sky;*
> *I had a lamp against the dark, and I was happy as a lark.*
> *I had a stove and a window-screen, I had a table painted green,*
> *Sat on a chair with a broken back, wearing a pretty potato sack.*
> *I had a rug upon the floor and roses grew around my door*
> *Though my estate was never high*
> *My house was snug, and so was I.*

Converse here sings only the main melody and lead lyric, but in her copyrighted lead sheet for the song (and in the "double recording" of it she made at home, overdubbing a second vocal part à la her recording of "Down This Road"), she sings with herself in a round. This only heightens the sense that the protagonist has a general feeling of blissful self-satisfaction.

The two voices in "We Lived Alone" are (a) the singer, and (b) the house, in which (and *with* which) she lives. This is objectively, and wonderfully, weird. After the first line of the song, the word *we* never appears again. The voice of the house chases that of the singer until the two come together at the song's finale, when they confront the destruction of their shared domestic paradise brought upon by the entrance of someone they both desire—next to whom all else pales.

> *I had a job; my wants were few,*
> *(They were until I wanted you),*
> *And when I set my eyes on you, nothing else would do,*
> *Nothing else would do!*

To drive home the story's unresolved drama, Converse ends the song on another major third chord, a trick she'd already employed in "Trouble." The life that she and her house have led until now—happy, serene, content—has been subverted. The major third represents the end of a chapter, a crossroads. What will happen next?

Converse lets out a little laugh at the song's conclusion. "I did it right that time!"

The one cover included in her set that day is her rendering of the traditional Scottish ballad "Katie Cruel." With its subject matter of regret, love, loss, and intrigue, the song dovetails well with her repertoire of original material. Its chorus also contains the sort of crafty wordplay Converse would make a hallmark of her own lyrics:

> *Oh that I was where I would be,*
> *Then I would be where I am not,*
> *Here I am where I must be,*
> *Go where I would, I cannot*

Converse gives a convincing, self-assured reading of the song, putting her own spin on it. The tune does not sound traditional in her hands—her peculiar chord choices and her overall treatment take it beyond the world of "folk"—but neither does it sound like an interpretation with ambitions toward high art. Instead, "Katie Cruel" seems like a template, one Converse may have used to continue to refine and articulate her compositional voice.

Next comes another stunning premiere. On the tape, a man says, "She has one that she hasn't sung yet." Converse is skeptical; she doesn't yet feel confident in her ability to put this song over—until someone suggests, "Why don't you just sing it, and we won't record it?" Converse gamely replies, "Oh, I can do that."

She clears her throat and begins fingerpicking the bluesy opening vamp of "I Have Considered the Lilies," playfully declaring over it, "This has a biblical text." The opportunity to unveil new material for such an eager, supportive audience may have been, in the moment, too tempting to pass up: Whether she knew it or not, Deitch's machine was rolling.

Yet again, a narrator attempts to break out of an unsatisfying reality. Like "Down This Road," "I Have Considered the Lilies" (or, as she titled it in her original transcription, simply "The Lilies") is another Cinderella-like take of being freed from the constraints of having to work a grim day job. But while the song is cut from the same narrative cloth as "Down This Road," it boasts a lyrical sophistication and compositional development that belie the mere three-odd years that had elapsed since that first wholly original composition.

> *I'm gonna take my working papers*
> *And turn them in . . .*
> *I'm handing over my pencil and pen,*
> *I won't be needing my broom again,*

I'll bloom by day,
I'll bloom by night,
And blooming will be my delight!

The lyric is both innocent and mature, and the music features experiments with form and harmony. "Lilies" not only bears the influence of rural American blues, but—in Converse's performance of it—also shows her further assimilation and mastery of idiomatic guitar techniques.

Barbara Bernal remembered being particularly impressed by the way Converse played her guitar, "with snap and aplomb."[20] You can say that again. From a guitar player's perspective, this song is a beast. Not only are Converse's technical chops eyebrow-raising, but the chord progression she uses is complex and unusual, making for some of the most breathtaking musical passages of all her guitar songs. The strains under the lyric "Look at the daylily, lemon lily, calla lily . . ." in particular combine to produce a sublime artistic moment—thrilling, transporting, full of easy rapture.

Like "Talkin' Like You," "Lilies" has something of a red-herring introduction before it opens up to take its surprising acrobatic vocal and compositional leaps, including a beautiful double-time section. Like "One by One," the song sounds as modern as it does timeless. Guitarist and composer Mary Halvorson, who approached it with her collaborator Jessica Pavone for a cover recording released in 2017, told me, "I'd never heard anything like it. From a songwriting standpoint, it just doesn't feel like there are any 'shoulds' in it at all."[21]

⌒

One window through which to understand the craft of an evolving musical artist involves tracking their approach to the same material over a series of years and decades. (See Glenn Gould, Nina Simone, Will

Oldham.) Variations in tempo, key, arrangement, lyrics, and emotional de-livery can differ widely. But, other than the duets and group sings heard on Deitch's recordings, there is almost no variation from one rendition to the next in Converse's existing performances of her songs.[22] No changes in feel or arrangement, no improvising of any kind. "She was always very precise in her renditions," Deitch told me.[23] His tapes bear this out.

So, while Converse produced a substantial and diverse body of mu-sical work, there are maddeningly few recordings of her actually per-forming it. None of the original individual tapes that she made for Phil and Jean of her guitar songs survive; after she made an anthology recording of that music in 1956, compiling most of those songs on the one big reel they kept, they recycled the older reels, recording over her ear-lier recordings.[24] There are few alternate takes, no public performances, and scant deep cuts, most of which come from what Deitch was able to capture.

One song she sings part of during one of her visits to his house is a setting for Walt Whitman's 1865 poem "When Lilacs Last in the Door-yard Bloom'd." Her performance on Deitch's tape begins with Canto 11:

> *O what shall I hang on the chamber walls?*
> *And what shall the pictures be that hang on the walls*
> *To adorn the burial-house of him I love?*

As with "With Rue My Heart Is Laden," Converse is again in elegy mode, attracted to verse that memorializes. What's particularly interest-ing about this composition is that it, like her earlier Chaucer setting, is clearly in the *lied*, or art song, tradition. It is what's known as "through-composed," which means that its melody and harmony continue to de-velop as the song moves forward.

The majority of non-classical songs that we know and love don't do this. They typically consist of a hummable verse and chorus—maybe an intro, maybe a bridge—but, in general, a familiar and easily identifiable, repeating structure. They're little pleasure outings—the experience of hearing them is like being on a boat that takes us out for a short ride, shows us some nice things, and then brings us right back to where we started.

Lieder are different, which can make them more challenging to listen to if what our ears are accustomed to is the pleasure cruise. Converse's "Father Neptune" gestures toward art song, but doesn't make the full leap. She throws us a few crumbs in it in the way of repeated motifs, and we soon become so captivated by her poetry that we fail to notice that the vessel we've climbed aboard is headed toward a place different from the one we disembarked from. When "Father Neptune" ends, we look around us in wonder: How did we get here? Songs like this one bring to mind a photograph of Converse taken at Deitch's at this time that shows her in mid-performance. She is feeling it, and the uncanny charisma that trans-fixed her listeners when she sang makes the picture frame vibrate. Converse looks like she's about to burst into flames.

But in "When Lilacs Last" she is well into the landscape of pure art song, and Deitch's recording contains only part of it. She stops herself after a few minutes and says, "It just goes on and on . . . ," and that's just how Gene Deitch described it to me in Prague. Deitch assumed the lyrics were hers, not Whitman's, and talked about the song in such a way that led me to think that Converse probably realized in that moment at his house that she was singing the right song for the wrong crowd.[25]

∽

If Gene Deitch and Phil Converse were right in believing that Converse was intentional about having a music career, who might her models have been? Her untrained, "natural" singing style is not so far from the delivery of someone like Dinah Shore, one of the most popular singers of that day. Listen to Shore's rendition of "Buttons and Bows," a song that reached the top of the pop charts in 1948. Shore has the same sort of flat, dry, smart tone to the timbre of her voice, the same slight nasality, the same plainspokenness. It's easy to envision her singing one of Converse's more lighthearted songs, but I can also imagine professional recordings of Converse backed by the sorts of orchestrations and arrangements afforded to Shore's numbers, had she only had the right handlers and support to make it happen.

Perhaps worse than not having more alternate takes of her performances is the fact that the one time Converse appeared on camera—when we would have been able to see the interplay between her singing and her guitar playing, clocked her body language as a performer, seen how she used her picking and chording hands—also was not preserved.

The Morning Show was a variety show that featured news, special guests, entertainers, and a puppet called Charlemagne the Lion.[26] The program, designed to compete with NBC's popular *Today* show, was in its first season of existence, and Cronkite, a fellow college dropout, was already an established name in the world of news and broadcasting.[27]

Television had become a big part of everyday American life by 1954. A full third of the country's households had sets, and watching shows beamed to them had the flavor of being visited by magic.[28]

The Morning Show was shot in a studio on an upper floor of Grand Central Station, site of Converse's oyster meeting with Phil years before. Broadcasts were transmitted from an antenna atop the nearby Chrysler Building, and were shown simultaneously on a large screen in the station's main concourse. Every commuter passing through Grand Central that morning would have had a chance to look up and see Connie Converse's television debut.[29]

But Cronkite was not Ed Sullivan, Converse was not the Beatles, and this was not prime time. *The Morning Show*'s slot was from seven to nine A.M. There would have been no hype about Converse leading up to her appearance. No one had ever heard of her, or her music. She was an unknown amateur with no professional credits to her name. She'd played no public engagements in New York and had never written a popular song. She had no recordings to promote and no upcoming concerts to speak of. That the appearance was scheduled at all is a head-scratcher.

Shows were broadcast live in that era. Not only is there no archival film footage of Converse's appearance, but CBS's archives have no production logs that include her name, nor copies of any contracts or releases she may have signed.[30] Her name is not listed in any of the *TV Guide* listings for the show from that time. The only evidence of Converse's one brush with notoriety is the series of still photographs that exist, their provenance unknown.

And yet, they contain information. Converse did not wear her glasses on the show, one of the few instances of her appearing before a camera without them. Maybe more significant, she seems to have been given the kind of makeover Barbara Bernal felt she was sorely in need of. Her hair is styled, and she looks to be wearing lipstick, mascara, and eyeliner.

But whatever she and Cronkite talked about, whatever she performed and however she performed it, even how she was introduced—as Elizabeth or Connie (or something else?)—seems to be lost forever. Though Cronkite was the host, the show's news anchor was Dick Van Dyke, who'd featured prominently in her "Sweet Amelia," written a few years prior. Did she playfully include this song in her set that day?[31] We'll probably never know.

The only remembrance of the show was recorded decades later by Kim Deitch, who recalled watching the program as a child and who grasped its significance in that moment. He recollected getting up early in the morning to catch the show, that Converse played two songs, and he remembers thinking then, *Well, this is it. We'll all be bragging "We knew her when" pretty soon.*[32]

But it was not meant to be. Converse's television debut did not inspire a legion of new fans hungry to hear more of her music. No popular singers approached her, excited to cover her songs. No record executives, music publishers, or talent agents beat a path to her door in the hope of signing this new talent. For all the excitement leading up to it, her television appearance went nowhere, almost as though it had never even happened.

And maybe this is not so surprising. The success that Converse was enjoying at that time was happening in tiny gatherings, where she could be herself and where the intimidating distractions of show business (lights, camera, action) were not at play. How her talent—delicate, personal, intense—translated to contexts with added production values, and how it might have developed had she continued to be presented in these ways, is also something we can only speculate on.

By the time she'd arrived at the Deitch salon, her songs had become polished gems, their brilliance enough to carry the day. But as far as the entertainment world went, she may not have been ready for prime time. The hair and makeup department at the CBS *Morning Show* were able to spruce up her looks, but how had her personality come across? Was she as irritated with Cronkite's questions as she'd been with Deitch's? Did her nerves cause her to miss chords or hit wrong notes in her television debut? Is this why her public performing career seems to have come to a dead stop after this appearance?

My guess is that it went like this: The Cronkite show represented the culmination of a campaign begun by Bill Bernal, who, convinced of her talent, had coaxed the unknown singer up to Westchester, where he could present her to his people. He'd talked Deitch into recording her, risking his reputation on this unusual young woman. The gamble had paid off; Converse managed to spellbind the Deitch crowd, who were now abuzz about her music. Bernal succeeded in getting from Deitch a demo to shop, and Converse began making the rounds to various apartments and homes around New York City, performing for small but excitable gatherings of people (some of whom were so blown away by what they heard that they could still recite the lyrics to her songs fifty years later, without the benefit of a recording).

Bernal probably tried to get gigs for her, too, but because the New York City coffeehouse scene had not yet begun, solo performers like Converse had few options other than the formal stage—in places like Carnegie Hall and Town Hall. And it's hard to imagine her appearing in such a context. (Dave Van Ronk's ex-wife, Terri Thal, who started coming to the Village in the early to mid-fifties, laughed at the idea that Converse could have been playing out in public. "There was no place to work!" she told me emphatically. "Nobody hired folk singers! Not until the coffeehouses came along much later.")[33]

Then, miraculously, the CBS booking happens. Against all odds, with no product or engagements to promote, Converse is offered a television appearance. As Kim Deitch recalled, there was a sense of kismet in the air, the feeling that Converse was about to blow up.[34]

But, for some reason, she didn't. And this must have represented a surprising and baffling disappointment to all of them: to Bernal, to Deitch, to her enthusiastic little following, and most of all, to Converse, who may have, at that moment, been disabused of the fantasy that she had what it took to make it in the music industry.

PART III

Connie's Piano Songs

In general the songs . . . are arranged solely with
an eye to change of key or pace. Were the composer
to employ a descending order of her own preference,
the first hundred feet of tape would be jammed with
indistinguishable sounds, followed by silence.

—From Converse's introduction to her
"Musicks (Volumes I and II),"
August 1956

Above: A gathering of Eatons, ca. 1901, including Converse's grandfather Emery (holding flower); her great-grandfather Daniel B. Eaton (third from right); and her great-uncle Joseph Smith Eaton (far left). Converse's mother, Evelyn, is likely the child seated closest to Emery.
Courtesy of Beth Day

Top right: Evelyn Eaton, college graduation, 1919

Right: Ernest Converse, undated

Ernest Converse's childhood home in Amherst, New Hampshire

(unless otherwise specified, all images are courtesy of Philip Converse)

Top: Evelyn Eaton and her pupils

Center: Ernest Converse and Evelyn Eaton (center) on their wedding day on August 11, 1920, in Meredith, New Hampshire

Bottom: Helen Converse with her mother, Mary, undated
Courtesy of J. Thomas Converse

Converse as a toddler

With her brothers, probably around 1930

"Me on the beach," 1933 and 1948

Cousin Edie

Frannie Flint, 1938
Courtesy of Humphrey Morris

Frannie and her brother, Bob
Courtesy of Humphrey Morris

Wins High Honor

ELIZABETH CONVERSE

Miss Converse Rates Highest In Scholarship

Will Get Full Tuition At Mount Holyoke As Result of Test

Elizabeth Converse, 17, daughter of the Rev. and Mrs. Ernest L. Converse, 9 Harvard street, has won Mount Holyoke's all-country regional scholarship, it was announced today by Miss Harriet Newhall, dean of admissions.

This means, said the dean, that the local girl received the highest average on her entrance tests for all Mount Holyoke candidates. Said Miss Newhall, "She seems to be an excellent student and we are glad that she is coming to Mount Holyoke."

The scholarship carries full tuition. Miss Converse will be graduated from Concord High school this month.

Above: Converse (standing, center) at Camp Northfield, summer 1940

Left: Converse's high school yearbook photograph, senior year
Author's personal collection

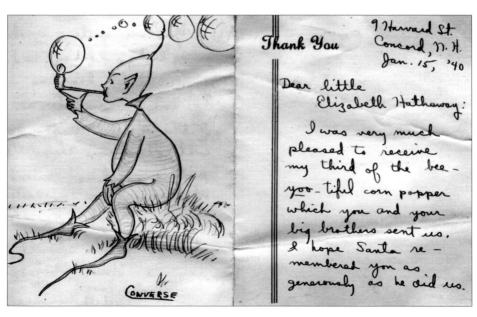

Thank You

9 Harvard St.
Concord, N. H.
Jan. 15, '40

Dear little
Elizabeth Hathaway:

I was very much pleased to receive my third of the bee-yoo-tiful corn popper which you and your big brothers sent us. I hope Santa remembered you as generously as he did us.

CONVERSE

Converse's illustrated card for her cousin Elizabeth Dunbar, 1940
Courtesy of Beth Day

Converse (third from left, front) and fellow "Volunteers"
Concord High School 1942 Yearbook

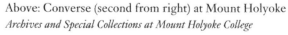

Above: Converse (second from right) at Mount Holyoke
Archives and Special Collections at Mount Holyoke College

Above right: Frannie Flint, undated
Courtesy of Humphrey Morris

Right: Riverside Park, April 1946
Photograph by Richard Aime, courtesy of Lois Aime

Converse, 1946

Photograph by Richard Aime, courtesy of Lois Aime

Adelaide Eby's 1945 bust of Converse
Courtesy of the Barkhorn Family

With Barbara and Adelaide Eby in Metuchen,
New Jersey, June 1946
Photograph by Richard Aime, courtesy of Lois Aime

"Igor," oil painting, ca. 1947

Sketch by Barbara "Ming" Eby, ca. 1947
Courtesy of Aime family

Detail from "City Night," oil painting,
ca. 1947

Undated Converse illustration

Converse's "Mask in Playdough, copper
sprayed," 1960

"The Old Songs," with the Eby sisters and Dick Aime
Photograph by Richard Aime, courtesy of Lois Aime

Self-portrait, ca. late 1940s

With Dick Aime, undated
Photograph by Richard Aime, courtesy of Lois Aime

Two photos likely from Converse's 1949 cross-country road trip

"I kept wondering why he didn't apply for unemployment insurance."

One of Converse's collaborations with Larry Rosinger, 1949

With Irene Conley Chang, undated (late 1940s)

Right: Johnny Hsing
Courtesy of Rita Chang

Below: Kuo-ho Chang and Johnny Hsing
Courtesy of Rita Chang

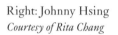

Schenectady, New York, Christmas 1955   In Ann Arbor, Michigan, 1957

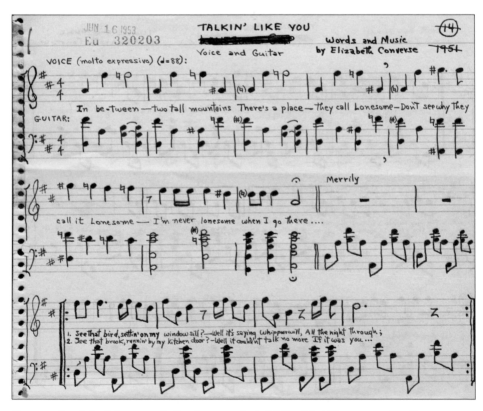

Converse's original sheet music for the song she initially titled "Lonesome Gap"
Courtesy of The Musick Group

Left: With Paul and parents, Woodville, Massachusetts, Christmas 1951

Right: Paul in window of Judson student house, 1953

Singing at Gene Deitch's home, 1954
Courtesy of Kim Deitch

Left and below: Converse's photographs of her Grove Street apartment

Converse with Evelyn, Ernest, and Paul, undated

Right: Box cover of Gene Deitch's
May 1954 recording of Converse
Courtesy of Dan Dzula

Below: Bill Bernal and Marie Deitch,
ca. 1954
Courtesy of Kim Deitch

Schenectady, New York, Christmas 1955

Left to right: Chris and Ada Ishii, Converse, Barbara Bernal, 1954
Courtesy of Kim Deitch

Gene and Marie Deitch, ca. 1954
Courtesy of Kim Deitch

MAY or JUNE 1954.

CBS

With Maude Brogan in Concord,
New Hampshire, August 1954

Visiting Evelyn and Ernest in Concord, New Hampshire, August 1954. Phil and Jean in back; Paul, Hyla, and baby P. Bruce next to Evelyn; Maude Brogan on far right

With Phil in Battle Creek, Michigan, August 1952

Top left: Visiting Ann
Arbor, Michigan, 1954

Top right: With Phil and
Jean in Schenectady, New
York, 1955

Center left: Studio portrait,
1956

Center right: At the piano in
the Harlem apartment, June
1958

Bottom: At work at Academy
Photo Offset, August 1958

First page of Converse's original sheet music for "Birthday Variations"
Courtesy of Library of Congress Music Division

Portrait of Jean Converse, 1958

Phil at the piano

Converse's rendering in oil

Top left: Bill Barss, undated
Courtesy of Taiya Barss

Top right: With Phil in Battle Creek, Michigan, August 1952

Left: Sarah Thompson, February 1959

Bottom left: Converse's sketch of Phil asleep, ca. 1956

Bottom right: With Phil at Ipperwash Beach, Ontario, August 3, 1958

Above: In Ann Arbor, Michigan, 1957

Right: With Phil and baby Pete in Ann Arbor, December 1957

In the Harlem apartment, June 1958

With Phil and nephew Pete in Ann Arbor, August 1958

From "Educating Henry" series of cartoons, date unknown

Above left: With Phil and baby Pete in Michigan, April 1958

Above right: Thirty-sixth birthday in Ann Arbor, August 1960 (with nephew Pete)

Right: With Jean and Phil, Ann Arbor, 1955

Below left: Visiting Larry Salisbury in Guilford, Connecticut, April 1960

Below right: Converse's photograph of Larry Salisbury at home, April 1960

In Ann Arbor, 1959

Ernest and Evelyn visit Ann Arbor, 1963

Above left: Notice in *The Michigan Daily*,
November 5, 1965

Above right: Converse's "Orfeo" (oil painting for
Maude Brogan, 1958)

Right: Converse's coding key for her slides

Below: From a series of photographs taken at
Converse's West 88th Street apartment on
August 22, 1959

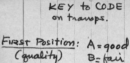

KEY to CODE
on transps.

First Position: A = good
(quality)   B = fair
             C = poor

Second position: 2 = mother, Dad (M,D)
(Subject
category)   3 = Phil's family
& 3d position   F = Phil
                   J = Jeaner
                   P = Peter
                   T = Stringothy
               4 = Paul's family
                   B = Brucie
                   H = Hyla
                   L = Lutli
                   P = Paul
               5 = me alone
                   or with others
               6 = Exteriors
               7 = Interiors
               8 = art shots &
                   closeups
               9 = other people
                   (by name)

C H A P T E R   T E N

There were sixteen whole balloons floating over the
kitchen table when the Snapfritzel family sat down to lunch
that day, and so many bottles of lemon soda-pop that Dido thought
perhaps she could try making it come out of her ears, the way
her father always told her it would if she drank too much of it.

"Hurray for Samp-
son Snapfritzel, the
promising young pic-
ture painter!" said
Priscilla as Sampson
dished out the spa-
ghetti. "Sampson
dear, you take this
bottle of lemon pop
--I think it's the
coldest one." And
she handed him the
pop bottle she had
secretly poured the
champagne into.

"Thank you, dear,"
said Sampson, "but
I think the ones I bought are even colder. Here, have one of
mine and I'll give this one to Henry. He won't mind if it's a
little warm, will you, Henry?"

Henry said, "I love lemon soda," that being the first thing
he had learned to say after Boo, and picked up the pop-bottle
that Priscilla had given to Sampson.

Priscilla remembered that that was the bottle she had poured
the champagne into, so she said quickly, "I think perhaps that's
a little too warm for Henry," and took Henry's bottle for herself
and gave Henry the one Sampson had given her. Then she tried to
think how to give Sampson back the bottle with the champagne in
it without spoiling her surprise.

Sampson cleared his throat hastily and said, "Well, I think
that one is a little too cold for Henry. You give me the one you
have and take back Henry's." The fact of the matter was that
Sampson had bought enough champagne to pour secretly into two
pop-bottles.

A page from "Snapfritzel," Converse's unpublished children's book

031 ⊕	6/12/58 ∞/M/- 15/4	Hudson River & Palisades Park, 8:30pm, from living-room window, 138 St NYC.	036 ⊕	6/14/58 ∞/M/- 60/5.6	Morning on 138 St, looking up toward Lewisohn Stadium.
032	6/12/58 ∞/M/- 4/5.6	Hudson River & Palisades Park, 8:30pm, from living-room window, 138 St NYC.	037	6/14/58 ∞/M/- 60/5.6	Morning view from Bum-bum Room, 138 St NYC. Southeastward.
033 ⊕	6/12/58 10/V/B 60/5.6	Elizabeth at piano, from window. Bumbum Room, 138 St NYC.	038	6/14/58 ∞/M/- 60/5.6	Morning view from Bum-bum Room, 138 St NYC. Directly opposite (south).
034	6/12/58 6/V/B 60/5.6	Elizabeth at piano, from doorway. Bumbum Room, 138 St NYC.	039	6/14/58 ∞/M/- 60/5.6	Morning view from Bum-bum Room, 138 St NYC. Southwestward.
035	6/12/58 4/V/B 60/8	Elizabeth as harried com-poser. Bumbum Room, 138 St NYC.	040 ⊕	6/14/58 ∞/M/- 60/5.6	Hudson River & NJ shore, shot hanging out Bumbum window, 138 St NYC.

A page from Converse's slide catalogue, using her coding method

Above: With Pete and Tim, ca. 1960

Right: Playing guitar for her nephews, undated

Below: In Ann Arbor, 1962

Converse (left) and Evelyn on their trip to Alaska, June 1969

Left: With cousins Helen and Edie and the Neffs in Oregon, 1969

Right: With Phil, Jean, Pete (standing, left), and Tim, 1973

Above: With Mary "Jill" Ault at the
1972 wedding of Riley Trumbull
and Bill Barth
Courtesy of Riley Trumbull

Right: The front door of 23 Grove
Street today
Courtesy of the author

Below: Large format passport
photograph, 1971

A Ghost, Again

In 2017, I took a few days off from all things Converse to journey up to the Berkshires for the Solid Sound Festival at the Massachusetts Museum of Contemporary Art, where the legendary, long-defunct Shaggs were performing their first full set in over forty years. I wanted to report a story about the occasion and looked forward to the brief palate cleanser before resuming my book research.

But, of course, I couldn't entirely escape Converse. As I drove up, I considered some of the things the Shaggs had in common with her. Like Converse, the Shaggs were born and raised in out-of-the-way New Hampshire. They, too, were women music makers, had grown up in a repressive household, and had created music that trafficked in the subjects of isolation and melancholy. Like Converse, they hadn't achieved commercial success or recognition during their years of activity, but were later discovered and fetishized by a cult of devotees.

I took back roads rather than highways up to Mass MoCA, making my trip twice as long and many more times beautiful. It was June, and the winding route I'd chosen took me through the lush green hills and valleys of summertime New England, replete with heart-stirring scenes: herds of animals peacefully grazing in fields, rivers rushing through forest glades, and tiny picturesque Yankee villages that seemed frozen in time.

My plans included a theoretical stop at at least one roadside farm stand on my way; I hoped to purchase some fresh produce and maybe a quart of local maple syrup. I passed by any number of candidates before choosing one at random, deep in the Massachusetts hills. As I climbed out of my car, I looked up and became momentarily paralyzed: There, directly above the front end of my vehicle, was a road sign that read CONVERSE CEMETERY.

To my right was a small, shady walled-in graveyard. The man at the farm stand across the street was staring at me and hollered a quizzical greeting. I may have been his first customer of the day. He may also have been responding to the fact that I appeared to be stuck.

Unable to take my eyes off the sign, I managed to stammer a question. Could he tell me anything about the cemetery? Might I go take a look?

"Oh sure," he said. "Go ahead."

Did he know any Converses?

"Nope. I just cut the grass in there sometimes when it gets too overgrown," he replied.

This place in the middle of nowhere, where I had arbitrarily chosen to pull over, also happened to be the site of a private family burial ground for a branch of Connie Converse's family tree. There were about a dozen headstones in there, many of them dating to the first half of the nineteenth century. I recognized names from my research into Converse's genealogy, but had not been aware that there was a cluster of relations who'd lived and died right near here.

What were the odds? Of all the possible New England family names I might have stumbled upon in such a circumstance, how could it be that it was Converse? Why had I chosen to stop here? Was I drawn here? By what?

I bought a few items from the man's farm stand. Then, still stunned, I got back in my car and continued on my way to see the Wiggin sisters' reunion.

CHAPTER 22

Nothing Else Would Do

In the summer of 1954, following her television appearance, Converse hit the road again. For the first time, she visited Ann Arbor, now the adopted home of Phil and Jean, who'd just returned from a year abroad.[1] She took along a new pal, a former college classmate of Jean's named Maude Brogan, who now worked in the music library at NBC in New York. The pair's travels that summer would also include a "pilgrimage" to Canada and a visit to New Hampshire.[2] If ideal atmospheric conditions were present during their drive to Michigan, the pair may have been able to pick up WHBQ out of Memphis and hear a song in heavy rotation that summer: Elvis Presley's "That's All Right," his first hit.

Brogan was going through some big life moments herself. Jean Converse told me that "Maude was in love at the time, but because she was a Catholic, she thought she would go to hell if she and the man consummated their affair. In the end, she felt it was worth it."[3] Given what Phil told me about his sense of his sister's promiscuity in New York, it seems that the women would have had more than one thing to talk about—

though, to be fair, I never heard about this side of Converse's personality from anyone but him.

A revealing photo from the Ann Arbor visit shows Connie Converse with a camera slung over her shoulder, her nose wrinkled, her smile broad. She is in the flush of life. Even if the recent excitement and attention she'd garnered in New York had not produced any further results, she loved to travel, to be with Phil and Jean, and had really bonded with Brogan.

After their brief stay in Woodville, Evelyn and Ernest moved back to Concord, and that August, Brogan joined Converse for a drive up there, too. The whole family convened: Phil and Jean, Paul and Hyla, and little four-month-old P. Bruce.[4] In a back-stoop family portrait, Converse sits in front of Brogan. She is the only one who does not look at the photographer (presumably Ernest).

When the two new friends got back to New York, Converse resumed her day job and, by night, began exploring new avenues for her music writing, her style about to take a radical turn.

Over the course of only a year, she'd gone from being an anonymous print shop worker with a songwriting hobby, to the darling of a small circle of Manhattan animation types, to a performer on television—but for whatever reason she now abruptly decided to move in a different direction. Phil told me that Brogan, a devotee of art song and opera, "discouraged Connie from writing more of those delightful guitar songs, and steered her toward more serious stuff instead. I sort of thought she was a bad influence."[5]

Whether her decision to abandon her songwriting for formal music composing just when she seemed on the cusp of breaking through was a terrible mistake or whether the music she would write in the third and final chapter of her New York years represents a courageous artistic leap forward is something only posterity can judge.

Having immersed herself in the worlds of poetry, prose, painting, political cartoons, and guitar songs, it was now formal music that seized her creative imagination, establishing a divide in what limited musical audience she had. Fans of her mostly catchy, mostly easily accessible guitar songs may have agreed with Phil that her turn toward art song was artistically alienating, just as aficionados of serious music like Brogan had little use for her guitar music. The two audiences were almost mutually exclusive.

Converse began her new explorations with a setting for a 1945 Jacques Prévert poem. "Just composed music for *Les Deux Escargots* [*sic*]," she wrote to Phil and Jean.[6] "Execution requires a voice, a recorder and two or three types of percussion. The result is a combination of Piaf and La Mère Oie [*sic*, she means Mother Goose]. I am waiting for my equipment for double-recording . . . and then I will be able to execute the execution myself. I am all loaded up with ideas right now."[7]

Maybe Converse had recently walked by the outsider composer and musician Moondog, performing his unclassifiable music on Sixth Avenue in Midtown, and had felt inspired to try something new. In her notes to the setting, she calls it "an experimental recording, included here for laughs. Instrumentation: two drinking glasses, two pencils, empty Kleenex box, alto recorder, guitar. I couldn't really concentrate on the singing part."[8]

In addition to the odd instrumentation, "Les Deux Escargots" is sung entirely in French. By the time she was finally able to record it, the process of doing so left her exhausted "from spending about 14 hours with a borrowed tape recorder."[9] The result is experimental indeed, like something Tom Waits might record decades later.

In her letter about the Prévert setting, Converse mentions going with Brogan to see a performance of a one-act Kurt Weill opera, which may have been as much research as it was cultural edification.[10] She was going to see more and more opera. Soon enough, with Brogan egging her on, she'd decided to write one.[11]

The first mention of Converse's opera dates to November 1954. Evelyn and Ernest were back in Manhattan for another Thanksgiving visit, and again stopped in at Grove Street with Paul and Hyla (this time accompanied by little P. Bruce). Once more, Converse recorded the encounter. This time there is no musical performance.

Converse seems to have recorded this visit without anyone's knowledge.[12] In a subsequent letter to Phil and Jean, she included a partial transcription of the conversation that ensued:

> MOTHER: (looking at sketch of stage set) . . . Does this opera take place in Cousin Helen's barn?
>
> ME: In a barn like that.
>
> MOTHER: . . . Well, who are the characters? Are they people, or are they animals? (General facetiousness) . . . Are they really people? (General affirmation) . . . But I don't see how they're connected with a barn?
>
> ME: Well, don't people ever go into barns?
>
> MOTHER: Yes, but they'd just be farmer people.

Remarks like this had to rankle Ernest somewhat. After all, a number of the Amherst Converses, including his father, had been "farmer people."

> HYLA: You mean farmer people can't be in operas?
>
> MOTHER: Why, I didn't s'pose they would.
>
> ME: . . . Almost the whole chorus and half the main characters are farmer people.

MOTHER: *(surprised and intrigued) Is that so! Oh my, that must be different. Well, there's a story to it? Well, is it exciting, or is it farmlike?*

ME: *(facetiously) No, it's very dull.*

MOTHER: *. . . How long is it going to be, Sister?*

ME: *About two hours.*

MOTHER: *. . . And they're all farmer folks?*

ME: *Not all.*

MOTHER: *I don't quite see how you get a plot. There is a plot, I suppose?*

PAUL: *(facetiously) That's what the barn is on. (Great general laughter.)*

MOTHER: *Well now, that's cute. (She dissolves into merriment.) . . .*

MOTHER: *Well now, this sounds most—what other questions shall I ask? The only way I find out is by asking questions.*

ME: *(defensively) Well, you get more answers than most people do, I'll tell you that.*

MOTHER: *So. Well, is it half-done, quarter-done yet?*

(My reply is an unintelligible mumble.)

MOTHER: *(repeating) "In some ways it's more than half-done"? And you have to write all the music, and all the words, and have a plot . . . (After considerable other talk) Well, what's the name of it, Sister? Or haven't you named it yet?*

ME: *Well, tentatively it's called The Prodigal Nephew.*

MOTHER: *The Prodigal Nephew! My sakes! . . . Is it sweet little ditties or is it very modernistic?*

ME: *(proudly) It's got everything in it.*[13]

That was Converse, subjected to and working through her mother's genuine if naïve attempts to understand what she's doing with her life. Evelyn seems to want to be supportive, but can't seem to help being patronizing and even a bit mocking.

Converse's transcription of the conversation for Phil and Jean may have superficially been intended to make light of their parents' provincialism, but there may, too, have been a deeper desire to find some familial validation for her new, more serious artistic ambitions. And she may also have craved some understanding for what must have been her disappointment at having her more serious musical ambitions subjected to ridicule by her own family. It wasn't as though Converse had received a commission to compose an opera. "The Prodigal Nephew" was as ambitious an endeavor as any she'd undertaken. And, like almost everything else she pursued, one done entirely on spec. If her guitar songs had seemed frivolous to Ernest and Evelyn, couldn't they now see that she was attempting to lift her craft to a new, more respectable level of art?

It was likely another painful activation of the competing narratives that seemed to buzz in the background of Converse's adult consciousness. On the one hand, she sought to distinguish herself from her parents as a modern freethinking woman, socially progressive and spiritually rebellious. She lived alone, in New York City, beholden to no one and nothing aside from the pursuit of her art and ideas. And yet, centuries of her family's culture were stamped upon her psyche. She was sensitive to her parents' judgment and wanted their approval, even as the decisions she made and the lifestyle she led were anathema to them. If anything, what she appears to have most wanted was for them to acknowledge that her choices were as legitimate as theirs.

It didn't happen. During this visit, Ernest says almost nothing. If he'd deigned to take a token interest in her music two years prior, when she had performed for them, his daughter's musical ambitions now prompted utter silence.

S tung by her family's failure to take her seriously, Converse canceled her annual December holiday visit to New England. "I'm going to stay home and make musics [*sic*]," she wrote to Phil and Jean. "I might even get stinking on the Eve. It's been long since I didn't go home for Xmas, so I guess I can take one year off."[14]

She made no attempt to mask her bitter feelings about Ernest and Evelyn. In a subsequent letter, she wrote, "Mother recently mentioned that you had invited them out . . . next summer. She also suggested to me that I might drive them out in their car if our trips could be made to coincide. This arrangement would be wise, kind, economical, and catastrophic. Could you in the early future count your beds and discover that you can't possibly put up three guests at once?" she asked them.[15]

But for all the corrosive psychological effects resentment can produce, it can also be a powerful motivator. Converse went all in on the opera project. Her immediate goal was to "get a passable demonstration tape" made of it. To do so, she tapped into the city's music community, rounding up a pianist and a few singers, whose services she hoped to pay for by passing a hat at her upcoming house concert appearances (evidence that she was still performing her guitar songs at this point).

"I have spent the most of two three-day weekends making musics [*sic*], with two parties squeezed in endwise and a remarkable shortage of sleep throughout," she reported in a letter to Phil and Jean a couple of days into 1955. "My opera is getting big! And healthy! And robust! Just like it ought to. There's an awful lot of work yet to do, especially working out the musical details on paper—I'm slow at that, and slower still without a piano. But nowadays I can lie alertly awake on Sunday nights . . . and run through the whole first act, or most of the second, word by word and air by air. Hoo."[16]

R eports of Converse's ambitious new project were, somehow, rippling through at least one part of the New York artistic community.[17] "A theater friend of mine informs me that Marc Blitzstein is eagerly waiting to hear my opera," she wrote, "or rather to see the MS. I keep telling people that nobody but nobody is eagerer than I'm."[18]

Blitzstein was a big shot in the worlds of musical theater and opera, having already achieved theatrical immortality with his controversial pro-union show *The Cradle Will Rock* in 1937. His translation of Brecht's *Threepenny Opera* was an Off-Broadway smash and had been playing mere blocks away from Converse in the Village since the previous year. (It may have been no accident that "The Ash Grove" had found its way into her guitar repertoire.)

That the well-established Blitzstein not only knew of the unknown Converse but had expressed active interest in her work is fascinating, as is the idea that she was now skirting the margins of yet another cutting-edge scene. Blitzstein biographer Howard Pollack told me he knew nothing of the pair's connection, and was surprised to learn of it, wondering whether their shared interest in left-wing politics and the fact that they were both living in the Village may have been what brought them together. "I really don't know Blitzstein to have taken much interest in younger composers," he wrote me.[19]

I consider this my doctoral dissertation in music," Converse wrote about "The Prodigal Nephew." "All my friends are so fascinated by the mere idea of my writing an opera that the finished work is going to be a helluva anticlimax."[20] The headiness surrounding the endeavor, piled on top of the recent television appearance, made whatever prose project she'd pursued in her early years in New York pale by comparison. "Writing a novel now seems to me the most pedestrian occupation in the world," she wrote.[21]

If there was any doubt about who was most responsible for Converse's new musical direction, she dispelled them for Phil and Jean, which may be what Phil remembered:

> *[Maude] and I may be worlds apart on many matters, but in the bannered fields of music she has been so just plain helpful . . . She was the one who dragged me to my first few operas. And when I suddenly announced that I was going to write an opera, she seemed less surprised than I was. She apparently believed from the beginning that I was really going through with it, and that helped take the edge off my feeling of temerity, even of rashness. Now I don't feel rash any more about it, just dogged, with occasional slight fevers of exultation . . . Thing is, I'm on top of the Hump in this particular artistic endeavor, and it's the first time I've been there with respect to an opus of this magnitude . . .*[22]

Today, the only complete lyric that survives from the opera's libretto is "Fantastic City," but there *are* two tape reels of informal sessions Converse organized at Brogan's house.[23] They feature Maude's roommate, a professional pianist named Virginia "Ginny" Gerhard, accompanying what sounds like a small chorus of three or four singers trying to muddle their way through the work in progress. The outside of the box of the first reel identifies the content as "Informal Chorus at Maude's . . . sight-reading selections from my 'The Prodigal Nephew.'" The other tape box reads:

> *Ginny tries out pieces of my opera:*
> *1. Randy + hired man (piano only)*

2. *"I Am Going Dancing"* [3:08]
3. *"Has It Made You Happy"* [4:35]
4. *"Fantastic City"* (piano part only) [7:24]

It's difficult to make out many of the lyrics on this tape, though the third song does feature the poignant lyric (set to doleful, dour music) "Has it made you happy / leaving home / living in New York? / Tell me how you like it." The soprano singing it might be a young Judith Raskin, then at just the start of her career.[24] Raskin and Brogan were close friends, and when Raskin's daughter Lisa heard the recording, she thought it sounded like her mother singing. Given her mom's close relationship to Brogan, and Brogan's close relationship to Converse and Gerhard, Lisa wrote to me, "It's hard to believe my mother wouldn't have known and maybe sung Connie's music."[25]

The first tape begins with a haunting chorus that features the weirdly prophetic lyric "Never had a husband / Never had a son / Dead at the age of fifty-one"[26] and a near-complete performance of what could be Converse herself singing "Fantastic City."

The song is included in her typed "Lyrics for Tapes" collection, its appearance there suggesting that she was happy enough with this one to call it finished:

> *Stand across the river*
> *And stare and stare at that fantastic city*
> *See how the sun makes it shimmer*
> *See how the sun makes it shine.*
>
> *All the ships of Tarshish are howling in the bay,*
> *They are howling at the city—*
> *Can you hear what they say?*
> *—Stay away, stay away.*

Nobody lives in that fantastic city,
They only eat and run
—And yet you never saw a town as pretty
Beneath the sun.

The corners are sharp,
The edges are hard,
Ante up and draw your card;

The gutter is wide,
The curbing is low,
Any street can be Skid Row,
Any street can be Skid Row.

You gotta watch it or you don't get what's coming to you
But then what's coming to you ain't worth a halleluia

Nobody loves in that fantastic city,
They only sleep and run
—And yet you never saw a town as pretty
Not one, not one.

The music is gay,
The music is loud,
Ante up and draw a crowd;

The faces are hard,
The fingers are cold
If you're cheap enough, you're sold,
If you're cheap enough, you're sold.[27]

The music, apparently still in progress, is prickly, full of odd meters and discordant passages. It's almost hard to understand how the composer of this song and "Les Deux Escargots" could possibly be the same one who wrote "Johnny's Brother" and "The Clover Saloon."

Her work on the opera would serve as a bridge between what Converse had composed up to this point and an entirely different corpus of music she was about to embark upon going forward—one just as distinctive, sure-footed, and compelling as what had come before.

In February, Converse wrote to Phil and Jean with big news—what she called "The Great Keyboard Solution of 1955." She'd bought an Estey miniature organ for her apartment: "It's about a foot deep, a bit over two feet high, a bit under two feet long, and quite light enough to carry . . . It has a range of 3 octaves, from the C below middle C on up. It works by electricity, but it is not, repeat NOT, one of those horrid electric organs with the cheesy vibrato . . . the tone is that of a real reed organ, because that's what it is . . . Now my apartment houses a recorder, two tape recorders, a violin, a guitar, and an organ."[28]

Equipped with this arsenal, Converse began writing a new cluster of songs, one that Phil had alluded to in "Connie's Guitar Songs."

But what were these songs, and what did they sound like? Phil told me that though he had no recordings of them, he did have his sister's original manuscript sheet music stored in his house somewhere, and that he'd be happy to send me copies of it if I was interested. I certainly was.

A Resurrection Project

In 2012, in New York City, I'd begun presenting performances of a theatrical work in progress about Converse's life, a project that grew out of my covering her songs and talking about her life at my concerts. This new show combined the fruits of my research to that point with her music and multimedia elements like her photographs, letters, and projected images of her artwork. One of the performers I included was soprano Charlotte Mundy, whom I'd enlisted specifically to sing some of Converse's more classical-leaning guitar songs, including the Shakespeare setting "O Mistress Mine" and "Where Are the Roses?," that curious song she'd written for Phil and Jean's wedding.

Charlotte was especially excited when she heard me mention Converse's art songs, and she gamely offered to learn a couple of them for the show with the help of pianist Christopher Goddard. Mundy and Goddard tackled what turned out to be two very different manifestations of Converse's mature, classical voice: her setting for the e. e. cummings poem "Anyone Lived in a Pretty How Town," and her own "Under a Lullaby."

But none of us had any idea what this collection of songs that Phil had sent me would sound like. Only one of them, "Vanity of Vanities," had ever been recorded by Converse, so we began by focusing on her demo of that song for guidance.

Unlike her guitar songs, the music Converse wrote for piano and voice had more than a hint of danger to it. In "Musicks," Converse describes "Vanity of Vanities" as "a daring innovation, very imperfectly rendered." She notes that it should be sung by a baritone, and in her recording of it, she sings at the bottom of her range, giving the performance an added measure of foreboding. In her manuscript sheet music for the song, Converse's one-word instruction for the performance of it is "gravely."

As in "The Clover Saloon" and "Johnny's Brother," we're again in the American West, this time in Tombstone, Arizona, site of the famous 1881 gunfight at the O.K. Corral. We come to town and encounter an alchemist, who instructs us to hand over our pocket change. Go "find yourself some scenery," he says, so that he may perform his magic.

We do as we're told and then get absolutely lost. Somehow, we eventually manage to find our way back to Tombstone, but it's as though we've been drugged; we have no recall about where we've been in the interim—only that it had involved "walking in the crystal air," and daydreaming of the treasure awaiting us upon our return.

But—what's this? Now the alchemist has been replaced by another figure imbued with transformative powers—one able to "preach sinners into heav'n." He wears a frock coat with a velvet collar and speaks a language we remember hearing "once before." Forget your dreams of wealth, he says, reminding us of Jesus's parable about the camel and the needle's eye. Finally, we leave Tombstone without any earthly riches, but "heaven-bound, and qualified to go."

The narrative is fever-like and hallucinatory, made more so by the music against which Converse sets it. It has a slow, hypnotic quality and, like its protagonist, we, as listeners, get lost—lost in the music's oddness, lost in Converse's discomfiting performance, lost even in what is really the relatively straightforward story being told. The chiming chords at the outset of the piece at first suggest a hopeful brightness, but the strange rhythm of the bass set against the song's 3/4 time, combined with the composer's written instructions to speed up and slow down at various intervals, throws the whole thing out of whack, making for an almost abrasive listening experience.

Converse had entered another territory—one far more outlandish than her guitar music, one that inspired her to visionary lyrical and musical language. She was no longer simply at odds with the popular trends of the day; now she was exploring a different universe altogether, one occupied by the likes of Paul Bowles, Mary Shelley, and Shirley Jackson.

And it may have been just as well. Rock 'n' roll was about to take over popular culture. The power and out-of-control nature of the music of Elvis, Little Richard, Jerry Lee Lewis, and company effectively sealed Converse's fate as commercial songwriter. Rather than continue to submit gentle, witty guitar songs as an alternative to this raging current of loud, lusty, extroverted man-music, she may have been opting to simply step away from the fight, freeing herself to go even farther in the other direction. As "Vanity of Vanities" and its brethren from this new phase of her composing life reveal, a shadow had fallen over the blithe spirit that infused "Down This Road" and "Talkin' Like You."

But I didn't know that yet. Aside from "Vanity of Vanities," I had no inkling of what the Converse songs contained in the package Phil had sent me were like. There wasn't a single recording or rendition of any of them—not anywhere. And we weren't talking about just a small handful of compositions, either: There were nineteen titles in all, more than half the number of the other Converse songs known to exist.

⌒

The bulky packet of photocopies Phil had overnighted to me were reproductions of his sister's handwritten scores, her instructions to both singer and pianist with regard to tempo, dynamics, and feeling specified in her thick, elegant penmanship. Over the course of some months, Charlotte and Christopher would eventually tackle all of them, making scratch demos and sending them along to me one at a time.

Hearing these songs brought back to life, probably for the first time in nearly half a century, was an experience unlike any I'd ever had. There she was again, the genie in the bottle, conjured, reconstituted, revealing herself—only, this time, in wildly new shapes and forms. Imagine being presented with a newly discovered trove of a favorite artist's work, one in which they express themselves in wholly new voice and form: a Mass by Hieronymus Bosch; a play authored by Charlie Parker; the ballets of Joan Didion. This was the feeling I had listening to Charlotte and Christopher's readings of songs like "Under a Lullaby" and "The Age of Noon," music so moving I almost couldn't breathe when I first heard it. Not only were too few people aware of Converse's brilliant guitar songs; even among them, none yet knew of this other, duskier side of her genius.

Charlotte and Christopher would go on to record the entirety of Converse's art song catalogue for an album I produced. In "Connie's Guitar Songs," Phil had written that he hoped one day to produce a recording of this music, but he told me he was now past the point of feeling up to the task. His vision had been to call it "Connie's Piano Songs," and that's exactly the title I chose, in tribute to him and his efforts.

CHAPTER 23

Harlem

There was another significant development in early 1955, one that Converse declined to share in her correspondence with Phil and Jean. She had met another friend of the Ishiis: William "Bill" Barss, a commercial illustrator who lived in northeastern Massachusetts but who made frequent business trips to Manhattan.[1] "Certainly the nicest thing that happened on my junket was meeting you," he wrote to Converse that April in a fawning letter that bears hints of what was to come (and what may have already been).[2]

Born in 1916, Barss was married, with three children and a fourth on the way. Like Bill Bernal, he was magnetic, a life-of-the-party guy, a romantic, and (according to his daughter Taiya) both "a skirt chaser" and an alcoholic. "He was a free spirit, a kind of hippie before there were hippies," she told me.[3] "My father thought of himself as a freewheeling bohemian, I think, wind in his hair, song on his lips."[4]

Caroll Spinney (Big Bird from television's *Sesame Street*) was Barss's longtime neighbor in Massachusetts, and remembered Barss as a bit "gruff," he said. "He had a studio in the top of our barn, where he would work and drink all day. He drank cooking sherry, and would try to hide the fact that he was drunk when he came in for dinner."[5]

Barss had more in common with Converse than merely a fondness for alcohol. His father had also been a man of the church, and Barss went to great lengths to hide his alcohol and tobacco consumption from his parents, even as an adult (something Converse and Phil both did and joked about, I learned). Barss, too, had been a precociously talented youth. He had a vested interest in politics, and had been a conscientious objector.[6] Maybe most important, Barss played guitar and sang. Like Bernal, he was struck by Converse's music and wanted to champion it.

"Hearing your songs . . . I guess I needn't tell you again how very wonderful I think they are, but the more I hear them the more enthusiastic I become. I think that you are the only one who should be allowed to sing them." He notes that he has played her recordings for an editor in the publishing world who, he said, "was ecstatic over your songs and immediately started to discuss the possibility of Houghton Mifflin publishing the lyrics, at least, as poetry . . . What I would like to see done, and [she] agrees, is to publish the songs with music (and with Barss illustrations naturally) in a very handsome, fine edition." He continues: "I think you are a very rare person and I would like to see something very good done with your things . . . I especially want to hear more about your folk opera."[7]

All of this had to have excited Converse. A successful illustrator was wooing her, making introductions to the publishing world on her behalf. Marc Blitzstein was interested in her opera, and she herself was overseeing rehearsals with musical collaborators to make that vision a reality. Though she was still working a day job, it must have felt to her, when these various moments of connection began to overlap, as though it were only a matter of time before she could become entirely self-supporting through her art.

⌐∽

Barss came back to New York for a return visit soon enough, and he and Converse had a romantic interlude. "It has been a week, and a long one, since our evening," he wrote to her, "and I have had more of those sleepless nights and thoughtful days . . . This writing machine is a poor means of telling you how very much I think of you, and I would probably sound maudlin if I tried," he wrote. "Anyway, I would rather tell you in person, although I didn't do so well Friday night. My heart runneth over . . . I wish that you had insisted that I stay at Grove St. I could have awakened you with a kiss instead of a telephone call." He bemoans the fact that he may not be back in New York for some months, but notes that when he is, "I hope your garden gate will be un-latched," which could simply be a reference to her lyric for "There Is a Vine," but also something more. "I would like to go on endlessly, tell-ing you how much you are to me . . . Know that I send my kisses. And my love."[8]

The affair continued through the summer, by telephone and in let-ters. "Dear Connie, come and live with me!" he exclaims in one. He fan-tasizes about the sort of artist patronage Converse would one day actually come to know, albeit briefly, in Ann Arbor:

> *I still think that my idea for The Benevolent Society for the Subsidization of Connie Converse is a good one. All I have to do is organize fifteen nice people who would put a weekly five dollars in the pot. You . . . could just sit in your rocking chair and turn out songs and operas like mad for years and years. The only difficulty is that all nice people seem to be nearly as poor as I am. I shall have to look for some not so nice people . . . I think you know how I feel about you. I want to tell you again and again how much you are to me. So I send my love.[9]*

Barss suggested that Converse stop off and see him and his family at their home in Bolton, Massachusetts, on her way to visit her parents in Concord that summer. His wife, he wrote, "is very excited over the prospect of your coming" (his daughter Taiya insisted to me that there was no way her mother would have known about the affair, much less condoned it). Later in the same letter, he mentions the possibility of having to be in Detroit for work around the same time Converse next planned to be in Ann Arbor to see Phil and Jean. "You must let me know where you will be staying," he writes, "your telephone number, how thick you like your steaks, the temperature of your beer."[10]

In typical Conversian fashion, her letters to Phil and Jean over these months omit explicit mention of the affair, though at one point she comes close. As her Ann Arbor trip got closer, she wrote to them, "I was planning to bring along an illicit lover, but it turns out he can't make it."[11]

The rendezvous nearly happened. "I was very much disappointed not to see you out there," Barss wrote to her shortly after, his wife now six months pregnant with their fourth child.[12] "I had been so pleased when I thought we would be in Detroit at the same time . . . I want to have a little time with you again. Wish you had your own habitat . . . I send my kisses and much love."[13] For reasons that may never be known, this note, and the aborted meet-up in Michigan, seems to have marked the end of their secret, short-lived affair.[14]

Converse revealed nothing more to Phil and Jean.[15] Instead, in her letters, she trafficked in her usual epistolary wit ("it isn't the heat; it's the people who say it's the humidity"), detailed the trip to Concord ("Maude went along to protect me in the parents' den"),[16] and wrote of joining Paul and Hyla for a trip to their upstate New York getaway at Tupper Lake.[17] It was there that the trio may have hatched the plan that would usher in a new, fraught era of Converse's life in New York—one that would eventually play a role in driving her out of the city for good.

⌒

B y 1955, Greenwich Village's Washington Square Park—a gathering place for folk music lovers since the late 1940s[18]—had become a simmering hot spot for guitar- and banjo-wielding performers, a place where "more than a hundred musicians, both amateur and professional" could be found every Sunday afternoon, jamming, exchanging songs, and performing for locals and tourists.[19] The complete eruption of the Village folk music scene was still a few years off, but this was a real place to be. And yet, in what now seems to have been another star-crossed decision, Converse vacated her Grove Street residence that summer, left the Village, and took an apartment with Paul and Hyla at 605 West 138th Street (between Broadway and Riverside Drive), in Hamilton Heights, a block away from Strivers' Row. She categorized the move as a cost-saving measure and guessed that it would last "for a year or a year and a half."[20]

It wasn't the Village, but the Village wasn't Harlem, either, which had its own dynamism. I like thinking about the kinds of music Converse may have heard in clubs close to her new apartment, like the Pink Angel (now St. Nick's Pub) and Smalls Paradise, and in the streets. Rev. Gary Davis, whose style seems echoed in Converse's guitar part for "Chanson Innocent," was a fixture on Harlem's sidewalks at that time, hollering his distinctive, soulful blend of gospel, ragtime, and blues and thumbing furious bass runs on his big Gibson. If Converse was indeed familiar with his music, maybe she crossed paths with Davis there and even spent parts of the occasional Sunday afternoon listening to his music?[21]

And then there was her decision to live with Paul, with whom she'd never been close and whose personality Edie Converse Neff had described to me in less-than-flattering terms.

⌒

Paul Converse died in 1993, and my attempts to talk to some members of his family were complicated. After he and Hyla divorced in 1964, Paul had no contact with either of his two sons from that marriage for almost twenty years; after that time, their interactions with him seem to have been emotionally freighted.

P. Bruce (who today goes by Bruce) was willing to speak to me, albeit guardedly, about his aunt Connie. But I had the sense that he did not want to discuss his father at all. Bruce's brother, Luther (named for Ernest's father), I learned, was reclusive and largely out of touch with the larger family. Phil told me that he was aware of these tendencies, and said he was at a loss for what lay behind them. My attempts to reach out to Luther were met with radio silence, and I was advised by other members of the family that it would be pointless to expect to hear from him.

Then, one afternoon some years into my research, I was stunned to receive a social media message from a young woman named Elizabeth Converse Roberts. This was Luther's daughter. "I am Connie's name-sake," she wrote to me, "but I never even knew she existed until very recently. I had no idea Connie had developed such a following, and would love to know any information you can provide to me about this beautiful woman. It really might explain some things!"[22]

Despite having given her Connie's name, Luther had kept his aunt's existence a secret from his own daughter. Elizabeth learned about her great-aunt only from Luther's half sister, Leslie, a child from Paul's second marriage. Elizabeth told me that when she confronted her father about his aunt, he completely shut her down. He would not discuss Connie, she said.[23] I told Elizabeth about my attempts to contact her father, the results of which did not surprise her. She agreed with the others that it was probably futile to try.

When I asked Elizabeth about her grandfather Paul, she wrote me, "My father only let us meet him twice," when she and her siblings were young. "We were not allowed to go to his funeral."[24]

~

I met Leslie Converse, the one who had tipped off Elizabeth, over coffee near her office in downtown Manhattan, not so very far from where Connie Converse had lived before moving to Harlem.

Leslie was close to my age, having been born when Paul was past fifty, four years after he married her mother. She had a brother, Robert, with whom she did not seem particulary close. Her mother had recently died.

Leslie's upbringing had not been easy. Paul was gainfully employed when she was very young, but he lost his job in the mid-1970s, around the time of her brother's birth. After that, he drifted from one line of work to another, including a stint with a "paper company" that kept him out of the house for long hours.

When she did see him, he seemed to her to exist in an oppressive cloud of doom and gloom, exhibiting what she called "a very grim, constant victim mentality." The family moved around between various low-income-housing situations, which included a lake cottage in upstate New York (which may have been the one he and Hyla visited with Converse) without heat or running water, and a trailer that Paul refused to heat during what Leslie recalled as a particularly "rough period."[25]

Leslie didn't know much about the Converse side of her family. She'd met her half brother Luther only once, when she was eleven—she described him to me as "religious" and "very devout"—and had never met Bruce. It wasn't until 2003, she said, when she and her husband took a trip to Michigan to meet Phil and Jean for the first time, that she first learned about her aunt Connie.

∽

The apartment in the Heights that the Converse siblings moved into together was in a large new building called the Stockbridge, close to the 137th Street subway stop.[26] Paul and Hyla had a room of their own, and P. Bruce (and, eventually, brother Luther) occupied another. A third bedroom contained an upright piano and was used as Converse's studio (nicknamed "the Bumbum Room" by P. Bruce, for the noises that would emanate from it). There was also a living room, and a dedicated study for Paul. Converse slept in an area off the kitchen just large enough to squeeze in a small bed and nothing else.

Harlem scholar John T. Reddick told me that due to the neighborhood's mixed-race makeup at that time (which included large Jewish and Irish Catholic populations), it would not have been in any way strange for a white family to move there, though historian Jonathan Gill wasn't so sure of that: "There were certainly cheaper places she could have chosen to move in the city, if money was an issue," he said, and suggested that Converse's move may have been something of a statement.[27]

Perhaps unsurprisingly, the situation in the apartment was tense from the get-go. Paul, like his sister, was no stranger to secret amorous activities. But while Converse's affair with Barss may have been socially improper, she had at least been at liberty. Paul, like Barss, was leading a double life, having an affair with a colleague and gone much of the time, leaving Hyla feeling overburdened, anxious, and resentful.[28]

Yet there were positives, too. With the fizzling of her romance with Barss behind her, Converse luxuriated in the novelty of having a work studio. Only, now, instead of the traditional songs she'd once looked to for inspiration, she was playing through the likes of Bartók, Ernest Bloch, and Roy Harris to hone her compositional skills.[29] Though female classical composers were still a relative rarity at the time, the work of Florence Price, with its use of American spirituals and folk influences, may have been on her radar as well (even if her contributions were—like Converse's—mostly neglected until recently) and she may have taken note of the Boulanger sisters, too.

What was such a relief to discover about this period of Converse's musical activity is that, unlike the first half of the 1950s, when her ambitions, practice, and methodology can be mostly only guessed at, her letters to Phil and Jean from her art song period contain real specificity about the music she was writing now and her struggles and triumphs with it.

"My one regret about my recent . . . visit is that you didn't hear 'Buffalo Bill's Defunct,' which I think you'd like," she wrote to Phil and Jean—yet another cummings setting, and one that does not survive. "I've been getting back into the opera, and plunging on a bit, besides trying to improve my manual dexterity. It *would* be nice if I could play my own music."[30]

And she continued to assign herself a prodigious reading syllabus. "I'm biding my time with such things as 'the Law of Civilization and Decay,' by Brooks Adams, the 1895 Spengler; and Ernest Jones on Hamlet and Oedipus. The IRT express"—the subway—"is usually too crowded to open up a newspaper in, so I've taken to paperbacks for commuter reading," she wrote to Phil and Jean. "Even so, some days the only way you could read would be to rest chin on sternum and hold the book open with one foot."[31]

As the family planned to convene in Concord for the annual holiday gathering, she wrote to the Ann Arbor couple:

> *My current simultaneous reading consists of:*
> 1. *Mullahy's OEDIPUS: MYTH AND COMPLEX*
> 2. *ANTHROPOLOGY TODAY, a huge symposium under Kroeber*
> 3. *Sir Chas. Sherrington: MAN ON HIS NATURE*

4. *Eagan:* ROBESPIERRE, NATIONALIST DICTATOR

5. *de Castro:* THE GEOGRAPHY OF HUNGER

6. *Condliffe:* THE RECONSTRUCTION OF WORLD TRADE

Ask me anything, anything. I am coming to Concord prepared to play for you three small piano pieces lately composed by mimi and none but me.[32]

hese would not be the last times she would reference thinking about Sophocles's seminal drama, whose hero's plight formed the basis for one of Freud's most discussed psychoanalytic theories, the Oedipus complex. "A good part of Oedipus's tragedy has always failed to fill me with the appropriate horror," she wrote to Phil after watching Tyrone Guthrie's film version of it. "Murder, yes, but not especially murder that is accidentally patricide or marriage that is accidentally incest. I guess I am seriously lacking in such atavisms as the sense of inexorable fate."[33]

Converse played piano for her toddler nephew and invented games like "Fishing for Mr. Smidgen's Hat," which involved the two of them going to a window that faced the street and dropping a long string down to catch the hat of this imaginary character.[34] At night, she used her lit cigarette to draw pictures in the air to illustrate the bedtime stories she told him.[35] She even composed and recorded a song for him called, simply, "Lullaby for P. Bruce"—one she would soon record as part of the "omnibus tape" she made of all of her guitar songs to date, for Phil and Jean, and for posterity.[36]

Entitled "Musicks (Volumes I and II)," the endeavor seems to be both a look back at where she'd come from and a declaration of where she was headed. The tape reel ends with the haunting "Vanity of Vanities," but this turned out to be only a hint of the compositional depths she was now exploring.[37]

‎onverse and her younger brother also sent audio letters to each other during this time, recording them on tape reels, with Phil sometimes including his recitation of bits of verse at her behest. After listening to one of these, she replied that his reading had left her "simply creamed with delight."[38] But his first attempt at a letter in the form of a tape recording, made that October of 1956, may be the most striking.

It's after two o'clock in the morning, and Phil sounds drunk. Either that, or the sort of silly, ridiculous "baby talk" tone he employs was how he sometimes talked to his sister. Speaking quietly (presumably not to wake Jean), he tells her that they'd hosted a party that night with friends, and had played for them some of Converse's new "Musicks" tapes, of which, he says, "we just love them and love them and love them.

"I'm just in an awesome sort of glow about your music," he says, and mentions finding new appreciation for songs he'd previously overlooked, like "Here Is the Door" and "Sweet Amelia," which he tells her he has "finally penetrated."

After about eighteen minutes of heaping praise on his sister for her talent, he closes by saying, "This music of yours is just out of this world," and that hearing it has engendered "traumatic fantasies about Schubert's songs turning up after he was dead and gone . . . Grim thought."[39]

The tape is spliced, and picks up again on another day soon after, with Jean joining in this time. Phil has some fun thinking about his sister and their parents all coming for a visit soon, and says, "We can put your ashtray on the studio couch, and we can make the kitchen a drinking room and they'll never come in. We'll build a little bar there . . . and you can sit on the other side of the bar and drink. You know, you can slouch across . . . You can keep your back of your head to the door." At the end of the tape, Phil sits at the piano and plays through some of Bartók's *Romanian Folk Dances* for his sister, a touching example of how they shared their love of art with each other.[40]

W hen she wasn't home, composing and being an aunt, Converse was availing herself of Manhattan's artistic offerings. She continued to spend time with Maude Brogan, with whom she took in operas by Orff, Stravinsky, and Verdi.[41] A testament to the fact that she had her finger on the pulse of the city's cultural scene, she attended José Quintero's epochal revival of *The Iceman Cometh* at the Circle in the Square, starring Jason Robards, and was favorably "struck" by O'Neill being "unlike some other modern (or perhaps MORE 'modern') playwrights when dealing with Grand Philosophy."[42]

Occasionally, she attended parties, like one that featured an impromptu steel drum duet by Pete Seeger and the Catalan composer Carlos Surinach. In yet another Zelig-like moment, she listened to a conversation between Surinach and a young student of Hindemith and Milhaud, and also talked directly to Seeger about music and activism. "Having seen P. Seeger several times on stage and several times in parlor, I continue to be impressed by the shining quality of his personality— unique among the solo entertainers I have seen," she wrote to Phil and Jean.[43]

A few weeks later, she reports, "You may recall suggesting [Dylan Thomas's] 'In My Craft or Sullen Art' as a possible song last summer . . . When I finished 'Recuerdo' I felt it might be a reasonable self-assignment to write one song a month for the next year or so."[44]

Phil wrote in "Connie's Guitar Songs" that she enrolled him and Jean as the charter and only members of her private "Song-of-the-Month Club" when she was writing and recording guitar songs, but it seems he may have been conflating two periods in his mind: Her move into formal art song appears to be when she inaugurated this regular practice, after she'd left guitar songwriting behind. If anything, Converse seemed even more serious and intentional in pursuing this new way of composing than she ever had been with her guitar music.

"I thought 'In My Craft' might be my assignment for December; and since it wasn't December yet, I thought I would take time to luxuriate in half-a-zozen [*sic*] possible settings before getting to work in earnest on it. Unfortunately, it jelled on me very suddenly at 8:03 P.M. of some night last week,—and all the other luxurious possibilities have perished by default, without a trial. But this is the chief hazard of art, what?"

"Sullen Art" sounds like an early study for the more mature, involved "Under a Lullaby" still to come. Like the narrators of "One by One" and "How Sad, How Lovely," this poem exists in a realm detached from the everyday world, observing humanity as though it comprised so many specimens in a jar. The poet labors by night, "when only the moon rages," not for the promise of wealth or fame, but for the innermost hearts of "the lovers" of the world (who, in almost Conversian fashion, are revealed by Thomas at the conclusion to be completely aloof to his efforts). Phil's suggestion that she set this text shows how well he knew his sister's mind.

Like "Les Deux Escargots" and the songs from "The Prodigal Nephew," "Sullen Art" is not designed to be something pleasantly hummed or sung along to. It is a quiet, reflective meditation, through-composed, with subtle authorial attention to tempo and dynamics.

When December 1 rolled around, Converse reports, "I stagger from the piano to the typewriter infatuated with the sound of my own composition . . . 'Sullen Art' is almost finished, and I do think it's the best thing I've done yet of this kind . . ." Then, a couple of weeks later: "I went back to 'Sullen Art' to polish off a few little details, and drat it all[,] but now the charm of the thing completely eludes me; yet I have changed it very little since the day I fell in love with it. This leads me to want to tamper with it further, but on the strength of my original impression I draw back . . . As for Recuerdo, after sending it to you I discovered that it is really fun to *play*, once you get up a little speed. It should be quite brisk. And dulcetly jazzy."

⁓

Despite this new artistic focus, Converse's guitar songs continued to have life, too. In July 1956, she signed a two-year contract with music agent Horace Linsley with the hope of getting a recording contract.[45] This refutes Gene Deitch's suggestion that her primary goal was to have other people cover the songs she wrote. Converse wanted to be a professional performing songwriter. Though she'd turned her back on composing guitar songs as an ongoing concern, she was open to the idea of performing them, or licensing them, or both, should those opportunities arise, even as her muse pushed her toward more art song.

"My agent rather manager phoned yesterday to say that he had a tentative display of interest from some recording co. I never hoid of," she wrote. "I'm sure he's had a number of turn-downs by this time but he remains cheerful."[46] Waiting for responses that never come from people in the business is a particular circle of hell that most working musicians have to endure. Converse did, too.

The verse of e. e. cummings, another hero, proved especially fertile ground for inspiration. "Apparently, January *is* going to be a Cummings [*sic*] month," she wrote. "I have got too far on 'Anyone Lived' to turn back now, though I had just about decided to do something less complicated; having just about so decided, I doodled another ten minutes[,] and off it began and up it grew . . . I'm afraid it's going to be an awful job and may run into February. But if it looks about to run that way, I'm going to pause and dash off something simpler, so as to live up to my new song-a-month motto."[47]

~

In the new compositions, exemplified by "Pretty How Town," the piano has a voice of its own, one that works in concert with the singer's, providing counterpoint, dynamic accents, and commentary on the vocal melody. As such, Converse's vision for how these songs could be ideally realized began to expand.

"... about Pretty How Town, I wish to note that it should really be performed by a mixed chorus in unison at the octave, so that the piano can grind along louder underneath and the tale gets a more Greek-chorus rendition."[48]

It's easy to see why the fragmented, witty language of cummings's original verse would have appealed to Converse, who often spoke and wrote in riddles:

> *anyone lived in a pretty how town*
> *(with up so floating many bells down)*
> *spring summer autumn winter*
> *he sang his didn't he danced his did*

There are themes here that are familiar to the Converse catalogue: children, animals, nature. The tone and flavor of the poem seems to point toward "The Age of Noon," an edgier song to come. And she adds a sweeping comic flourish to the end, giving it a fortissimo, two-octave, descending glissando—the musical equivalent of the singer falling down.

Dylan Thomas and cummings have long since achieved canonical status, but at the time that Converse was setting their words, their work was still quite fresh. Both were hugely popular among the art crowd—another example of her placing herself in the vanguard of contemporary writers ("Pretty How" was first published in 1940).

Satisfied with this one, she now wrote to Phil and Jean:

> *I stumbled through both Recuerdo and Sullen Art for Maude recently and she said she was impressed by the development of my accompaniments since the bumpty-bum days on the guitar. But she feels I'm not paying enough attention to "vocal quality" in the voice parts . . . One part of Pretty How Town is going to be pretty how vocal, or it seems so to me. What she means by vocal, in case you don't know, is a soaring, sweeping melodic line that a good singer can really go to town on.*

The remainder of this particular letter is a convoluted, humorous account of a conversation she'd had with a co-worker who'd had a fight with his wife over the fact that he'd kiddingly called her a fat pig:

> *I should explain that this cameraman is quite intelligent, that he is trying to build up his own printing business, and that his wife is fat. Anyway, he went on to ask me, "If anybody called you a fat pig would you get mad?" I said it would probably depend on how it was said and who said it. He said There you go, that's how a woman thinks. So I asked him to explain the Common Sense reaction to being called a fat pig. He said, in the first place his wife knew he was joking, but she got mad anyway. But in the second place, and more fundamentally, if you are NOT a fat pig, and who is?, why should you get mad when somebody calls you one? The truth is, he went on, if you do get mad it means you are not Well Adjusted. "I," he said, "am well adjusted. Know what that means? It means that there are only two ways in which anyone can hurt me: one is breaking my bones, and the other is taking my money. Suppose somebody tells me I shot a lousy half-tone. That doesn't hurt me; if it's true, so what? I usually do good work. If it isn't true, well, it just isn't true; it's no skin off my nose."*

> *I congratulated him on his adjustment. He asked me if I was well-adjusted*
> *and I told him no.*

Converse uses the episode, and the man's defense of his position in the matter, as a springboard for examining his conception of "Common Sense," the differences between reason and emotion in men and women, respectively, and for her critique of same. In her exegesis, she takes to task "the culture of it's-smart-to-be-slim and all-men-wish-they-were-married-to-Marilyn-Monroe."

She closes the letter with "Emotion is *not* always the herald of unreason . . . in fact it's much more likely to be the herald of deep reason, and should be treated with the greatest respect and attention—the more unreasonable it seems, the more attention it deserves."[49]

A couple of weeks later, in a "Bulletin for SOTMC members," Converse writes to Phil and Jean, "Your Yeats collection fell open at a short poem called The Peacock; I mean I knocked it off the table, so it really was an accident. So I glanced at the poem . . . and it framed itself perversely in a sort of brisk dry Handel or Purcell-type air, except not so pretty; and with no wet rocks or heather in the music at all; so I'm trying to make the music all peacock instead, and all I can say is, isn't it a pity I'm not Handel or Purcell because I'm getting sort of fouled up in the feather-adding . . ."[50]

The up-tempo "Peacock" is one of Converse's more effervescent art songs, which may have reflected the flavor of her neighborhood at that time, described to me by Harlem scholar Jonathan Gill as "a place apart—vibrant, colorful, and family-oriented." Unlike the Village, Hamilton Heights was filled with children, mom-and-pop shops, and observant people of many faiths.[51]

"The Peacock" boasts florid accompaniment for the voice—one she expected her younger brother to learn. Converse now often included homework assignments for Phil in her letters: "Rather than send us a tape [of the piano songs] where she would try to sing and play at the same time," Phil told me, "she required me to practice each song well enough to send her a tape I had made of each item, once I had them 'mastered.'[52] And she would grade me out, totally generously, you understand . . . [This] accounts for why I had all those scores in the basement!"[53]

But even if she'd chosen Phil as her willing performing avatar for these songs, he again told me that he was privately confused by her new direction. "I felt a lot of the 'folk' charm did not survive the piano," he wrote, adding, "There is a rather heterogeneous quality to this set."[54]

"Hallo! I am me. Are you somebody too?" Converse wrote, apparently unaware of anything less than enthusiasm from him. "Can you see over the top yet? *Is* there any top?" (a direct reference to Emily Dickinson, one of her spiritual forebears).[55]

"I'm in a lousy mood myself, wherefore plunge we into the calm chaos of the intellect . . . I am boggled down over both current songs and fearful for my deadline. February is such a SHORT month and often dreary . . . I see a black cloud coming, no bigger than an elephant's behind, so excuse me while I run for cover. Tally ho, Lady Chatterley's Mother."[56]

⌒

The increased frequency of correspondence between the two siblings resulted in not one but two long letters, both of them noteworthy, that had issued from Converse's typewriter on January 18, 1957. The first, entitled "NOTICE TO MEMBERS OF THE SONG-OF-THE-MONTH CLUB," informed her two-person fan club that:

All members who contract for three songs in any given three-month period receive a Free Song-Dividend if the weather holds. Following is the schedule assigned to you:

> *November: RECUERDO*
> *December: SULLEN ART*
> *January: PRETTY HOW TOWN*
> *Three-Month Dividend: THE RAINMAKER*
> *Tentatively Planned for Feb.: UNDER A LULLABY*

> *Just between us members, we've had a hot week here at headquarters. Monday night we solved the chief problem of Pretty How Town by dumping the fifth and sixth verses entire . . . Tuesday morning at the shop I took an anonymous English quatrain of the 15th or 16th century[57] and built around it some additional American folk-type lyrics . . . I brought the result home with me that night and sat down at the piano, determined to set it in all the beautiful cliches I could think of; and that is exactly how the melody has shaped up. That night it kept me awake two hours by running through my head as I polished up the lyrics. This is The Rainmaker.*
>
> *Wednesday night I worked over both numbers a bit more, and then retired at a reasonable hour; whereupon still another song—the lyrics, for a start—began dribbling over my roof-brain, and I like the idea so much that it will fairly certainly be my February number.[58]*

Whatever the issue was she'd been having with "Pretty How Town," one of the two verses she omitted was one that deals with marriage, something she would bring up soon with Phil.

∽

Under a Lullaby"—Converse would later retitle it "She Devises a Lullaby," repurposing it for her Cassandra Cycle—takes the uncomfortable, itchy darkness of "Vanity of Vanities" and ups the ante. If "Lullaby for P. Bruce" was intended to gently lull a child into peaceful slumber, "Under a Lullaby" is its evil twin, conjuring such unpleasant images as a screaming train, creeping tigers, floods that breach broken levees, and bleeding, deadly wounds—all of which seem to make up a turning "dark, slow circle" at "the center of the world." It's another nightmare, but unlike with "One by One," there is not even a sliver of hope here.

The song, with its almost postapocalyptic feeling, stands in stark contrast to "The Rainmaker," which may be the most melodically accessible song in Converse's piano catalogue. "The quatrain on which it was built," Converse wrote to Phil and Jean, "was given to me verbally by an acquaintance a year or more ago with the suggestion that it might make a nice song; the original wording, as I scribbled it down, is:

> *O West Wind, when wilt thou blow,*
> *That the small rain down can rain?*
> *Christ, that my love were in my arms,*
> *And I in my bed again."*[59]

Converse takes the evocative phrase "the small rain down can rain" and the romantic, windswept yearning of the original and transposes the action, and the spirit, to Harlem:

> *I'm going over Sugar Hill to help them do the haying*

Depending on which historian you talk to, "going over" to Sugar Hill for Converse would have either meant a walk of less than ten minutes to the northeast, or else was the very neighborhood she was living in. The designation "Sugar Hill" for the Harlem neighborhood today thought of as adjacent to the one where she lived with Paul and Hyla had been coined in the 1920s and referred to the life that migrants from the South had found there. As Harlem scholar John T. Reddick put it, "Imagine moving up from a shack in Mississippi with no amenities, and now you live in this big row house in New York with a living room, and a dining room, and two or three bedrooms."[60]

Converse transposes the action of the Renaissance-era English quatrain to modern times, though "the haying" she refers to seems anachronistic. One clue may lie in the song's title. N. Richard Nash's 1954 play of the same name had recently been adapted into a hit film starring Katharine Hepburn and Burt Lancaster. Converse may have seen one or both versions of a story about a spinsterish young woman whose family is concerned that she will never marry.

Some old crow is calling after me but what can he be saying?

Once again, a bird is talking to Converse. This time, it's the symbolically ominous crow, rather than a whippoorwill, and an old crow at that. And unlike the warbler in "Talkin' Like You," who conjures for the singer an erstwhile lover and also keeps her company, this bird's message is vague. The singer tries to make sense of it on a pleasant, sunny morning, even if the weather has generally been dry and hot. What everyone needs most is some relief:

Morning words and morning birds and sunshine in the lane
West wind, when wilt thou blow
That the small rain down can rain?

The song seems a companion piece to another new composition from this time, Converse's setting to "Somewhere I Have Never Traveled," also by cummings, with that poem's famous last line, "Nobody, not even the rain, has such small hands," keeping company with this new creation.

"I didn't take much pains with the accompaniment," Converse wrote of "The Rainmaker," with typical modesty, "just using whatever seemed handy phrase by phrase of the words so that it isn't very integrated; but since the whole thing is cliches anyway, and the general air of the ballad is the thing here, I trust none of us minds."[61]

As if. Her gift for melody and musical savoir faire is on full display here. Despite her claims to the contrary, Converse was not selecting random notes and motifs lying fallow in her consciousness. What sets this song apart from much of her piano works, most of which take advantage of that instrument's superior harmonic versatility to the guitar's, is that it's not difficult to imagine "The Rainmaker" as a guitar song. It's mostly all folkish major chords, and not many of them, either. "I will let slip the secret that I liked this one all the way, and still do," she wrote. "It cost me no sweat, except for the night I couldn't get the tune out of my head."

> *I'm going over Sugar Hill to do the raking after*
> *All the hay we made until today should reach the highest rafter*

As always, there are multiple entendres in her lyrics. She's talking about making hay, which may also mean that she and her neighbors are seizing an opportunity. But then comes the startling couplet:

> *Not a haze for seven days, the sky as bright as pain*
> *West wind, when wilt thou blow*
> *That the small rain down can rain?*

More trouble—a sky as bright as pain to go with the old crow that's heckling her in an indecipherable language. In contrast to the song's lilting, carefree-sounding melody, Converse's lyric for "The Rainmaker" suggests something else. After "railing at the weather," she calls again for the wind that will bring rain—though, this time she includes the reveal, the wish that lies underneath all else:

> *Then shall my love be in my arms, and I in my bed again*
> *West wind, when wilt thou blow,*
> > *That the small rain down can rain?*

And then, just like in "Trouble," and "We Lived Alone," she ends the tune on an unexpected chord. This time, though, it seems to ring with optimism.

⌒

Converse's other letter of January 18, 1957, had been atypical—a confessional, private attempt to bridge an emotional disconnect she was feeling with Phil.

"The following is an act of faith," she wrote, phase two "of a project which I set for myself after my visit . . . last summer. Phase #1 was getting acquainted with your extraordinary wife; *really* acquainted, I mean. In the past five months or so we have exchanged autobiographies at considerable length . . ."

This first phase had been the easier of the two, she explains, because "Jeaner *is* more verbal in personal matters than either you or I, for one thing; and for another thing, sometimes it is easier to get to know someone you've never known before than to get to re-know someone you have once known well and whom you like to think you still know well, no matter how much water has gone under the bridge." Whether that water was time, or her and Phil's experiences growing up as Converses, we'll never know.

She then describes her most recent visit to Michigan, a time in which she felt that "prolonged exposure to [your] wedded bliss made me hypersensitive to my own hard lot . . . well, I do find my lot hard," and a "shut-out-ness" due to the fact that both Phil and Jean were busy with work, but also (more important) "that there lay under us a sea of things that were not being said and should be said."

The letter is a rare instance of the self-reliant, individualist Converse expressing vulnerability outside her music. "What I wanted to demand, and would not be caught dead demanding, was a few swims in the sea of unsaidness," she wrote, sounding as though she were reciting lines from Susan Glaspell's play *The Verge*. Converse relates an episode of bursting into tears over some trivial matter during her visit: "The funny thing is that even if we were in perfect harmony in all matters, and I simply turned to you and said 'you are my brother,' I'd probably burst into tears just the same—not out of misery, not out of fear, but because my own deep affections, when I try to express them, do sometimes make me weep instead. I do not call upon you to understand this; but you do not know me if you do not know this . . ."

She goes on, expressing the idea that had resonated with Edwin Bock when he'd read my essay about Converse and thought about her out on the ledge:

For the best communication, the most satisfactory human relationship . . . it seems now to me that knowing and being known are prerequisites . . . Being a complex and inward personality, I have always found it difficult to make myself known. Well, by and large it has never too much disturbed me that I generally turn outward to each communicant only one, or one-or-two, phases of my own personality; that I generally conceal my own problems and listen attentively to those of others; that, indeed, without enjoying your apparent lack of inner conflict, I often turn toward the world a face much like yours—serene (or at least strong and cheerful) and imperturbable. But with you two, whose affection I value very highly, I wish to be known better and to know you better . . .

Rather than her typical tongue-in-cheek sign-off, she closes with, simply, "Love—Sis."[62]

Phil's response, a few weeks later, met with her satisfaction (many of Phil's letters to her were in her filing cabinet; this one was not). "My act of faith is richly justified," she wrote to him a few weeks later. "If your letter had been merely pleasing, I would have thought much less of it. As it is, it has evoked great pleasure, mild annoyances, several 'yes-buts' . . . and—not least—an objective admiration of your little mind. (Little here being, of course, strictly affectionate.)" She promises to make more allowances for Phil's busy schedule, as far as his side of the correspondence goes, and expresses gratitude for his understanding and his acceptance of her desire to be more known to him. "I feel very resonant today and high as a kite," she continued. "Lability is unsettling but I would not exchange my own temperament for rubies."[63]

❧

Converse's music continued getting deeper, too—more personal, even closer to the bone. When she mentions her new "Song for Old Wars" (a composition she would later retitle "She Hears of Old Wars" and include in her Cassandra Cycle), she tells Phil and Jean: "I almost feel as though somebody else wrote that one."[64]

The lyric points directly at the words of a poem she'd already written music for: Whitman's "When Lilacs Last in the Dooryard Bloom'd," once again suggesting that her settings for work by other writers sometimes served as rough drafts for what she eventually wanted to express herself. Here is Whitman:

> *And I saw askant the armies,*
> *I saw as in noiseless dreams hundreds of battle-flags,*

> *Borne through the smoke of the battles and pierc'd with missiles I*
>   *saw them,*
> *And carried hither and yon through the smoke, and torn and*
>   *bloody,*
> *And at last but a few shreds left on the staffs, (and all in silence,)*
> *And the staffs all splinter'd and broken.*
>
> *I saw battle-corpses, myriads of them,*
> *And the white skeletons of young men, I saw them,*
> *I saw the debris and debris of all the slain soldiers of the war,*
> *But I saw they were not as was thought,*
> *They themselves were fully at rest, they suffer'd not,*
> *The living remain'd and suffer'd, the mother suffer'd,*
> *And the wife and the child and the musing comrade suffer'd,*
> *And the armies that remain'd suffer'd.*

Yet Whitman's gruesome scenes of death and dying seem almost quaint next to Converse's, which involves a massacre of soldiers while they sleep, and imagery that ventures into the realms of frightening fantasy and metaphor:

> *Dark horses flew among them with wings like knives;*
>   *They roused the sleepers up where sleep had flung them*
>   *And seized their lives.*

Converse word-paints in the music. We see "lakes of shadow / where the sun was drowned" in her melody and piano accompaniment, the music taking on an ethereal, unworldly quality, like the soundtrack to a story from Ray Bradbury's *The Martian Chronicles* in which explorers encounter a world with its own rules and phenomena, eerie, strange, outside anything they've ever known.

The frosty feeling of the song found its parallel in the mood clouding the Harlem apartment. Paul and Hyla's situation, for its part, had only gotten worse, and they'd begun receiving professional marriage counseling.[65] By the time Luther Philip, their second child, had been born the summer before (in June 1956), there was near-constant stress and friction.[66] Even with the presence of Converse as her housemate and confidante, Hyla was on the brink of mental collapse. "If it had not been for your understanding and objectivity and moral support," she later wrote to Converse, "I might have cracked up."[67]

Converse continued to witness her older brother's ugly behaviors up close, and to be aghast. In addition to his philandering, he was stingy, slovenly, and unwilling to work for long stretches.[68] And he put Hyla through psychological torture. On two separate occasions during Converse's time living with them, Paul packed Hyla and the kids into their car, drove them to far-flung locales (once, to the Northern Adirondacks; the next time, to Hyla's sister's home in Monroe, Louisiana), and simply left them there, speeding away in the dead of night.

Baby Luther was only weeks old the first time Paul pulled this stunt. Because Hyla didn't drive and had no savings of her own, she and the infants were stranded for months on both occasions, with no means of transportation, no money, and little contact with Paul. Converse pleaded with her brother to recognize and amend the insanity of this behavior. She got nowhere.[69]

During Hyla's second exile, in Louisiana, Converse wrote to Phil and Jean, "[Hyla's] life here must look somewhat dimmer, narrower, and wearier. And colder; O frigid northland, O icemen without hearts of fire, O well-adjusted bank accounts, O pigs. Speaking of pigs, I hear that Hyla's sister's husband (south-born) does not favor racial integration."[70]

The domestic strain was also reflected in "The Night Is Freezing Fast," another A. E. Housman setting, one she gives music as chilling as the poem's title. Unlike "With Rue My Heart Is Laden," this poem comes from the end of Housman's career, but it shares themes with that earlier work. Death is conjured, the departed are memorialized: in this case, one friend now wears an overcoat "made of earth and sea." Housman's words here imply a gentle stoicism and acceptance about the inevitable cycle of life, but Converse hears something different. The forthright, plain folkiness of her "With Rue" setting has here given way to a piercing feeling of dismay.

With Hyla and the kids gone for long stretches, and Paul's comings and goings ever unpredictable, Converse's solitary time at the piano continued. On March 4, she wrote, "If my tape recorder (one of them) is still working that well, I will chatter on the back side of the poetry tape when I send it to you in a week or two if I could only read. So don't erase me unlistened, I would feel dreadfully demagnetized and all. Yrs, the Third sparrow from the left."[71]

A June 4 letter announces to the two members of her "Song-of-the-Month Club" "that There Will Be NO Song For July," as "the composer will be out viewing society from various apices."[72]

A few days later, she thanks Phil and Jean "profoundly for your various letters of cheer" about the music she was sending. "They fair turn my head." A discussion of a problem that Phil was having "'working out time' in the songs" follows, which advises him to look at the second hand of a watch to "count out various beats by trial and error for one-quarter or one-half minute to approximate a reading" if he does not have a metronome handy. "I don't have a metronome either," she writes. "In fact I'm an orphint [*sic*]."[73]

E rnest and Evelyn stopped off in Harlem en route to see Phil and Jean.[74] Discussing their impending arrival in Michigan, Converse gave Phil a green light to play for them any of her songs he saw fit. By now, she either finally felt confident enough about her music, and independent enough as a person in the world, to detach from Ernest and Evelyn's judgment, or else she had ceased to care about it entirely. She also mentions that she'll be heading out to see Phil and Jean again the following month; Ann Arbor was becoming a home away from home for her.[75]

On at least one of these visits, Converse performed at a small backyard party. The son of someone who would later become one of her closest friends in Ann Arbor told me, "My one strong memory, through the lens of a child, was seeing Connie sitting quietly, not quite part of the conversations. My Mother said that Connie was shy in the extreme, and particularly about singing in front of others. The only way to get her to sing was to ply her with wine. When she finally agreed, I was given to understand that this was a special occasion, and importuned to come down to be with the adults so we could listen. She sang for a long time once she began."[76]

That shyness may have been what kept her hopeful that her songs might be taken up by other singers. That summer Converse reported: "Every few months my guitar stuff hits some new periphery of the entertainment world and I have to meet people, copy off lead sheets, etc."[77]

This happened now as a result of her attending a cabaret performance by a contemporary, the vocalist Annette Warren, at the Blue Angel, a supper club on East Fifty-fifth Street co-owned by Max Gordon (founder of the Village Vanguard) and unique for being desegregated. Katie

Lee had performed her clever, original folk-like songs for voice and guitar there recently, to great success, which may have piqued Converse's attention.

With the increasing popularity of groups like the recently reunited Weavers and the up-and-coming Kingston Trio from San Francisco, demand for folky material was in the air as an alternative to the rock-'n'-roll trend. Perhaps this augured a place for Converse's earlier material after all. After Warren's set that night, mutual friends introduced them, and Warren expressed a desire to try out some of Converse's songs.[78]

Converse sent Warren handwritten sheet music for "Roving Woman," "The Witch and the Wizard," "Talkin' Like You," and "Playboy of the Western World." About the last, she wrote to Warren, "I have an idea that you might want to trim or rearrange the verses; I'm quite open to suggestion on things like that."[79]

As an aspiring commercial songwriter, she was nothing if not practical. "After you phoned today I got to thinking about stronger endings for the other three songs, and I thought up a possible substitute for the last verse of 'Witch & Wizard':

> *The witch settled down, and the wizard as well*
> *And both began raising the devil in hell—*
> *The devil is happy I guess;*
> *The witch can't stop witching, the wizard feels low—*
> *He can't tell his wife where to go, where to go,*
> *Because Hell is their legal address"*[80]

The song is a humorously grim take on marriage and parenting. Despite the fact that it was written in 1954, while Converse was still living in the Village, Phil often referred to it as his sister's thinly disguised portrait of Paul and Hyla's bitter domestic situation.

~

L ike others whose memories were suddenly unlocked when Converse's name was mentioned, Annette Warren let out a sharp gasp when I explained over the phone why I'd tracked her down at her home in Los Angeles. Although she was nearing her ninety-fourth birthday, Warren sounded decades younger.

"Oh my *god*," she declared. "Is she still alive? I *loved* her. She wrote songs for me, two songs . . . well, not *for* me, but she sent them to me, and I sang them for years!" Warren told me that Converse's songs had been showstoppers for her and that she knew she could always pull one of them out to bring down the house.[81]

It was strange and sad to learn that Warren had had success with Converse's songs for so many years and that Converse likely never even knew about it. After initially reporting to Converse that "she had used Playboy with success on the West Coast in nightclubs," Warren ceased to keep in touch with her.

She continued to perform Converse's songs, however, though she never made commercial recordings of them (nor was Converse paid royalties for Warren having used them in her act). When I told Warren of Converse's fate and her disappearance, there was a long silence on the line. Then, quietly, she said, "That just makes me sick." A tremble in her voice, Warren vowed to engage a psychic to find her.[82]

Still, she had gone to bat for Converse after they'd met in New York, and had set her up with at least one music industry audition. As Converse wrote to Phil and Jean:

> *I have to go play my guitar stuff to some wheel in a music publishing company owned by (Most Happy Fella) Frank Loesser. This type of thing always curdles me like a dentist appointment, and I've done it often enough to predict the*

verdict—"lovely, but not commercial"; and I wouldn't bother except that opti-
mistic people keep making appointments for me. This one was by the (girl)
night-club singer I told you about. While I was in A[nn]A[rbor] I forgot to
think up new endings for Playboy and Roving Woman, so I had nothing to offer
her when she called today. She is beginning rehearsals on her act today, but I
still don't know whether she'll use any of my stuff . . . She said she liked the
alternate ending I made for Witch & Wizard . . . If I am going to support
myself in my old age maybe I will have to be commercial.[83]

Sharon Sheeley was about to become one of the earliest (and youngest)
female songwriters of the rock-'n'-roll era with "Poor Little Fool"
(written for Eddie Cochran), but trying to imagine a similar treatment of
a Converse song like "How Sad, How Lovely" or even "Love in the Afternoon" makes it possible to understand why music executives kept showing Converse the door. Melodically and harmonically, many of her songs
occupied a similar place. But in terms of their emotional content, they
were worlds away.

Still, Annette Warren was not the only singer who expressed interest
in Converse's material. Sometime later, Elly Stone, another cabaret
singer, wanted to add "How Sad, How Lovely" to *her* repertoire.

Converse offered Stone the exclusive right to perform it for a year, for
which Stone offered her a royalty of fifty dollars. With no prompting,
Converse volunteered to accept half that, suggesting the lower fee might
act as incentive to have the song professionally arranged.[84] But unlike
Warren's abiding love for Converse's material, Stone's interest in it
quickly waned. She took the song, paid Converse the twenty-five bucks,
and then ghosted her.[85] When I tracked Stone down in 2014, she had no
recollection of the interactions, the song, or the composer.[86]

Stone had also never heard of a song called "A Thousand Shapes and

Shades," a "Voice and Piano" sketch that Converse copyrighted in 1957, and another of her originals for which no recording exists. It's a title that, on its own, could describe Converse's entire life.

The composition is a song of praise, and it sounds like one when played, even if the object of her devotion is human and not divine. Like in "Love in the Afternoon" and the soon-to-come "Andante Tranquillo," Converse's narrator is singing to someone she adores:

> *The color of your eyes never fades*
> *And you're only as tall as you are tall*
> *But your heart has a thousand shapes and shades*
> *And I know I shall never learn them all*

The melody is reverent, the chords behind it church-like. The singer tells her love that "to study your grief would take a while, for your tears have the colors of the sea" and that others fail to "see the hues that make you rich and bright."[87]

~

It's unlikely that Converse would have shared a delicate, stylistically out-of-fashion paean like this with singers like Warren or Stone, but whatever effect those showbiz nibbles had on her increasingly jaded attitude about the music industry, one aspect of her life that continued to bring Converse joy was her relationship with Phil and Jean. Returning from another jaunt to Ann Arbor, she detailed scenes from her flight home to them, which she deemed "quite satisfactory, even though I had only my nose and one eye above gin level."

> *You must just squirm and shuffle while I thank you for a distinctly superior*
> *vacation including the rendition of my music and the Grand Bender and Beef*

Stroganoff and Discursions and just the right amount of gin and tonic. Dear people, I miss you very much and think it most unkind of you to vanish into thin air like this each year, and hide behind six hundred miles of moonlight and snow pudding.[88]

Converse's efforts to get closer to Phil seem to have been working. He visited her (and, presumably, Paul) in New York just a few weeks later, and she was back in Michigan again a month after that.[89] About his trip to New York, she wrote to him, "I have extra keys so you can come and go and there are clean sheets and eggs in the ice-box. There might even be gin and tonic by that time. Turn about [*sic*] is fair play and you will have to consume about two quarts of gin while you're here to even us up."[90] When Phil's firstborn, Peter, arrived in December, she was out there once again.[91]

⌒

At some point in 1958, Converse would have learned that Sarah Thompson's older sister, Frances, had drowned herself in a Massachusetts lake. Perhaps this, combined with the greater intimacy she was feeling with Phil and Jean, led her to pay tribute to her brother and sister-in-law in two canvases she painted that year. As her fellow New Yorker Lorraine Hansberry once wrote: "One either writes, paints, composes or otherwise engages in creative enterprises . . . on behalf of humanity—or against humanity."[92]

Phil and Jean were successfully establishing themselves in Ann Arbor, upwardly mobile and in the market to buy their first home. But in her painterly tributes to them, Converse instead celebrates their respective, solitary artistic pursuits.

Phil plays piano, and while Converse renders him in almost saintly fashion, the squares of primary colors behind him suggesting the stained glass panes of a church window and the light falling on his face and upper torso causing him to stand out against the earthiness of his surroundings, we can't see his hands. His sideways glance gives the painting an edge of discomfort—that and a single red pane suggesting some unspecified conflict.

In the painting of Jean, the subject is sculpting, her focus directed intently on the bust of the head of a young child. A sculpting tool rises in her right hand, while her left hand grips her worktable for balance. On her table are a bright red pack of Pall Malls, a tall ceramic mug, another sculpting knife, and an ashtray with a cigarette at rest. Like Phil, Jean appears against a darker backdrop, her pale yellow blouse a contrast as light streams in from just beyond the canvas's edge, bathing the artist at work in a kind of ennobled light. But again, there is a note of subtle discord; Jean's sculpture, cool in contrast, looks away from its creator.

Converse loved to share her artistic expression with the people in her life. She made a painting for Maude Brogan, too, entitled *Orfee,* a work as atypical for her as it is striking. Her subject here is a Black banjo player, imposing and confident, one of his large, powerful hands frailing his instrument's strings. The musician gazes off past the outer limits of the canvas, his expression open, the billowing swirl of his bright red tie suggesting warmth and passion. Like her ongoing friendship with Sarah Thompson, Converse and Brogan remained close.

In one sense, Converse was reenacting her early days in New York, when she'd been fanning out in various artistic directions at once. In addition to these paintings, her musical activities now included a small professional job (recording "The Twelve Days of Christmas" for a company called Motivational Methods[93]) and even more ambitious piano-based composing: an opus written for Phil, called "Birthday Variations," and a new work entitled "Andante Tranquillo."

As with "Love in the Afternoon" and "A Thousand Shapes and Shades," "Andante Tranquillo" finds the narrator at peace, with both herself and in her feelings for the object of her affection. Its narrator, once again, is in love, but this love stills and calms her—something unusual to her experience, and seeming to build on the mere praise of those earlier songs:

> *My love, how is it that the arms of love*
> *Can clasp in quietness myself*
> *That stirs and runs about the world?*

Love somehow has the power to "still the grinding stones that sharpen me," softening her. It "loosens the hard tug of the earth on my delight; it slays all things away, even the vast and imperceptible flight of stars." This is luminescent language—the singer caressed by gentle, warm waves of serenity and acceptance—that brings to mind Roland Barthes's "I love the other, not according to his (accountable) qualities, but according to his existence; by a movement one might well call mystical, I love, not what he is, but *that he is*."[94] She closes the song by professing her admiration for her beloved's intellect: "How skillfully thy learning moveth me."

Learning was on her mind. "Birthday Variations," written to commemorate Phil's thirtieth birthday, is unlike anything else she composed, before or after—a long-form instrumental piece for solo piano that she delivered to him accompanied by a lecture/demonstration on how she'd come to conceptualize and compose it in the form of a nearly hour-long tape recording made especially for him.

On the tape, Converse explains to Phil that the composition is the result of her having assigned herself the song "Happy Birthday" as a jumping-off point, and had then turned the song inside out and upside down until it became something entirely her own. The influence of Gershwin, one of Phil's favorite composers, is heard throughout.

As pianist Christopher Goddard helped me understand, what Converse accomplished with it shows characteristic complexity, surprise, and innovation. Goddard explained that the relative looseness of the "variations" form, by definition, allows composers to highlight their unique range of expression and imagination. But Converse doesn't really do that here in the piano writing itself ("perhaps out of limitations on her part," Goddard guessed). Instead, the kinds of variations she explores are atypical for the genre.

"Primary among this is tonal contrast," Goddard wrote.

> *I honestly cannot think of an example from the repertoire that employs so many key changes, so often. Usually tonality stays consistent in variations because it's the only way we retain a connection to the main theme once the melody goes away. But the melody doesn't really go away here, it just takes on different shapes. There seems to be a sort of "developing variations" technique happening, a term coined by Schoenberg to describe Brahms's music, primarily.*[95]

Converse takes "Happy Birthday," smashes it to bits, and then sets about playing with the pieces—tossing and kicking them around, stomping on them, and then experimenting with different ways of putting them back together. In songs like "One by One," she'd yearned for a reality in which she could shine. Here, we see it, and the result is spectacular.

On her taped master class for Phil, Converse notes that the end of the "Variations" piece "reels off into space." She wasn't kidding.

The relationships Converse had with her brothers had moved in completely opposite directions. Her intense bond with Phil continued to grow, while whatever connection she'd had with Paul now fell apart. By early 1959, Converse was ready to get out of the Harlem apartment. Hyla had already left for New Jersey.[96] Bad scenes continued there during Paul's visits, including domestic abuse calls to the police and at least one hospital visit for Hyla.[97]

Converse, increasingly alarmed by Paul's behavior, joined forces with Phil to tell their parents about it. The two siblings each wrote to Evelyn about their older brother, detailing their reasons for taking Hyla's side as she sought legal remedies against him. Paul caught wind of it, resulting in a complete rupture between him and his siblings.[98]

"Paul was a difficult guy," Phil's son Pete told me, noting that he and his brother, Tim, did not see their uncle again for a quarter of a century, long after their aunt Connie disappeared.[99]

Converse moved into new digs at 46 West Eighty-eighth Street, just off Central Park—her final address in New York. There is no evidence that she and Paul ever spoke to or saw each other again.

CHAPTER 24

Cassandra

Whatever the real source of Phil's discomfort with his sister's art *lieder* was, it reached its apex around 1959, when she completed most of her first and only formal song cycle, her most far-reaching compositional endeavor since "The Prodigal Nephew." Happily, most of this one survives.

The shifting grounds in Converse's world being what they were, it's tempting to read into this set of songs what she may have been feeling at the time. She'd been surrounded by—and ultimately, had ejected herself from—the noxious living situation in Harlem, detaching physically and emotionally from her older brother, whom she now knew to be capable of heinous behavior and abuse toward both her nephews and her sister-in-law. She was living alone again, and now in the sixth year of her employment at Academy Photo Offset. And the source of one of her greatest joys—the relationship she had with Phil and Jean and their newborn—was about to be situated even farther away than usual; they were going abroad for a year, to France. To top it off, she was on the cusp of turning thirty-five, just like that.

Phil described this music to me as a "very personalized and often very opaque, autonal [*sic*], song cycle named ominously 'Cassandra.' One has no trouble seeing this latter subset as the early stages of the gathering massive depression that came to cloud her later professional work and produce her final disappearance."[1] In video footage provided to me by the musicians Betsy and Ryan Maxwell (who'd visited Phil in Ann Arbor a few months before I did in 2011), the camera focuses on Phil as Betsy sight-reads some of the Cassandra songs on his piano.[2] He grimaces and becomes visibly agitated, pacing the floor, hands thrust into his pockets or repeatedly looking at his watch, each note played seeming to press on a raw nerve. Watching it, I remembered what Phil told me when I'd first contacted him that same year, that he and his family were "long past the main grieving" regarding what had happened to his sister. That didn't seem to be the case here.[3]

I n Greek mythology, Cassandra is wooed by the god Apollo, who bestows upon her the gift of prophecy (in some versions, this is accomplished as her ears are licked clean by snakes while she sleeps). But when she then spurns Apollo's sexual overtures, he amends the gift with the provision that no one will ever believe her, a situation that eventually drives her mad.

Cassandra appears in Aeschylus's *Agamemnon.* When she speaks, as playwright Joseph Shragge explained to me, the play's lyricism "famously breaks down into a series of sounds—*otototototoi popoi da*—that are beyond human speech" (an idea that also fascinated Virginia Woolf, who devoted time and energy to translating Aeschylus's original Greek in her own study of the text).[4] Shragge described it as "broken language," and said, "It's possible that it was originally sung in a weird and unmusical or onomatopoeic way like a birdsong."[5]

Like Converse, Cassandra is an outsider, a misfit, a freak. Her "life story tells of repeated marginalization in every respect: sexual, social, cultural, and linguistic," Dr. Emily Pillinger has written. "Her marginalization is a result of her exceptional prophetic knowledge, but it is not the knowledge itself, so much as the fact that her message is never fully understood by her peers, that keeps her apart."[6]

∽

C onverse begins her cycle with a bold, theatrical fanfare to introduce "Cassandra's Entrance." It sounds like a processional, the sort of thing played by horns in a courtly palace to announce royalty. Yet the lyrics are anything but triumphant:

> *Here she comes, wearing her web of days, gone past the gossamer;*
> *Over the meadow fly the bees, to bud and blossom her*
> *Yet she is never content with spring; And must refashion it*

If these songs can indeed be understood as thinly veiled autobiography (as Phil suggested was the case), then Converse's self-esteem at this point in her life—either never high to begin with or never something with which she even bothered concerning herself—had now begun a slow descent into depths from which she was eventually unable to surface.

Cassandra's history, as Converse paints it, has been a bad one, and the cycle begins with a disgusting image: the singer encased in her days, which—rather than stretching backward and forward in straight lines— are instead wrapped around her, a mass of filmy, sticky spiderweb. Even the beauty of the spring, with its promise of renewal and rebirth, meets with her dissatisfaction. It's not enough for her. Nothing is. Many of Converse's narrators have wanted reality to be different, but this one makes her demands explicit:

That robins wait for words to sing; that truth be passionate;
That time and promises be one, giving eternity no mention;
That rogues do business in the sun,
Though sweet deceit be their intention;
That every gossamer be spun,
    from filaments of comprehension . . .

She wants birds to talk. She wants truth to have feeling to it, not just logic. She doesn't want to wait for heaven to receive life's promises. She wants men to reveal their intentions plainly, even if they're no good. She wants the world to make more sense than it does.

She is the husbandman's despair,
These many seasons;
Bright she may blossom, but she will bear,
Nothing but reasons

The "husbandman" reference here (typically a farmer, or one who cultivates) is ambiguous, but the last lines of the song are not. She's fertile, and biologically there is nothing to prevent her from being able to reproduce. And yet the singer gives birth only to reasons.

Reasons. Converse lets the word echo and shimmer uncomfortably by having the singer repeat it several times as the piece concludes. Converse's stand-in, like her, is childless, capable only of producing things that the world she lives in deems worthless.

Quickly, we leave Cassandra's world (as it is traditionally known) for the cycle's next entry, "The Age of Noon"—what may be the most artistically dazzling of the entire project. And also the most mysterious.

The song's literal plot involves a "she" and a "little boy" who take a walk in the woods together. There alone, amid the forest's natural wonders, "their ages were reduced to one," and they connect with each other in a way that lifts them beyond the particulars of their individual human experience. Boundaries fall away, nature compels them to relinquish their concerns, and suddenly, "The humming blood beneath the skin / Was louder than their words had been," and "The afternoon around them burned."

The song contains the most carnal imagery in Converse's entire oeuvre, right down to its title—possibly suggesting puberty, and "noon" representing both hands of a clock standing straight up and sexual awakening.[7] As in most of the Cassandra songs, the sensual, nature-driven poems of William Blake seem a likely inspiration here, though Converse's intimations of inappropriate physical intimacy that happens in private as a surrender to animal instinct make this tale her own.

And "The Age of Noon" is also filled with greater compositional complexity than any Converse song outside her "Birthday Variations." It has bold tempo changes and pensive fermatas. When, finally, "to his separate age the child returned, and she to hers," the two come full circle, finishing their outing as they began it, returned to earth as it were and talking "of the things they knew, vague and particular, sad and amusing, false and true."

Converse may have been missing her nephews P. Bruce and Luther. She may have been thinking about her newest nephew, Peter, some six hundred miles away in Ann Arbor. She could have been re-creating a scene from her childhood. Or the entire enterprise may be a work of fiction. The song concludes with a thrilling wordless outro for the piano, a lush and transcendent flourish. Converse was pulling out all the stops with these songs, giving to them everything she had as both poet and composer.

S he Warns the Children" returns us, however tenuously, to the world of Cassandra, who tells her young charges that they will come to understand how with "shrugs and frowns / To hide your wounds less they be counted." One's true self must remain hidden, Converse's narrator imparts, only a couple of years removed from her letter to Phil about aspiring to greater transparency and vulnerability. Almost as though she were using that very letter as a template, she tells the children to "Notice that your conquering brothers / Never cry and groan," and implores them to "discern the hurts of others / And conceal your own; Bleed and die alone; So save yourself from being known."

The singer's harsh, cautionary advice continues. She tells them to "beware of danger everywhere impending," that "suspicion breeds the thing suspected," and to "think of love as man's invention, prone to fail."

Embedded in this lyric is the idea that the narrator has only herself to blame for her troubled state of mind. "Love and hate," she warns, "are verdicts on your vice and virtue." If what she means is that virtue breeds love, and vice hate, it's possibly yet another commentary on the situation with Paul and Hyla, or else further evidence that Converse is still wrestling with the lessons of her Baptist upbringing. If the latter, it makes one wonder: What *were* the vices she was engaging in that produced these acrid, poisonous feelings? Was it merely the cigarettes and alcohol, or was she including her inappropriate relationship with the married Bill Barss (and with whomever else she may have been secretly involved)? She finishes her guidance with "Show your teeth to all your brothers / Let it be a sign / You are even with the others / You have paid your fine."

Teeth. On her cross-country road trip in 1949, she'd had to see a dentist in Arizona about a lost filling, and there is the mention in her letter to Phil and Jean comparing her having to go to an audition to the pain of a visit to the dentist. Later, the checkbook registers she left in her filing cabinet, beginning in 1968, reveal a long pattern of dentist bills, culminating with a large one in 1973 that was likely for either major repairs or even replacement.

For whatever reason, Converse did not take good care of her teeth. In the few color photographs she saved in which she can be seen smiling with her mouth open, they are grossly discolored.[8]

Again: "Show your teeth to all your brothers," her narrator sings. "Let it be a sign / You are even with the others / You have paid your fine."

Converse hadn't merely ventured into a new stylistic realm with these songs; the power of these lyrics, the mastery with which she draws these lines from her linguistic quiver and then fires them with expert precision show her in complete demand of her creative voice, her Cassandra swooping down like some vengeful god come to slay her tormentors, to tell the furious truth no matter who is listening, no matter who believes her or can even understand her. Unlike most of Converse's guitar songs, she is after the subconscious with the Cassandra Cycle. If this was to be her final artistic statement (which, in essence, it was), she was going to slam the door shut on her way out. As the writer, translator, and performer James Harrison Monaco told me, these lyrics are "as complex, rich, and endlessly analyzable as the best poetry of her time. Once you start digging into them, they become like a whirlpool in a way that makes them cosmic."[9]

⌒

A series of six pictures taken by an unknown photographer on August 22, 1959, show Converse in her new apartment, striking a series of poses: looking over her shoulder, a milk bottle in her hand; sitting next to her bookcase and record player with her legs crossed, smoking a cigarette and reading the back of a tape reel; staring at the photographer in note-taking mode, a clipboard on her knee; holding the receiver of a red telephone to her ear while draping an arm on her mantel. They look like the kinds of pictures intended for someone else, but in her coding of them there's no indication of whom, or why.

Then, in a moody shot that looks like it was taken later that night, Converse sits on her sofa and lights a cigarette. The clipboard is by her side, as is her pack of cigarettes. There's a different bookshelf, an ashtray, a drinking glass, and some sort of object with a strap behind her—maybe a pocketbook. A cheap-looking table lamp hangs sideways from her bookshelf, casting her in a muted, golden glow.

The photo is hypnotizing, a microcosm of her life. Converse is the camera's focus, but she is turned away and into herself, her gaze down, her attention intense and focused. She seems to inhabit a private, impenetrable space. We can see her, but we can't reach her. She is untouchable, unknowable. She's not there.

❧

No music survives for the cycle's next entry, "The Spinner in the Bone,"[10] but the psychologically excruciating lyrics do not let up. There is little light to any of these songs, little to celebrate, little to be happy about. Perhaps it's no wonder that Phil seemed to wince whenever these songs were mentioned, that he had the reaction he did when Betsy Maxwell played them for him. Maybe it's even why he never produced his own "Connie's Piano Songs" recording.

In "Spinner," Converse again employs spiderweb imagery, this time to describe the "riddles for the young" that she produces. "But still beneath the bone she sits and spins / Within the bone shell, dim by day and night." More macabre horror, more unease. In the span of a half-dozen years, Converse has gone from merely having a bed made of stone and an eye burnt by a star to being a creature trapped inside her own bone shell.

"Spinner" appears to explicitly address Converse's upbringing: The singer "ruined the cloth of all her hand-me-downs," choosing to cut away what she'd damaged rather than try to mend it. Here, again, is her rage at Ernest and Evelyn and at the constraints of the world they inhabited, occupied by "men with gods" and "the lives of women bound."

But this is Cassandra, too, condemned never to be believed. "Nor will the young / Fathom the webs and riddles of her tongue; / So in a devious way the curse is kept" as she continues to see the future in the webs she spins, not stopping to sleep "even as young lust moved her bones to dance."

In "She Thinks of Heaven" the singer once again expresses her world-weariness to a child. "I cannot learn to love / Visions of paradise," she sings, where she will have no voice, no lips, no blood, no heart. And yet:

> *The eyes of God would flicker in surprise,*
> *For I should weep although I had no eyes.*

The first lines of the cycle's Bach-like penultimate song could almost be Converse's epitaph. "A woman plagued by thought / Must cure herself with pain." Greek tragedy scholar Rachel Kitzinger wrote me: "Clearly, to me at least, Connie Converse found in the myth of Cassandra a story for her own sense that her voice cannot be heard, that her words, her songs, belong to a different sense of time and reason, that as a woman who sees with infinite clarity and deep perception she has to be an outsider. It's so moving."[11]

The singer is in pain, yet the only remedy is more pain. Here is the songwriter revealed as a masochist who tortures herself for her imperfections, for her inability to fit in, for the overactive mind that does not suit her, "or so most men maintain." If any of Converse's writings could argue for her status as a feminist, it's this one. Aligning herself again with Cassandra, "she dwells / In the markets of the mind, / Possessed by spells and bargains of a kind, that might confuse / A wiser woman's head."

The song ends with the singer's "tough hypothesis" that the only solution left her is to continue to allow herself to be tortured by her own thought. The first verse repeats, making for a repetitive loop from which she cannot escape.

In a 1963 letter about the Cassandra Cycle, Converse indicated that she considered it unfinished. Musing about how it might be realized in performance she wrote: "I should like to see a very small instrumental combination (bass-and-snare drum, and two—hopefully French—horns) used in place of the conventional piano," and suggested that "little fanfares between songs" could be used. "I would propose rounding off the cycle with a ninth item," she wrote, "which would be essentially a reprise of the opening song with some appropriate revisions."[12]

What distracted her from putting the finishing touches on her magnum opus when it had been her focus may have been a friend's unexpected offer: the opportunity to record her guitar songs properly, once and for all. At long last, Connie Converse was going to make an album.

CHAPTER 25

"Connie Converse Sings"

At this point in my research, if anyone knew Converse's music, they'd either heard her performing it live, decades ago, or they were in possession of hissy, probably off-speed second- or third- (or tenth-) generation dubs of recordings made by Deitch (in 1954) or by Converse (using her Crestwood machine). These were the tapes that producer Dan Dzula sourced when he was preparing *How Sad, How Lovely* for release in 2008.

But Dzula was also privy to an unsubstantiated rumor that the master recording of an unreleased Connie Converse *studio album* had once existed and been lost. Allen Swift, the voice actor who may be the one heard dueting with Converse on some of Deitch's tapes, told Dzula he was certain that "someone" had produced a session for Converse at National Recording Studios, but he couldn't remember the details. Only when Dzula was in Ann Arbor in 2014 to help consolidate Converse's papers did he unexpectedly strike gold: there it was, added to the pile of her other tape reels, something Phil had found in a box in his house somewhere, the rumored studio recording. It was labeled "Connie Converse Sings."

Even then, Dzula knew nothing else about it, though the tape box offered clues: It included eleven songs, all of them featuring her guitar and voice, and was made in 1960, another pivotal year in Converse's life—another inflection point, another radical decision, another series of events that demolished the plot of her story to that point.

Even as her focus was on her *lieder*, and specifically her Cassandra Cycle, Converse had continued to make the rounds with her guitar, performing at dinner parties hosted by people like the Ishiis and the Bernals. This was how she'd met Peter Cooper, a commercial adman with a passion for folk songs.

"There'd be a small group there," Cooper told me when I found him, painting a picture not unlike the one Barbara Bernal had remembered. "Maybe ten or twelve people." He recalled at least a dozen occasions when both he and Converse were present.[1] "She was always by herself," he said, confirming what others had told me about Converse being a loner.[2]

"Dinner would be followed by an informal presentation when music would be performed." Like the Bernals, the Deitches, the Crippens, Merle Edelman, the Ishiis, and who knows how many others back then, Cooper was transfixed by Converse's talent. And like Bill Bernal and Bill Barss, he felt compelled to do something about it.

Converse's contract with manager/agent Horace Linsley had expired by then, without any indication that he'd found even a nibble of real interest for her music from record labels. Cooper felt that if no one else was willing to make a proper Connie Converse studio recording, then he would do it himself.[3] Through his advertising and jingle work, he had access to studio time and called in a favor.

That February of 1960, Cooper brought Converse into National Recording Studios in Midtown Manhattan for her only known professional recording date, producing the reel that Phil had left for Dzula. Cooper remembered that though the proceedings went well enough, they were not particularly auspicious.

"I was a novice," he told me, "and she was shy. The number of takes we did of each song was limited—maybe two or three each. She had her way of doing them pretty set, so there wasn't much need to do more than that." The entire session took a few hours at most, he said.[4]

The tape box lists the album's contents as follows:

1) Down This Road (with Connie's layered/overdubbed vocals)
2) Honey Bee
3) Lullaby for P. Bruce
4) The Witch and the Wizard
5) I Have Considered the Lilies
6) One by One
7) Man in the Sky
8) Playboy of the Western World
9) Roving Woman
10) Talkin' Like You
11) We Lived Alone

"These recordings were just made for us, for archival purposes," Cooper told me. "I think by that point she'd pretty much given up on making it with her music."[5]

But Cooper was in failing health when I spoke with him, and he told me that his memory was spotty. Maybe they were indeed intending to put the record out, or at least shop it around? Two years later, Converse's former AIPR boss, Larry Salisbury, would write to her, "I have bought a turntable and will buy your LP record as soon as it is on the market."[6]

On the tape, Converse is singing her guitar songs again, a half-dozen years removed from that moment in her life when anything had seemed possible. As an artist, she'd since moved on from this body of work.

Hearing her revisit playful tunes like "Roving Woman" and "Talkin' Like You," with their youthful defiance and insouciance, it's hard not to read new things into these performances: regret, wistfulness, even a hint of shame. She doesn't sound invested. Rather that this being a triumphal, belated arrival for her music, the session instead represented a diminuendo, the flicker of a flame that had once burned bright.

~

Peter Cooper was not the only one trying to do something, anything, for Converse's moribund music career around this time. As if to add insult to injury on the occasion of her finally getting to record an album of her guitar songs past their emotional expiration date, Bill Bernal got in touch with her to commission Converse to compose the title song for a project he was co-producing for the Asthma and Allergy Foundation of America—an animated educational short called *Nothin' to Sneeze At*. She took the gig, which turned out to be a collaboration between her (as composer) and bandleader Turk Murphy, who arranged and performed the music with his Dixieland ensemble (with perhaps predictably gauche results, TV and radio personality Steve Allen provided the narration). Bernal must have known that Converse could use the work, and she was probably grateful to get it for strictly financial reasons, but as if to signal how artistically insignificant she deemed the gig, Converse didn't even give the song she wrote for it a proper name, calling it simply "Allergy Ballad."[7]

Part of the confusing eddy of activity in Converse's final year in New York involved her former boss and onetime nightlife escort Larry Salisbury. Salisbury was now living in Guilford, Connecticut, a small, conservative coastal village fifteen miles east of New Haven. He came to visit her in New York that February, the same month Cooper produced her session at National, and may have stayed with her in her new Upper West Side flat. "It was a pleasure to see you again," he wrote upon returning home. "You are improved by your hairdo and heellessness [*sic*] . . . I expect to see you here in April or May."[8]

Salisbury had not featured much in Converse's life since she left the AIPR almost ten years earlier. Now semiretired, he was pursuing various writing projects and engaging Converse as a freelance editor for his work. He, too, tried to help her, suggesting to the *Outdoor Life* writer George Heinold, his friend in nearby Madison, that Heinold's work could also profit from her editing services.[9]

Salisbury's correspondence had always been laced with innuendo— not unlike the kind of dialogue heard in *Seven Keys to Baldpate,* that creaky play already dated when Converse appeared in it in high school. A Valentine's Day invitation to visit him in 1956 had failed to move her ("You will have to bring someone with you if you stay the night[,] or risk gossip,"[10] he'd written), and a holiday card at the end of that year read, "I think I must abandon Victorianism and suggest (or recommend) that you visit me without a chaperone."[11] These entreaties continued, along with offers to underwrite her travel to see him,[12] but it wasn't until late 1959 that they really began spending time with each other again in earnest. "I am really anxious to see you and listen to you," he'd written to her that November.[13]

If the two had begun (or resumed, or continued) a May–December romance around this time, it's hard to pin down. His letters, ticklish though they be, don't offer real evidence. He could have been as much a mentor or a father figure for her, or an old flirt, as anything. As Salisbury's friend Sir Laurence "Laurie" Martin told me, "I find it hard to imagine him wanting to share his life on a full time basis with anyone."[14]

But Converse was going to see him in Guilford, and would stay at the new home he'd just had built there. She documented a springtime visit to him in April of 1960, taking photographs of Salisbury and the house and property. She had him take a picture of her as well, and the beaming smile on her lips suggests that, at the very least, something about being there made her happy.

If they were romantically involved, it may have been an arrangement built on mutual benefit. Converse's intense devotion to her nephews was clear in her letters and photographs from that time, and she may well have been feeling the biological imperative to have children of her own.

For his part, the lifelong bachelor Salisbury may have been looking for assurance that he would not spend his final years living alone and isolated in small-town Connecticut. Converse's relative youth and vitality might have counteracted what Martin described to me as his gloomy tendencies at this point in his life.[15]

This seemed too much of a stretch to consider until I corresponded with one of Salisbury's close friends from this time, Betty Bouallegue. Bouallegue and her husband met him abroad in the late 1950s, and she recalled Salisbury telling them about a much younger woman with whom he was involved, who lived in New York City and would come to visit him in Guilford.[16] When I offered a capsule biography of Converse's life to that point, and particulars about her beliefs and endeavors, Bouallegue wrote to me, in no uncertain terms, "I feel sure it was her."[17]

I pointed out the vast age discrepancy, but Bouallegue would not be dissuaded. "They were both idealists, purists, and had worked together on Asian Affairs," she wrote. As for Salisbury's mild-mannered letters to Converse, she said, "Larry did not wear his heart on his sleeve! And in my experience did not show any interest in attracting women as a pastime." She told me that though he was indeed getting on in years, he "was young in heart and spirit."[18] She insisted that Converse was the person in question, the woman in Salisbury's life.

As she was traveling to and from the Connecticut shoreline, Converse also seemed to be looking for something, anything, that might anchor her to New York, something to signal to her that she had a place there, that she belonged. She applied for membership to the music publishing organization ASCAP, perhaps hoping that it might assist in getting her songs greater visibility, or help her collect royalties from the few singers who were performing them, but her application for membership was denied. Converse was not qualified, the organization determined, because none of her compositions had yet been commercially recorded or published.[19]

The help that was available was the wrong kind, almost comically so—Bill Bernal commissioning her to write an educational jingle about allergies; Salisbury finding her a gig editing a writer's local stories about fishing and hunting; maybe worst of all, National Recording Studios had managed to lose the master recording of the session that Cooper had produced. He told me that he felt "terribly embarrassed" about this, but because the studio had "done it for nothing," he said he "felt badly about giving them a hard time about losing the tape."[20]

Then there was Susan Reed.[21] Reed was an established musical contemporary of Converse's. She'd gotten her professional start at a young age, debuting at the popular Café Society in the late 1940s while still a teenager—Converse may even have seen her act while living on nearby Grove Street—proving such a success that her initial two-week engagement was held over for two years. Reed went on to play at Town Hall and appear on Broadway, on television, and in film, in addition to having several major label releases to her credit.

"She was a sort of premature prototype of Joan Baez," Dick Weissman told me, known for her plaintive, genteel versions of traditional Anglo ballads that Baez would soon record, like "Black Is the Color of My True Love's Hair," "Lord Randall," and "Go Away from My Window."[22]

No less an authority than Alan Lomax had praised Reed in the same breath as stalwarts of the day like Josh White and Woody Guthrie.

But others, especially those in the new folk scene, were less enamored. "Poor Susan Reed," Ellen Stekert told me of Reed's reputation for being out of step with the folk trends of the time. "Everyone made fun of her."[23] Terri Thal told me similar things. Thal and her soon-to-be husband, Dave Van Ronk, were at the center of the scene at that point, and knew everyone. "Susan Reed was older than us," Thal said. "A five- or seven-year difference in age was like a generation back then. She was one of those performers who gave formal concerts in concert halls. It didn't sound like folk music to us."[24]

Converse's songs somehow found their way to Reed, and Reed took an active interest in them. But it was yet another example of the right idea paired with the wrong fit. Reed also inhabited a musical gray area that made it challenging for the industry to know how to market her: not gritty enough for folk; too folky for pop. Her politics didn't make things any easier. Having come to the notice of the House Un-American Activities Committee, Reed had been blacklisted.

By the time she got in touch with Converse, Reed was living in West Nyack, New York, with her husband and child, a situation that removed her even further from the new burst of folk music that was happening in the Village.[25]

But Converse's songs inspired her; Reed fell in love with them and wanted to help find them an audience. Converse mailed her omnibus tape to her, prompting an invitation to visit Reed in Nyack. Converse, ever wary but always game, accepted.

Over the course of a few days, the two women collaborated on demos of Converse's music, recordings that featured Reed's vocals and Converse's guitar playing.[26] When I began my research, Reed had just recently passed away, but I was able to get in touch with both her husband, Jim Karen, and their son, Reed Karen, the latter of whom told me that his mother had been a pack rat and that her effects were buried in heaps of uncategorized clutter.

Miraculously (and after some gentle but persistent prodding), Reed Karen put his hands on the tape reel his mother and Converse had made together, a one-of-a-kind artifact that he generously sent to me to digitize and preserve.

The tape features a nice sampling of Converse's guitar songs, with Reed taking the lead vocal on all of them, and Converse often capo-ing her guitar to accommodate the singer's register. Reed misses a note here and there, and seems to lack the sense of timing and dynamics that these songs demand, but her dedication to the material is clear. Still, there's a saccharine quality to her readings of Converse's material that serves to smooth out their rough edges, and that eliminates something essential. (Even "Trouble" gets resolved in Reed's rendition. Rather than landing on that uncertain major third chord, Reed's version instead ends on the obvious chord our ears expect. Maybe worse, on the last of several takes the duo does of this song, Reed affects a kind of hick southern accent.)

What's most interesting about these recordings are the new lyrics that Converse adds to a couple of the songs, the kind of tinkering she'd told Annette Warren she was open to. "Man in the Sky" gets a new second verse:

> *The man in the sky is made of stars*
> *He drinks from the dipper and fights with Mars*
> *His name's Orion and I can tell*
> *If once he'd love me, he'd love me well.*

Converse also tweaks "Talkin' Like You," adding a new, second B section ("Down in town, you bicker with everyone / Sounds just like the rooster in my chicken run"), but it doesn't seem to do much to improve upon the original.

The one keeper here may be "Sun, Go Down," a song Converse never seems to have recorded herself, but that Reed tried twice—once here, and once again a year later, on a demo she made with a professional accompanist. The song has the sort of all-purpose lyrics that Converse mostly eschewed in her songwriting. It's just right for a singer like Susan Reed:

> *Sun, go down, no use for you*
> *I got a man staying, never had a man so true.*
> *Moon rise up, and hear my song*
> *I got a man staying, never had him stay so long.*
> *Roses wither, and birds take flight*
> *But love's forever, if it lasts all night.*

The song is simple, harmless, and lovely, and in Reed's recordings of it, there is a brief window into another kind of musical career Converse might have had, had she only stuck around. As Gene Deitch had said about her "Incommunicado," "Sun, Go Down" sounds like a show tune, the sort of thing that would have been right at home in Jones and Schmidt's *The Fantasticks,* a production that debuted that same year.[27]

~

Betty Bouallegue recalled that it was around this time that things with Larry Salisbury and the younger woman he was seeing had come to a head. Salisbury "felt trapped and couldn't go through with it," Bouallegue told me. "The situation too greatly upset his well-guarded equilibrium." As she recalled it, the break came suddenly. "They were on the verge of getting married when he called it off."[28]

Married? Was it possible that Converse was talking about matrimony with Salisbury, and that her upcoming, abrupt decision to leave New

York was, in part, a reaction to his breaking things off and that not even Phil knew about it?

Though almost everyone who knew Converse in New York during this time is gone, many of those she was close to in the 1960s, after she moved to Michigan, were still around during my research. And though few of those people knew her to talk about her life in Manhattan, one of her closest Ann Arbor friends, Marcia Barrabee, evinced a knowing causticity about it. When I asked whether Converse ever reminisced about the kinds of things she was going through during the end of her time in New York, Barrabee replied, "Why the puzzle about Connie's inner life? Just listen to her music. You can tell that someone had done her wrong."[29]

At the same time, Phil and Jean had now been in France with little Pete for the past year. It had been a long separation from them, and from Michigan, with greatly diminished communication—and maybe that, too, had given her some new perspective.

Her Ann Arbor cheerleaders were set up for upper-middle-class respectability: Phil, especially, had gained real traction in academia, and was about to achieve international renown in the political science world with *The American Voter*, a book he co-authored (and one that became a touchstone text for the study of voting behavior in the country). Jean was now pregnant with their second child. The family was due to arrive from Paris with a sporty new car they'd purchased abroad and about to move into a new house as first-time homeowners.[30]

What was Converse's life, in comparison? Five years of working and hobnobbing with a scholarly crowd devoted to humanitarian goals that left them all running for cover because of their idealistic beliefs; a novel that had gone nowhere; ten years of trying to make it in the music business, including an appearance on a television show that had been a nonevent; a musical résumé of almosts and not-quites—nothing that had traction, nothing close to stability or professional success.

She was unaffiliated with the burgeoning folk music scene now centered in Greenwich Village. None of the people I reached out to from that milieu had even heard of her. Not Joan Baez, not Ramblin' Jack Elliott, not Ellen Stekert, not Judy Collins, not Happy Traum, not David Amram, John Sebastian, Carolyn Hester, Terri Thal, Barbara Dane, Luke Faust, or Dick Weissman. The name Connie Converse meant nothing to Peter Stampfel, nor to Paul Prestopino, Ethel Raim, Bob Yellin, Barry Kornfeld, or Chip Monck. Not even to Izzy Young, whose legendary Folklore Center on MacDougal Street, which opened in 1957, was considered a hub for anyone making anything resembling folk music in those days. Young told me that he felt he knew absolutely everyone back then (he was probably right). He'd never heard the name Connie Converse, nor Elizabeth Converse, nor of any Converse related to the scene.[31]

After one or two secret affairs, Converse was single and approaching middle age. Her daily existence consisted of punching in to a full-time job at a print shop, a hand-to-mouth existence. She was a skilled painter, illustrator, poet, and writer, but none of those things had provided her with a means of income. As her cousin Edie wondered aloud to me during one of our conversations, "Maybe it was frustration that she could do so many things that was the obstacle?"[32]

Some artists are able to spend their entire lives this way, swimming against whatever adverse currents happen to come their way. Very few of those people succeed in spectacular fashion, compromising not at all while enjoying great financial success and notoriety. (See Marlon Brando, Werner Herzog, Patti Smith.) Another, perhaps larger group finds ways to succeed on their own terms, choosing art over creature comforts and trading economic stability and renown for personal freedom and expression. (See most working artists.) But the grim reality is that many buckers of convention reach a turning point when they realize that the costs associated with following the uncharted way will only increase, probably exponentially, and things begin to feel unsustainable.

Every artist whose accumulated body of work has not made them a household name knows something about this. The lens changes. Instead of seeing the world from the vantage point of steadfast confidence and endless possibility, of song after uniquely personal song, of one happy project after another, we look around and see a landscape littered with accumulated effort, and attendant disappointment. Bitterness begins to gnaw. Despair sets in. A sense of deep, demoralizing defeat descends, especially if the realization happens to occur (as it so often does) at the onset of middle age. Suddenly, life is half over—an awareness that eclipses the bright vitality of youth with breath-stopping speed, the horizon fast growing dark. Our physical bodies begin to wear down. Those previously wide-open roads leading to success and achievement narrow into overgrown paths, their destinations now indistinct, some simply dead ends.

Add to this the indignities involved with being a workaday resident of New York City. If you've ever seen a beleaguered person of a certain age rushing to squeeze between the closing doors of a subway car during rush hour, a frantic look in their eye and an embarrassed look on their face, you know what this means.

I remember what it was like, as the child of working-class parents, to visit the homes of my friends whose parents had real money. Consciously or not, I noticed the accoutrements with which they surrounded themselves: the fancy hand soaps; the shiny appliances; the heirlooms, the antiques; the gourmet foods in their cupboards and the expensive artwork on their walls. After I'd had my first taste of professional success, in my late twenties, I remember making my first "adult" purchases, luxury items I'd always associated with people who had made it: a brand-new mattress, home delivery of a daily newspaper, my first brand-new suit, a used car.

As Converse entered her late thirties, she had few such things to call her own. Economically it was still very much a man's world (just one of any number of examples: When the first credit cards had been introduced two years earlier, in 1958, a woman was generally not allowed to apply for one unless a man co-signed on her behalf). Although she was never one to place much emphasis on the importance of possessions or creature comforts, she had to know that, unless she changed the story somehow, her daily life in New York was going to get only more difficult, only more uncomfortable. She was still young enough to try a new way, but it had to be soon, and it had to be quick.

Two of her contemporaries, Nelle Lee and Diane Arbus, both faced their own kinds of crossroads in 1960. Lee, a struggling writer supporting herself with a job as an airlines reservation clerk, completely overhauled the novel she'd been working on for years, adopted the first name Harper, and published *To Kill a Mockingbird*. Arbus, a fashion photographer, opted to trail writer Joseph Mitchell as he documented the city's underbelly of freaks and outcasts—a project for *Harper's Bazaar* that radically altered the focus of her work, leading to the indelible images that propelled her to the forefront of avant-garde photography.[33]

But Converse had already done her artistic about-faces, morphing from aspiring fiction writer to performing songwriter of catchy tunes to composer of serious, challenging art song. Nothing had worked. As she'd written to a friend in France earlier that year, "I am still a printer, an aunt, and a struggling middle-aged artist; no news on those fronts."[34]

Maybe the music world was not where she belonged. Maybe New York wasn't, either. Maybe she could do something different. Maybe somewhere else, as someone else.

Whether for these reasons or others, at the end of 1960, Converse began telling people, friends and co-workers, that she was taking a "sabbatical" to Ann Arbor. This was pure subterfuge. As she'd done a decade and a half earlier at Mount Holyoke, she was pulling up stakes, abruptly, and not telling anyone why.[35]

"We were surprised that she wanted to move," Phil told me. "We had the sense that something had happened that made her want to leave New York."[36] When I asked him what that might have been, he said he had no idea.

N o idea." This was the same answer Phil had given with regard to her dropping out of college, to what she'd done in the year before her arrival in New York, to what her love life had been like (other than his winking references to her being promiscuous), to how she'd landed on TV, to why she had suddenly stopped making music. Why wasn't Phil able to answer these basic questions about his sister? He told me that she never once spoke to him about her reasons for the move.

When pressed on the subject, and whether there might not be some clues in the letters she wrote to him at the time, he replied, "Any self-revelation on Connie's part is very hard to find," something that sounded true and also very not true.[37] Had he forgotten her letter to him about knowing and being known?

Phil's son Pete told me he felt it entirely possible that the rift between his uncle Paul and aunt Connie may have been a contributing factor to her decision to move to Ann Arbor (and to stay there, rather than return to New York). And Bruce Converse, who was there for her departure from the city, all of six and a half years old at the time, remembers his aunt Connie saying goodbye to him, his brother, and Hyla. "She left when Phil and Jean came through New York en route from Europe. They'd brought a Renault with them, in which they were all going to drive out to Ann Arbor together.[38] Her departure was upsetting to all of us—Connie included. But she was a decisive person. She told us, 'It's better for me to make a fresh start. I know it's hard for you to understand, but this is something I have to do.' She was weeping as she left."[39]

If it's true that one of life's great paradoxes is that the essence of a thing can hold two opposites, then the tears Converse shed as she left New York for good may have been ones of both sadness and joy. As she packed up her belongings in preparation for the life that waited for her in Ann Arbor, it may have felt freeing to think of finding new homes for whatever furnishings she'd accumulated during her moves from two different apartments on the Upper West Side, to the Village, to Harlem, and then back uptown once more. Maybe she even put some things out on the street for neighbors or passersby to pick over: a floor lamp that had never worked right, a chair with a broken back, a vase that once held flowers.

Ann Arbor, a place she loved to visit, her home away from home, would now *be* her home, with its gentler pace, its quieter atmosphere, and its socially and politically progressive community. The world was changing. After back-to-back Eisenhower terms, John F. Kennedy had been elected president. He wasn't much older than she was.[40]

Converse never explicitly called her departure from New York the abandonment of her musical ambitions, but for all practical purposes, that's exactly what it was.

It wasn't that her guitar songs had failed. They'd made lasting impressions on the consciousness of people who became her lifetime fans— people like the Deitches, the Ebys, the Bernals, the Crippens, the Ishiis, Peter Cooper, Bill Barss, Merle Edelman, and Cliff Roberts—but none of them was well positioned enough to be much more than that.

The people who championed her songs professionally—Elly Stone, Annette Warren, and Susan Reed—had done so within their own limited followings, but none achieved a level of favor for them that might have held any real promise for Converse's future as a composer of popular songs.

Her opera had gone nowhere. Maybe Marc Blitzstein saw the score, or heard parts of it, or both, but there's no record that he offered her any help or guidance with it. Or maybe the distractions of working a full-time job, living in a dysfunctional household with Paul's family, and whatever was happening in her well-guarded private life had sapped the energy Converse required to complete such a large-scale project.

Her art songs, culminating with the Cassandra Cycle, the pinnacle of her poetic voice, may well not have made it past the ears of an audience of a tiny handful of people: Phil and Jean (who told me they didn't much care for them), Maude Brogan, Ginny Gerhard, and whoever those singers were.

As E. B. White once wrote, "The residents of Manhattan are to a large extent strangers who have pulled up stakes somewhere and come to town, seeking sanctuary or fulfillment or some greater or lesser grail. The capacity to make such dubious gifts is a mysterious quality of New York. It can destroy an individual, or it can fulfill him, depending a good deal on luck. No one should come to New York to live unless he is willing to be lucky."[41]

Converse was anything *but* lucky. And in a lifetime that contained what can be seen in retrospect as a few profoundly ill-advised decisions, this one may have been her most star-crossed. There was no way for her to know that at the precise moment she chose to abandon New York for the Midwest, that very same month, a young man calling himself Bob Dylan would come roaring into town from the opposite direction.[42]

Dylan brought with him the willful notion that someone armed with no more than a guitar and an un-showbizzy voice and look could not only write and perform idiosyncratic, introspective songs filled with poetry and literary references, but that it was possible to succeed and even become wildly popular doing so, and without sacrificing a shred of artistic integrity. It was a fight that Converse had been waging, unsuccessfully, for more than a decade—a fight she now had surrendered.

The connection was clear to Ellen Stekert. After I first sent her some of Converse's music, and with no prompting from me, she said with absolute amazement, "She was the female Bob Dylan. She was even better than him, as a lyricist and composer, but she didn't have his showbiz savvy, and she wasn't interested in writing protest songs."[43] Dylan was in the right place at the right time. Converse was not.

Because Converse's music was largely unknown, her direct influence on what happened next in American music is impossible to establish. She existed outside the culture, outside musical history. None of the surviving people from those early days of the folk boom had heard her, and there's no way to prove that those who have passed (Van Ronk, Odetta, Leonard Cohen) or any of those who may have influenced them ever heard her music, either.

But they may have, or their friends may have, or both. Music can infect and permeate consciousness in ways that seem to defy logic. Look at the memories of the Crippens, of Merle Edelman, of Barbara Bernal.

Without a single commercial recording or public concert appearance to her name, is it a leap to say that her music could have influenced the singer-songwriters who followed in her wake? Sure. But then, she lived in New York City, in Greenwich Village, in the 1950s. She performed a slew of private concerts for admirers who were infatuated with her music, against a backdrop of tremendous cultural and intellectual activity. Blitzstein, at least, knew who she was. So did Seeger. If laypeople who'd heard her back then could still recall her songs five and six decades later, what kind of unwitting influence might those same songs have had on the influential working musicians of her day, or on the people who knew those musicians? However nonexistent her professional successes were, the music she made was out there, in the ether. It couldn't have existed in a complete vacuum.

Converse and Dylan, each of them a virtual unknown in that frigid January of 1961, effectively swapped places. They could practically have waved to each other from the road as their paths, and destinies, crossed, missing contact by the narrowest of margins.

Yuri Gagarin became the first human to fly in space that year, Kennedy ordered the failed Bay of Pigs invasion, the Berlin Wall started going up, and Roger Maris overtook Babe Ruth as the home run king. By late October, Bob Dylan would be signed—by John Hammond for Columbia Records—to record his first album.

The singer and songwriter Connie Converse was exiting, stage left. But to only suggest that Converse could have been another Bob Dylan is insufficient, and diminishes her activities and achievements in other realms that were still to come. Connie Converse the musician was checking out. Elizabeth Converse the woman was heading west, and moving on.

PART IV

The Twentieth Twentieth

The mind is a jungle with little wars going on in it,
and sometimes an Armageddon.

—ELIZABETH CONVERSE,
"The War of All Against All"

CHAPTER 26

The Nearest Star

A nn Arbor, Michigan, in the 1960s was, according to local historian Alan Glenn, "a wild and wooly place that regularly made national headlines" and "a key center of political and cultural revolution that rivaled the better-known Berkeley, Madison, and Columbia."[1]

Phil Converse told me that, once his sister had settled in here, she was eager to join the fray.[2] Alongside Jean, she volunteered for Ann Arbor Women for Peace[3] (the local chapter of the national Women Strike for Peace movement) to protest agianst the threat of nuclear testing in Ann Arbor airspace. This was where she met super-activist Marcia Barrabee, who'd spoken to me about what she understood to be Converse's romantic troubles in New York.

Barrabee was a leading voice of dissent in the community, so central to it that she played host in her home to the likes of Martin Luther King, Jr., and Dr. Benjamin Spock. (She would also make her basement available to draft dodgers en route to Canada during the Vietnam War.)[4]

I found Barrabee in her mid-eighties, living in an assisted-living facility in Pennsylvania. Over the course of a series of lengthy telephone conversations, she had a good deal to say about her old friend. "Everyone was in awe of her," Barrabee told me. "She was so smart. It seemed like she was from another world. She was unusually soft-spoken, very rational, would rarely raise her voice. And she would often come in at an odd perspective on things. She always made me feel intelligent. If she ever made a suggestion about something, or corrected me on some fact or other, she would never do it in a disparaging way."[5]

If Converse's move to Ann Arbor was a reset, an attempt to start from scratch, she was also effectively erasing her decade and a half in New York. She was once again unemployed and working on a novel, just as she'd once been, fifteen years before, only now in decidedly less stressful Michigan. She was again living in a small studio—in what Phil told me was essentially student housing, near the university.[6]

Converse did not advertise herself to her new community as a composer, a songwriter, or a performer. Save for a small number of the countless people I spoke to from her thirteen-odd Michigan years, people there had little inkling of her musical accomplishments. Most knew her as someone who kept to herself and about whom they knew little personally.

But Barrabee and Converse had been close, and Barrabee did sometimes see this other side of her friend come to the surface. "When things would get rough at our meetings, Connie would pull out her guitar and play," she told me. "And sometimes when I would visit, while we talked, she might pick up the guitar and fiddle with it or hum a little, but she never *sang* any songs that I can remember. I was not aware of her New York experiences at all. I just had the sense that she'd had a terribly sad love affair there. But I had no clue that she'd had this other life of trying to write music,"[7] or that Converse had anything simmering back in New York.

"Susan Reed has a tape of her concert, which she would like you to hear," Hyla wrote to her sister-in-law eight months after Converse left.[8]

Whatever tape that was may have featured Reed singing a standard repertoire of old folk songs, but it may have also been a warm-up for the more ambitious presentation she was about to give in Manhattan.

On Saturday, November 11, 1961, as part of the 92nd Street Y's Saturday evening "Folk Concerts" season at Kaufmann Hall in New York City, Reed appeared in a headlining concert, accompanied by guitarist Victor Messer.[9] Her program was organized into thirds; the first and last sections were devoted to various folk songs of Irish, Cajun, and English origin.[10] But the literal centerpiece of the show was listed as "The first performance of... a group of original songs by Elizabeth Converse." This was a major engagement, and the most significant public exposure Converse's music had been given since her *Morning Show* appearance nearly seven years prior.[11] Reed performed eight Converse originals, but in her refined, affected way—representative of the old-fashioned style that Bob Dylan and company were musically rebelling against.

"It was a full house and it was splendid," Converse's friend the author Ruth Karen wrote to her from New York. "My own personal preference, since no one asked me, is still for a more gutty, sophisticated rendition of your sophisticated songs... Reed's renditions were pure and lovely—only. The audience went most for the 'Playboy of the Western World,' for which it screamed a repeat request ... Your populus was sensitive, responsive, well dressed, well behaved ... Summary: it was a successful concert."[12]

Reed continued to promote Converse's songwriting. Two years later, Bill Bernal recorded his impressions of another of Reed's Converse-centric concerts, writing to say that the Ishiis and the Robertses and Merle Edelman had been there, too—what he called "the faithful Converse nucleus." Bernal reported that Reed did not perform "Talkin' Like You" ("to everyone's disappointment") but that "she did a goodly number, a whole section of the show." He, too, however, sensed the disconnect between material and performer: "My own feeling about Susan Reed is that her voice is great ... but I think you need a female Ed McCurdy—a throatier, more visceral singer . . . Susan is too refined . . . She said your songs had 'a bit of earth in them'—but she left it out."[13]

Sarah Thompson wrote to say she'd hoped to be at this concert, too, but a case of chicken pox had prevented it. In her letter, she reported "news of the old gang," which included two of the three Eby sisters (the third, Pat, had long since moved west with a gold prospector). "The news is none too good," she wrote; one of them "sounded quite drunk (just a little after high noon)" when Thompson had recently phoned, while the other had recently fallen off the wagon and was receiving shock treatments.[14] Neither of the Eby sisters seemed to be in a condition to attend Reed's concert, either.

"Nothing exciting happened after the tryout of your songs," Reed wrote to Converse after the show. "My friends liked them. I guess *your* friends didn't . . . It hurts my feelings." She continued, "I still love them & the people whom I trust love them. We just have to find our audience."[15] Unfortunately, Reed's star went into rapid decline. Within just a year or two, she would retire from the music business entirely, devoting most of her time to running an antiques store in Nyack and eventually sinking into dementia.

⌒

But Converse's attention was elsewhere. If she had kept open the possibility of returning to New York City and resuming her life there, her activities during her first year in Michigan didn't reflect it. She seemed here to stay, and she was.

Maude Brogan, Converse's former road-tripping pal who'd spurred her to develop her classical composing chops, wrote from New York to ask, "Are you reveling in your independence? It's nice that you were able to get settled with relatively little added expense . . . Have you been able to get accustomed to having free time? . . . I forget how it is, not working."[16]

Indeed, Converse was now at liberty in her new town and able to follow her whims. She embarked on a number of simultaneous projects, including one she'd begun in her final months in New York—a "Statistical Study of 1000 Melodies."[17] It ranks next to "The Prodigal Nephew" and the Cassandra Cycle as one of her most industrious, and quixotic.

IBM card — 80 columns, 12 rows

Cols. 1, 2, 3, 4 = letters of lead-in notes, if any (12 positions, 12 possibles)

Col. 5 = letter of note of first major accent (blank if accent is silent)

Cols. 6 = durations of note in Col. 5 in standardized eighth-notes :

Row 1–	2 eighths	Row 7–	8 eighths
" 2–	3 "	" 8–	9 "
" 3–	4 "	" 9–	10 "
" 4–	5 "	" 10–	11 "
" 5–	6 "	" 11–	12 "
" 6–	7 "	" 12–	13 or over

If col. 6 is empty, the note endures one eighth

Col. 7 = letter of 2ND note

Cols. 8 & 9 = distance (in half-tones) and direction (up or down) between note in col. 7 and preceding note:

COL. 8				COL. 9	
Row 1–	1 up	Row 7– 4 u	empty cols. mean same note	Row 1– 7 u	Row 7– 10 u
" 2–	1 down	" 8– 4 d		" 2– 7 d	" 8– 10 d
" 3–	2 up	" 9– 5 u		" 3– 8 u	" 9– 11 u
" 4–	2 down	" 10– 5 d		" 4– 8 d	" 10– 11 d
" 5–	3 u	" 11– 6 u		" 5– 9 u	" 11– 12 or more u
" 6–	3 d	" 12– 6 d		" 6– 9 d	" 12– 12 or more d

these can be re-analyzed by the letter in col. 7

Col. 10 = duration of note in col. 7; proceed as in Col. 6.

Col. 11 = letter of 3RD note
Cols. 12 & 13 = halftone intervals as in Cols 8 & 9
Col. 14 = duration as in Col. 6

— And proceed with 4 cols for EACH NOTE UP THROUGH 12th note – 50 cols
(14th note – 58 cols
16th note – 66 cols)

4th note – Cols. 15–18	9th note – Cols. 35–38
5th " " 19–22	10th " – " 39–42
6th " – " 23–26	11th " – " 43–46
7th " – " 27–30	12th " – " 47–50
8th " – " 31–34	

Uses for remaining columns :

1. duple or triple time ?
2. coding for type of song ?
3. letterwise progress of major accents ?
4. harmony ? modulations ?

Sample page from Statistical Study of 1000 Melodies

The study appears to be an attempt to understand, scientifically, what makes a successful song. Converse was essentially doing by hand, ear, and an early computer what programmers a half century later would do on platforms like Pandora and Spotify, when they put computers to work analyzing a song's "data" to predict what other songs like it might appeal to consumers. "She was predicting the future," professor of psychology Dr. Susan A. Nolan told me. "She was *tagging*!"[18]

Converse wasn't interested in the business side of the equation (i.e., What will *sell* a song?); but rather: What is it that makes a good song *good*? What are the musical attributes that enduring songs share? And what did they have in common with *her* songs (all of which she included in the study; see Appendix A). The degree of imagination mixed with fastidious, formulaic intellect and minutiae she applied to investigations like this seems to inhabit the same universe found in the work of creative geniuses from Leonardo da Vinci to contemporary cartoonist Chris Ware—a level of inquiry and obsession so complete that the mind just stops in awe to behold it.[19]

It was clear from how Phil talked about his sister that he recognized this. But if Converse had imagined that living in close proximity to him might ignite some collaborative sibling energy, she now had a rude awakening. Though Phil was knowledgeable about the science of statistics, and though she sought to engage his interest in her project, he shut her down. "I might have been a little impatient with her," he told me.[20]

Instead, it seems, most of the time she got with his family was spent with his two young boys, Peter and now Tim, born within a few months of her move to Michigan.[21] "We were so busy with our jobs and raising our kids," Phil said. "We didn't have a lot of time for keeping track of what Connie was getting herself involved with." They had no idea, for example, that she'd also recently completed writing and illustrating a children's book.

⌒

S napfritzel" survives as a thirty-two-page, single-spaced typescript with illustrations. It tells the story of a young family comprised of a struggling artist father, a breadwinner mother who works as a plumber, and two small children named Henry and Dido.[22] When I showed Converse's illustrated manuscript to children's book author and illustrator Sophie Blackall, she was impressed by its level of artistic accomplishment. It's "completely charming and disarming and of its time but also somehow fresh," she told me.[23]

The story was mostly created, and meant, as a balm for Hyla's kids, P. Bruce and Luther, who were experiencing the trauma of their parents' ugly split—a drama in which Converse continued to be enmeshed, even from a geographical remove.[24] Hyla wrote to tell her that she and the kids loved it and that they all read it together every night. She'd formally asked Paul for a divorce that summer of 1961, and Converse offered what moral support she could, even returning to the East Coast for a brief visit, in late 1962 or early 1963.[25] She remained close to P. Bruce and Luther for the rest of her known life, faithfully sending them presents and cards for their birthdays and holidays every year, no matter how precarious her financial state. When Bruce was still young and just learning to play violin, she shipped him hers. He told me he'd played the instrument in the school orchestra all through junior and senior high school and in the pit orchestra for high school musical productions.[26]

Hyla wrote to Converse that Paul's secretiveness had been a large part of their problem, a pattern identified and shared with her by his psychologist. Paul would not tell Hyla where he was when he went away on business, nor even what his salary was. Even when I talked with Leslie Converse, Paul's daughter from his second marriage, she told me, "I never really knew what my father did for a living."[27] And then, of course, there was his ongoing affair, which he conducted at the apartment of his mistress.[28]

But obfuscation wasn't an ongoing behavior unique to Paul. Converse and Phil hid their drinking and smoking habits from their parents. Converse seems to have engaged in secret relationships with several people. Even now she was pretending to her New York friends that her time in Michigan was temporary. And Phil—Phil had gone out of his way on several occasions to privately share with me details about sexuality and his sister.

Secrecy. Converse's uncle dying of psychosis in a state hospital; Edie Converse Neff being allowed to live her life thinking that her mother, Helen, was actually her sister; whatever was in those photographs Albert Converse's widow burned in the driveway after he died; the fact that Converse kept the details of her life in New York City, and her musical persona, from most of the people she befriended in Ann Arbor; Luther Converse naming his daughter after Connie while simultaneously concealing his aunt's existence and then refusing to talk about her when it was discovered; whatever was in all those files in the cabinet that Phil had dumped; whatever really happened to Connie Converse.

All families have secrets. For this family—or at least some of them—curating those secrets was an ongoing activity of their lives.

∾

Whether one of those secrets for Converse was an affair she'd once had with the married Bill Bernal (as my conversation with Gene Deitch had suggested), the two continued to keep in touch well after his divorce from Barbara. Having commissioned her "Allergy Ballad" for *Nothin' to Sneeze At*, Bernal now wrote to her about another short he was making, one he hoped she'd help score with a new song. "I've written in the ballad parts in rough form . . . [and] the producer likes the song as I have roughed it in," he informed her.[29]

This has to have been something called "House," a demo she self-recorded for Bernal that first February in Ann Arbor, when she was also finishing "Snapfritzel" and working on the "Statistical Study."[30] The incomplete composition is a surprising return to the guitar song form she'd started with a dozen years earlier and the first of these she seems to have written since "Empty Pocket Waltz" in 1955.

Bernal's persistence may have driven her to compose on guitar again—that, or she may just have needed the money. (For all its triteness, the modest fee she received for the "Allergy" commission represented the financial high-water mark for her songs to that point.) And the absence of the disapproving Maude Brogan, who had discouraged her guitar song making, may have had something to do with it, too. For whatever reason, Connie Converse the clever songsmith now briefly twinkled back to life, one more time.

She begins it with a spoken introduction over some arpeggiated chords:

> *To some people,*
> *A house means a tent.*
> *To some people,*
> *House means rent.*

The verse then begins, as she sings:

> *But when you start to make your score*
> *Home means something more . . .*
> *A house, a house, of wood or brick or stone,*
> *A place to call your own*

> *A house is home.*
> *A house, a house, a bit of grassy ground,*
> *With roses all around*
> *A house is home.*
>
> *Home is where you spend your finest hours*
> *Home's the place to grow your hearts and flowers*
> *Watch the kids grow tall,*
> *Winter spring and fall*
> *A house, a house, to hold your joys and tears*
> *To mellow with the years*
> *A house is home.*

Another set of verses continues in this same vein, extolling the pleasures of a house that can be "shelter from the cold," "a happy journey's ending," and a place for "sheltering your dreams."

Unlike with her earlier home recordings, which document only completed works, in "House," a bit of her process is heard as she engages in trial and error, trying to get it right. The fact that there is no final take (and that the words seem unusually mired in clichés) suggests that this was a work in progress, one she may never have finished to her satisfaction. The words may have just been placeholders, and no further correspondence with Bernal about it exists. What's touching about the lyric, given where she was in her life, is that it expresses in the simplest, most direct terms the singer's longing for something she never seems to have found: a safe place for her to relax and feel at peace.

❧

Brogan wrote again to update Converse on doings back east, and asked, "I thought you were coming to New York in the late spring?

What happened?"[31] Journalist Amy Schaeffer, another New York friend, sent a note reading: "Congratulations!! And all that jazz. I know a bar mitzvah is supposed to be a solemn occasion. But yours is, I don't know, somehow different... I hope the sabbatical works out well in every way."[32] (The "bar mitzvah" reference is unexplained.)

Schaeffer and Brogan were part of a cluster of Converse's New York City friends who did not seem to subscribe to gender norms of the day—a group that also included Brogan's former roommate Ginny Gerhard (who'd played piano for the 1955 rehearsal of "The Prodigal Nephew").[33] Each of them spent their lives unattached to men, at least in a romantic sense. Gerhard's relatives described her to me as "asexual," and Barss's daughter called Schaeffer "mannish." Brogan, with whom Converse took numerous extended road trips in the 1950s (and who appears alongside her in multiple photos taken during that time), was referred to me by Judith Raskin's daughter Lisa (who called Brogan "family"), as having "a shroud of privacy" around her private life and "possibly gay."[34] And then of course there was Sarah Thompson, who lived most of her adult life as an openly gay woman.[35]

Converse was also friendly with two openly gay men (the playwright Andrew Burris and the artist Merle Edelman) and had at least some connection with another (Marc Blitzstein).

It seems safe to say that, if nothing else, Converse was accepting of ways of being in society that were alternative to the norms of her time.

I happened to mention this while talking with Dr. Catherine S. Forest, the daughter of Hanne Sonquist, one of Converse's close friends in Ann Arbor. Dr. Forest is an academic physician with a specialty in gender spectrum care at UC San Francisco residency. We'd been talking about Converse's reclusiveness, her intensive focus on cataloging and organizing, her unusual physical presentation, and her seeming lack of romantic partners. Dr. Forest thought it possible that Converse may have been what today is called neurodivergent. When I brought up this particular circle of Converse's friends, Dr. Forest suggested that "it would have been easier for Connie to be with other people who did not present in stereotypical gender norms," but was careful to say that "there is no way to diagnose her in retrospect."

A nother letter from Schaeffer asked: "Have you had more inspiration out there than here? I certainly hope so after making the big change you did . . . I miss you very much; miss not being able to jump up and call you, curse you out and make a date for dinner and a show."[36]

Schaeffer was not the only one longing for a dinner date with her self-exiled friend. One of Converse's former colleagues at Academy Photo Offset—someone I'll call Anthony to protect his identity—was writing to her as well. He now sent her a check for an undisclosed amount, writing, "I hoped it could have been more . . . Take it, Connie, and please don't mention it."[37]

Why was Anthony sending Converse money? Was it just another instance of people sensing that this was someone who needed help? A family member told me that Anthony "always took care of people," and that "he was always there for anyone who had a problem."[38]

After sending whatever money he did, Anthony wrote to tell Converse that he would be in Detroit soon, for a bowling tournament. He offered to take her to dinner while there, if she happened to be interested and free.[39]

Apparently, she was both. In mid-May, he wrote again:

Just a few words to let you know what a wonderful evening it was and do hope there will be more. I made the hotel just in time, and the boys were all packed and waiting. The only thought in my mind was, why did I let the fellows talk me into a train ride—when I could have had so much more time if I flew there. If I did not disappoint you and if you should come East will you get in touch with me? Ed [Pierry, one of their co-workers] asked me if I saw you and I told him you couldn't make it to town and we just spoke over the phone . . . If you care to answer this letter this time[,] write Ed's name on the envelope and write him a few lines. This way, in case you do write me in the future—well, you know what I mean. If you do write to Ed—just write somewhere in the letter that you'll take a rain check on that dinner I promised you and that will be my answer that you care to see me again.[40]

Shades of Larry Salisbury. Shades of Bill Barss. Shades and more shades.

Converse saved these letters from Anthony, despite the fact that, outside of their long stint together at Academy, the two didn't seem to have much in common. Family told me that Anthony had grown up in Bergen County, New Jersey, in a large Italian American family that included six siblings. As a young man, he was accomplished at sports and had flirted with a career in professional baseball. He got married in the early 1940s before serving on the front lines in World War II; when the war ended, he settled into domestic life and began raising a family and working at Academy. Anthony had never been to college, and his letters reveal him to be a fairly straightforward man of the day—a bowler, a numismatist, handy around the house, a gardener, and a devoted husband and father. The affair, such as it was, had clearly been conducted in secret, and there's no telling whether it was a continuation of something that had begun while she was still at Academy, or if it was instead the brief consummation of a long-standing office flirtation.

Anthony wrote again in mid-August to say that Ed Pierry was going on vacation and would not be back until after Labor Day. "So if you are up to it, I sure would like to hear from you in the next two weeks. The reason I say this is because I won't have to share your letter with Ed—I know I'm selfish—but maybe you would want to tell me something just between us." He tells her of the problems they're having at the shop in her absence and urges her to consider returning to her old job. Then he writes, "Thanks for writing that letter to Ed, I hoped some of it was indirectly meant for me. The reason I said to write Ed last time was so [as] not to make things look so—you know, when Ed is around he wants to know everything about everyone. No one knows about us and no one will. In your letter, you said you were running out of money and will have to go to work soon."[41]

But when Ed Pierry wrote to her at around the same time, his making mention of a development at Academy suggests that there was more than one lingering office intrigue involving Converse. The letter begins with his telling her how much they missed her, personally and professionally. "[Anthony] said that you have had quite a rest and it's about time for you to come back." What follows is the eye-opening content: ". . . When I think of the proposal you received I'd like to wring your neck. If you were to meditate just a little and say very, very slowly: 'Mrs. Nate Turkel, MMrs. NNate TTurkel, MMrss. NNaattee TTurr . . . horrible, isn't it?"[42] Had Nate Turkel, the owner of the company, proposed to her? Was Ed interested in her as well, and was this the reason for the steps taken by Anthony to hide their involvement?[43]

It sounds like the makings for a novel, which is exactly what Converse was now close to completing a draft of—one that had progressed to the point where she was ready to begin shopping it to publishers. Schaeffer and Barss were on the case, acting as her unofficial literary agents.[44] Barss, who'd advocated for getting Converse's poetry and lyrics published during their affair in 1955, had gotten a green light from a Houghton Mifflin editor for her to submit her manuscript. But nothing came of it, and the novel appears to be lost.[45]

O n the fiction project, I got 'encouragement' but not enough, and have given that up again, at least for a while," she wrote to her friend the author and historian Ellen Joy Hammer in January 1963.[46] She must have also written as much to Salisbury, who continued to keep in touch, though his letters to her in Ann Arbor now contained none of his previous innuendo. "I am very sorry to hear that your fiction work has not yet impressed a publisher toward publication,"[47] he wrote to her now. "With encouraging comments from publishers, you ought not shelve your fiction permanently. Remember, 'Good Earth' went to 22 publishers."[48]

In another letter, Salisbury wrote, "If you have suspended fiction, have you not been able to wangle [*sic*] a degree from your present associates? You are insufficiently hardboiled in your own interests."[49]

Converse was a step ahead of him. In 1963, at the age of thirty-nine (and now twenty years removed from her last classes at Mount Holyoke), she decided to go back to school.

T he book on Connie Converse, as it has generally been known in the years since her music was released in this century, has it that her move to Michigan represents a quick fade to black. This is wrong. It would be more accurate to say that she'd found an environment that seemed to better suit her at this point in her life, one that was aligned with what she wanted now.

"I have no desire whatever to live in a metropolis again," she wrote to her friend Hammer; "it's just not my cup of tea."[50] She now moved into a new apartment, one also not far from Phil and family, on whom she could drop in at any hour, just as they could drop in on her. Time spent with this set of nephews took place in a happy atmosphere, unclouded by the sort of corrosiveness that hovered over some of the relationships in Paul's family.

Most of all, she was returning to earlier passions, including working to make the world a better place. And where better to do this than in a town like Ann Arbor—essentially, a big, extended campus of the University of Michigan, infused with broad-minded energy, seriousness, and youthful idealism, and one of the country's hubs of liberal thought and activism?

As she wrote to Hammer: "I got fascinated by the problems of conflict definition, and conflict resolution, decision theory, and all the New Thought in the social sciences some years before I came out here, and didn't really realize when I came that this would be such an ideal spot for it." Enrolling in the bare minimum at the university (one economics class) allowed her to establish academic status at the school, but this was a means to an end—footing that would allow her the chance to have ideas she'd been working on to be considered for publication. "I have no expectation of plodding on to a degree."[51]

Her reasons for selecting a course in economics probably had less to do with the subject, per se, than with the man who oversaw that department. Kenneth Boulding had been at the university since 1949, and was a leading economist of his day, even as his theories marked him as an outlier in that field. Boulding was brilliant and formidable, "half Milton Friedman, half Mahatma Gandhi." Like Converse, he was an artist with a broad range of interests; in addition to his scholarly work and innovative insights, he wrote poetry, painted, and would "sing entire Gilbert and Sullivan musicals from memory."[52]

Boulding had also helped found the relatively new Center for Research on Conflict Resolution (the CRCR), housed at the school.[53] The Center's quarterly, *The Journal of Conflict Resolution*, was becoming an influential publication in academia during the escalating conflict in Vietnam, its contents later described by Boulding as "the beginning of the Peace Research movement."[54] *The Journal*'s intent, he'd written in its debut issue, was "to devise an intellectual engine of significant power to move the greatest problem of our time—the prevention of war."[55]

The Center's personality reflected Boulding's: it was bold and innovative. Freedom Rider (and author of the Students for a Democratic Society manifesto "The Port Huron Statement," just drafted in 1962) Tom Hayden had an office there, and his fellow SDS members regularly came and went. The Center's staff operated, as one of them told me, with a sort of "cowboy happiness," and the atmosphere was exciting and loose, with students coming in, without much oversight, to make use of the Center's phones and copy machines for their activist agendas.[56] There was a sense that something was happening there, something cool, something important.

Converse noticed, and she made sure they noticed her, too. The work that the Center was doing was not that far removed from the work she'd been doing at the AIPR when she'd first arrived in New York. She befriended Boulding and his wife, Elise (who would become as important and influential in peace studies as her husband—each of them would be nominated for the Nobel Peace Prize),[57] and was soon hired as his personal secretary.[58]

But Converse was interested in more than taking memos. Ten days before the Cuban Missile Crisis broke out, she submitted a paper to him describing a "game of ideas" she'd been working on, hoping it might be considered for publication in the *JCR*. She also sent it to Anatol Rapoport, leader of the university's Mental Health Research Institute—another example of the kinds of connections she was making. A Russian-born mathematical psychologist, Rapoport (who began his career as a pianist and composer in Vienna, and was a one-time member of the American Communist Party), was a leading figure in systems sciences, and studies in conflict and cooperation, and peace research.[59]

In "Modular Dialog: A Game of Ideas," Converse describes the parameters, rules, and function of a game that could be put to use on a societal level as a way to study the nature of conflict, and as "partial compensation for the information explosion" in which "even highly-trained people may find themselves ill-equipped to understand social controversy outside their immediate fields."

Converse was proposing a paradigm in which conflict between players could be studied, broken down into data, and then analyzed for the greater good.[60] She gives examples of different kinds of ideas that could be debated, how the players would be scored, and a way of coding the results of each game played.

> *If the game is to be widely useful, however, special installations would be required. The simplest installation would consist of two mutually soundproof rooms with an intercom system between them and some equipment for keeping records . . . recording the formal moves as they are made (verbatim statements and code numbers); for keeping track of the sequence of moves and signaling the available alternatives at each juncture; and for keeping a cumulative and visible record of the progress of the game for the benefit of both players and of bystanders.*

Those games that Converse had invented for her and Phil to play as children, and the ones she later devised for her nephews, had nothing on what she was proposing here. In her description, she writes that her "game, if found both playable and useful," could "become in itself a little institution." She proposes "to establish this game of ideas in the public consciousness."[61]

Connie Converse created a game that she wanted to institutionalize and make part of our everyday American life, in order to mitigate (or even solve) human conflict.

The essay was not selected for publication. What survives is a condensed version of whatever she originally submitted—a revised draft prompted by Rapoport's suggestion that she winnow it down. In her cover letter to Boulding, she notes being anxious to mimeograph, at the very least, seventy-five to one hundred copies of "the detailed game manual . . .

I could supply the labor for this," she wrote, "but not the stencils and paper, because I'm too broke."[62] The "complete . . . original long version" of the project, including her game manual "and extras," was among the items in Converse's filing cabinet that Phil "dumped."

A new acquaintance—likely someone she met working with Ann Arbor Women for Peace, for which they both volunteered their services—somehow learned about Converse's musical output and expressed an interest in it. This was Mary Critchell, described by her son Peter as a "whirlwind of volunteer activity" and someone who was always eager to help people in need.[63]

In the fall of 1963, Critchell wanted to try to get the Cassandra Cycle into the right hands. But with all the activity and excitement happening around the Center, Converse almost couldn't be bothered. In a letter, she tells Critchell that it has been suggested to her that "these songs might well be re-arranged for a women's chorus . . . [but] I am so overloaded with non-musical chores that I doubt I could manage it myself this year."[64] (See Appendix B.)

In a repeat of her trajectory at the AIPR, when she'd gone from doing clerical work to writing scholarly articles in what seemed like no time, Converse quickly moved up the ranks at the Center. Just after the Kennedy assassination on November 22, and only a year since she'd begun doing secretarial work for Boulding, Converse was offered the position of managing editor of the *Journal*.[65] Phil, an academic world away in the political science department, later said "she went her way, and I went mine, professionally speaking. I had no idea what she was doing."[66] He admitted to me he was "astonished" when he learned about his sister's rapid and assured ascent.[67]

The *Journal* post was anything but glamorous, but it was important. Converse was in charge of a concern with international prestige, one built on promoting ideas and understanding. She had a title. She had an office. She had a staff. Maybe even, for the first time since her days at the AIPR, she had the sense that what the world wanted of her, and what she wanted to offer, were in agreement.

Converse threw herself headlong into new role, not only reading and editing manuscripts, but also overseeing the business of printing, advertising, and managing subscriptions. She attended board meetings and worked closely with both university and Center staff.

"Peace research was a relatively new idea," the Center's former director Robert Hefner told me. "And we were in the process of becoming the most important journal on world peace and international relations in the world."[68] As they did, Converse—amazingly—was at the helm. She now focused all her energies on reading and thinking about peace, and on being part of the solution.

Riley Trumbull, in her mid-twenties then and a generation younger than Converse, began working at the journal around this time, and had clear memories of the first time the two met. "I liked her from the beginning," Trumbull told me.

Trumbull is a visual artist, her observations and memories more detailed and vivid than those of most people I spoke with. Converse "seemed like a grown-up" to her, someone she respected and admired.[69] "Elizabeth was a really good, safe person who didn't need anything," Trumbull told me. "She was complete." Like Barbara Bernal, Trumbull took careful note of how Converse looked:

Her complexion was rather pale and thin-skinned—as a strawberry redhead might have. She had somewhat freckled arms which could get a light tan but never dark, and the hairs on her arms were very pale golden in the summer, and her eyelashes and brows were also pale and gold-ish. Her eyes were a pale blue. Her posture was rather tight even though she had a slouch—her arms often crossed and her shoulders hunched as if holding something in, or hiding behind. It was in the manner of an ill-at-ease preteen. Shy. Afraid to be exposed, almost afraid to be seen. Being frightened in a deep sense if not in the immediate situation.

Her intelligence, wit, and good humor could be seen and felt. That kind of plainness, purposeful dowdiness can be a protective shell against being found attractive. Or it could be just bewilderment at what it takes to understand the marketing of prettiness[,] i.e. "how to be a girly girl." I remember that she often rocked a little on her heels when standing.

There was something solid in her presence/bearing. I always felt she was smart, kind, funny, and deep. When I picture her[,] it is often with that defensive posture of arms crossed, but I didn't perceive that she was lacking. Because I thought of her as complete, I didn't think of her as lonely.[70]

Riley Trumbull now became my Virgil for understanding the Ann Arbor scene at the time, and Converse's role in it, both professionally and socially.[71]

"Everything at the Center happened by merit," Trumbull told me. "It makes sense that Elizabeth would be given that job. It was massively important, but she was capable, well-organized, so smart, and willing to do it!"[72] Like a lot of Ann Arbor people, Trumbull referred to Converse as Elizabeth (or, less frequently, Liz). Converse was a different person here from who she'd been in New York.

Converse received little outside recognition for her work at the Center, and her pay was paltry compared with what men there were making (or compared with other kinds of employment she may have pursued). But what she did was having an impact. She was making one of the most important journals in the world run and grow, and everyone involved knew it.[73] Hefner described her to me as "brilliant" and as "the keystone figure that kept everyone together," an idea supported by every other colleague of hers with whom I spoke.[74]

She spent a lot of time with Boulding. "She was devoted to him," Trumbull told me. "And they were together a lot. There may have been some tensions with [his wife] Elise. Ken Boulding was a handsome man."[75]

John Tropman, on faculty at the time, told me that Converse was "unique as a woman leader," and that she had "a bemused disdain" for some of the heads of the various movements on campus who "seemed in it for themselves as much as for the causes."[76]

Jerry Hinkle, whose office was three doors down from hers, told me that Converse "stuck to her knitting. She wasn't someone to engage in small talk with, and she wasn't someone drawn to parties. Her office was staid, serious. If you went in there for something, you had the sense that you were disturbing something important. But she had everyone's respect. The *Journal* was her life."[77] Trumbull said almost exactly the same thing. "She held everything together. She was on call every minute. She *was* that Center."[78]

⁓

Whether she was conscious of it or not, part of Converse's motivation for going back to school and working at the Center may have been to advance that part of her story, even to prove something to Ernest and Evelyn. Ever since Converse's decision to abandon her Mount Holyoke studies, her mother had been vocal in her disapproval of her choices. Evelyn poked fun at her songwriting endeavors and belittled her attempt to write an opera. She generally couldn't understand what her daughter was doing with her life. Relatives told me that Evelyn expressed disappointment to them about the fact that Converse had become an "old maid."[79] And Ernest's stony silence when it came to her activities may have been his own kind of rebuke.

But now Ernest's health was declining (the result of Parkinson's disease), and maybe Converse saw an opportunity. If she could not resolve her lifelong differences with her father, maybe she could at least come to terms with them, and him, while there was time. She may not have been the daughter he'd hoped for, but she could now finally boast of having a real career, of having achieved some fast and irrefutable recognition in her new position, of having done things her way and succeeded. She'd even become a featured lecturer in town, and was giving advertised talks at two established, intellectual gathering places for activism and discourse: Guild House and at the First Presbyterian Church (Converse's copies of these lectures were also among the items discarded by Phil). As John Tropman told me: "She had community prominence."[80]

And she was doing it in Ann Arbor, which continued to be at the center of the national conversation. When Lyndon B. Johnson made his "Great Society" speech on May 22, 1964, he'd chosen the University of Michigan's commencement as his venue. That next spring, when Converse's fellows Boulding and Professor Bill Gamson helped others to organize the first "teach-in" at the university (an overnight protest staged in repudiation of the Vietnam War on March 24, 1965), she was there helping, too, on the front lines, a witness to history. The event had generated bomb threats, made national headlines, spawned more teach-ins and protests around the country, and has been cited as the start of the national antiwar movement.[81] After it helped fuel the idea to hold an international conference that September in Ann Arbor, "Alternative Perspectives on Vietnam," Converse would be one of its primary organizers.[82]

She was at the center of all this, working, protesting, organizing, editing, lecturing, watching, while also helping to anchor the Center's activities and publications. Unlike during her creatively exciting time in New York, when—as a songwriter— she'd been a few steps ahead of the moment, Converse in Ann Arbor was now a part of it.[83]

Until now, it had been as if her natural inclinations had brought penalties rather than rewards. Her left-wing ideals of the late forties, her guitar music, her cartooning, art song, fiction, and unavailable romantic partners—all these things had burnt her eye. But now—at age forty— she was succeeding.

It hadn't been a straight line. But in the summer of 1965, it seemed as though the prodigal daughter could, for the first time, feel sanguine and even a little confident about returning home for what might be her final visit with her ailing father.

Alas, what could have been a moment of some closure for her instead became something else. While she was en route to Concord, Ernest Converse died.[84]

CHAPTER 27

Markets of the Mind

A parent dies, and our sense of time, even of ourselves, undergoes transformation. A person who's always been there, present in our earliest dreamlike memories, a part of the fabric of our consciousness—someone who has never, not for one second of our existence, *not* been there—is gone, and no matter how inevitable the moment may be, no matter how we've prepared for or imagined it, we can't understand the impact it will have until it happens. Because in that moment, we get older. In that moment, something in us goes away, too.

Phil and Jean came to New Hampshire for the funeral. Whether Paul—who was not speaking to his siblings—was there, too, is unknown. Claire Eaton Motschman—recently married to Converse's cousin Everett D. Eaton—recalled the day. Her husband, she told me, had no relationship with his Converse cousins at all, and had in fact never even mentioned them to her. The funeral was Claire's first (and only) interaction with Connie Converse, whose attire that day she remembers taking note of, describing it to me as "rather masculine, which included ankle-high black shoes with thick heels that were not the style of the day." When the two were introduced, Converse "barely said hello" to her. "In fact, she just kept walking by."[1]

Converse stayed on in Concord to help Evelyn get her affairs in order. Maybe she took the opportunity to walk by the house at 9 Harvard Street on a warm summer day, to breathe in the fragrance of a more innocent time in her life, to catch a glimpse of the ghost of her childhood self peering out the window and wondering what her future might hold. Maybe she walked up and down the block and then around the corner and across the street to Concord High, where she'd been valedictorian of her class, where she'd been made fun of and gossiped about by her schoolmates. Maybe she stopped by the campus of St. Paul's School, where Frannie Flint's father had taught and where the Flints had lived for at least part of her childhood in Concord. Maybe she visited the town cemetery and stood by Franny's gravestone—one Flint shared with *her* father. Or maybe she did none of these things.

After Converse returned to Ann Arbor, she dove back into her work. Both she and Phil moved, around this time, to new living situations, each one representing a modest upgrade (and both still relatively close to each other).[2] Converse's dwelling was the upper floor of a two-family home at 733 Oakland Avenue; Phil's, a proper house at 1312 Cambridge Road—right next door to a family named Burns, whose sons, Ken and Ric, Phil told me, delivered their daily newspaper.[3]

Given all this, receiving a letter about her music from Peter Cooper (the man who'd produced the stillborn "Connie Converse Sings" LP) must have come as an unexpected surprise.

Cooper wrote that he'd had the idea to make a short film adaptation of "Playboy of the Western World."[4] When I asked him about this, some fifty years later, Cooper recalled to me that he'd continued to have great affection for Converse's music and that the project was mainly just an excuse to collaborate with her again.[5]

A telephone conversation between the two ensued, and terms were discussed. "I understand that you wish to make certain alterations in the song for this particular purpose," Converse wrote to Cooper afterward, "and I am willing to trust your judgment in this regard."[6]

The film took Cooper a little over a year to complete; when it was finally finished, in August 1967, he sent Converse a print.[7] Excited to see it, and eager to share this bit of rare artistic activity with family and friends, she rented a room at the Ann Arbor Public Library for an informal screening.[8]

The soundtrack to the roughly nine-minute short entitled *Connie's Song* features a radical rearrangement of Converse's original composition, now reimagined as a dulcet, easy-listening fantasia.[9] Professionally scored and orchestrated, it features long passages of instrumental music occasionally interrupted by an unidentified female singer intoning snippets of Converse's lyrics, the song smoothed out and neutered.

"That was quite a surprise package you sent me last week," Converse wrote in response. "I managed to combine a projector, a projectionist, and a dozen friends to view the film, and I expect to show it again when some other friends get back from their vacations."[10]

Dan Dzula remembers screening the live-action short on loan from Phil and that it was "a lot of a woman looking at a man, a man looking at a woman, and closeups of flowers . . . maybe a car crash or something that happens offscreen but you don't see it, you just see flowers or grass blowing in the wind."[11] Whatever the film's cinematic merits may have been, the musical component was another artistic mismatch, this treatment of Converse's work even more desultory than Susan Reed's had been. Cooper's intentions were good, but his sense of aesthetics—perhaps dulled by years of work making television commercials for products like Jell-O and Quaker Oats—less so. *Connie's Song* managed to squeeze every ounce of charm and delight from "Playboy of the Western World."

"It's more 'elegant' than I'd expected," Converse continued in her reply:

> *By the way, that first shot of the Playboy himself is perfect—I would have known him anywhere, and it's obvious that he could even conjure up an ocean in the middle of Central Park. My compliments to the people on the music end too. The changes in the song were interesting, and if I only say "interesting" you know it's just because the songwriter inevitably clings to the "Original" like an old barnacle . . . It is a treat in itself to hear my music elaborated on and "done up" professionally.*

In closing, she notes that she was "amused and touched" by the title of the film, and by "the fact that Peter kept the song on the back burner of his nice mind all these years and really Did Something With It . . ."

∽

Phil and Jean mentioned to me that, during this time, someone dropped in on Converse—an episode they recalled with some mirth. Jean Converse said that she'd been driving past Converse's house very early one morning and saw Charles Thomas, a well-known Black activist in town, walking to his car. She and Converse, she said, pretended not to see each other, given the implications of his being there at that hour.

"Charlie Thomas was wild and peculiar and scary as all hell," Marcia Barrabee said when I brought this up. "I can't imagine any kind of love relationship or anything soul-satisfying could come of [a relationship] with him."[12]

In all my exchanges with people who knew Converse in Michigan, this story is the only one that even hinted at a romantic involvement. But that, and the fact that no other interest appears in her letters from this point forward, doesn't mean she didn't have one. As evidenced again and again in the narrative of her life, what other people saw and what was actually going on could have been vastly different things.

"It was almost as though she truly didn't see herself," Riley Trumbull had told me about Converse's outwardly asexual presentation—a nearly exact echo of what Barbara Bernal had once said.

The sexual revolution was now in full bloom in Ann Arbor, a town as freethinking as any in the country. "Partner swapping was prevalent," Phil told me. He said that when he attended parties thrown by his department, young women would frequently approach him, saying "their husbands were out of town for some months, and would he come and visit?"[13]

Ruth Zweifler, another person from Converse's Michigan orbit, confirmed that the atmosphere had been loose. "There were a lot of hormones in those days," she told me. "A lot of fluid relationships to go along with everyone's passionate political concerns."[14] Trumbull said that get-togethers in the Victorian-era houses occupied by faculty at the time featured copious amounts of whiskey, weed, and tabletop dancing.[15]

Certainly, in that scene, Converse might have seemed like a fish out of water. If her fashion choices and personal aesthetic had made her seem like a hick in cosmopolitan Manhattan, they now made her appear older than she was, odd and even more out of step. "She dressed strangely," Marcia Barrabee's daughter, Lisa, told me. "Old-fashioned, almost Amish/Mennonite. Dark clothes, hem lengths long, hair in a bun. For the 60s, that was really strange."[16]

But there may also have been another explanation for Converse's habits. When I mentioned them to psychologist Michael D. Kahn, author of *The Sibling Bond,* he wondered if Converse had been abused at some point. Kahn, who has dealt professionally with such cases for over six decades, told me that "victims of sexual abuse will often go to great lengths to make themselves appear unattractive to the opposite sex. It can be both a self-protective measure—to ward off potential predators—and also a way to signal to the world that they are, essentially, 'damaged goods,' unfit for, and unworthy of, receiving love or affection from others."[17]

"She stood out because she didn't want to stand out. When you walked into the office [at the Center for Research on Conflict Resolution], there was all this youthful energy. Women in heels and short, short skirts, things like that. And then there was Elizabeth. She didn't care about appearances—hers, or others'," Trumbull recalled. "She was interested in content. If you sat down with her, and she started talking, nothing she said would be like what she looked like. All of her color was in her talking, in her humor, her language. Then she wasn't the grandmother wearing the dowdy housedress at all. She was hip and cool. And the brightest thing about her was her smile. You almost couldn't see her until she smiled."[18]

But Converse occasionally made appearances at those parties, often arriving with the CRCR's assistant director William "Bill" Barth, a man Trumbull would marry in 1972, and then divorce soon after.[19] "Bill was this wild hillbilly-in-a-suit, good-natured and promising good times . . . refreshingly open and unpretentious in a crowd of very pretentious ambitious people. In a suit he was elegant, refined, polished and handsome, and a relentless negotiator, which was the Center side of him. When he got to the parties I'm talking about, he would pull off the tie, throw away his suit coat, roll up his sleeves and string up his washtub bass. Class went out the window," Trumbull said.

He and Converse made quite the pair. "She would often be sitting to the side, drink and her ciggy in hand, watching Bill's antics and laughing.

She had a silent laugh which was all big smile and heaving shoulders. Bill was an athletic sort of musician while playing, legs and arms and howls. A show-off. I remember her sitting and listening, very drunk but obviously enjoying all these quirky people doing a LOT of drinking, and laughing a lot with and at Bill for his whooping it up sort of antics."

Trumbull did not think Converse and Barth were anything more than friends. "He was always very warm with her but like a pal, not like a Woman, and she treated him like a lovable and sometimes annoying pet. Looking back I see them as very protective of each other—in some way they each felt like an imposter, I think. Bill always worked to overcome not being a member of the Real Academics Club. And here was Elizabeth, plump, frumpy, and plain, with a thin colorless braid wrapped around her head, bangs, matronly, that same mousey gray dress, Peter Pan collar, sitting in a sea of mini skirts and big eyelashes and big earrings."[20]

Occasionally, Converse joined Barth on guitar. These weren't performances, per se, just the two of them (and whoever else happened to be around) singing and playing in a corner. Trumbull couldn't remember any of the tunes they chose, only the flavor of them. "Bill was from the Ozarks, so the music they made seemed to be sort of country-bluesy to me."

Trumbull told me that there was nothing unusual in the outwardly square, quiet Converse picking up a guitar or sitting down at the piano in such settings. "She was eccentric," Trumbull said, "but everyone was eccentric in those days, so it didn't register as odd."[21]

But, more often, Converse hewed to her loner, isolating ways. Barrabee told me, "I would often drop by late at night if I saw that Connie's light was on. At ten or eleven, even after midnight. She would often be up, playing her guitar, and smoking. She smoked three or four packs a day. And she might be drinking." When I asked Barrabee if she considered Converse an alcoholic, she dismissed the idea. "Oh no," she told me. "She might be a little tipsy, but I never saw her drunk or anything like that. She just liked to drink. There was only one time that I can remember when alcohol may have been a factor. It was at a party, and she got into a ferocious political argument with a guy I was fond of, and her words started to slur."[22]

Alcohol and cigarettes were often mentioned by people who knew Converse in the 1960s.[23] Some talked about these habits as simply endemic for that time. Trumbull remembered that Converse was "a hard, heavy drinker" and that, like many, "she kept a bottle in her [office] desk."[24] At least one person—an Ann Arbor friend named Nelle Chilton— was more direct. "We all knew that Connie was drinking a little more than she should," Chilton said.[25]

When I asked Barrabee to expand on what she recalled from those late-night visits, she said, "Sometimes I would talk with her about the love affair I was having. She would get a sad, dreamy look on her face. She was somewhat mysterious that way. Wistful."[26]

Phil and his family were really the only ones who saw Converse's musical self on any kind of regular basis. Her nephew Pete told me that nearly every Sunday she would come to their house for "informal musical performances, singing songs that all were familiar with—the Beatles, Bob Dylan, Pete Seeger, and chestnuts like 'Oh! Susanna.' Kids from the neighborhood would join in," and Converse would alternate between guitar and piano.[27] When it came to her awareness of contemporary music, I like to imagine her browsing the aisles of Discount Records near campus, maybe even asking for recommendations from a young clerk there named James Newell Osterberg, Jr.—the future Iggy Pop.[28]

CHAPTER 28

Reasons

As managing editor of the *Journal of Conflict Resolution,* Converse did everything. This meant not only reading and responding to every manuscript and proposal that came in (solicited or not), but also continuing to be responsible for more thankless jobs like soliciting and maintaining subscriptions, interfacing with suppliers, raising funds, meeting print deadlines, attending staff and board meetings, even licking postage stamps. "The men whose names appeared above hers did little of the work, but had no problem taking the credit," Riley Trumbull told me.[1]

As if that weren't enough, in the latter half of the 1960s, Converse began a project that would devour what free time she might otherwise have had, a complete and thorough written study of the entirety of the *JCR*'s contents, from its first issue to its most recent. Her goal was to analyze and understand the trends, themes, and ideas put forth in its pages in its first decade and then synthesize the whole for readers. It was, essentially, a self-assigned dissertation.[2]

"Nobody asked me to do it," Converse later wrote. "I wanted to do it . . . I did most of the review work on unpaid time, and I was taking economics courses for credit as well"—though, by 1967, she'd ceased her undergraduate studies to devote herself fully to the project.[3]

Robert Hefner thought that it may in fact have been Phil who suggested the undertaking to her, perhaps seeing it as a way for her to further solidify her standing and prove herself professionally.[4] If this is true, it's another sad and striking parallel with the story of Frannie Flint, who two decades earlier had felt pressured by *her* brother to overextend herself academically, leading to her emotional collapse and apparent suicide.

T he world around Converse—the one she cared so deeply about, that she was dedicating her life to trying to improve—had begun to rip apart. The convulsions of 1968 brought more riots; the assassinations of Martin Luther King, Jr., and Senator Robert Kennedy; the chaotic Democratic National Convention in Chicago; the escalating conflict in Vietnam; and Richard Nixon's ascendancy to the White House. It's sad and painful to imagine the empathic Connie Converse struggling within and without against the backdrop of these seismic events. In the coffeehouses of Ann Arbor, both Joni Mitchell and Neil Young gave concerts that year. Did Converse attend one, or was she too consumed by her work to even notice?

I n August, Converse received a letter from Evelyn, written on what would have been Ernest's eighty-fifth birthday. "It still seems strange to me that he is gone beyond recall," she shared. Phil told me that their mother was worried, both about Connie's mental state and the fact that she was still unmarried. She now had something significant she wanted to propose to her daughter:

I can't wait to tell you something I've been thinking of lately. Could you get away for 3 weeks next June, say, so that you and I could take a trip to Alaska? Don't gasp—I really mean it. I would pay all your way as I'm sure I can spare $2000—which it would probably cost for us both (together I mean). I would like to go to West Coast and then take inland boat passage. I could come to A[nn]A[rbor] and there from Chicago I'd like to go by train . . . Then I had another idea—perhaps cousin Helen would like to go with us to Oregon to see Edith [Converse's cousin Edie] while we go on to Alaska. I think it would be much better than us two older ones going alone—to have a young person like yourself sort of manage us. Helen I think is 81 or so now. You know much more about travel than either of us. Well, you just think it over![5]

To Converse, the prospect was horrifying.[6] Besides her feeling that she could ill afford to take that much time away from work, Phil told me that she viewed the idea of spending three weeks with Evelyn as anathema even as she knew she'd probably have to agree to it. She told Phil: "I want to go to Alaska with mother about as much as I want to go to the basement."[7]

⌒

Converse's treatise "The War of All Against All: A Review of *The Journal of Conflict Resolution, 1957–1968*" was published that December in a special anniversary issue. "The Hobbesian title chosen for this review is intended to express my surprise, after such a long immersion in conflict studies, that anybody gets along with anybody," she wrote in her conclusion.[8]

Like every other one of her investigations, her *JCR* review was broad and comprehensive. Once she'd committed herself to it, she was all in. Hefner described the end result to me as "a Herculean effort."[9] Kenneth Boulding, having since moved on to the University of Colorado, wrote an introduction to the issue in which her study appears. "In any enterprise there may be inspirers and legitimators, but the crucial question is who really does the work. In this case the answer is clear . . . *The Journal* is largely the creation of Elizabeth Converse, whose article in this issue . . . adds substantially to its significance."[10]

"The War of All Against All" is not lay reading. Converse's audience here was a scholarly one, the essay essentially an insider's guide to an insider publication. Her prose, analytically dense and academic, would be rough sledding for anyone without a social science background. During an informal video conference I convened with thinkers from various disciplines to weigh in on Converse's scholarly projects, research expert Ivan Bojanic asked me to forward him this essay so he could skim through it as the group of us spoke. I did and, while others were talking, tracked his reaction, watching his jaw first go slack, and then land on his sternum.

"Um, you guys?" he interjected after some time. "This is not what I expected. I thought it would essentially be a synopsis of each article, in chronological order. But this is *analysis*, this is *personal perspective* . . . She sat down and . . . holy shit! . . . just took *every single article* in this journal and just connected all the dots." He paused, momentarily speechless. "That . . . is just . . . beyond imagination. She took all these disparate pieces of research, from people who were studying a million different nooks and crannies of this nascent field, and tried to create a single unifying narrative out of it!"[11] And he was right.

After the essay's publication, Converse descended into a "postpartum depression" and began devoting significant time to volunteering with the Ann Arbor chapter of People Against Racism (PAR), a coalition of mostly students.[12] "You had to wonder what she was doing there," Rob

Hovey, one of the group's early leaders, told me. "She was twenty years older than the rest of us. We were all proto-hippies, but she was straight."[13]

Some years before, in the fall of 1963, Converse had written a letter to the editor at *The Ann Arbor News* voicing her support for a group of activists who'd been arrested for protesting "our town's feeble legislation on fair housing." A couple of them, she offered, were friends of hers, "two young mothers . . . sane, socially respectable, educated, civic-minded, comfortably situated, and devoted to their families. They . . . are prepared for fines—and even jail if necessary—in order to call our attention to the plight of Negro families in our town." She closed the letter with a provocation: "If we don't want to cope with the problems of discrimination, our police blotters may become a directory of the finest people in town."[14]

It was these same tensions that had given rise to the nearby Detroit riots of 1967, shaking the nation. Now, in May 1969, a new incident occurred right there in Ann Arbor, again spurring Converse to action.

Raymond Chauncey, a Black staffer for the town's Human Relations Commission, had gotten wind that the Star, a campus bar, was engaging in discriminatory practices. When he went to see for himself (and without divulging his official capacity), sure enough, he was denied service. Chauncey peacefully asserted his rights. When asked to leave, Chauncey refused, and the police were called. He'd then been hauled off to the station, and was knocked unconscious, requiring hospitalization.[15]

Protests ensued, and Converse took a leadership role. A meeting between concerned citizens and city officials on May 21 resulted in her being chosen as one of five to form a steering committee that would then meet with mayor Robert J. Harris about establishing a civilian review board to address police brutality. Five decades before George Floyd and the Black Lives Matter movement became part of the national conversation, the group that Converse helped lead was calling for greater police oversight and accountability, and for new educational initiatives on racial equality.[16]

As the result of the incident, Chauncey's job security became tenuous. "They were trying to get me fired," he told me, "and if it wasn't for people like her, they would have done that. We need a million more like her."[17]

Converse now submitted a memo to PAR, outlining her "personal opinions which can be safely regarded as controversial" (see Appendix C). When I forwarded it to renowned American activist, feminist, and scholar Peggy McIntosh, she described it as "remarkable," and confirmed that "for 1969 in the U.S., I feel Converse was thinking about mobilizing group power deeply, intricately, carefully and well ahead of her time."

Converse's "I" is remarkable, for starters. "We," often as a pompous overgeneralization, is used for persuasiveness by leaders in speaking about planning and policy-making for a group. The "I" that Converse uses in the A-section could be for a pledge that each member might make individually, but by section B2 ("I think it must be . . .") it has evolved into a testimonial and autobiographical "I" that traces and makes public her own intricate processes of thought. (B6: "I have come to believe . . .")

These processes are as complicated as she is; they contain many hedges and qualifications and statements about contradiction. She is doing social and psychological analysis and is quite accurate in saying academic life does not prepare us to do what she is trying to do. In this document, she is using her intellect in a way that the society has not given her permission to do. She is letting her group members watch her thinking, not learn her (frozen) "thought."

Converse's rare use of "I" to think aloud in public about leadership makes me think maybe she left Mt. Holyoke after two years because academic frames in the 40s did not welcome or even allow the "I." Many still do not.

She is deeply influenced by three French analysts of power and colonization:

Aime Cesaire, Frantz Fanon, and Albert Memmi . . . But these three men were not as ingenious as she is in their discussions of the psyche. She is onto her inner complexities, and in using down to earth and startling words like "frozen" she is original.[18]

Robin DiAngelo, author of *White Fragility*, had a simpler response when I sent Converse's memo to her. "My goodness!" she wrote. "It is indeed remarkable for its time. It would be remarkable even now, given the degree of nuance and self-awareness she displays. Just wow."[19]

The PAR memo had been sent to me by a former member of the group named Patricia Murphy, along with a cache of Converse's other writings and thoughts about addressing bigotry in America. Happily for us, Murphy had retained copies of these in her files. Everything that Converse had saved in her own filing cabinet related to her thoughts on race were among the items that Phil eventually discarded.

❧

But having had found her footing in mid-sixties Ann Arbor, however briefly, Converse was now, once again, slipping between the cracks, once more somewhere between being in her time, ahead of her time, and out of her time.

Aside from Boulding's nod to her in the *JCR* there doesn't seem to have been much contemporary recognition at all for the kinds of contributions she was now making. She was becoming invisible again.

Then-student Peter Meyers, Converse's friend and fellow PAR activist, got married that May, and Converse wrote and performed a song for the occasion. Meyers described the outdoor event as "a big hippie wedding." And there was Converse, with her guitar:

Oh, I am yours,
You are mine,
We are one . . .

(Spoken): Dearly beloved, we are gathered here together in the sight
of one another to consider a mystery: God created the world in
six days exactly as he wanted it—and on the seventh day,
while he was taking his nap, uncertainty crept in. So that:

Nobody here can say never,
Nobody here can say forever,
Nobody knows the winning horse,
Nobody knows the wisest course—

(Spoken): Behold, I tell you a tragedy: there are as many laws
against loving as there are against hating. So that:

Thou shalt learn to hate thy brother,
Thous shalt compete with one another,
Thou shalt learn to fight and kill,
Thous shalt learn to work thy will—
 Still, I am yours,
 You are mine,
 We are two,
 But we are one . . .

(Spoken): Dearly beloved, we are gathered here together in the
sight of one another to celebrate a miracle.

Celebrate a miracle passing
Our common understand of:

Out of my rage came forth sweetness,
Out of my sorrow came forth love—
   Oh, I am yours,
   You are mine,
   We are two,
   And we are one—
   Or are diminished into one . . .
Amen[20]

Neither Meyers nor Vicki Peters, the woman he married that day, have a recording of the song, recollections of how Converse performed it, or any memory of what the music sounded like.[21]

❧

Now, in the summer of 1969—season of the moon landing, the Manson Family murders, the Stonewall Riots, Woodstock, and Converse's own efforts to address systemic racism in America—she was hitting the road again, with her mother.

It was Converse's first journey west since the cross-country drive she'd taken twenty years earlier. What a difference two decades had made, something Converse had to be thinking about, especially when she, Evelyn, and their octogenarian cousin Helen (she of the Old Home Place back in Amherst, New Hampshire) arrived in Seattle, their first stop.[22] It was here where Converse had once visited her peer and fellow aspiring poet Carolyn Kizer. Kizer had since gone on to a literary career of some renown, something Converse could still only dream about.

Evelyn kept a diary of the trip, which Converse typed up for her after they'd returned. "We went at once to the Hertz car-rental place where Elizabeth had reserved a Ford Fairlane," Evelyn wrote, "and, with all our bags stowed away in it, we three set out south toward Oregon and Edith

Converse Neff."[23] Other than inserting a few humorous asides in the typescript she later prepared, Converse did not document anything about the trip. No breathless accounts of dramatic changes in landscape this time, no captivated thoughts about interactions with strangers met along the way. Nothing.

"They didn't really have kinship or common interests," Jean Converse told me about the mother–daughter relationship. "I mean, Evelyn was interested in nature and flowers and birds and Connie wasn't interested in these rural pursuits . . . They didn't have the easy sharing of interests."[24] Marcia Barrabee agreed with this assessment. Evelyn "didn't seem to be a loving mother," she told me.[25]

F rom Seattle, the trio of women drove for nearly six hours, to the coastal town of Tillamook, where they met up with Edie and family. Converse had not seen her cousin since Edie had gotten married and moved west in the late 1940s.

"I could hardly recognize her," Edie told me. "She had changed, her personality had changed—I had the feeling that something was wrong, that something had profoundly changed about her."[26] This impression may have been exacerbated by the stress Converse was feeling as the result of being in constant company with Evelyn. Phil told me that the trip took a real toll on his sister's psyche.

Their visit with Edie was a short one, its main purpose being to hand Helen off with her sister/daughter while Converse and her mother went north. They would see the Neffs again in a few weeks, when Helen would rejoin them for the journey home.

Converse and Evelyn checked into a motel, en route back to Seattle. The following morning, they returned the rental car, took a bus to Vancouver, and boarded a cruise ship, their home for the next eight days (and from which they would disembark briefly at various ports of call). Evelyn was tracking birds and fauna. Sometimes between stops, she and Converse played Scrabble.

Their rapport during the trip can only be guessed at, but some hints can be found in Evelyn's years of emotionally distant letters to her daughter.[27] And as Phil pointed out to me on numerous occasions, his sister's need to hide her twin dependencies on alcohol and nicotine from their mother made these weeks particularly rough on her.

Whatever tension there was between the two, or if the experience at times offered moments during which they bonded, no clues can be found in Evelyn's travel diary.[28] Entitled "Notes on a Grand Tour," it could not make for drier reading.[29] Converse's role in it is limited to the one who makes their practical decisions. Evelyn, meanwhile, holds forth at great length about flowers, mountains, lakes, and streams, and the various pleasant people they meet on trains and at shared dinner tables. Not once is there a glimpse into the emotional state of either woman—what either is feeling, what it meant to them to be with the other at this moment in their lives, what they were inwardly thinking about. We learn that Evelyn was delighted with almost everything she encountered, but next to nothing about Converse.[30]

When the ship docked back in Vancouver, the pair took a train to Banff for a fortnight before heading back to Seattle. Then it was down to Eugene, their appointed meeting spot to reunite with Helen, Edie, and family. There, they took a couple of days to explore the area, including a trip to a redwood forest. A snapshot of the group of them there (presumably taken by Evelyn, who is not in the picture), shows a smiling Converse wearing a dark blue trench coat and sunglasses, a cigarette in her hand. She stands below and apart from Helen and the Neffs. In the series of photos to which this one belongs, there is not a single picture of just the two formerly close cousins together.

When I asked Edie what else she recalled about this experience—the last time she and Converse ever saw each other—she reiterated, sadly, her feeling that Converse "seemed almost numb, emotionally. She didn't seem right—smoking a lot, and drinking," which would suggest that —at least by the trip's conclusion—Converse had finally given up on trying to hide these habits from her mother, as evidenced by her posing while holding a cigarette in that final photo with the Neffs. "The way she talked was strange. There was not a warm feeling about her."[31]

These were tangible outward signs of the psychological difficulties that had been developing within Converse—difficulties she was now unable to conceal, and that would soon overtake her completely.

CHAPTER 29

The Hard Tug of the Earth

Converse returned from the trip with Evelyn physically and emotionally depleted, really sinking now into the depression she'd begun experiencing after publishing her *JCR* review. It was a state that would define the final years of her known life. Even her appearance now seemed to undergo a significant transformation, her face's formerly angular features becoming rounder and bloated, her hair gone thin and wan, her frame showing signs of substantial weight gain.

Converse had developed what she dubbed "a Sisyphus complex" with regard to her job, something she described in a letter to her colleague and friend Clinton Fink: "I remember telling Bill Porter[1] in January or February 1969 that I was suffering from postpartum depression with regard to my monograph. That was really the first scream of the meemies . . . but of course I screamed too quietly to the wrong person."[2]

Her mental state wasn't helped by the fact that the Center was undergoing a marked change in character. Boulding's absence had an impact. A half-dozen years or so since Converse had begun working there, the

Center had now become less freewheeling, more academic. As Riley Trumbull told me, "The humor had gone out of it."[3]

A small victory for Converse manifested when she was given a modest raise as a token of appreciation for her *JCR* review.[4] But it was too little, too late. Feeling unable to continue managing the entire operation herself, she resigned her post and took on the title of co-editor and research associate.

As the 1970s began, more symptoms had begun to accompany Converse's general feeling of listlessness. It wasn't until Jean insisted she get medical help and made appointments for her that Converse agreed to be professionally evaluated.[5]

As she later confided to Fink:

I knew my psychosomatic potential for work was declining, and I went to doctors and clinics to find out if there was some relatively simple medical remedy for this decline. I found out that I was not anemic, nor tubercular, nor diabetic, nor a dozen other interesting things; all I had was a nonmalignant fibroid uterine tumor which might or might not require surgery at some indefinite later date. Toward the end of 1970 I began to realize that I might have to believe the unbelievable: that the basic nerve and will by which I had always been able to survive my difficulties may have worn out or broken and might not be readily reparable. It was a very strange feeling and I kept retreating into disbelief.[6]

Fink and Converse had met in the mid-1960s, when he was first published in the *JCR*. He described her to me as "knowledgeable and competent, intelligent and well read. She was a friendly person, not formalized in her behavior. She was casual—didn't dress up, or look like an administrator."[7] They'd formed a friendship that grew when he began to share some of her managing editor responsibilities. Fink was also an amateur pianist and one of the few people in Ann Arbor with whom Converse *did* share her experience of being a songwriter in New York City. She even lent him manuscript copies of some of her songs, including "Under a Lullaby" and "Birthday Variations," along with her piano transcriptions of "Playboy of the Western World" and "Fortune's Child."[8]

Whatever torpor Converse was experiencing, she still spent time with Phil and his family. Her nephew Tim, who told me that he was closer to her than his brother was, said that around this time, when he'd been eight or nine years old, he decided to run away from home in order to escape his oppressive piano lessons.

"I hit the road on an early evening of a bitterly cold night," Tim told me, taking with him nothing but a handful of Oreos and a ten-dollar bill. A search party was formed, and it was Converse who'd found him. He was persuaded to come home only after she'd promised to give him piano lessons herself.

And she made good on the offer. Tim told me that these lessons were of a different order from those of his former teacher. His aunt had him focus on chords and on improvisation, using standards like "Heart and Soul" as starting points for exploring melody, harmony, and rhythm.[9]

Tim, who would go on to write songs when he got older, said he'd often go over to his aunt's house to spend the night, and that they would then stay up late and play board games like Risk. ("Connie immediately moved all of her forces to Iceland, isolated and without access to supplies, to teach him a lesson. 'Don't get caught up in war games,'" he remembered her saying.)[10]

One night, quite late and for no particular reason that he could recall, Converse fetched the omnibus tape reel of her performing her guitar songs, cued it up in another room, and pressed play. Tim, now ten or eleven, had often heard his aunt playing guitar and singing, but he understood that this was something different, something he "found sort of odd and baffling."[11]

The scene made quite an impression on his young mind. For that brief, dumbfounding moment, a curtain was lifted, and his aunt Connie became someone else in his eyes, someone with a secret history, someone even more special than he'd previously understood.

It was the one and only time she ever played her own music for him. Did Tim see a gleam in his aunt's eye as she traveled back in her mind to her Grove Street apartment, imagining what it would be like to have that life again? Or was it the sting of regret he intuited in her, a self-lacerating series of questions about choices made and promise unfulfilled?

❧

Maybe it was the fact that Converse was planning a trip back east that brought her former persona back to mind. In 1970, she took it upon herself to organize and execute a surprise birthday gala for her disapproving mother. Evelyn's seventy-fifth would be celebrated in Concord, and Converse contacted everyone in her mother's orbit, doing all the behind-the-scenes work from afar. When the time came, she flew in for the occasion with Phil and Jean, Evelyn unaware until the last.[12]

And Converse engineered other memorable parties in the early 1970s, in Ann Arbor, often for the benefit of Phil and Jean's social circle, many of whom Converse was friendly with, but who did not claim to know her very well.

"You would be told via invitation that you were to arrive with some piece of writing about something," neighbors Helen and Joel Isaacson told me. "Connie was behind this, but never wanted anyone to notice her. She would have made a good spy!"[13] Converse sometimes composed pithy poems and short, humorous songs for these occasions, copies of which she would distribute to invitees, enjoining them to sing along and, if they felt so inspired, contribute their own.

At work, she went through the motions, her psychological struggles unabated, but by March 1971, all bets were off. She drafted a letter to Hefner informing him of the "imperative for me to spend several months in a complete change of scene and with complete freedom from immediate obligation . . . [as] my personal situation is rapidly becoming untenable and a drastic step is required." That step was to resign completely and collect her retirement funds. "I may try to spend the summer in England, puttering about," she wrote, which would "probably include work on my English history project."[14]

For whatever reason, the letter was not sent.[15] Instead, she requested a six-month leave of absence without pay. "Virtually all of my so-called vacation time . . . over the past eight years, has been largely work-ridden rather than real holiday. Not because the Center required it of me, but because I have been much involved in my work and perhaps took on more than I should have."[16]

Then, a few weeks later, came her extraordinary letter to Fink, the one that referenced her postpartum depression and one she expected him to show their Center colleagues "who deserve an explanation of my recent uncharacteristic behavior." In it, she describes having had

half a nervous breakdown following a year or more of the inaudible screaming meemies, accompanied by short but increasing Erfurt periods[17] . . . spent partly in extra sleep, since sleep has become the most tolerable condition of my life, but also partly in rather systematic thinking about certain things I want to write, including fiction as well as nonfiction. And it is that second part which keeps me from giving over entirely to sleep. As a long-time novelist manquée, I have one more plot in my bag which I have to shake out before I go . . .[18]

She writes of being "regretful and ashamed" at having created "the small havoc that now confronts you and Jill [Ault] in keeping the *Journal* going . . . You know, or don't know, that one must keep the dignity of responsibility for one's own acts. At least, that's the only dignity I have been able to achieve in this world and I am extremely reluctant to let go of it." Marcia Barrabee illuminated this for me: "Connie was absolutely determined to have control over her own destiny. She took full responsibility for the way she lived her life, and she never played the victim. She was fierce about that. Personal dignity was the only thing of value to her."[19]

Converse's seven-page, single-spaced letter to Fink goes on to address gender inequality in the workplace, especially when "the division of labor breaks down between men and women in organizations—specifically journals—especially after the predominantly male creators . . . [have] withdrawn their intellectual penises and 'let nature take its course.' . . . I am putting it more sharply than I would ordinarily do, because of the women . . . who will come after me."

Converse mentions her intention to give up her apartment and move into Phil and Jean's attic until she gets things figured out. "I have given myself one last chance . . . and failed. So it's all over." She closes the letter to Fink with: "Your line (and Jill's) must of course be that MISS CONVERSE HAS SUFFERED A NERVOUS BREAKDOWN AND WE ARE TRYING TO PICK UP THE PIECES."[20]

❧

B arrabee was aware of all this and quickly seized upon an idea: to take up a collection for Converse that would allow her to spend her sabbatical in England. "I had gone to the British Isles and organized family trips there," Barrabee told me. "And each time I came back, I went to Connie with my slides and maps and told her all about the adventures, and she would sigh and say how she longed to go and then the idea came and I started talking it up and everyone wanted to DO SOMETHING FOR CONNIE. Before we knew it, we had a list and a bunch of money from people who really owed her for special favors or who wanted to cheer her up."[21]

That April, shortly after her letters to Hefner and Fink were delivered but before the move to Phil's attic, Converse's colleague (and washtub bass accompanist) Bill Barth arrived at her apartment with a gift from those friends, co-workers, and family whom Barrabee's initiative had brought together. The group, calling itself the Committee for Sponsorship of Independent Scholars and Educators, presented Converse with a letter and a generous check, which they called an Award in Recognition of Her Unique Contributions to Scholarship, Education, and Human Individuality. (See Appendix D.)[22]

The letter salutes Converse's editorial work at the *Journal,* her treatise "The War of All Against All," her participation as a speaker at a recent series of talks given by scholars from the Center for Research on Conflict Resolution, her work as an activist, and a series of "informal lectures" she gave "on the problem of human exploitation" that were "eagerly attended, especially by young activists." The letter continued:

> *These lectures are indicative of the enormous work in serious education that Elizabeth has done over the years—independently, without the financial support of any institution, given freely out of her talent for crystallizing and communicating complex ideas and her concern for the human condition.*

Converse, they write, is:

> *a genuine teacher—by pleasuring in the development of other people's minds . . . she rejoices in the brilliance of the accomplished; she encourages the diffident and the uncertain. She immediately communicated the sense that everyone's*

experiences and ideas are important. Her belief that each person is unique and
worthy is not just a Principle: it is a total behavior, the natural response of
delight in another's thought, experience, and individuality.[23] *

⌇

These particular sentiments get at essential elements of Converse's character that never came through in the recollections of people like Gene Deitch and Barbara Bernal, who'd also felt it important to clarify to me that they did not consider her a friend. To hear them tell it, she was aloof, judgmental, a bit arrogant. Even Jean's feeling that it was her sister-in-law's intimidating intellect that kept potential romantic suitors away suggests an aspect of snobbery about Converse—something alluded to in her cousin's wife's recollection of meeting her at Ernest Converse's funeral, and even in Edie Converse Neff's memories of their encounters in Oregon.

But that's not what I heard repeatedly from people in Ann Arbor, and it's not at all how Converse is written about in this letter from her friends and colleagues.

Jean, surely aware of this being a rare and significant validation of Converse's mostly unsung activities in Ann Arbor, sent a copy of the award citation to Evelyn, who then wrote to her daughter that it had "set my thoughts a-soaring . . . I am sure it is well deserved, and it is very pleasant to have recognition . . . And to be sincerely appreciated gives one a good feeling of doing something worthwhile."[24]

Converse was stunned by her friends' and colleagues' gesture. In response, she wrote a letter to the group titled "Report on a Bridge

---

*For the complete text, see Appendix D.

Built over Troubled Waters (and other metaphors)." In it, she refers to the "Blue Funk" under which she'd been operating—caused, in part, by her feeling that "women of my age are very likely to get intimations of mortality that make them wonder whether there isn't something more and different that they'd like to do before reporting to the undertaker."

She then goes on to use language that foreshadows an all-purpose letter she would write three years later explaining her need to disappear: "I began to realize that in order to survive at all I had to have a change of work, a change of scene, and a drastic reduction in current obligations... I was hung up between what was tolerable to me and what was sensible to my affectionate friends and relatives."[25]

Close reading of the two letters would seem to offer the possibility that Converse was actually preparing to disappear in 1971, and that those intentions were upended by the sudden, unexpected display of loving support from her community.

Her first instinct, she wrote now, had been to refuse the money. But, thinking it through, she was able to reframe the gift not as an act of charity (intolerable to her), but as "an investment in my present... What you have done with your contributions is to turn my Blue Funk and Dilemma box over on its side so that I can escape through the floor."[26]

∽

And escape she would. This was the moment when Converse tidied and organized the papers, writings, photographs, artwork, documents, and music that would comprise the contents of the filing cabinet I looked through in Phil's garage. It was also when she typed up her fastidious "Guide to Contents of Five-Drawer File" finding aid.

Now she got her first passport. The large-form photograph she had taken to accompany her headshot shows a hefty, short-haired, middle-aged woman, attired in the sort of garb her friends remember her frequently wearing.[27]

She sold her car, deposited the proceeds in her bank account, and consolidated all of her belongings (including her filing cabinet) in Phil's attic. And then she bought a one-way plane ticket to London.[28]

CHAPTER 30

The World and Time and Space

Converse's flight on June 4, 1971, had an overnight layover in
New York—what appears to have been her first time back since
her move to Michigan ten years earlier.[1] The city that had
played such a transformative role in her life, that had been the setting for
her early hopes and ambitions, was now a place on a flight itinerary, a stop
on the way to somewhere else.

She checked into a cheap motel there, probaby close to the airport in
Queens. She felt "rather dazed and exhausted on arrival . . . napped, ate
dinner, made up a list of NY friends to call—and never called them at
all!"[2] She did not contact people like Maude Brogan, or Sarah Thompson,
or Bill Bernal, or the Eby sisters, or Larry Salisbury, or Amy Schaeffer,
or the Ishiis, or Peter Cooper, or the Changs, or anyone from her fifteen
years of life there.

Converse arrived in England on June 6. "Haven't had a drink in
24 hours," she noted in a letter to Phil and Jean upon her arrival.[3] During
her first week in London, she bounced around from one budget accom-

modation to the next.[4] She took a bus tour, wandered the city, went to the British Museum, and attended a matinee of Agatha Christie's long-running play *The Mousetrap* ("the length of its run is the only extraordinary thing about it").[5]

A week later, in a letter to her Ann Arbor benefactors, she described soaking up the everyday scene—sitting in a park watching "children fish for tiddlers and grown men flying handsome kites" and people "with their remote-controlled model yachts." London reminded her of New York City, she wrote. "I only felt country-bumpkinish for about 24 hours. I have taken to the underground like a duck to water . . . [and] I find little difference between underground London at the rush-hour and subway New York at the rush-hour." She notes visiting a bar, "a 'local' on Praed Street," where she ordered a beer and joked with the bartender.[6] By the start of her second week, she'd secured long-term housing in mostly Irish, working-class Kensington: "I am finally ensconced in a bed-sitter that costs only £5.50 a week . . . the room is large, appropriately scruffy, and livable."[7]

~

By June 25, Converse reported, "I find it hard to describe my internal state after this sudden change of life (pun intended). Certainly the texture of my days has become more interesting and much more tolerable than it was in the months before I left . . . The overurbanization that helped drive me out of Manhattan ten years ago is evident here too, though not to the same degree . . ."[8]

When I traveled to London to get a sense of what life there might have been like during that time, I was surprised by how far Kensington was from the center of the city—a couple of hours by foot, a little less than half that by Tube.

Today, the neighborhood she chose is a charming and affluent one, evidenced by the current state of the very residence she occupied. What was once essentially a boardinghouse, with rooms to let that would have included shared bath and kitchen access, has since been converted into a luxury single-family home. Though Kensington had real literary cachet—the playwright John Osborne wrote *Look Back in Anger* there, and T. S. Eliot, Ezra Pound, James Joyce, and Henry James were all residents at various points—the woman who was now living in the house where Converse once stayed told me that in the early 1970s, the neighborhood was run-down ("like Notting Hill," she said) and dangerous.[9]

In interviews that Phil gave in conjunction with the release of *How Sad, How Lovely,* he described his sister's time in London as a complete disaster, one in which she essentially hid out, drunk. He told me the same thing. "One of Jean's bosom buddies from high school was living in London at the time," he wrote to me, "and Jean asked her to look up Connie. Which the friend did, and came away with the intelligence that she seemed totally holed up in her room."[10]

And this was true on some days. "I have converted all London into my private Mercywood," Converse wrote to friends back in Michigan, a reference to Ann Arbor's psychiatric hospital and an acknowledgment that she knew that they knew that the true purpose of her time there was to recover from a breakdown. Months later, she wrote to her friend Torry Harburg: "As a self-tending patient, I have found my inexpensive roof, and trudged countless times to my local supermarket, newsdealer, laundromat, and post office, and bank, and wineshop . . . The point where one's madness stops being mainly painful and starts being mainly enjoyable may or may not be the upturn to recovery; I only came to that point last week so I don't know yet."[11]

But at other times Converse was quite active, even adventurous, and more unbound than at any time since she'd left New York. After her friends sent me copies of the letters she'd sent them, I began to under-stand that Phil had a limited picture of what that time was like for his sister—maybe even his own agenda for portraying her as having become a pathetic figure. Contrary to his accounts, she did things.

Having effectively established a home base in Kensington, she took a five-day trip to Paris in July. There, she walked the city, saw friends, practiced her fluent French, and visited the cathedrals and museums.[12] "The first thing I saw at the Louvre was that incomparable sound of wings at the top of the stairs," she wrote. "Oh, wow. Lump in throat. Worth everything else put together."[13]

Her lengthy letters back home weighed in on a variety of topics, in-cluding American politics, the Pentagon Papers (which had just been published), her wide-ranging thoughts and preoccupations, and updates on her condition.[14] By the end of her second month abroad, she wrote to Vicki Vandenberg (another Ann Arbor friend):

Of myself I can only say that I have Not Recovered Yet. And my workaday future is in such a state of doubt that I can't even cope with it yet as a problem (which it certainly is). The last time somebody asked me (in Paris) what my future plans were . . . I broke out in a fit of hysterical laughter, without the slightest overtone or undertone of wretchedness (I haven't got that far yet); it was just plain amusing. Who knows?? . . . I can always resort to my retirement money, which the Pretty Committee including youse guys saved me from resorting to before. The future is blanker to me now than it has been in a long time; but blankness has its advantages as well as its despairs. I can only tell you that going back to the Journal is about the last thing I want to do.[15]

But Converse may have been optimistic in thinking that a *Journal* job would even be available. That August, what appears to have been a puni-tive campaign by the university's right-leaning administration forced the

CRCR to close up shop. "We were closed because we supported the Black Action Movement," Robert Hefner told me flatly.[16] The university's move was unexpected and sudden, and though the school signaled that it might be open to at least keeping the *JCR* housed there, the publication's future was now in doubt.

And then there was her novel, which she'd hoped to use some of her time in London to work on. Like Frederick Rolfe, the obscure writer who is the subject of Symons's *The Quest for Corvo* (a book Converse had read and admired while living in New York), she had spent much of her adult life longing for a reality in which she could simply be an artist, relieved of financial burden. Now that she had it, procrastination and creative paralysis set in. As Symons had told it, after the long-suffering Rolfe had at last found the patronage he'd dreamed of: "The way was clear at last for the man who had so long cried out that, given time and money, he would write and write and write. Both were given him, and he did nothing: it was too late."[17]

In August, Converse dedicated what must have been a substantial chunk of her forty-seventh birthday to typing an eleven-page, single-spaced letter to Jean. Entitled "Just for Jeaner," the discursive missive touches on Vietnam, women's lib, sexual morality, Ann Arbor gossip, her own lack of a sex life, and a topic the two women bonded over: middle-aged depression.

> *Your Blue Funk is of course especially crisp to me, and although some professionalism is involved I competitively state that my Funk is funkier than your Funk but I am glad to hear details of your Funk because it makes me feel a little less singularly Funky, you being generally lifetime-wise less prone to Funks than me, and if you fall into even a Small Funk—et cetera. All this is to be sung to the tune of "My dog's bigger than your dog."[18]*

That fall, she traveled the English countryside, looking for sites and grounds related to her ancestral heritage, exploring tiny villages and areas that had literary associations for her (Jane Austen, John Fowles, Shakespeare), and visiting a few "shrines." Arriving in West Amesbury she found that—because it was the off-season and tourist buses were not running—she had to walk the couple of miles each way to Stonehenge ("to me, that is devotion, and I hope the Druids appreciate it").[19]

In the early 1950s, Converse had composed a heavenly-sounding song for two voices, set to the lyrics for Shakespeare's "O Mistress Mine," from *Twelfth Night*. Like in "Down This Road," "We Lived Alone," and "Where Are the Roses?," she overdubbed herself singing the second part on top of her original vocal in the recording she made of it. I like to think of her strolling around Stratford-upon-Avon, singing her tune quietly to the playwright's ghost. She described the visit to his birthplace as devoir similar to the one she took to Salisbury Cathedral "except that I am fonder of William than I am of Jesus."[20]

Converse visited twenty-two counties in eight days and seven nights, traveling as inexpensively as possible "all by train, bus, and shank's mare," and staying in low-cost lodgings. "For weather, I picked the worst week in October: lots of rain, and recurrent gale-force winds." The one time that she shared dinner and drinks with anyone—a young friend of a friend of a friend she'd met in transit to Salisbury—"both of us clearly put some value on traveling . . . alone, and when by chance I arrived at Stonehenge at a point when she was about to leave, we said hello cheerfully but dodged apart like electrons."[21]

By December, she was ready to vacate her Kensington place, aware that her time in England, and her sabbatical, were coming to an end.

Mary Shurman, a friend and former student of Jean's, temporarily put her up.[22] Shurman told me that she was busy with the task of juggling three young children at holiday time:[23]

We saw Connie only very occasionally when she would come for supper or for a walk on the Heath . . . She was a warm guest and took an affectionate interest in the children . . . I sensed that she wanted to keep her life at a distance and I didn't want to intrude. I assumed her appearance was not of importance to her. She struck me as dowdy but not falling apart. But I did sense an emptiness. Maybe that was just my comparing my own busy, happy state with her situation, alone in a London given over to family celebrations at Christmas . . . I don't know where she intended to go when she left us.[24]

A t this moment in the movie version of this story, "Wild Horses," a hit for the Rolling Stones that year, plays in the background—Mick Jagger's keening, melancholy vocals essaying broken faith, not having much time left, and a "dull, aching pain"—as Converse wanders the streets of London, gazing inward, smoking, knowing that 1971 is drawing to a close and that the resumption of her real life now beckons from the other side of the Atlantic.

"I dragged myself kicking and screaming to the PanAm office in Piccadilly and bought myself a ticket home," she wrote on January 5, 1972. "I'm sure I wouldn't be so fond of London if I had a job here; but I feel that if I did have a job here I'd like this city better than I liked New York in the late 1950s. A matter of temperament and texture, social texture."[25]

W hen she got back, Converse followed through on her plan to live in the third-story attic of Phil's house. Ever since she'd left for college in 1942, the siblings had been engaged in a sort of magnetic dance. First, there had been Phil's adventuresome visits with her in New York City, the two finally freed from the restrictions of their childhood home.

Then came the faithful correspondence between them and her sharing with him (and Jean) the results of her artistic pursuits. Then more and more visits to Michigan as her life in New York became less and less satisfying—the period during which she wrote her confessional letter to Phil about her desire to be closer to him, to really know him. Next, she'd moved to Ann Arbor, and began working on the campus where he was making his career, living in housing never more than a mile or so away from him.

Now, in 1972, no physical distance between them remained. She'd moved in. She bought a used VW Beetle, to replace the one she'd once had,[26] and tried to get a feel for what might be next.[27]

Things here had changed, and quickly. Suddenly, the Center was gone, and now the university began making moves to push the *Journal* out as well, recommending that it be given to the University of Texas. "I am astonished by this recommendation and disturbed by the odd decision-making process that seems to have led to it," Converse wrote to the University of Michigan's dean in response.[28] When the *JCR* ultimately went to Yale, Converse was not consulted about it, nor were her editorial services considered as part of the publication's future.[29]

Where that left her, by her own estimation, was unclear, but Converse did not seek to leverage her decade of experience at the *JCR* into potentially similar professional opportunities. Robert Hefner, who knew nothing of her music life, chuckled when I asked if he had a sense of what her ambitions were at this point. "In those days," he said, "we just didn't pay that much attention to the aspirations of the women on our staff. I honestly don't know whether she had any"[30]—a sad echo of Gene Deitch, another man of influence unable to see Converse in ungendered terms. Even Phil, when I asked him about what kinds of things she could have gone on to pursue, framed it this way: "She had no real credentials to bring to a new place."[31]

"Elizabeth's prospects were not completely eliminated," her former

CRCR colleague Dee Wernette told me. "But with her rather withdrawn personal style, her support network was likely very limited. More important, I'd suggest, was likely her need for making a meaningful contribution to the still-hopeful political-social-economic scene. Just any academic job would not have offered such. So I have little difficulty imagining why she would choose to 'bail out,' first figuratively and later likely literally."[32]

Wernette told me that the CRCR's antiwar stance and lefty activism had always guaranteed its status as a stepchild of the university and that working at the Center had "all the security of a floating crap game." After I'd described Converse's lack of outward success in her previous life at the AIPR, and then as a composer and performer in New York, he saw a parallel with the closing of the Center, writing to me that it "likely felt like a repeat of her NYC experience. Little payoff/recognition for high-quality work leading to a perceived and actual dead end."[33]

But Jean Converse had a different take: She was "quite sure" that Converse was offered other jobs "that she did not take, not because she was being fussy but because she felt she actually couldn't do them."[34]

Converse's temporary living situation in the attic soon became a permanent one, and she began paying rent to Phil and Jean.[35] When she typed up her CV that summer, she listed her current employment as "freelance."[36]

&

I n 2013, at a concert I gave in Portsmouth, New Hampshire, I included the short set of Converse's music I'd continued to develop, introducing and framing her songs with narration about her life and the significance of her work—an early draft of which would become my play, *A Star Has Burnt My Eye*. This particular show had special resonance for me: To my knowledge, it was the first time Connie Converse's music had ever been performed on a stage in her home state.

During the lobby meet and greet afterward, a man approached me and said—as though he couldn't believe it was true—"I knew Connie Converse in Michigan."

This was Joel Kostman, who'd come to my show that night not only ignorant of the fact that I'd be performing Connie Converse's music, but also that there was even such a thing as Connie Converse's music. He'd met and gotten to know Converse in Ann Arbor, after her return from England, when he was only twenty years old. As the concert that night progressed, he'd slowly started to realize that I was talking about the same woman[37] and was spooked by the coincidence. "Listening to you tell her tale on stage the other night brought shivers down my spine," he wrote to me a few days later.[38]

Kostman was a young friend of Marcia Barrabee's and a fledgling songwriter in his own right when he knew Converse.[39] He told me that Barrabee always had "wonderful, interesting friends, and I think she wanted to 'offer' them up to me as it were."[40] This squares with something Helen Isaacson told me—that "it was difficult to be a single person in Ann Arbor back then" because the community was made up of mostly "married people with children."[41] Barrabee was trying to play social matchmaker for her two single, music-minded friends.

"Marcia had talked me up to Connie. I had just started writing songs, and she thought Connie and I might hit it off. We had dinner at Marcia's house, and I remember talking about my songs, which Connie seemed interested in. Never did she mention her own songwriting." A decade or so earlier, Converse might have been open to sharing some of her music, maybe even to playing a few songs for Barrabee's young friend. Not now.

"We had a connection," Kostman told me about Converse. "She just had that something. You know it when you see it and . . . I saw it. Marcia had a lot of smart friends, intellectual and extremely conversational. Her friendship with Connie made perfect sense although they were yin and yang. Connie soft-spoken with the driest wit around, Marcia high strung, political, never quite finishing her sentences because her brain worked faster than her mouth. They were both part of a 'scene' back then. Connie was one of them but different from the rest."[42] As Peter Meyers—the student whose 1969 wedding Converse sang at—told me, "She calmed a lot of us younger people down."[43]

Like everyone else who knew her in Ann Arbor, Meyers and Kostman both expressed regret that they had been unaware of Converse's musical accomplishments when they knew her. Even Riley Trumbull, who "felt close to her," told me, "I didn't get that she had a huge other life and world of riches and needs of her own."[44]

If no one was privy to Converse's songwriting talents, Helen Isaacson at least succeeded in engaging her music-making spirit. Isaacson kept a small drum kit at Phil's house, next to his piano. In a tableau delicious to imagine, the two women sometimes got together to play popular songs of the day, with Isaacson on percussion (which included various bottles, pots, and pans) and Converse at the piano. Isaacson told me that they never performed for anyone—that it was just for them.

This seems to have been Converse's final foray into music of any kind. The end of the road for her as a performer did not involve her showing up to play an open-mic session at the popular local acoustic venue the Ark; nor her giving an informal house concert of her guitar songs, showing them—as she'd done when she played her tape for Tim—another side of their favorite aunt; nor even of making more home recordings for posterity. Instead, the last time anyone remembers Connie Converse making music, she was banging out covers of the latest pop hits on her brother's piano, with her friend improvising accompaniment on a drum kit and with various kitchen implements.

⌒

As I turned my focus to the end of Converse's time in Ann Arbor, I found myself reflecting on my 2011 trip there and my encounters with Phil. That visit had ended with a concert I'd lined up in town for my quartet, at the Kerrytown Concert House, half a mile from Converse's last known apartment. People like Trumbull, Barrabee, Isaacson, Chilton—really, all of Converse's local friends—weren't even blips on my radar screen yet. Had they been, I'd have invited them to be my guests at the show.

Phil and Jean were there for it, though, and that seemed momentous enough, and emotionally freighted. Not only was I performing in the town where she spent the last known fifteen years of her life, but the two people closest to her were sitting right there in the front row. As I introduced the segment of the concert devoted to Converse, it seemed like an almost sacred moment.

I polled the audience, as I always did, asking them to clap their hands if they were familiar with the name Connie Converse. Other than Phil and Jean, the room was silent. The two of them quietly applauded—and if there is such a thing as apologetic clapping, that's what theirs was. My voice caught in my throat as I tried to imagine how the two of them must have felt knowing that, even here, her musical legacy was completely unknown. By the time I got to the final song of the set, "How Sad, How Lovely," I could barely make it through. I'd been scared to look at Phil and Jean throughout, but when I stole a glance during an instrumental passage, I saw tears streaming down both their cheeks.

The song may be Converse's most poignant. If the lyrics of "Talkin' Like You" and "Roving Woman" suggest that Converse had, at times, been happy as a single person, "How Sad, How Lovely," written in 1952, relates to "There Is a Vine" and "One by One" as the inverse expression of that feeling:

How sad, how lovely,
How short, how sweet,
To see that sunset
At the end of the street;
And the day gathered in
To a single light,
And the shadows rising
From the brim of the night.

Although the first eight bars of the song hew to a familiar chord progression (virtually the same one as in "Roving Woman"), the vulnerability of the lyric, the melody, and her recorded performances of the song set it apart.

Some popular songs from Converse's youth, like Hoagy Carmichael's "I Get Along Without You Very Well" (from 1939) and Rodgers and Hart's "My Funny Valentine" (from 1937), contain the germ of the sort of feeling Converse conveys here. But those songs were sung mostly by polished singers, and recordings of them featured backing by band or orchestra arrangements that protected the listener from the sort of raw, exposed emotion heard in Converse's delivery. Even Carmichael, a rare instance of a pop songwriter from that day who also performed his own material, sounds as though he's performing a role when he sings "I Get Along Without You." It's not that his renditions of the song sound insincere; there is simply a remove in the way deep sentiment was expressed in that era, hidden under a maudlin, superficial veneer—something Converse stripped away when performing her music.

Like many of her compositions, the bridge of this one, again, takes a sharp turn from where the song seemed to have been headed:

Too few, too few
Are the days that will hold

> *Your face, your face*
> *In a blaze of gold.*

We get a key change, a minor tonality, and a lyric in which a mysterious other (with whom she cannot be united) is once again addressed. Then:

> *How sad, how lovely,*
> *How short, how sweet,*
> *To see that sunset*
> *At the end of the street;*
> *And the lights going on*
> *In the shops and the bars,*
> *And the lovers looking*
> *For the first little stars.*
>   *Like life,*
>   *Like your smile,*
>   *Like the fall of a leaf—*
> *How sad, how lovely,*
> *How brief.*

It's a heartbreaking series of images. The setting sun—maybe the one setting over Hudson Street as Converse once gazed west from the doorstep of her apartment building on Grove—instills in the singer a rush of feeling that threatens to overwhelm her entirely. There in the words, with stoic clarity, is life's most profound paradox: its boundless enormity, and its tiny insignificance. The sunset pierces her heart with its beauty as she comes face-to-face with her existential apartness. She watches the human activity in the street. She sees couples holding hands and gazing up into the night sky, gazing as one into the heavens, in which they see their future's promise.

But the singer is separate. She does not belong. The spirit and energy of the great world move and thrum without her. She is alone, unable to do else but note the terrible beauty of it all: nature, a setting sun, a single leaf, a lover's smile. She wants, desperately, to seize the beauty, to grasp it, to share it, to keep it from passing, but she cannot. It is a song of surrender, as gentle as it is shattering. In Converse's voice, we hear all the love we don't have in our lives, all the love we do have but don't know how to express, all that is beautiful that we don't know how to take in. Beauty so strong it's painful; radiance so fierce it hurts.

After the concert was over, I noticed Phil walking toward me as I stood talking with some audience members. I tried to extricate myself from the conversation so that I could speak to him, but he motioned for me to continue, coming close and offering me his hand. His eyes were still wet. "Thank you for what you did," he said quietly, looking at me from what seemed to be far way. "We have to get going."

CHAPTER 31

Out and Out

R eacclimating herself to Ann Arbor life after her time in England, with nothing to anchor her professionally and no home to call her own, was challenging for Converse.

"Connie didn't take good care of herself," Marcia Barrabee told me. "My sense was that she just picked up meals here and there. I always suspected they weren't even meals, unless she was invited somewhere, so I often made soup for her and left it on her doorstep."[1]

Barrabee led me to Irene Schensted, another Michigan friend, "someone Connie admired a great deal because they both lived in special worlds of their own making."[2] Schensted remembered a long-standing Monday lunch date she had with Converse, one that went on for years. They often went to a local buffet, where she told me that Converse "preferred to take drinks, rather than food." Once, the conversation turned to the subject of mortality and how, if given the choice, each would choose to go. "She told me that her wish would be to simply disappear, to minimize problems with her family," Schensted remembered.[3]

Converse's final couple of years in Ann Arbor were a series of misfires and nonstarters that happened as both she and the country were undergoing a paradigm shift. As the United States tried to regain its footing after the cataclysmic end of the 1960s, many found themselves unmoored and adrift. The Vietnam War had split America in two, the Pentagon Papers had kneecapped people's trust in government, Kent State had happened, and the Watergate scandal was gaining steam. Anomie was again gripping the culture, but this time, unlike in the early 1950s, Converse did not try to process it through her creative gifts.

"There's this primary America of freeways and jet flights and TVs and movie spectaculars," author Robert Pirsig wrote in a book he was then trying to get published, *Zen and the Art of Motorcycle Maintenance*. "And people caught up in this primary America seem to go through huge portions of their lives without much consciousness of what's immediately around them. The media have convinced them that what's right around them is unimportant. And that's why they're lonely. You see it in their faces. First the little flicker of searching, and then when they look at you, you're just kind of an object. You don't count. You're not what they're looking for. You're not on TV."[4]

Those who, back then, refused to accept this reality found themselves cast as outsiders and misfits, a danger to the status quo and to themselves. Think of Ken Kesey's *One Flew over the Cuckoo's Nest*; of the protagonists in *Easy Rider* and in Hal Ashby's *Harold and Maude*; and of a film that a young David Lynch had begun to shoot called *Eraserhead*. Think of Charles Bukowski writing his first novels; and of the films of John Cassavetes, whose seminal *A Woman Under the Influence* tells the story of a middle-aged woman whose refusal to play by the rules of standard, polite human interaction leads to her being institutionalized. Think of Barbara Loden's *Wanda*, a portrait of a lost, disenfranchised single woman whose lack of direction leads to a relationship with an abusive psychopath.

Ashby, Loden, Pirsig, Bukowski, and Cassavetes were all Converse's contemporaries. Like her, they had not completed college, had struggled with depression or mental illness, and were considered outsiders in their fields. Unable to attract studio interest in his films, Cassavetes financed most of them himself. Loden wrote, directed, and starred in *Wanda,* using a skeleton crew of three. Pirsig's consciousness-shifting book was passed over by 121 publishers before one decided to take a chance on it. Ashby found a kind of cult success for his films, and Bukowski was finally able to quit his job as a postal clerk at age forty-nine after he'd found a bene-factor.[5] But all had the experience of being told time and again, in various ways, that their art was not commercially viable, that there was no audi-ence for it. And as all artists working outside the mainstream must, they had to contend with demons who told them their work was insignificant, irrelevant, or just no good.

But each of these artists eventually succeeded on their own terms. Both *Zen and the Art* and *A Woman Under the Influence* were released in 1974, the year Converse would disappear, and became sensations. Ashby and Bu-kowski are now revered and have been canonized. Loden's film took home the award for Best Foreign Film at the Venice International Film Festival in 1970 and, though it never found proper distribution in the United States, is now regarded as a landmark of American cinema. Had Converse been able to hang on a little longer, if she had had the tools with which to keep going, might she have finally broken through as well and had the same sort of effect on our culture as these artists did? Could she have joined other marginalized figures like Elizabeth Catlett and Alice Neel, who achieved greater recognition for their work only later in their lives?

And what did Converse think of the way Dylan and the Beatles had made pop music smarter? (What did she think, for that matter, of the incendiary early rock 'n' roll that preceded them, when she was still try-ing to make it in the New York music scene; or of the harder, grungier sounds of artists who came in their wake, like the Velvet Underground and Janis Joplin?) Had she a way to get her songs to a label like Warner Bros.—which repeatedly took chances on "uncommercial" artists like Randy Newman and Van Dyke Parks because of the artistic prestige their work lent—could the climate have been right, finally, for a series of Connie Converse albums?

Pete Converse told me that his aunt's open-ended stay at their house during this period was something his parents endured rather than enjoyed. "If it had happened ten years later, my dad probably would have popped for an apartment for Connie, at least for a while," he said.[6] As it was, her presence caused the mood in the house to sink. She had become "irritable and sad," mostly keeping to herself except for meals.[7] When she did emerge from the attic, she was "fairly intoxicated at the dinner table."

His brother, Tim, told me that alcoholism ran in the family and that drinking was a regular feature of the household.[8] When Evelyn would come to visit, for example, his parents and Connie drank their liquor out of teacups so she wouldn't notice, but such hijinks were the lighter side of what was generally a dark, dispiriting, and tense domestic atmosphere.

As anyone who has lived aroud alcohol dependency knows, in such environments, secrecy, unpredictability, and bursts of chaos are commonplace, and something to guard against. The drinker's behaviors and moods are often disruptive, upsetting, and destabilizing, causing sober members of the family to feel they have to walk on eggshells.

Tim remembered one particularly contentious argument between his aunt and his parents over the fact that there was no fire escape leading out from the attic. As the confrontation grew heated, Converse expressed her underlying feeling that Phil and Jean did not have her welfare and best interests in mind.[9]

Having not quite hit adolescence, Tim may have found it easier to deal with the situation in the house at a time when "she was around a lot, and we had great affection for her."[10] This was in contrast to Pete's decidedly less rosy perspective. The third-floor storage space their aunt had taken over had previously been his, and he was now forced to room downstairs with his brother. The two siblings and their aunt shared one bathroom, "which got pretty old, quick," Pete told me.

Pete described Converse during this time as gaining a lot of weight, smoking a lot,[11] and generally being down and depressed, and he called her "quite literally, the crazy aunt in the attic" and a "source of shame and embarrassment" to the family.[12]

"She would sigh a great deal, and was less and less kempt," Marcia Barrabee remembered. "It looked like she was falling apart. She was drinking a lot, and her hands seemed to tremble. She was despondent about the world." In another echo of Barbara Bernal's recollections of her encounters with Converse in Gene Deitch's living room two decades earlier, Barrabee revealed "I wanted to hug her, but she didn't seem to invite that sort of contact."[13]

⁓

This is where Converse's final chapter starts to slip off the rails before ultimately plunging headlong into a mysterious, seemingly unknowable black hole.

Both Pete and Tim Converse told me that she lived in their attic from the time she returned from England, in January 1972, to the night she was last seen, in August 1974. But on January 1, 1973, Converse moved into a new apartment, at 544 North Main Street, in the heart of what was then an almost entirely Black neighborhood—one that is now an Ann Arbor African American historical area.[14] It was an address of which neither Pete nor Tim says he has any recollection.[15]

What Pete did suggest was that, for his parents—both of them under strain from the high-pressure world of academia, and with two growing boys in the house—the tension of harboring Converse, at this point, had become almost too much to bear. At one point, a lengthy marital spat had ensued, during which Phil and Jean communicated with each other only through letters—something Pete told me was common practice for them. In one missive, from which he would read me only a short excerpt over the phone, Jean wrote Phil of her complete exasperation with his sister, whom she judged "desperate," and wondered "whether she will even be alive a year from now."[16]

This is probably why Converse felt compelled to move out of the attic. She was no longer welcome—a feeling that would have outweighed all other considerations, including the fact that she had no money, no job, no prospects of any kind.

Converse appears to have briefly taken up residence at the Bell Tower Hotel, and then moved into her new North Main Street apartment,[17] where she began paying rent by the week. By the time I turned my attention to this address hidden in plain sight (it had been right there in the filing cabinet, printed on a set of canceled checks from her bank account), Phil and Jean had both passed. It seemed odd that their sons could not recall Converse's moving out, or this residence, at all. Pete insisted that he had no recollection of his aunt's ever having her own place in Ann Arbor after she came back from England. Tim, also, seemed to know nothing about the North Main Street address.

If Converse's presence in their house, and her living in their attic space, had so upset the family dynamic, how could the brothers have failed to notice that she'd moved out or, at the least, was spending time elsewhere? And if they'd been as close to her as they say they were, how could they have gone for nine months or more without ever once visiting their aunt in her new living situation? Something didn't seem right.

And it didn't stop there. After I'd gotten to know Riley Trumbull a bit more, it was clear not only that she wanted to contribute in any way she could to the understanding of Converse's story, but that she also had long-suppressed memories and impressions of which she sought to unburden herself—ones that would color my understanding of Converse's final phase in Ann Arbor.

"I had a sense of Phil's aggression, and Elizabeth's fear," she told me. "He seemed like a bully to her. *He* was the smart one in the family, and she was not to be smarter than him." Trumbull said that she had a bad feeling about Phil, going so far as to call him "a snake." It was a sense that was reinforced when, in the context of my ongoing conversations with her, she'd brought up Phil's name to her friend and colleague Jill Ault (Converse's onetime assistant at the CRCR). Ault told Trumbull that she'd "always avoided Phil because there was something creepy about him."

Trumbull went on: "I will say that Elizabeth and Phil seemed very close, or at least very bound together. It was accepted that they were an unusually close brother and sister."

"I always thought that she and Phil were married," John Tropman told me. "They were a pair."[18] More than one person I reached out to from the Ann Arbor community of that time told me they thought the same thing. I did not elicit such memories from them; they were offered without any prompting.[19]

"They were accepted at the time as close like twins," Trumbull continued. "And yet I never could see how they were alike—some facial resemblance, but in character, not at all. I found Phil friendly, yes . . . but underlying it was something unpleasant, not forthright, and I avoided him when I could. I felt he had a rather unhealthy attachment to her," she told me, and sensed that Phil was also "secretive and sly."

Trumbull then related the following anecdote:

At someone's house, at a party, in the dimly lit hall to the kitchen, I had to walk by Phil, who had his back in my direction, and he was talking to someone, leaning in very closely. It was a crowded party, but the hall was empty except for Phil, and the person I couldn't see. He was holding a bottle like soda or beer, and his arm was flailing about, making points, and splashing liquid back and forth. I hesitated to go by because I didn't want to get that close to him. From his bent back, which was all sweaty (summer, no AC), it seemed threatening, but as I dashed by, I saw the other person was Elizabeth and I felt relieved because then it seemed it might be "safe." As I went by he turned to look at me with a smile that was too big, and rather leering, so he must have been very drunk. I remember Elizabeth as having a placid expression. Not peaceful but flat—not matching his at all.

Trumbull said this incident had occurred probably between 1967 and 1969. She told me that the two were "knee to knee" and "if it had been another woman I would have thought he was putting the make on her. It certainly looked like that to me," she said.[20]

Now, with my new understanding that Converse was not living in Phil's attic during her final chapter in Ann Arbor, a remark he'd made to me years before seemed to take on greater significance. It had been in the context of his bringing up with me, again, that episode he'd first told me about on our private walk in Ann Arbor—the one about what he considered to be nothing but playful fooling during an overnight with his sister and her roommate, when they were much younger.

This time, Phil and I were on the phone, and in *this* recounting of the scene (which was, once again, not initiated by me), he included some additional thoughts: "Let them enjoy it," he told me he remembered thinking at the time, and that "Connie remembered these sexual explorations" for years to come. Also: "I never slept with her or anything."

But then, continuing, he'd said something else: "I have cursed myself in later years for not visiting her alone in Ann Arbor. I wonder if it would have made a difference."[21]

I have no reason to believe that there was anything inappropriate going on between the Converse siblings in their relationships. Any of them. But my responsibility as a writer is to report what I discover, even in those moments when I can't fully grasp its greater meaning.

Phil worked closely with me for several years, consistently making a point of offering me information he thought I should know, even when he didn't always fully explain the details. I don't know why he said these things to me. In the end, the fact that he did, and that he returned to them more than once, was not something I felt I could completely ignore. Phil knew I was writing this book. For whatever his reasons, I understood he wanted these details to be part of the story.

∾

H aving her own place again seems to have temporarily lifted Converse from her gloom. In 1973, she took on a new initiative: helping to form and raise money for a local Learning Exchange (based on a successful model that had begun two years prior in Evanston, Illinois—Ann Arbor was just one of a number of locales that took up the practice).[22] She and her fellow organizers were given an office and a telephone at Guild House (where she'd lectured in the mid-1960s) and they began building up the community service.

In text that she helped prepare for an informational brochure, the Exchange is described as "a free educational matching service to help people . . . share their knowledge, skills, and interests." It was designed to be open to everyone "from preschoolers to senior citizens," the idea being that interested parties would call in during office hours, and explain what they were interested in and available for. The Exchange was intended to be a grassroots way of bypassing the institutional education model, the politics of which had effectively helped to end Converse's career in academia.

Over the course of most of that year, Converse helped put together over two hundred topics on which the exchanges could focus, including: Far Eastern religion, medicine, yoga, men's consciousness-raising, music, jamming, French, witchcraft, sign language, tropical fish, sales techniques, legal self-defense, sailing, folk singing, science fiction, videotape, marriage counseling, and parakeets, all of which had either people willing to teach or people wanting to learn, or both.

"If you are offering to teach, you are given the names and phone numbers of people who want to learn your subject. If you want to learn, you are given the names and numbers of people offering to teach that topic. If you are interested in just getting together with others who have the same interest in a particular topic, you are given the names and numbers of appropriate people."[23]

Converse wanted people to connect with one another, to share interests and passions, to strengthen, grow, and learn as a communal body. "The basic idea . . . is that any sizable community has human resources of information and skills which are not readily available for sharing by way of regular schools and colleges," she wrote in a fundraising letter to friends, even as she apologized for making what she promised was a onetime ask for small donations. "Even adult education classes . . . do not fill the bill for people who want and need flexible schedules, one-to-one teacher-learner relationships, or topics that are unusual."[24]

Converse's volunteering duties included answering the phone when interested parties called in during office hours, matching people's interests to the appropriate teachers or learners, publicizing the Exchange with ads in local newspapers, putting posters up around town, writing and mailing brochures, fundraising, and sitting at an information booth at the local farmers market with the hope of signing people up.[25]

"She was the one, the catalyst who brought the Learning Exchange to life. Of course she was," Sally Ryan wrote to me. Ryan's husband, Desmond, helped to publicize the Exchange on his weekly Sunday morning radio show, and Ryan remembered the central role that Converse had played. "Her leadership abilities were outward, right out there ahead of everyone, but her inwardness made her unable to stand alone. Classic female duality. I got a strong sense of her kindness by her inclusiveness. She revealed her love of others by selflessly working for peace and cooperation in communities. She would be quite protective of other peoples' feelings, would never say mean or sarcastic things. She was an extremely rare kind of person who doesn't feel the need to constantly be better than anyone else, who isn't easily threatened by others or constantly competing. She was very well liked."[26] The Learning Exchange was "really unusual, and it really worked!" Ryan told me.[27]

So, it seems that if you lived in Ann Arbor in 1973, you could have encountered Connie Converse manning a booth at the farmers market. And if you had a skill or area of expertise she was interested in learning more about—a likely proposition—you could probably sign up to teach it to her in exchange for a lesson in guitar, or in French, statistics, folk singing, games, history, learning, music theory, nonviolent action, piano, poetry, political systems, offset printing, social problems, or writing—all of which she listed as subjects available for exchanges.

～

Mary Critchell, the woman to whom Converse had sent the Cassandra Cycle a decade earlier, had gotten the music to opera soloist

George McWhorter, who in turn passed it along to Nelson Keyes at the University of Louisville.

Keyes was a music professor and composer, his work now mostly forgotten. His take on Converse's magnum opus reads as follows:

> *I believe that the music does not reach the level of the poetry. The main weakness is rhythmic—the words are often set in a literal, square way, as if reading the poetry in a mechanical, plodding manner. I haven't examined all of the songs all the way through, and some good qualities may have eluded me, but on this brief look[,] the composer appears to be a talented but inexperienced amateur qualified for the study of composition but not at this point ready for professional exposure.*[28]

Converse preserved the letter in her filing cabinet. A pattern of repeated rejection over many years is enough to wear anyone down, but with Converse now in a state of flux, Keyes's dismissive feedback, after all this time, may have represented something even more to her. At the very least, it had to have been yet another blow to her morale.

Nineteen seventy-four saw the publication of Jean Converse's academic textbook *Conversations at Random: Survey Research as Interviewers See It*. It featured Connie Converse's illustrations—her last known creative effort, other than a theme party she organized and had written satirical texts and songs for, to be read and sung by attendees. Previous festivities had been humorous tributes to "Ex-Saint Christopher." (As Helen Isaacson's daughter Elise explained to me, "Saint Christopher's status changed in the Catholic church . . . apparently, [they] realized that he had never been canonized and took him off the calendar, so he no longer has a feast day. The impetus for the party was the ouster of the saint . . .")[29]

This time, however, Converse had chosen for the festivities' subject "Ex-Saint Philomena," a teenager who'd taken a vow of chastity and spurned the advances of an emperor (echoes of Cassandra), who submitted her to various forms of torture before finally decapitating her.[30]

Philomena was another saint who'd recently fallen out of favor with the Church (when it was discovered that her historical remains might not be hers after all), but as Converse wrote in the handout she prepared for the party:

It is clear enough that Philomena has always been in charge of workaday Wonders & Verities. And God wot, may she, as ex-saint and patron of mortals, keep right at it, making sure

> *that it snows outside only*
> *that flowers grow up, and visible*
> *that good spirits are available*
> *that the years of fertility are finite*
> *that some wine is red, and all dragons are green*
> *that there are half-sizes*
> *that children are younger than their parents and, for a time, smaller and weaker*
> *that Orion keeps watch in winter*
> *that people are for celebrating . . .*[31]

⁓

As she continued to try to find a place for herself, Converse began helping a pair of locals named Ernie Harburg and Rick Burgess, who wanted to purchase a downtown hotel called the Earl and a large garage next to it. The two already owned the much-beloved Del Rio Bar across the street and the idea was to buy that building and convert the other ones into a multi-use venue that would together serve as the centerpiece of a neighborhood revitalization effort.[32]

Burgess was a local jazz musician, and Harburg (son of song-writer "Yip" Harburg, and husband to Converse's friend Torry) worked at the university's Institute for Social Research, where Phil held a leadership position. They'd opened the Del Rio in 1970 and made it into a communally run establishment whose regulars included many of Ann Arbor's artistic and eccentric personalities (Converse was one of them).[33]

Converse was excited about the project, and wrote and illustrated a pitch letter for it. "We envision . . . a downtown area that is lively with people during the afternoon and evening; that is well lighted but not garish; where walkers far outnumber cars; where a wide range of citizens feel comfortable (and are not outnumbered by tourists); and where, within a short radius, people can find many interesting things to look at, listen to, taste, use, and talk about."[34]

It was a model for the very type of green-space, pedestrian-friendly urban renewal projects that have since sprouted up everywhere in this new millennium, and Converse was there helping it along with her energy, her imagination, and her passion for trying to make life better for humanity.

Converse hit up Jean Converse for a personal loan that would be returned with interest, but—seemingly out of character—her sister-in-law cast aspersions on Converse's entrepreneurial ambitions, pointing out that there was a difference between "running a business vs. running around in the peace movement."[35]

Bruised, Converse retreated, and soon abandoned her role in the enterprise altogether. In April 1974, in a short note to Jean and Torry, she wrote, "I guess it's clear I'm not competent for such a tricky and delicate operation . . . I think you'd better regard me henceforth as a bad risk. I'll be working on my own alternatives."[36]

Harburg told me that, around this time, he remembered Converse "was having some problems" and had become "a floater" at the Del Rio—maybe even one of the number of people who were given "spot jobs here and there" at the bar as a means of helping them out.[37] It was probably around this time that Jean Converse discovered that her own father had begun to secretly send Converse personal checks, "some five hundred dollars at a clip," amplifying the tension between the two women.[38]

At a low ebb, Converse took a clerk job working for Clint Fink's wife, Berenice Carroll, a former CRCR colleague who'd opened a bookbindery. But that, too, did not last long. Fink told me that Converse's poor hygiene torpedoed her employment there. Not much had changed, apparently, since Barbara Bernal registered this same detail. When Converse was told that her unpleasant odor was off-putting to customers and that she ought to start wearing deodorant, she replied, "They should get used to it. This is the natural way that people are, and you don't go out of the way to make yourself something that you're not."[39] Robert Hefner's wife, Leslie, told me, "That attitude fits perfectly with how I remember Elizabeth. She wasn't rude; she just wasn't going to capitulate to something that didn't fit with her beliefs or values."[40] Fink told me that his wife felt she had no choice but to let Converse go.

"It was a time when you could walk through a crowd of people and smell human bodies," Riley Trumbull said about it. "That doesn't happen now. By the end of the day, Elizabeth smelled like a person. But I never had the sense that she was unclean, or dirty. I think she liked naturalness because it wasn't deceitful."[41] This brought me back to a remark that Ellen Stekert once made when discussing why Converse's reputedly bad hygiene may have been "one of the major determinants as to why her music was not accepted" by the gatekeepers in New York. "There's nothing worse in our culture than something that smells," Stekert told me. "In our culture, everything is scrubbed clean. We don't smell anything."[42]

Trumbull told me that Converse's drinking now "sure took its toll with some broken blood vessels and ruddy cheeks . . . and her hair had grown rather thin. When she was tired, she just looked washed out, a sag in her face." Converse "became dowdy and dumpy and yet she was not unpretty."[43]

It may have been during this time that Trumbull received an "out of the blue" phone call from Converse.[44] "She sounded nervous, anxious, and sad. She was in her cups; I could tell because her words were a bit slurred. But she'd heard about a recent local incident involving my now ex-husband, [the washtub bass player and Converse's colleague and friend] Bill Barth, who'd charged into the MSU Library in nearby East Lansing with a gun, threatening to shoot the man I left him for. And Elizabeth wanted to apologize, because years earlier she'd encouraged me to marry Bill. I remember her telling me, 'I'm down on my uppers,' which I took to mean that she was broke and at loose ends. That's the last time I ever spoke to her."[45]

⌒

Converse's unceasing restlessness, her curiosity about everything, her obsessive compulsion to constantly do her part to help make everything she touched better understood, more logical, and fair, had at last brought her to a total personal and professional rock bottom. At one point, she told her nephew Tim, "I would just like to get a job at a Woolworth's as a cashier and work nine to five, so I could just go home at the end of the day," but even that now seemed impossible.[46]

In another effort to lift her daughter's spirits, Evelyn suggested a sequel to the Alaska trip for the two of them—this time up to Nova Scotia and the easternmost part of Canada. Phil told me that this idea—one more wretched journey with her mother—on top of everything else (which also included an impending surgery on a fibroid tumor that would shut the door on the possibility of her ever having children[47]), may have represented the last straw, the thing that finally drove Converse over the edge and into thin air.

But there may have been other factors at play.

~

The only thing that's certain about the months leading up to Converse's fiftieth birthday in August 1974 is that she made a decision to leave Ann Arbor—to enact whatever plan she may have been envisioning in the spring of 1971, before it was short-circuited by the generosity of her friends and their campaign to send her off to England. This time, there would be no saving grace, no cavalry charging in at the last moment to save her, no second thoughts.

Anyone who's ever heard the elevator-pitch version of Connie Converse's story latches on to one incontrovertible fact: that she disappeared without a trace. This is never accepted at face value. No one ever says, *Oh, that's interesting* and leaves it at that. They need to confirm that they've understood correctly. *She vanished?* It's the first question that everyone who knows anything about Converse asks me. *People don't just vanish,* they say. *There must be more to the story.*

There was, and there is.

CHAPTER 32

The Disappearance

As Converse approached turning fifty—momentous and symbolic as that number can be—she seems to have taken stock of her life, and understood it to be broken. Her friends saw this, too. "She was in ill health at the end," Helen Isaacson told me.[1] Converse's existence, such as it was in Ann Arbor, had become claustrophobic to her, a pitch-black dead end.

On two separate, previous occasions in her life, at age nineteen and again at thirty-six, Converse had made dramatic, risky, and unpredictable exits from courses she'd carefully plotted and followed until she couldn't any longer. It was time to do so again.

Fifty a half century ago was not what fifty is today. Fifty then was the beginning of old age. Life expectancy in 1974 was only seventy-one years. Fifty may have represented to Converse one last chance, one more reinvention, one more setting a bridge ablaze. If her life was to have a fourth act, she had to move again, and quickly. This one was finished.[2]

Phil and Jean's account of what happened next, repeated in numerous interviews, is considered the current story of record. It goes something like this:

In early August 1974, they took their annual summer vacation to Glen Lake, in the northwest of Upper Michigan. They always took the kids with them and invited Converse, too, and she always declined. But this time, something had seemed off.

"We were really worried about her and concerned about leaving her alone," Jean told me, so they were in part relieved when Pete announced that he wasn't going with them, preferring to stay home instead.[3]

But Phil said something very different: "I really think that was in a period where we weren't seeing her a lot . . . Sometimes when she was living with us we saw her a lot and then we saw her less when she was living away," which seems to be a reference to the North Main Street address, one I hadn't picked up on at the time because the timeline kept getting confused in their recollections, and I thought that perhaps Phil was mixing up her various addresses in Ann Arbor.

"Uhh, I never, we never, you see, she was out there at this new place for some few months before she disappeared. But we never had been there. So that tells you something about that frequency . . . Neither of us had ever stepped into that place."[4]

Phil said that when they returned, Pete informed them that "Connie had gone away on a trip in her Volkswagen." Immediately, they'd sized up the situation: She'd seized upon the opportunity of their being away to pack up and leave without having to have a scene of any kind. "She wanted to get away before we got back," Phil believed.

A note she'd left behind explained that she was off to find a new way of living somewhere, with specific instructions for Phil to pay her health insurance, but only until a specific date, unless they heard from her otherwise. Phil said that once he read that note (the whereabouts of which he said he'd lost track), he knew, instinctively, that she'd gone "to do away with herself."

Soon after, concerned phone calls came pouring in from friends who had received their own cryptic letters and notes, all of them imparting a similar message about her going away and starting over.

Both Phil and Jean were fond of repeating a detail, reported to them by Pete, that Connie had kept delaying her departure because Nixon's resignation was imminent and she wanted to witness his downfall on television, in real time. But the entire episode nonetheless blindsided them, leaving them "devastated."

Yet that's not the story Pete told me.

Pete said that in the weeks leading up to her fiftieth birthday, on August 3, 1974, Converse had let it be known to her community of friends and family that she was intending to return to New York City, the place of her early artistic triumphs and of her freewheeling young adulthood, to try to get her old job back and make a fresh start.

An unremarkable celebration had been held in her honor, a combination birthday/bon voyage party. Pete told me that part of the intention of the party was to raise money for her so that she could get herself set up again in New York[5]—but no one else I talked to remembers anything else about it.

In direct contradiction to what Phil said, Pete told me that his entire family "certainly knew she was leaving," so they knew perfectly well she would not take them up on their offer to join them on the trip to Glen Lake. She never went with them anyhow, but this time she had a trip of her own planned.

Pete told me he'd stayed behind mainly "to avoid my parents."[6] He recalled that in the days leading up to his aunt's departure, he saw her packing and organizing her things, but said that this didn't seem unusual in any way. In fact, it made complete sense. "I was a teenager at the time," he told me. "I was thinking about girls and not really paying too much attention to Connie. I mean, we all knew that she was leaving, and I assumed that I would see her or hear from her again soon."

This contradicts another detail that Phil repeated to me, and to others—that because Converse had schemed to pack her things and sneak away while the family was gone, Pete's last-minute decision to stay home had somehow added an unforeseen complication to her plans, causing her to fabricate a story for him. "She told Peter that she'd decided to take a trip," Phil said, her story for why she was packing all her things up. According to Phil, such activity would have "raised suspicion" because no one was yet aware of her intentions.[7]

⌀

A nd then: Tim later told me that *he* may actually have been the one who stayed behind in the house and watched Converse leave and that it had been *Pete* who went on the trip with their parents.[8]

None of this makes any sense. If everyone knew she was leaving, and if a bon voyage party had been held in her honor, why would she have been upset that Pete (or Tim) stayed behind, ostensibly throwing a wrench in her plan to pack in secret? Why would Phil and Jean have been surprised to find her gone when they returned from vacation, as Phil recalled on numerous occasions, if that's exactly what she'd told them she was going to do?[9] If the community was aware of her plans to move, why would the goodbye notes she wrote to everyone, dropped in the mailbox on her way out of town, have caught everyone off guard, as Phil and Jean said they had? And why didn't the brothers' memories of who watched her leave match?[10]

The Ann Arbor weather was pleasantly mild that second week of August. The Watergate hearings had reached their peak, and Pete indeed recalled to me how his aunt's eyes were glued to the television set as she packed. She hated Nixon with a passion, a sentiment dating back to his role in the anti-Communist hysteria of the late 1940s and early '50s that had impacted so many of her former AIPR colleagues. She wanted to watch him get his just deserts. Pete repeated the story that she held off leaving until there was some closure to the case.

On the evening of August 8, 1974, all three major networks carried Nixon's resignation speech. There's a one-in-three chance that Converse watched anchor Walter Cronkite deliver the news. She may have mentioned to Pete then, or at some other juncture during nonstop coverage of the hearings, that she had once, only twenty years earlier, sat next to Cronkite in a television studio, in front of a live camera, as a featured guest on the CBS *Morning Show*; that she had performed her songs for him and for countless unseen audience members; that she'd been a star for a day.

More likely, and more characteristically, she didn't mention it at all, keeping to herself thoughts of an opportunity that had never borne fruit, if she thought them at all anymore. She'd played the tape of her singing her songs that one night for Tim, not for Pete, who told me that it wasn't until many years later that he learned his aunt had even written and recorded music of her own. And, given what Pete told me about where his attentions were focused at that time, she was probably watching the television alone.

Then, knowing Nixon had been disgraced, Converse enacted her exit. She said goodbye to her nephew, Pete told me, walked out to her Volkswagen Beetle (already packed with her guitar and some few belongings), set her bag down on the passenger seat, and started the engine. Pete told me that he remembers her waving goodbye as she drove away, the car quietly receding into the soft summer night.[11]

~

Over the next few days, her goodbye notes and letters landed in the mailboxes of her friends and family. Each had its own distinct flavor and tone, with references unique to its recipient. None of the envelopes that enclosed them had a return address. Here are excerpts from the letters I was able to track down.

To Marcia Barrabee:

August '74

Dear Marcia—I'm off to NYC for a while. I'm glad I didn't have a chance to say goodbye to you because goodbyes are desperately harrowing to me, though I know others NEED them. O temperaments rather than O mores.

And your soup at my door and your nice evenings with new people (never got to hear Joel sing!) AND your many phone calls to me out of the blue, with a useful suggestion and/or just the sense of friendly concern. Thank you very much, Miz Barrabee. Please just ramp around your clinics till your situation is decent and comfortable and then leave for some job even more so.

Love,
Connie[12]

Barrabee told me that when she got hers, "I called Jean and said, 'I got the strangest note from Connie.' She said, 'We all got one,' and I thought: *Uh oh.*"[13]

Vicki and Ed Vandenberg, a married couple who were two of Converse's close Ann Arbor friends, each received goodbye notes. Ed, a guitar player, had worked with Converse on the Alternative Perspectives on Vietnam conference she helped to organize in the 1960s, and had recently lent his legal aid to the downtown neighborhood revitalization effort that he, his wife, and Converse were all working on with Ernie Harburg and Rick Burgess. They'd also been key participants in Converse's "Ex-Saint" parties over the last few years.

To Vicki Vandenberg she wrote:

> *. . . You've been an exceedingly gentle friend to me over many years, and I wish I didn't have to give you up.*
>
> *Parting shot at one of your Figures—I am too an Ethnic! I sweat like a pig, I don't feel at home in the WASP establishment, and my passions leak out frequently, and, and. So there, you calm Pole! Luv (Anglophile spelling)*
>
> *Connie[14]*

Unlike almost the entirety of her voluminous correspondence, these notes were handwritten. It is as though she wanted to leave behind some last, personal trace of herself.

Ed Vandenberg's read:

> *Dear Edward—*
>
> *WHEREAS: After my warning to my own family not to observe my birthdays, you and Vicki have persisted in doing it; and*
>
> *WHEREAS: You have at least twice failed to bill me for Legal Aid Rendered; and*
>
> *WHEREAS: Your particular forms of wit and humor have always endangered my personal dignity in that they often crack me up; and*
>
> *WHEREAS: You persist in forming and communicating interesting and informed opinions on a number of interesting subjects; and*

THEREFORE, regardless of your long years of service to the Community at Large, I the undersigned do complain of these particulars and represent that you have been too kind, too funny, and too sensible.

YOU ARE THEREFORE SUMMONED to appear not later than 12 noon, August 2, 40 years from now, along with your manifold co-conspirators, at the Bar of Heaven (20 years grace period) to answer to these charges.

Complainant (Plaintiff) Connie[15]

Helen and Joel Isaacson got a note that included:

I have to leave town for another while (NYC this time, trying to rejoin my old union and get a job)—and just thank you for being the Isaacsons in my life . . .[16]

To her nephew Tim (which would seem to be an argument for its having indeed been Pete who was in the house when she left):

Just like Bilbo Baggins, I have to go away.[17]

To another friend, named Nancy Williams:

The hymn you picked for my birthday card really hit me in the solar plexus, because I'm about to "brave another cruise," though I can't claim to know whose wind is drying my vain tears and filling my rifted sail. Anyway, I'm off to NYC to try to find a livelihood . . .[18]

One more Ann Arbor friend, Rose Wilson, told me that her letter from Converse was "two or four sentences that said she was going back to New York," she said. "It didn't seem significant at the time."[19]

〜

Most of these notes are dated, vaguely, "Aug. 1974," but the one Converse sent to her mother had a specific date: August 10, 1974. After a paragraph of small talk, she wrote:

> *I have just vacated my room and disconnected my phone and am about to leave Ann Arbor for NYC to see if I can get back in my old union and get a job there.*
>
> *It may be some time before I can get settled somewhere and get back in touch. In any event, it would be pointless for you to worry. I just have to try some new way of getting along instead of being a burden on my relatives and friends.*
>
> *Take care of yourself and get all the enjoyment you can out of life.*
>
> *Love—Elizabeth* [20]

What must Evelyn have thought? Her only daughter—who, from an early age, had shown such promise, for whom everyone had predicted such great things. How had it come to this? Did Evelyn feel any responsibility for her daughter's decision, or read anything into the final lines encouraging her, her *mother*, to take care of herself? [21]

〜

There is only one typewritten farewell from Converse that I'm aware of: a one-page all-purpose letter left in her filing cabinet. At the top of it, she scrawled:

> *8/10/74—This was just one of several efforts, none adequate.*
> *A sample.*

Then she addresses the world, in all caps:

"TO ANYONE WHO EVER ASKS: (If I'm Long Unheard From)"[22]

This is the thin hard sublayer under all the parting messages I'm likely to have sent: let me go, let me be if I can, let me not be if I can't. For a number of years now I've been the object of affectionate concern to my relatives and many friends in Ann Arbor; have received not just financial but spiritual support from them; have made a number of efforts, in this benign situation, to get a new toe-hold on the lively world. Have failed.

As an overeducated peasant I've read a good deal about Middle-Age Depression and known several cases other than my own. I know there are temporary chemical therapies and sometimes "temporary" is long enough. Experts agree it's not a single isolable mental disease. Probably it's a few simple humanities mixed up in a pot of random concomitant circumstances.

In the months after I got back from my desperate flight to England I began to realize that my new personal incapabilities were still stubbornly hanging in. I did fight, but they hung in. Maybe my time in England, financed largely by my friends, was too benign a treatment; at any rate, it's the only sustained period in my life that I now look back on in the silliest detail as "fun," unproductive fun. Not getting anything done. I did sit in my bedsitter very often in bemused despair, but also I had fun.

Since then I've watched the elegant, energetic people of Ann Arbor, those I know and those I don't know, going about their daily business on the streets and in the buildings, and I've felt a detached admiration for their energy and elegance. If I ever was a member of this species, perhaps it was a social accident that has now been cancelled.

To survive at all, I expect I must drift back down through the other half to the twentieth twentieth, which I already know pretty well, to the hundredth hundredth, which I have only heard about. I might survive there quite a few years—who knows? But you understand I have to do it with no benign umbrella. Human society fascinates me and awes me and fills me with grief and joy; I just can't find my place to plug into it.

So let me go, please; and please accept my thanks for those happy times that each of you has given me over the years; and please know that I would have preferred to give you more than I ever did or could—I am in everyone's debt.

Elizabeth (Connie) Converse

The Volkswagen she drove away in on August 10, 1974, has never been found, nor has any trace of its contents, or her body. What people can't believe is true *is* true: Elizabeth "Connie" Converse was never seen or heard from again.

Walking in the Crystal Air

I have dozens of fans all over the world.

—Connie Converse,
attributed by Phil Converse

CHAPTER 33

Past Recall

In 2011, when I first raised the subject of Converse's disappearance with Phil, at his home, I asked if he had reported her missing. He told me that, at one point, he spoke to "a tracer of missing persons" to gain an understanding of what would be involved in looking for her. As Phil told it, the private detective informed him that everyone has the "legal right" to disappear if they want to—that is, hypothetically, were the detective successful in finding Converse, he would be bound *by law* (Phil's emphasis) not to reveal her whereabouts if she didn't want to be found.

How Sad, How Lovely producer Dan Dzula told me that Phil relayed this same information to him, more or less verbatim, in their early conversations. "It did seem a little odd," Dzula said. "I mean, isn't that what private detectives do?"[1]

But, as far as Phil had been concerned, that was that. After receiving this information from the detective, he didn't pursue the matter any further. Phil felt that to do so would have run counter to his sister's wishes to be left alone.

Phil did not recall Jean's detail that his sister had left instructions with him to pay her insurance and bills up to a certain point "and only to that point," but he agreed with his wife that it must have been so.[2]

Converse's long-ago statement about Frannie Flint's death had stuck with him, he said to me, a reminder to him that his sister had long considered suicide a viable option for herself. Converse had always loved to drive out to the farthermost ends of land, where it met large bodies of water, he said, and she had a particular fondness for Tobermory, Ontario, a tiny town at the end of Bruce Peninsula on Lake Huron (site of numerous famous shipwrecks). He wondered aloud whether she'd arrived there, or someplace like it, and then simply driven her car "off a cliff or something," straight into the water. Phil said that this was the reason he did not report her disappearance to the police and why he did not go looking for her. There hadn't seemed much point.

Nevertheless, a few weeks after her departure, Phil wrote to the medical examiner at Bellevue Hospital in New York:

> *I have lost contact with my sister whom I believe to be somewhere in the New York City area. At the moment I am not completely alarmed, as her dropping out of sight was intentional and announced to me in advance. On the other hand, I know her to be despondent over several problems, including a health difficulty, so I felt I should file some identifying information with you . . .*[3]

Bellevue replied a month later: She had not turned up there. Both letters were in Converse's filing cabinet. Presumably, she had not put them there.

"If anyone could have disappeared without a trace, it would have been Connie," Helen Isaacson told me.[4] Her husband, Joel, added, "It wouldn't make any sense to me, if a beloved sibling disappeared, not to go looking for them."[5]

Pete Converse told me that it was his feeling that children reared in repressive and emotionally stunted households, like that of the Converses of Concord, New Hampshire, sometimes develop nonverbal ways of communicating with each other and that his father and his aunt had always seemed to share a private sort of code. It was his sense that there was something about the way Converse left, or however she expressed herself in her goodbye letter to him (the one that got lost), that led Phil to understand intuitively, or at least to believe, what her true intentions were.

After Converse had been missing for a month, Evelyn wrote to Phil and Jean about her "concern and perplexity about Connie's departure to New York, and the silence thereafter."
Jean replied:

I would be very surprised if anyone understands Connie's current move... We are all hoping to hear from her, all quite certain that we will not hear for quite a time, all concerned and yet hopeful that she will find a way to set her life in order...

... Connie has a genuine work crisis. Perhaps she will find something in the printing business. But perhaps she's found something at Kresge's or a soda fountain, which she may use to tide her over. If it's some utterly dull, or even demeaning job, I think she'd rather have this tiding over period to be a rather private one. Privacy, and pride, and the need to try out the current experiment, whatever it is, without any audience at all.

... Philip mentioned that you wondered whether she was "mentally unbalanced," mindful that menopause has given many women anxiety and depression... I do not think ... that Connie's state of mind is something nonrational or really disordered ... Philip and I ... think of Connie's state as depressed.[6]

J ean told me that Evelyn "somehow felt guilty herself and had said, 'Oh we never talked about Frannie Flint' and somehow she felt culpable that if they had talked about Frannie Flint it wouldn't have preyed on Connie's mind and that this alternative wouldn't have been so . . ."[7]

According to Phil, Evelyn took to looking through phone books from across the country. At one point, she found an Elizabeth Converse living in either Oklahoma or Kansas City—he wasn't sure which, and this was what had prompted him to seek out the detective he'd spoken to, the one who told him that people have the legal right to disappear if they want to.

When Everett T. Eaton was a teenager, around 1974–75, he would often visit his great-aunt Evelyn in Concord. Eaton told me she never once mentioned that she had a daughter who'd recently gone missing.[8]

In July 1977, in a note to her cousin Marion Dunbar, Evelyn wrote, "We have not heard from our Elizabeth for many months and do not know where she is. We think her age and physical conditions are partly responsible."[9] Evelyn's niece Claire remembered learning that Evelyn "suspected she was on a secret assignment . . . She never seemed upset."[10]

Evelyn lived until age ninety-five, never knowing what had become of her daughter. Her death notice included the fact that she would be buried next to Ernest in Meredith, New Hampshire, and that "it would be helpful if those planning to attend notified Paul Converse" and listed Paul's then-current address and phone number. Apparently, Phil and Paul were still not on speaking terms, thirty years after the rupture in that relationship.

Paul's elder son, Bruce, was studying abroad in France when he heard from Hyla that Converse was missing.[11] Bruce felt certain that his aunt was not dead, that she'd simply made up her mind to go somewhere else, the same way she'd decided to leave New York fourteen years earlier. On his way home from Europe, Bruce stopped off in Concord to visit Evelyn, staying for a week or so shortly after the disappearance. He does not recall a single mention being made of his aunt Connie during his visit.[12]

Years later, after he'd moved to Phoenix, Bruce found an "E. Converse" in the local phone book and drove to the address to see if it was her. It was not.[13] He then told me about a conversation he had had with Phil in California in 1989, after Phil had taken a post at Stanford.[14] When the subject turned to Connie, Phil told Bruce then that she had once written to him, "If I need to go down to the sea, I trust you will let me."[15]

Converse was never officially reported missing. Phil and Jean told me that each of them received goodbye letters from her, too, but they couldn't seem to find them. Phil Converse died in 2014; Jean, in 2018. Connie Converse's farewell letters to them have never surfaced.

Myths and legends have a way of cropping up around unexplained events. Marcia Barrabee's son, David, who was a teenager in 1974, recalls hearing that Converse had "gone off to find an old boyfriend from the Navy . . . something to do with a man and the sea."[16] Tom Converse remembered hearing that Evelyn went to a fortune-teller at some point (against her Baptist beliefs) and was told that Converse was alive and well and living a new life in Brazil.

The story of her disappearance, as it was relayed to Tom by his father, included the following tableau: Cousin Elizabeth had not been heard from in some time, and the police were summoned. "It was the middle of winter. Her car was found still running in the driveway, there was breakfast on the stove, and the back door was wide open."[17]

Upon learning that this was a fiction created out of whole cloth by members of his extended family, Tom chuckled. "Well, are you sick of the Converses and their peculiarities yet?" he wrote to me. "I sometimes think we're like something out of Hawthorne, or maybe Flannery O'Connor. Or *The National Enquirer*."[18]

And contrary to what Phil and his sons told me, his nephew Luther's ex-wife, Barbara, remembered that Phil "talked about hunting for Connie" and that this was "a theme for the whole family. Phil would go to oceanside places to see if they had any unidentified bodies."[19]

So many clues added up to so many questions, and then there were the clues that just *weren't* anymore. During my visit to Phil in Ann Arbor, I'd finally asked him straight-out why he'd decided to "dump" so much of the contents of his sister's filing cabinet decades before. At first, he protested, claiming he would never do such a thing. But when confronted with the evidence—the cabinet's original "Guide to Contents of Five-Drawer File" with "dumped" written in pencil next to so many items—Jean, sitting next to him, said, "That *is* your handwriting." There was a long pause. Phil seemed either confused or embarrassed, or both. "I guess it is," he admitted.

Phil's getting rid of entire swaths of his sister's papers, including big chunks of her writing and diary entries, may not have been Ted Hughes's burning of Sylvia Plath's journal, but it seems to live in that same neighborhood. Why would he have done this? He would later memorialize his sister with "Connie's Guitar Songs," so he was well aware of her artistic accomplishments and had even positioned himself as loyal keeper of the flame. He knew that, eventually, people like me (and the world) would be interested. He'd not only invited me there to look, but had been as gracious and forthcoming as he could be, offering me unfettered access to her effects, granting me permission to quote from her writings and include her photographs in my work, making himself available for my every question, every phone call, every email, cheering me on in my research and encouraging my endeavors. But if his actions and behaviors with regard to his beloved sister seem complicated and imperfect, let those whose lives are neither make those judgments.

I did finally hear from Paul's son Luther, the one who'd named his daughter Elizabeth in tribute to his aunt. After a decade of having my requests for his participation go unanswered, he texted me out of the blue one afternoon. There it was, on my phone: a message from Luther Converse (I think he now goes by Luke). He apologized for his long silence, told me that he preferred not to talk on the phone, and that he didn't want to get into anything related to his aunt Connie other than to say that he'd come to a place of peace regarding her, that he was aware of my efforts on her behalf, and that he wanted to offer me blessings. These brief but gentle messages, coming as they did in the final days of completing this manuscript, somehow felt providential.

After Phil died, I asked Pete how the trauma of his aunt's disappearance had been handled within the family unit in the months after she left. Pete told me that his parents were not emotionally open with him and his brother, and that they "shielded us from stuff." He recalled that "within six to twelve months," there must have been some conversation in which the subject was addressed, but he did not recall any specifics.[20]

Tim told me that it was not until late adolescence that he began to accept that Connie was not coming back.[21] Neither nephew offered much in the way of revelation about the aftermath of the disappearance. If anything, both downplayed it, as though it were not a particularly extraordinary event.

This tendency took a turn a few years later. On an April morning in 2018, I checked my inbox and noted a new email from Pete, written the night before, at 11:40. "Something's come up that I need to talk with you about," it read. The subject line was "Can you call me?"

Everything about this was unusual. After Phil died, Pete had been put in charge of his aunt's estate, and he and I corresponded frequently about a variety of matters related to my various Connie Converse–focused projects. These exchanges had never before had any urgency attached to them. In all that time, Pete had never once asked me to call him, and the late time stamp on his email and the fact that he'd made a point of including his cell phone number (which he knew I had) indicated that this was something important.

Sometime before, in the context of talking about the disappearance, Pete had told me that his uncle Lee Cross, (Jean's brother-in-law, based in Indianapolis) had once hired a private investigator to look for Connie.[22] Pete's unusual email, I soon learned, had to do with this.

That uncle, I'd found, was long dead, but his wife, Susie, was still alive, and I'd recently emailed Pete to ask him to put me in touch with her to see what she remembered about that investigation. Pete now explained that my request had led to a discussion between him and his brother about Connie's fate. Pete told me that, five or six years ago, he himself had been contacted by the Michigan State Police about a murder case that involved some remains that had been found in Tennessee. The detective whom he spoke to thought the remains might be his aunt. If so, Pete was told, he would be notified. If not, he would never hear from the detective again. According to Pete, that was the end of it.

Why was Pete telling me this? And what did it mean? Five or six years prior, Phil had still been alive. Why would the police contact Pete and not Phil? And if nothing had ever come of that case, why even tell me about it?

These were the questions in my head as Pete went on to tell me that, before his mother died, the subject of the disappearance had come up. He explained that Jean felt, emphatically, that "Connie did not want to be found," that she was a very smart woman, and that if she wanted to remain vanished, that was how it was going to be. Pete wanted assurance from me now that my book was not going to focus on solving what happened to her. I answered that this was not my agenda: Indeed, his aunt remained vanished.

The idea that her story continued is engrossing; the idea that it ended, tragic. At the very least, and without engaging in conspiracy theories, it seems not unreasonable to wonder whether there are people who may know, or did know, something about exactly what happened to Converse.

Beginning in 1969 until records of her checks stop in September 1973, Converse began writing monthly checks to "Cash" in what were objectively large amounts of money (on average, about twenty thousand dollars annually in 2022 money, adjusted for inflation).[23] Because she wrote checks for her groceries, rent, utilities, insurance, magazine subscriptions,[24] alcohol, etc., and lived in the cheapest housing available in Ann Arbor, that cash is largely unaccounted for.[25] Why did she need it?

Many who now love Converse's music have expressed the hope that maybe, just maybe, she managed to slip off the grid, and lived out her life in isolated peace and quiet among the wildflowers, birds, and animals that appear in her songs. Maybe she was saving money to do just that. Maybe it's possible that, though she did not vanish on the wings of glory, Connie Converse's life continued somewhere else, maybe even *as* someone else.

For now, the only thing that can be said for certain is that Converse was last seen in Ann Arbor, in August 1974, her final, furtive act utterly consistent with how her life might be described: unpredictable and inevitable, opaque and mesmerizing, complete and unfinished, and almost unbelievable.

AFTERWORD

Connie Converse's life was ruled by a battle between two opposing forces: a longing to make herself known and an instinct to hide, to be invisible. The extremity, the gravity, of the last thing that we know about her continues to suck us in with a kind of morbid fascination, but it's hardly the most interesting thing about her. Her disappearance is simply the exclamation point she left at the conclusion of her known life.

What does it mean that the Connie Converse we can now see remains incomplete? It does not diminish her appeal; if anything, it may even increase it. The outlines of her life intersect with so many of today's cultural trends and preoccupations, and with so many evergreen ones, that it would not surprise me to see, in time, entire books devoted to: Converse's work around the issue of race in America; her Cassandra Cycle and how it relates to both Greek myth and twentieth-century art song; her work in conflict studies and as a political thinker, both in Ann

Arbor and in New York; how she fits into twentieth-century narratives about gender; her output of visual art, including her drawings, paintings, illustrations, and photography; her explorations into community learning; and her "Statistical Study of 1000 Melodies" and Modular Dialog projects. These books could and should be written. I want to read them all. Maybe a copy of the game manual for Modular Dialog will be found. Maybe we'll all be playing it someday.

For me, this is a story about questions, not answers. The questions about Converse remain endless. But what about the questions about us? How many more Connie Converses are there out there—marginalized talents waiting to be heard; artists and thinkers lacking the emotional tools, the encouragement, the self-esteem, the community, needed to thrive? And what price do we pay, as individuals and as a culture, by continuing to use fame, wealth, property, and power as our primary metrics for success?

In America, by the time we're old enough to start thinking about what we want to do with our lives, we've already been indoctrinated into the notion that the value of art is monetary. We're repeatedly shown examples of artists who've "made it," by which is meant that they're fantastically rich and famous. It's a competition; there are winners and losers. To be a winner means making a lot of money with one's art. To be a loser means not making a lot of money with one's art. Merit, talent, and genuine expression are not the major factors in this equation.

My father, Harvey, may he rest in peace, was a violin prodigy. When kids his age were out playing ball and going to parties, he was home alone with his mother, a depressive woman whose greatest joy may have come from listening to him practice his scales, études, and arpeggios. My dad went on to be concertmaster in every orchestra he played in, and was offered a scholarship to attend Oberlin Conservatory of Music, but by then he'd become convinced that a career in music and achieving success were mutually exclusive endeavors. He wanted to be able to support the family he and my mother, Myra, his high school sweetheart, were planning, and to have a chance to do so in some comfort.

So, my dad, the son of a poor Ukrainian immigrant father and a first-generation Austrian American mother, stayed close to home, got a B.A., and went into business. He put his violin on the shelf, where it stayed for the rest of his life. He did well, first as a salesman, then as a stockbroker, and finally as a retailer. And though we lived frugally in a modest suburban home, he sent me and my brother to expensive colleges and made sure our family was never wanting for any essentials that money could buy.

But other things, money couldn't buy. Though he had the bulwarks of family and a stable business, and though I know he derived great pleasure from those things, peace of mind eluded him. On those exceedingly rare occasions I can remember him picking up his old violin, my dad became a different person. His technical skills had deteriorated, of course, but the talent, the soul, was still there—in the warmth of his tone, in his lustrous vibrato, in the feeling behind every note he played, in the expression of who he was. For those brief, glowing moments, he seemed to be who he actually was.

Yet for whatever reason he wouldn't, or couldn't, resume his creative practice, and I wonder whether the inability to fill the void left by its absence with material possessions is what helped feed his lifelong internal struggles. What was it like to have had this gift, and to have then consciously buried it? What was it like for him to hide this innermost part of who he was, not only from the outside world, but from his family and even from himself?

To truly internalize the message that one's purest form of self-expression doesn't matter, that it has no value in the world, must be a kind of spiritual death. I have to believe it's what contributed to Connie Converse's final surrender to the idea that she had failed.

We need art. It is an essential human language, a notion that gets steamrolled every time funding for arts education is cut or eliminated. For some, art is the only language they're capable of speaking with fluency. I might count myself in this number. Art is how I talk. It's how I understand my place in the world, and it's how I communicate *with* that world. Whether the marketplace assigns it value has nothing to do with the purpose for which I make it: to express, to be understood, to belong.

In my early twenties I lived in New Orleans, and one of the countless characters I befriended there was the sculptor and painter Roger Wing, who regularly hosted "art parties" in his apartment. They were potluck affairs, and community-minded. Roger would put on some music for inspiration (I particularly remember late Coltrane and Ornette Coleman being in heavy rotation) and the people who showed up would be encouraged to make use of the spread of art supplies he had on hand. The purpose was not to make work to show or to sell; the purpose was to prime the pumps of our own individual engines of creativity, to prompt us to engage with our own true spirits.

How might Connie Converse have fared had she lived in a society in which everyday creativity was honored, and all took a genuine interest in the things one another made? The famous artists we love and admire are one thing, but what about that healthcare worker down the street who writes poetry on the side? What about that aunt who paints watercolors as a hobby, or that high school teacher who curates a gorgeously thriving garden, or is experimenting with new culinary creations, or who just wrote a new song—not to upload on social media to get hits, but simply for the sake of doing something beautiful, as Converse did throughout her life? In today's trend toward everything local, can we take more of an interest in local art, too? Can we find a way to celebrate one another, and the creative spark that resides in each of us?[1]

People who knew Connie Converse talked to me about her being unlike anyone else they'd ever known. They've used phrases like "It was as though she'd come from another planet" and "She had one foot in another world." It's a compelling idea, one that gives so many details about her a sense of unreality. It's almost as though Connie Converse's entire life is a sort of urban myth, a legend for us to consider, the manifestation of some kind of collective nightmare still haunting us, a harbinger of the culture of falsity, incuriosity, self-absorption, and numbed-out isolation we now inhabit. A warning.

⌒

It's my hope that there will eventually be a revised edition of this book. As Converse's music gains in popularity, as treatments of her life are inevitably adapted for various media, as more people find her life and work worthy of further study and appreciation, I expect any number of people to come out of the woodwork with their own recollections of Converse—their correspondence with her, their photographs of her, maybe even private recordings she made for them. Maybe people who met her after she left Ann Arbor for the last time will come forward. Who knows?

The sheet music for some of the songs for which we have only titles (like "Cousin Jane's Blues" and "Sun, Weary of Swimming") may turn up, or recordings of her singing more of her piano compositions. Maybe the manuscript of her novel will be found, or her opera, or any of the creations missing from her filing cabinet—even if the deliriousness of considering what qualities these and other unknown items possess may prove more thrilling than the items themselves. I hope it all comes to light. I hope we get to know more and more about Converse. And more, and more.

Given what we now know about how meticulous she was, it's clear that there was real intentionality as far as what she left behind goes. She could have easily disposed of all the letters, the pictures, the projects, the folders containing her THOTS and her TRIES. She could have tossed out the tapes, the manuscript sheet music, the drawings and paintings.

She could have brought that filing cabinet out to the curb on the night she left. She could have effectively erased her life.

But she didn't. She knew that she'd lived with purpose, that she'd made contributions that might, one day, be appreciated. She wanted us to see them, and have them, and know them. She knew that what she'd done had value, even if few in her world could see it. It is *we* who are in *her* debt.

Don't ask how Connie Converse disappeared. Ask how she lived. Listen to her recordings, hear her voice, play her songs. She's still right there—just as she's there in the photographs she left behind, in the drawings, in the correspondence, and in the fingerprints left on her goodbye letters. She's there in the passionate, Cassandra-like thoughts she recorded about America, and conflict, and race, and the war of all against all. She's there, too, on the steps of 23 Grove Street, in her old Village haunts and peering out a Harlem window, in a few random London pubs, and on the tree-lined blocks of Ann Arbor. She's there, at this very moment, in the massive shadows and rippling echoes of all she left behind— out on a windy hill, wearing her web of days, waiting behind a gate and beneath a tree, and living in between the two tall mountains of her life: the eternal one to which she always belonged and the earthly one she could never comfortably inhabit until, perhaps in some small ways at least, now.

The Fall of a Leaf

After the inevitable *Did I hear that right?* questions people tend to have about the disappearance, the next most common (and logical) thing I am asked is: *If she never made it as a professional musician, and if she vanished long after trying, how does anyone even know about her and her songs today?*

This has mostly to do with something that might be called "The Revelation Visited upon the Pilgrim Dzula Whilst he did Rove upon the Turnpike in the Land of newest Faire Jersey."

On Sunday, January 9, 2004, WNYC radio host David Garland introduced his *Spinning on Air* listening audience to his featured guests that evening: none other than Gene Deitch and Deitch's son, Kim, a long-established underground comic book artist. The two had come on the show to promote the release of a new book they'd co-authored.

Garland knew about Gene Deitch's history as an amateur recording engineer, including his early recordings of John Lee Hooker (sessions that had recently been released on a European label). So, in addition to helping father and son promote their book, Garland was interested in highlighting these other accomplishments and wanted to play some of Deitch's homemade recordings on the air.

Prior to the appearance, Garland asked him for a sampling of his favorites. The CD-R Deitch then sent was, to Garland, not terribly exciting.[1] One track, however, stood out: It was performed by Connie Converse, singing alone, quietly, accompanied by her acoustic guitar.[2] At first, Garland thought he recognized the song as something he'd heard long ago, but he could find absolutely no information about Converse anywhere he looked.[3]

Puzzled, he asked Deitch for more details. Who *was* this Connie Converse?

Deitch replied that the recording had been made by him at his home in Westchester in 1954. Converse had been a stranger to him, an odd young woman who simply turned up with her guitar one night to a listening party he was hosting. She played a number of songs that evening, all of them her own highly unusual compositions. Though the music did not "fit" stylistically with the jazz, blues, and folk preferred by Deitch's gang, Converse succeeded in stunning everyone in attendance with her songs. Deitch lost touch with her soon after. Years later, he heard, she had become depressed and had literally vanished.

Knowing a good yarn when he heard one, Garland told Deitch that he intended to highlight the homemade track on the upcoming show and that he wanted Deitch to talk a bit more about this Converse person. Deitch said he'd be delighted to do so, eager to give her music its introduction to a radio audience some fifty years after he recorded her. The Converse song that Deitch had sent Garland, and that Garland was going to play for his listeners, was "One by One."

～

Spinning on Air was in its seventeenth year at that point and had its share of devoted followers. Among them was a young Dan Dzula, a twenty-year-old college student studying film and television production at New York University's Tisch School of the Arts.

Dzula was driving to his parents' house on the New Jersey Shore on a chilly Sunday night in January when he tuned in to Garland's show.[4] Upon hearing Converse's performance of "One by One," Dzula had a visceral reaction commensurate with the one I would have at a holiday party some years later, when I heard "Talkin' Like You" for the first time. He pulled his car off to the shoulder of the New Jersey Turnpike and sat listening in stunned silence as a ghostly, unpolished voice sang of alienation, of yearning to connect but not knowing how. Like "Talkin' Like You," "One by One" seemed impossible to place, untethered to any musical era or style. Like that other song, this one featured music that was measured and spare, but it was an even heavier cut, the darker, smudgier side of the same coin.

That the song did not follow any sort of traditional musical song structure was not what immediately drew Dzula in. There was something else he heard in its two minutes and six seconds—something direct, uncanny, something vital. Dzula fished in his glove compartment for a pen, scribbled "Connie Converse" on the back of his car registration, and made his way back onto the turnpike.

～

A total of about five minutes of Garland's broadcast that night was devoted to Converse (including the duration of the song itself). Deitch recalled how, back in the 1950s, when he was living in New York, he often had musicians showing up at his house parties happy to have their impromptu performances recorded for posterity and that, one day, this woman had simply appeared. Deitch described Converse as "modest," said that "she had thirty or thirty-five songs." He recalled that "we all fell in love with her music."

He also related that Converse seemed to have "frustrations in her life," that she'd "never had success," and that he'd later heard that, one day, she left a note for her family and friends that said "I'm going somewhere else." Deitch described her on the program as a "lost genius" and said he held out hope that perhaps someone might take up the cause of gaining attention for her music, perhaps by covering her songs today. He and Garland then moved on to other topics.[5]

When Dzula got home that night, he powered on his computer, pulled up the WNYC website, and captured the stream of the broadcast he'd just heard.[6] Then, as I and so many others similarly affected by the power of Converse's music have done, he began scouring the internet for more information. Like Garland, he found absolutely nothing. Zero. Not a single entry. There was no one named "Connie Converse." Dzula tried every conceivable alternative spelling. Nothing came up.

Second-guessing himself, he listened again to the webstream and found the short section devoted to Converse. Yes, that was the name Garland and Deitch had used: Connie Converse. Dzula listened to the song one more time that night and then, puzzled, turned out the light and went to bed.

Nothing immediately came of Gene Deitch's radio pitch for the "genius" of Converse's music. Shortly after Deitch and his son appeared on Garland's program, Deitch the elder flew back to Prague to resume work on his various projects, and Garland went back to hosting his eclectic weekly radio show. The Connie Converse phantom was back in her bottle.

———

D zula now had access to that bottle, however, and over the next few years, he would release the apparition it contained again, returning to his bootleg capture of "One by One" to play for friends. He periodically searched online for mentions of Converse, assuming that, eventually, someone, somewhere, would release of the rest of her music. "I kept thinking, *I can't wait to buy that album,*" he told me.

Dzula graduated from college, moved to Queens, and began supporting himself by writing music for a jingle house and working as a technician at a local recording studio while continuing to make music with his brother.[7] A promotion he was given at the studio to the position of engineer fed into a burgeoning passion he'd developed for doing his own mixing and producing.

As Dzula's role there increased, he was able to help his friend and former college classmate David Herman get a gig there, too. One afternoon, during a lull, Dzula cued up "One by One" for Herman.

Dzula took note of his friend's reaction to the music, watching as Herman had the requisite emotional response. Herman was dumbstruck and wanted to know and hear more. Dzula told him the little he knew, but where he was nonchalant about assuming that Converse's music would eventually be released, Herman saw an opportunity. If no one else was going to undertake the mission, he said, why couldn't the two of them put out the recordings themselves? Why not get hold of more of her songs and release Connie Converse's debut album, using the intrigue of her disappearance as one means of generating interest? Converse's music now had the marketing hook it had lacked in her day.

In September 2007, more than three and a half years after "One by One" compelled Dzula to pull his car off the highway, he wrote to Gene Deitch offering to help gain attention for Converse's songs. Deitch responded with glee and offered to express a package to him that same day. Neither Dzula nor Herman had any inkling of the impact that the contents of that package would eventually have on so many lives.

⁓

Dzula, in particular, has always been a collector of the musically rare and the hard to find. Just the idea of getting his hands on the virtually unknown recordings of Connie Converse, an artist more obscure than any other he'd ever encountered, gave him goose bumps. In addition to his curiosity about the quality of her music, he was also just excited to have in his possession recordings to which almost no one else anywhere had been exposed.

But the originality and power of Converse's other songs jolted Dzula and Herman. Toward the end of 2008, they began to move forward with their idea to release her music commercially. They had the blessing of both Deitch and (soon after) Phil to proceed, but they wanted to be sure there was a market for what they envisioned as a small-run batch of CDs, complete with artwork and extensive liner notes—something that would involve an outlay of some capital. Being music heads and audio engineers was one thing; going into the record-producing business was something else.

Their first step was to release three Converse songs as a digital-only EP: "One by One," "Talkin' Like You," and "Father Neptune." They posted a link to it on social media with a short blurb about Converse's story and then sat back and waited. The response surpassed anything Dzula and Herman had hoped for. "We weren't really prepared for the level of excitement that the EP generated," Dzula told me. "We knew that some of our friends would be into it, but people totally flipped out."[8]

This was all the validation they needed. Within weeks, plans were set in motion to release a full-length album of Converse's recordings. The duo incorporated as a new record label for the express purpose of bringing Connie Converse's music to the world for the first time.

Deitch had made the original tapes, and had included "One by One" in the curated playlist Garland included on his show. Phil Converse had continued to send copies of his "Connie's Guitar Songs" booklet and CD to anyone who expressed an interest in hearing her music. But it's safe to say that were it not for Dan Dzula and a series of occurrences that can only be described as miraculous, it's likely that Converse's work would still be lost, relegated to the dustbin of American musical history. Instead, because Dzula happened to have his ears and his mind open on one particular, random night, a great artist was rescued from obscurity. And now she belongs to all of us.

How *Sad, How Lovely* was released in 2009 in the most modest of rollouts: two thousand units were pressed, and sold mainly online.[9] Gene Deitch and Phil Converse wrote the liner notes. David Garland produced a feature-length episode of *Spinning on Air* devoted to Converse's music and her story. Word began to get around, and it hasn't stopped.

A year later, I was at a holiday party when a song came on that sounded both entirely new to me and as familiar as my own skin.

Rewind. Stop. Fast-forward. Record. Pause. Play.

The Songs of Elizabeth "Connie" Converse

Known songs, arranged here by approximate date of composition:

With Rue My Heart Is Laden, 1949*

Down This Road, 1950

There Is a Vine, 1950–51

Trouble, 1950–51

Honeybee, 1951

Chanson Innocent, 1951*

Man in the Sky, 1951

Sorrow Is My Name, 1951

Sweet Amelia, 1951

Talkin' Like You (aka Two Tall Mountains), 1951?

The Moon Has No Heart, 1951

Where Are the Roses?, 1951

Chaucer: Introduction to "The Canterbury Tales," 1952*

How Sad, How Lovely, 1952

Johnny's Brother, 1952

Roving Woman, 1952

When I Go Traveling, 1952

Sad Lady, 1952–53

Fare You Well (aka Walkin' Shoes), 1952–53

Father Neptune, 1952–53

O Mistress Mine, 1952–53*

John Brady, 1953

Love in the Afternoon, 1953

Playboy of the Western World, 1953, revised 1960

Thunder Mountain, 1953

The Clover Saloon, 1954?

Fortune's Child, 1954, revised 1960

Here Is the Door, 1954

The Lilies (aka I Have Considered the Lilies), 1954

One by One, 1954

The Witch and the Wizard, 1954

We Lived Alone, 1954

Les Deux Escargots, 1954*

Songs from "The Prodigal Nephew," 1954–55
    Fantastic City
    Randy and Hired Man
    I Am Going Dancing
    Has It Made You Happy?

Empty Pocket Waltz, 1955

Frère Philippe, prior to 1956 (lyrics only)

Vanity of Vanities, 1956

An Eliot Fragment, 1956

In My Craft or Sullen Art, 1956*

Incommunicado, probably 1956–57

Anyone Lived in a Pretty How Town, 1957*

She Hears of Old Wars, 1957

She Thinks of Heaven, 1957

Somewhere I Have Never Traveled, 1957*

The Rainmaker, 1957

Under a Lullaby (aka She Devises a Lullaby), 1957

A Thousand Shapes and Shades, date unknown, copyrighted 1957

She Warns the Children, probably 1957–58

Lullaby for P. Bruce, probably 1957, copyrighted 1960

She Warns Young Women (aka A Woman Plagued by Thought), probably 1957–58

Cassandra's Entrance, probably 1958

The Age of Noon, probably 1958

Andante Tranquillo, 1958

The Spinner in the Bone, probably 1958

Birthday Variations (piano solo), 1958

Sun, Go Down, prior to 1960

Allergy Ballad, 1960

House, 1961

Song for Peter Meyers's Wedding, 1969

* An asterisk indicates a setting (music only)

? Question marks are Converse's and represent her guesses regarding date of composition. Dates that say "probably" are the author's best guesses.

SOME OTHER CONVERSE SONGS

In her unfinished "Statistical Study of 1000 Melodies," Converse listed the name of every song she chose as her sample for the study. Included were *"numbers 908 thru 999 [which] are my own melodies"* (she did not include a one-thousandth song).

These are the titles from that list for which no music or lyrics have ever surfaced. Settings for other writers' poems have been indicated here with brackets, but the song names listed in parentheses are as they appear

in her original typescript. She left no indication regarding the significance of the parentheses.

Ale and Beer

Apple Tree Dance

Berceuse

Buffalo Bill's Defunct [setting for poem by e. e. cummings]

Chestnut Vendor

(Cold and Stony)

Cousin Jane's Blues

Dark River

(David's Valley)

(Green Velvet Glove)

Lily Ladle

Long Have I Wandered

Mary Was a Quiet Girl

My Father Was a King

One Child Have I

Passengers: Arthur Had a Garden

Passengers: Am I Too Shy?

Passengers: She Looks So Nice

Passengers: So How's Chicago?

Queen of the Western Isles

Recuerdo [Edna St. Vincent Millay setting]

Sun, Weary of Swimming

There Goes Henry Jones

(Trumpeter)

Vin d'Anjou

When the Old Man Comes

(Where Leander Drowned)

(Wrap Me in My Father's Cloak)

APPENDIX B

The Cassandra Cycle

E. E. CONVERSE
309 THOMPSON
ANN ARBOR, MiCH.

November 10, 1963

Dear Mary Critchell:

Enclosed herewith are copies of eight songs whose words and music I have written. I also enclose separate copies of the words so that you can get a quicker sense of the verbal content.

Six of the songs were written for a "Cassandra" cycle which I had not yet finished; the other two were written independently of the cycle but can, it seems to me, be aptly included. I would propose rounding off the cycle with a ninth item which would be essentially a reprise of the opening song with some appropriate revisions. The order of the songs would be like this:

1. Cassandra's Entrance

2. The Age of Noon

3. She Warns the Children

4. The Spinner in the Bone

5. She Hears of Old Wars (now "Song for Old Wars")

6. She Devises a Lullaby (now "Under a Lullaby")

7. She Thinks of Heaven

8. A Woman Plagued by Thought

9. Cassandra's Exit (revised reprise, not included here)

Mrs. Wiers has suggested to me that these songs might well be re-arranged for a women's chorus, and conceivably she might be persuaded to undertake this job herself. I am so overloaded with non-musical chores that I doubt I could manage it myself this year. If it were arranged for chorus, I should like to see a very small instrumental combination (bass-and-snare-drum, and two--hopefully French--horns) used in place of the conventional piano. There are little fanfares scattered through the cycle, and other bits that could be handled very effectively by two horns, and we might even use little fanfares between songs. But perhaps this notion is too ambitious.

I shall be glad to have you show these things and this explanatory letter
to anyone you think might be interested. I'd appreciate getting the music
back eventually since copying is always either tedious or expensive!

Thanks very much for your own interest.

> Sincerely,
>
> *Elizabeth Converse*
>
> Elizabeth Converse

1. Cassandra's Entrance

Here she comes, wearing her web of days,
Gone past the gossamer;
Over the meadow fly the bees
To bud and blossom her.

Yet she is never content with spring
And must refashion it
That robins wait for words to sing;
That truth be passionate;

That time and promises be one,
Giving eternity no mention;
That rogues do business in the sun,
Though sweet deceit be their intention;
That every gossamer be spun
From filaments of comprehension . . .

She is the husbandman's despair
These many seasons;
Bright she may blossom, but she will bear
Nothing but reasons.

2. The Age of Noon

When they were weary walking they sat down on a stone,
She and a little boy, in the woods alone;
And so began talking of the things they knew—
Vague and particular, sad and amusing, false and true . . .

>*Their noise was questioned by a thrush,*
>*But they were deaf, and would not hush*
>*Such chatter as descends and climbs*
>*The slope between their separate times.*

And then along the forest path
The noontime swept in radiant wrath;
Sounding the cricket drum and fife,
It slew them with the heat of life.

A dragonfly stitched up their words
And they were still as nesting birds;
The doleful, deft, and decorous air
Arranged their clothing and their hair;

Down from the highest springs of spruce
The sun shook golden circles loose
To seal their eyes from all concerns
And light the little wicks of ferns.

Then, blind to all but green and gold,
They heard the crumbling of the mold;
They heard a caterpillar pass,
And beetles roaring in the grass;
The humming blood beneath the skin
Was louder than their words had been;
Their ages were reduced to one—
One crossing of meridian . . .

The afternoon around them burned the pines and firs,
But to his separate age the child returned, and she to hers,
And so began talking of the things they knew—
Vague and particular, sad and amusing, false and true.

3. She Warns the Children

Since you must, be green and tender,
And complain
Of every pain you can remember.

Now you can be understood,
While you have no understanding;
Faces that are made of wood
Are more commanding.

You shall learn in shrugs and frowns
To hide your wounds lest they be counted
And enemies invade your towns
Upon this information mounted.

Notice that your conquering brothers
Never cry and groan—
Then discern the hurts of others
And conceal your own;
Bleed and die alone;
So save yourself from being known.

Still disown your dark pretending,
And beware
Of danger everywhere impending.

Soon the dragons of the mind
Will explain your worst mischances;
Fear you ill and ill you'll find
Your circumstances.

You shall learn the subtle way
Suspicion breeds the thing suspected;
The wolf will take the fattest prey—
Can you expect to be selected?

Health is said to be contentment;
Let your health increase;
Confidence has no resentment—
Let your fancy cease;
Set your mind at peace;—
So every wolf shall wear his fleece.

Think of love as man's invention,
Prone to fail,
And then bewail each new suspension.

Love is the immortal touch
Blessing us in life's probation—
How would it be left to such
Improvisation?

You shall learn that love and hate
Are verdicts on your vice and virtue;
Acknowledging your mean estate,
Is love unjust if love desert you?

Show your teeth to all your brothers—
Let it be a sign

You are even with the others,
You have paid your fine.

—Call that love divine,
And so distinguish it from mine.

4. The Spinner in the Bone

. . . Such is the way of her speech, and so her tongue
Reels out her webs and riddles for the young—
Whose patience ceases where her sense begins.
But still beneath the bone she sits and spins—
Within the bone shell, dim by day and night,
Where her two eyes let in her only light
And her ears sing entangled histories.

When she was young, the way she wore her gowns
Ruined the cloth of all her hand-me-downs;
Where she would rest, the roughness wore it through;
Where she would run, the brambles always grew;
Nor would she mend—she kept her scissors sharp
Snipping at life and teasing out the warp
In puzzled filaments and mysteries . . .
  The little difference of peas and pods,
  The odds of wagers made by men with gods,
  The lives of women bound in silken covers,
  Eccentric orbits run by careless lovers,
  The postulates a child's remark discloses
  The elementary particles of roses . . .

These she kept spinning, spinning, under the bone,
Within the dim shell where she sat alone
The while she walked in endless companies.

Such is her way of speech, nor will the young
Fathom the webs and riddles of her tongue;
So in a devious way the curse is kept.
Yet she has never ceased, not while she slept,
Nor while she paced the lawless squares of chance—
Even as young lust moved her bones to dance—

Still she kept spinning, spinning, under the bone,
Within the bone shell, dim by day and night,

Where her two eyes let in her only light
And her ears sang entangled histories.

5. She Hears of Old Wars

Beyond them,
Beyond them lay the lakes of shadow
Where the sun was drowned;
And pausing,
And pausing in a perilous meadow,
They set their tents all around.

Dark horses flew among them
With wings like knives;
They roused the sleepers up where sleep had flung them
And seized their lives—
Swept them from the perilous meadow,
Plunged them in the lakes of shadow—
And brought word home to their wives.

. . . We found them,
We found their campfires dry for lighting
Under ancient thorns;
And pausing,
And pausing in the smoke of our fighting
We heard the sound of their horns.

6. She Devises a Lullaby

This is the center of the world's dark circle—
A dark, slow circle spun by the loving stars . . .
Like myself, all things adore you;
Close your eyes—I will keep watch for you;
Sleep . . . in the world's dark circle,
The dark, slow circle . . .

Do not listen to the screaming train—
It will run down after a mile or two;
Do not worry the moon is on a chain—
It can only smile at you;
In cities where tigers creep
They've put away the tigers—

Sleep . . . in the world's dark circle,
The dark, slow circle . . .

    Now all thunder muffles up its riot;
    Broken levees keep their flood;
    Now all armies stand apart in quiet;
    Deadly wounds hold back their blood—

Of all things I, at least, adore you;
Close your eyes, I will keep watch for you—
In the center of the world's dark circle,
The cold, slow circle
Spun by the stars.

7. She Thinks of Heaven

Child of this world, I cannot learn to love
Visions of paradise. Transcendent joys,
That might entice me to be dreaming of,
By deadly logic must transcend my voice.

Only the dust can lend the wind a note;
All music lives upon a time and tide,
And must be gone along with wind and throat
When our small dust and time are swept aside.

And then what rhyme could lipless language make
To crack that silent range, if I met you,
Bloodless and strange, without the heart to ache
For all the words and music that we knew?

The eyes of God would flicker in surprise,
For I should weep although I had no eyes.

8. A Woman Plagued by Thought

A woman plagued by thought
Must cure herself with pain,
For nothing to be bought
In that demure domain
Can deck her as it ought,
Or so most men maintain.

Within her swells
The pitiful conceit
That reason smells
Most exquisitely sweet,
That learning is a grace,
That proofs may be displayed
Around her pensive face
Like ivory and jade.

And so she dwells
In markets of the mind,
Possessed by spells
And bargains of a kind
They might confuse
A wiser woman's head—
Which she pursues,
And so comes late to bed.

Far better to go bare,
So she must quickly find,
That publicly to wear
The purchase of her mind.
Let her retain
One tough hypothesis
To tease her brain,
And let that one be this:

A woman plagued by thought
Must cure herself with pain,
For nothing to be bought
In that demure domain
Can deck her as it ought—
Or so most men maintain.

9. Cassandra's Exit

("There she goes, wearing her web of days . . ." revised reprise)

Converse's "FEDD" Memo

One of several memos and papers Converse wrote and distributed to her fellow members of People Against Racism (PAR) around 1968–1969.

AN EXPERIMENT TOWARD "IDEOLOGICAL" CONSOLIDATION

This is a slightly revised version of a paper used as a basis for discussion at the AA-PAR spring retreat, first session. The first page (the A-series of statements) was intended to express some sort of minimal ideological agreement already existing in the group. The succeeding series (B through E) include an increasing amount of the writer's own personal opinions which can safely be regarded as controversial.

It was of course not possible to cover all the points raised in this paper within a single discussion-session. There was general agreement on the A-series as a minimal common ideology. There was considerable interest in the "FEDD" notion as developed in the C-series (we have come to pronounce it "fed"). There was some discussion of the scarcity/uncertainty idea (C-3); the writer should probably elaborate and clarify this if the matter comes up again.

-- E. Converse

Appendix C

ME AND   A-1   I want to help eliminate white racism from my society. I take "white racism"
MY GOALS   to mean the white assumption of racial superiority and the white arrogation
of power and privilege in relation to people of color.

HOW   A-2   I realize that white racism is pervasive in my society. I keep spending a
SOCIETY   little time learning how it works--keeping up with the facts of the relative
WORKS   welfare of whites and blacks; studying the history of white racism; and trying to
understand how both individual attitudes and institutions serve to perpetuate the
status of black people as perennial losers in my society. I know this understanding must include
processes that are called "psychological" and others that are called "political" and "economic."
Public and higher education rarely provide people with the skills of critical social analysis.

MYSELF IN   A-3   I know I participate in behaviors with racist effects every time I participate
SOCIETY   in the major institutions of my society, and that's often. This confronts me
with a choice: to go on participating in my society while working for radical
change in it--or to withdraw my complicity in racist actions by withdrawing from daily participation. For the time being, at least, I have chosen the first course. This is because (1) real withdrawal is technically very difficult if not impossible in the long run; and (2) building full-fledged
separate communities that meet the range of human needs requires powers and resources that I and
my friends do not have now. A third, more feasible alternative may be the gradual building of
parallel institutions--not for escape from complicity but for learning and demonstrating a desired
and feasible future.

REFERENCE   A-4   To stay in society and act against white racism, I need to associate myself
GROUP   with other people who feel approximately as I do about it. We need to work
together both for the sake of our humanity and for the sake of concerted action.
We need to develop interpersonal trust and some minimal "ideological" agreement. Sharing
decisions, knowledge, and experience will help us do that.

STRATEGIES   A-5   There is probably no one "correct method" of combating white racism.
Neither racism nor society itself is that simple. I can see several major
kinds of strategy, each with infinite variations in concrete situations. One is attention-getting,
which ranges from shouting in the streets to martyrdom; it does not attempt to communicate much
beyond the fact that we feel outraged about racism. Another is education/conversion, in which we
--by both words and acts--we try to communicate the substance of our beliefs about racism. A
third is political combat, in which we test our kinds and amounts of social power against the
social power of people whom we view as hard-and-fast opponents. A fourth is physical combat,
a specialized test of relative powers to disrupt, damage, or destroy the physical and personal
bases of an opponent. A given action may have more than one component, but we should learn
to identify these components and match them with both our capabilities and our goals.

CONSTIT-   A-6   All human beings have internal contradictions which make them liable, in
UENCIES   some degree under some circumstances, to radical changes in their cogni-
tions, beliefs, and values. Most human beings are also directly involved in
societal contradictions as well. So I cannot be certain, just by looking at a white person or
knowing his socioeconomic status or his institutional role, whether he is my potential contituent
or my hard-and-fast opponent. I should be guided by probabilities, but not uncritically.

B. FIRST EXPANSION OF BASICS   B. FIRST EXPANSION OF BASICS

B-1   Rather than taking white racism as self-evidently bad or immoral, I must try to under-
        stand why I, a white person, want to help eliminate white racism. After all, most white
people in my society take white superiority to be self-evidently true. I grew up white (nothing
can change that) and I find some aspects of my native culture positive or useful--if I don't think
so, I should probably think again. I need to understand my own anti-racism.

B-2   For most white people in my society, white racism seems to fill identity needs ("psycho-
        logical"), and/or consumption-security needs ("economic"--and not just electric carving
knives but also where the next meal is coming from), and/or control-security needs ("political"
--even sheer survival requires some control of one's environment, including other humans). I
think it must be "economic" scarcity, or the appearance of it and the fear of it, which drives
people to seek consumption-security by depriving others; and more generally it must be the
uncertainty of human life which drives people to seek control-security at the expense of others;
that is, by arrogating the labor-power and the decision-making power of other people. These
are probably the real and material conditions which lead people to aggrandize their own identity
as a justification for controlling and exploiting other people.

B-3   I think my own struggle against racism in my society must take account of its material and
        psychological bases; I cannot afford to view it as sheer malignity or perversity on the part
of bad or stupid people (do I really believe in demons and angels?). Also, however, I cannot
afford to expect that the black victims of white racism will see white racism as anything but
demonic--at least when they first come to view it as a total social process rather than something
which is "their own fault." The black experience of destroyed identity, economic want, and
political helplessness is ten times more intense than anything we white middle-class people are
likely to have felt. So whenever I engage as an ally of black liberation against white racism I
must expect a degree of conflict within that alliance.

B-4   The question asked in B-1 above applies to my whole anti-racist group. Are we just nat-
        urally good and decent while others are not? Or are some of our basic human needs
already being filled in ways that we have not yet accurately identified and taken account of?
This question bears closely on our strategies and constituencies.

B-5   I have come to distrust the simple combination of fury and good intentions as a guide to
        "the correct strategy" against racism, and displays of righteous anger as the sign of true
commitment, and the rejection of historical experience as the prerequisite of revolutionary
courage, and the rejection of the scientific method as the proper anti-academic attitude. Real
history, carefully dug out from what passes as history, can help us avoid some absurd, wasteful,
and even criminal errors in our choices of strategy at various junctures. The scientific method,
stripped down from the mishmash of what now passes for social science, is the safest method we
have of testing our "self-evident" assumptions and hypotheses, our "correct" strategies. It takes
time and it can often lead to painful conclusions (what did we guess wrong about? why did we
make that particular wrong guess?).

B-6   I have come to believe that most people, apart from the very rich and powerful, both want
        change and fear it. They want it because they know in their bones that they could be
freer and better off than they are; but they fear change because they know they cannot design
and control "THE" revolution, "THE" radical change; they distrust the people who are going to
design and control it--those with least to lose, most to gain; in anti-racist change here today,
the blacks. They fear brash ignorance on the part of revolutionaries (result: chaos and losses for
everybody); and they fear the self-interest of the revolutionaries (result: just a change of
masters). This is a psychological/societal contradiction which probably pervades any white
constituency we are likely to deal with.

Appendix C

C-1 I am coming to realize that the essence of racism is a "frozen" pattern of exploitive
       domination/dependency between persons and between groups. By "frozen" I mean   FEDD
institutionalized, self-perpetuating, not aimed at ending in independence or in mutually
beneficial interdependency. "Exploitive" simply means more beneficial to the dominator
than to the dominated, which is why the dominator wants to perpetuate it. (But we should remember that submission usually has some rewards.) "Domination" means the arrogation of
decision-making power from the dominated to the dominator. It is the freezing--usually,
institutionalization--which makes exploitation likely.

C-2 I now realize that, besides racism, there are a number of other FEDD relationships in our
       most central social institutions. Traditional sex roles seem to stem from or depend on such
a FEDD relationship between men and women. Our own government and, historically, the white
national governments of Europe have established large-scale FEDD relationships with nonwhite
nations (imperialism). The central relationships of capitalist economic organization, based on
the legal convention of ownership and buttressed by the essentially military power of the law,
seem to be distinctly "FEDD."

C-3 Uncertainty and its special economic case, scarcity (in a here-and-now sense, not in an
       absolute sense), are quite adequate conditions to explain the predominance of FEDD rela-
tionships in the major institutions of Western (at least) civilization. Genuine, overt, and
ongoing conflict among human individuals and groups absorbs time, energy, and other "scarce"
values, so in a condition of scarcity conflict is readily viewed as wasteful and inefficient.
Genuine, non-predetermined conflict increases the amount of general uncertainty in an ongoing
social system, while--in contrast--the establishment of FEDD relationships predetermines who
will win in a nominal social conflict. These apparent practicalities of human society are what
I am up against if I take a stand against FEDD relationships including racism.

C-4 Many people who do not like racism do believe in the necessity, if not the sacredness,
       of other kinds of FEDD relationship. They cannot conceive of a workable social structure
without a backbone of FEDD. If anti-racism in our group is going to expand to an anti-FEDD
position, we will have to help one another (1) to identify present myths and self-evident assumptions about FEDD relationships, and (2) to begin thinking about alternative kinds of organiza-
tional, institutional, and ultimately social structure.

C-5 I think a broad anti-FEDD position and commitment are "revolutionary" in that radical
       social change is implied. A pure anti-racist position and commitment are not neces-
sarily "revolutionary" in that sense. For this reason I think our group will be stuck with
short-term, ad hoc decisions about strategies and constituencies unless or until we have some
group consensus of choice between these two positions and commitments. Choosing the anti-
FEDD position (which I myself prefer) would almost automatically answer a couple of our current
questions about strategies and constituencies (see C-6 below, and the D- and E-series beyond).

C-6 If it is true that the elimination of white racism (were it possible to do that alone) would
       require some sacrifice of material advantage for all or most of our possible white constit-
uents, we might still get some of them to work with us on moral grounds (but see the B-series).
On the other hand it seems extremely unlikely that white racism can be eliminated all by itself,
without other social changes of a radical nature. These other changes may offer hope of long-
term benefit to many whites as well as blacks. But--again--we need to choose our basic
position before we can really identify and work with our potential constituencies.

D. THE PROBLEM OF REVOLUTION D. THE PROBLEM OF REVOLUTION

D-1 One oddly hopeful thing about dominators in FEDD relationships is that they usually need
to justify/rationalize their domination ("I know what's good for you and you don't"; "If
I don't dominate you, you'll dominate me"). Of course they usually do it by "dehumanizing"
the people they want to govern and use. It is oddly hopeful only in that most people seem to
understand, deep down somewhere, that you don't deal with real equals in this FEDD way.
The difficult point here is that, if I am really anti-FEDD, I must avoid adopting tactics and
strategies and programs based on FEDD-type rationalizations and justifications.

D-2 It seems to me that both our society and "the movement" are still some distance from the
verge of creating radical social change. The perceived legitimacy of our major social
institutions is still huge and strong in the main sectors of our society. "The movement" is in a
real sense "pre-revolutionary" because--outside of something vaguely called socialism and not
very well understood--it is not yet offering an alternative skeleton for large-scale society. I
disagree with those who say we will only develop our positive program through our own struggle.
I think we must also have a very good and deep understanding of what we are against and how
it came about and know it works. We must have some small practical basis for believing that
society can function with a non-FEDD skeleton instead of a FEDD skeleton.

D-3 If I want the FEDD structure of society to be changed, other people are going to call me
revolutionary whether I choose that term for myself or not. But there is an extra difficulty
in my position. The main thrust of conventional, main-line revolutions comes inevitably from
conditions of intense scarcity and uncertainty--the very conditions which historically breed
FEDD-based social systems (C-3). Thus if I make a determined effort to develop new strategies
of struggle that really match my anti-FEDD position, my behavior may often be viewed as
unorthodox and wicked both by the Establishment and by some main-line revolutionaries. I
have to be ready to cope with that both emotionally and intellectually.

D-4 It seems essential to me that our group recognize the smallness, peculiarity, and painful-
ness--as well as the possible long-run importance--of any role most of us can have in
something called "making a revolution." In our lives we may only be able to add a few significant paragraphs to the presently discouraging end of Memmi's famous chapter on "the
colonizer who refuses." Commitment and ingenuity strike me as the two most important characteristics for people in a group like ours.

D-5 I think we must slowly increase our short-term actions inspired by immediate events (but
guided by our long-term views). Given the "pre-revolutionary" situation, I think we
are mistaken to try to use a mechanical "reformist-versus-revolutionary" criterion for such acts.
Furthermore, we cannot engage in significant political combat (see A-5) without forming ad hoc
coalitions with other groups who do not share all our beliefs--and we can do this. But a better
criterion for specific actions, at present, would be whether they may help a few other people
to see the emperor without his clothes. And a good criterion for internal education would be
whether it is aimed at the problems mentioned in D-2 above. Some portion of our group resources should always be used for slow, in-depth recruitment and consolidation. This requires
the patience and optimism of a long-term outlook.

D-6 We must try to get past the mechanical classification of our constituents and opponents
in globs under labels that have some initial analytic usefulness but which tend to impede
further analysis and have the quality of sculpture rather than of motion. Not all high school
students are alike, nor all dirty workers, nor all "libs," etc., etc. (see A-6). Actually we
all have this common sense and common experience, but we shouldn't drop it out when we are
trying to be "political."

Appendix C

E-1   I should not judge radical effectiveness--mine or others'--by the number of jailings or
        beatings by cops. At least for the present there are better criteria (e.g., see D-5).
I should also probably beware of play-acting the stance and rhetoric of main-line revolutionaries, those who are right now resisting intense oppression. Such play-acting detracts from
the reality of my own past and present and, in the end (I think) it detracts from the validity and
dignity of the stance of those who are intensely oppressed. My time will probably come but
when it does it will be very real and I won't have to worry about play-acting

E-2   Increasing repression of various groups including ours seems almost inevitable, but we
        should understand and take account of its strategy and tactics as we do our own. As far
as I know, the only full-fledged and ready-made social analysis which focuses on FEDD relationships is the Marxist one, and this is also a full-fledged and ready-make spook even for
nonpolitical people. In any case, I need to use Marx's model discriminately (his class
analysis, for instance, is not at all easy to apply to our society). And I need to use the
20th-century Marxist models of political revolution discriminately, since none of them have
occurred in a highly industrialized society. Furthermore, I shouldn't allow myself to discount
the Russian revolution simply because it "went wrong"--that's how unscientific views of
society are created and maintained.

E-3   We should realize that conditions of increasing repression directed against our allies and
        against us will also increase our own sense of scarcity (of resources) and uncertainty (of
short-term outcomes). This raises the possibility of FEDD creeping into our own organization,
and even of repression being used within "the movement." The justification always is that
such measures are necessary to diminish conflict and get concerted action of the kind we want
(see C-3). But that's what the other side says too, and they usually add, "We'll stop shoving
as soon as you guys stop pushing, and then the period of necessary repression will be safely over."
I think we should stop viewing this problem as an insoluble moral dilemma of revolution, and
start examining it as a scientific matter involving recognizable social processes for which
alternatives may be possible.

E-4   I must learn to regard myself as a resource for my group and vice versa. Our resources
        are still very small and we can't afford to squander them unless all seems lost anyway.

E-5   Real revolutions are happening right now without our intervention, assistance, or control.
        We should perhaps think of ourselves as "special forces" (sorry about the term) way off
from the real bases of operation. That requires flexibility and ingenuity of strategy. The laws
of our jerry-built society have many interstices, "grey areas," and internal contradictions. We
need to learn more about them and use them to advantage--work on the loose cement of
institutions rather than seeking head-on collisions with the stonework (except under selected
circumstances). This will not save us from repression but it can help us not to squander our
resources.

E-6   I believe we have, and should carry out, a peculiar obligation to any and all of our
        putative constituents, whether they are just "ad hoc" or whether we hope presently to
get them into our group. I think this obligation is inherent in the kind of group we claim to be.
We must never dehumanize these people by deceiving them "for their own good" or "to teach
them a lesson," or regard them as pawns for our battles. Such tactics always boomerang
eventually and there is every reason why they should. We should recognize that the tempta-
tion to use such tactics is bound to be recurrent and strong. We should understand why they
must be firmly rejected.

APPENDIX D

Converse's "Award" Letter

This letter accompanied a lump sum check representing the total amount collected on Converse's behalf to underwrite her 1971 sabbatical in England. A list of contributors follows, with Converse's handwritten annotations. Both were among the effects in her filing cabinet.

AWARD

to Elizabeth Converse

in Recognition of Her Unique Contributions

to Scholarship, Education, and Human Individuality

by the Committee for Sponsorship of Independent

Scholars and Educators

April 1971

Elizabeth has combined disciplined scholarly inquiry with a rare, broad sympathy and understanding of people -- a kind that sometimes eludes many of us who have spent so much of our lives in the academic world.

We are appreciative of her years as Managing Editor, and then Editor, of the JOURNAL OF CONFLICT RESOLUTION, which has received so large a measure of her time, talent, and devotion. While doing the demanding work of an editor -- nurturing authors, attending to the innumerable details of bringing out a quarterly journal -- Elizabeth somehow managed to pursue her own independent studies in the social sciences, including a remarkable article which appeared in the December 1968 issue of the JOURNAL. This article, entitled "The War of All Against All," is a review of all the literature published in the JOURNAL, analyzed in the light of a concept which Elizabeth called the "control paradigm," the desire of individuals and groups to bend their universe to their purposes. This broad-gauge analysis is only one of several independent studies that she has undertaken.

Elizabeth is one who can communicate fundamental ideas in simple terms. We recall that some years ago a group of scholars from the Center for Research on Conflict Resolution presented a series of talks about the Center to a local church community. The series as a whole was well-received but it was Elizabeth who struck the most responsive notes with the audience -- that marvelous phenomenon called communication.

In another unique role, Elizabeth has penetrated the barriers that so often separate scholars from activists dedicated to social change. As both scholar and activist, she has participated in social movements -- for new directions in the social sciences,

for peace, for the abolition of racism, for broad political change,
for the continuing development of the free individual. She has
given generously of her talents in writing, editing, organizing,
graphics and layout (not to mention the inevitable licking of
stamps and running of the mimeograph machine). More importantly,
she has made systematic intellectual contributions to the <u>thinking</u>
of these action programs which no one else could have provided.
She has given generously of her <u>ideas</u> -- a contribution which many
reserve for the formal presentations upon which academic reputation
and rank are based. For example, some of us had the privilege of
attending a series of informal lectures which Elizabeth gave on the
problem of human exploitation. There was no academic credit for
the attenders (and needless to say, no honorarium for the lecturer)
but the sessions were eagerly attended, especially by young activists.
These lectures are indicative of the enormous amount of work in
serious education that Elizabeth has done over the years --
independently, without the financial support of any institution,
given freely out of her talent for crystallizing and communicating
complex ideas and her concern for the human condition.

There is still another sense in which Elizabeth is a
genuine teacher -- by pleasuring in the development of other people's
minds. For all her own originality, her analytic and artistic powers,
her competence in realms of science or periods of history, she rejoices
in the brilliance of the accomplished; she encourages the diffident
and uncertain. She immediately communicates the sense that everyone's
experiences and ideas are important. Her belief that each person is
unique and worthy is not just a Principle: it is a total behavior,
the natural response of <u>delight</u> in another's thought, experience,
and individuality.

We do not hope to do justice to Elizabeth's intellectual and personal contributions. We only hope that this Award may in some way help her to continue with her studies of the human condition and with her work in communicating her insight to others.

Awarded to Elizabeth Converse

in tribute and affection   April 1971

The Committee

ok ——• Marcia Barrabee
ok ——— Lisa
ok ——— David
ok ——— Ruth & Andy Zweifler
ok ——— Janet & Peter Klaver
ok ——• Irene & Craige Schensted
ok ——• Hanne & John Sonquist
ok ——— Rose & Gene Wilson
ok ——— Nancy & Greg Gendell + Julie
ok ——— Helen & Phil Isaacson + Joel
    ——• Ed & Vicky Vandenberg
ok ——— Connie Janssens ——— thru Vicky
ok ——— Torry & Ernie Harburg
ok —• Peter
ok —• Timo
ok ——— Phil & Jean Converse
ok ——— Gail Kellum
ok —• Mara Julius
ok —— Joan Lind
ok ——— Nell & Bill Chilton
        (Kathy Dannemiller) OK TO THANK

Add: Kelman Susie & Lee

Ad: Jane & Roger Barney
    Wendy Roe
ok —Dan Katz + Christine
ok ——Kenneth & Elise Boulding
   - Anatol & Gwen Rapoport
ok ——Bob Angell + Esther

ACKNOWLEDGMENTS

From the start of this process—during which my dedication to Connie Converse became first a concert, then an album, then an essay, then a play, and now at last, this book—what nourished this quixotic-seeming quest was the very thing she herself often seemed to have such a deficit of: connection. Mine was with the brilliant, questioning, open spirit that resides in all she left behind, with the people who knew or knew about her, and with friends old and new who offered help, support, and guidance.

First and foremost, I am indebted to the total cooperation of the late Phil and Jean Converse, who, from our first exchanges, fully supported this project. And to Dan Dzula, whose assistance, patience, gentle good humor, and dedication to the larger goal of gaining wider exposure for Converse's songs helped me immeasurably. Dan, I salute you.

The extended Converse family probably heard far more from me far more often than they would have liked, but Pete, Tim, Bruce, Leslie, Elizabeth, Rob, Barbara, Ron, and Jenna Converse, and Edie and Sally Neff (on the Converse side) all contributed to my research, as did Everett T. Eaton, Beth Day, Lori Wood, and Claire Motschman (on the Eaton side). J. Thomas Converse was especially gracious and kind in helping me to better understand the New England Converses. And the genealogists Carolyn Converse and Alan Cooper over in England were a great help, too.

Dick Mullavey and Jean Crowley, Concord High School alumni class of

1942, shared memories with me that were more than seven decades old about Converse and Frannie Flint, and Flint's relatives Jeanne Paradise and Anne Lee led me to Humphrey Morris, caretaker of Bob Flint's papers. I am greatly indebted to Humphrey for sharing them with me, first by mail, and then during my visit to his home in Cambridge, Massachusetts. Retired police chief Robert Irving, of Wayland, Massachusetts, helped me to better understand the circumstances surrounding Frannie Flint's death.

To contextualize Converse's early days in 1940s Manhattan, Jonathan and Ivan Barkhorn, and Adelaide and John Aime—all children of the Eby sisters—shared their memories, thoughts, and ideas with me, and Linda Duffy offered information about her aunt Sarah Thompson. Lois Aime talked to me about her late husband, Richard, and gifted me with some of his fantastic photos of Converse. Andrea and Sukey Lilienthal and Nadya Chang helped piece together the early New York years, too, and Edwin Bock became the deus ex machina of that part of this book near the close of my research, providing previously unknown details that brought back moments from that time in glorious color. Thanks, too, to Matt Diffee, who connected me with the illustrators I spoke to about Converse's cartoons, and to Michael R. Anderson, for taking me to school on the IPR and the AIPR.

Converse in the 1950s was easier to track with the help of people like Kim and Seth Deitch, Julia and Fred Crippen, Lindsay and Victoria Bernal, Taiya Barss, Naka Ishii, Howard Pollack, Peter Cooper, Greg Gerhard, Katy Carter, Juana Culhane, Lenore Stadlen, John Formicola, Jr., Andréa Mahee, and Merle Edelman. Lisa Raskin contributed valuable memories about Maude Brogan, and Nan and Gay Talese, Nick Pileggi, Edward Field, Penny Jones, and Maggie Berkvist all offered wonderful recollections of New York City in those days (thanks to Michael Minichiello, who introduced me to the latter three). Sir Laurence Martin, Betty Boualegue, Joel Helander, and Sean Cosgrove offered important perspective on Larry Salisbury. Ron Gordon and Tim Inkster shared their insights into the printing industry back then. And so many people from the early days of the folk revival in New York City offered me their thoughts, but Happy Traum, Dick Weissman, and Terri Thal warrant special mention, along with Reed Karen, who located and forwarded me the tape reel of his mother, Susan Reed, singing with Converse's guitar accompaniment.

Among the many who shared with me about Ann Arbor in the 1960s, I want to especially thank Zelda Gamson, the Isaacsons (Helen, Joel, and Elise), Sally Ryan, Peter DiLorenzi, Joe Falkson, Ernie Harburg, Peter Meyers, Frank Joyce, Patricia Murphy, Jerry Hinkle, Sam Friedman, Catherine Forest, Raymond Chauncey, Peter Critchell, Wil Cummings, Dee Wernette, Bob and Leslie Hefner, Jacques Bude, Ed Haber, Frithjof Bergmann, David Cole, Ruth Zweifler, Craig Hammond, Mike and Tom Harburg, Heidi Gottfried, Russell, Bill, and Philip Boulding, Nelle Chilton, Joel Kostman, Jill Ault, Ed Vandenberg and Benita Kaimowitz, Gayle Rubin, Lenore Weissberg, Anne Remley, Shirli Kopelman, Tony Rapoport, and Rob Hovey.

All librarians, teachers, mentors, and volunteers should be thanked every day of their lives for what they do, but Caitlin Moriarty and Madeleine Bradford at the Bentley Library in Michigan, Sarah Patton at the Hoover Institution Library, Willa Vincitore at Vassar, and Caitlin Miller and Bryan Cornell at the Library of Congress archives deserve extra-special thanks for their indefatigable efforts on my behalf. John Hopper of the Meredith Historical Society took time out of his schedule to show me around Evelyn Eaton Converse's hometown. Special thanks, too, go to my erstwhile English teacher Bertha Strauss, with whom I happily reconnected in recent years, and to the late Donald Faulkner and Arthur Gelb, who both offered me nurturing guidance at the start of this process. In moments of self-doubt, it was often the voices of these angels that I heard.

The morning after I presented my first Connie Converse documentary-style concert, in July 2011 at Joe's Pub in New York City, I received what turned out to be one of the most significant fan letters I've ever gotten. Peter Wilderotter, president and CEO of the Christopher and Dana Reeve

Foundation, had been at the show, and urged me to develop it, offering his help and advice. That led to further iterations of what became *A Star Has Burnt My Eye*, which so many helped with in its various incarnations, including my great friend and longtime musical collaborator Russell Farhang; the saintly presenters Joe Melillo and Amy Cassello at the Brooklyn Academy of Music; and a team of burning stars that included (among so many others): Paul Lazar, Nic Adams, Jean Rohe, Charlotte Mundy, Liam Robinson, Jay Wegman, Jennifer Conley Darling, Shanta Thake, Sandy Garner, Osei Essed, Dina Maccabee, Christopher Heilman, Dallas Estes, Meghan Lang, Anastasia Barzee, Susan Oetgen, Nick Webber, Lindsay Bowen, and Philip Caggiano, many of whom helped me to parse out what belonged in the play and what needed to wait for this book. In addition to his terrific dramaturgical skills, James Harrison Monaco really helped me understand Converse's poetry. And when Skidmore College offered us a residency to develop the show further, Paul Calhoun, Gary Wilson, Sue Kessler, and Jared Klein were a big part of making that a gratifying, uplifting experience.

Christopher Goddard, Matt Kanelos, Marie Lewis, Chris Parrello, Lily Holgate, and Kyle Sanna all helped me hear what Converse's never-recorded music is supposed to sound like. And people with their own Converse projects were generous in sharing some of their thoughts and research, too, including Dan Dzula's pal and business partner, David Herman; Betsy and Ryan Maxwell; David Garland; Andrea McEaneney; and Adam Briscoe.

When I first starting knocking on publishing industry doors about this book, one editor told me that since my subject was a complete unknown, I ought first to try to place a magazine article about her to generate some interest. I wrote 6,000 words and sent them to *New Yorker* staff writer Sarah Larson, an early champion of my play, hoping for feedback. Sarah not only set aside time to read the whole damn thing, but offered edits, suggestions, and an offer to read a revision. To my amazement and wonder, she sent my next draft to editor Michael Agger, who saw fit to publish the piece (parts of which have been repurposed here, in the book's opening pages) the start of my becoming a contributing writer there—a dream.

I'm grateful to my trusted agent, Susan Golomb, for delivering me to Dutton, and into the hands of my editor there, the good and great John Parsley, who has been a godsend from the get-go. John immediately grasped not only the importance of this story, but the unconventional ways I wanted to tell it. His nuanced understanding of the various themes and ideas that run through this book has always been absolutely clear. Fortune smiled not only on me, but on Connie Converse, when John and I began our work together. I'm also thankful to Linda Friedner at Penguin Random House, who offered her wise and expert counsel, to copyeditor Jenna Dolan, for her perceptive and careful handling of the manuscript, and to LeeAnn Pemberton, Frank Walgren, and Rob Sternitzky for rolling with a first-time biographer's goofs and snafus.

In the world of words and ideas, I'm grateful to Sam Sifton, Tina Fallon, Sam Roberts, David Rowell, Matt Weiland, Sarah Fan, David Lida, Elianna Kan, Renee Zuckerbrot, Julia Eagleton, Rick Moody, Elizabeth Gaffney, Daphne Kolatay, Seth Rogovoy, Marc Woodworth, Lary Bloom, David Hays, Eric Marcus, Simon Lipskar, Hugh Ryan, Howard Sherman, and Marisa Silver, all of whom heard me talk through anxious moments of this process and offered support and guidance. While I worked on completing my manuscript, I was blessed with fellowships at the Vermont Studio Center, the Horned Dorset Colony, the Hermitage Artist Colony, and the Dora Maar House, each of which provided me with ideal environments in which to write.

Just about every friend I have has, in some form or another, cheered this project on, but some warrant special mention for their enthusiasm. These include: Michael Benanav, Roger Wing, Sarah Byrne-Martelli, Maxim Matusevich, Alina Reznitskaya, Susan Nolan, Ivan Bojanic, Kelly Goeddert, Ed Schmidt and Sophie Blackall, David Sykes, Ash Martin, Alan Katz, Toby

Nitschke, Phil Satlof, Dave Gandin, Eddie Schmidt, Alexander Nemser, Matthew Perry, Ruth, Mike, and Ben Kahn, Catherine Talese, Barrett Temple, Riley Jason, Bob Hemmer, Brennan Cavannaugh, Naomi Person, Matt Licari, Dave Thrasher, Trey Lyford, Sean Gallagher, Kathleen Kolb, Francesca Normile, Jason Gardner and Carrie Angoff, and Julie Sanderson.

My brother, Adam, has believed in every project I've ever undertaken, and has kept me laughing all the way. I'm so grateful to him; to his wife, Indre; and to my little nephew, Henry, who brings me unending joy and who will one day be not so little and able to read this book. My aunt Janet and uncle Eric Cramer, and cousins Rim Mierowitz and Fran Pulver have also been terrific cheerleaders.

Lastly, and maybe appropriately, it was the abiding interest, generosity, and understanding of a handful of women that gave me the strength to bring this book to the finish line. Early in my research, I put out a call on social media for a research assistant. Karen Lamb replied that she had a little extra time on her hands, and that it sounded like a fun project. The two of us had been part of the 1997 class of the Lincoln Center Directors Lab and, while we were certainly friendly, I wouldn't say we knew each other particularly well. Little did I know that Karen would become my most trusted ally on this book, sleuthing out details and information, tracking down contacts and gamely allowing herself to tumble down one rabbit hole after another. This book would not have been possible without her.

Riley Trumbull, Ellen Stekert, and Rita Chang became more than just people who appear in these pages; they became dear friends who lent their spirits, imaginations, and hearts to the greater goal of honoring Converse's legacy. Sarah K. Williams (a luminous artist in her own right) patiently listened to me read page after page to her during our long months of COVID lockdown, offering insightful critiques, comments, and questions; when I accepted Dutton's offer to acquire the book, I think she was even more excited than I was. And of course my mom, to whom I owe everything, who makes time for a phone call with me every morning, who always tells me she loves me and to keep up the good work.

This is far from a perfect book. From the moments when I first became aware of the vastness of Connie Converse's universe—not only the projects she pursued and the worlds she was ensconced in, but just how much of it was hidden, or lost, or gone—I have felt unequal to the task of understanding it all with any degree of completeness. I still do. I know that there are things I've missed, or failed to understand, or both, in ways that left me feeling inadequate. But now it's time to let Connie Converse go. My hope is that I have somehow at least served as a worthy shepherd, and that others will follow along, joining in the parade behind Converse as she makes her way at last to the place she belongs, to the table of great American artists and thinkers. Her seat is there, waiting for her.

NOTES

All Connie Converse references here are indicated by the initials CC. All other Converse family members are cited by their given name followed by a C.

Materials sourced from Converse's filing cabinet are indicated with the initials FC and are used courtesy of Philip Converse.

EPIGRAPH

1. CC to Phil C. and Jean C., Jan. 3, 1955, FC.

PRELUDE: A STAR HAS BURNT MY EYE

1. CC to Phil C. and Jean C., June 4, 1957, FC.

CHAPTER 1: PAST ALL DREAMING

1. *Hear that lonesome whippoorwill / He sounds too blue to fly / The midnight train is whining low / I'm so lonesome I could cry.*

    Another, perhaps more obvious source may be Stephen Vincent Benét's 1925 poem "The Mountain Whippoorwill," with its verses:

    Up in the mountains, it's lonesome for a child, /
    (Whippoorwills a-callin' when the sap runs wild.)

    and

    An' I heard the sound of the squirrel in the pine, /
    An' I heard the earth a-breathin' thu' the long night-time.

    Benét (1898–1943) was a Pulitzer Prize–winning poet, fiction writer, and dramatist best known for his book-length narrative poem, *John Brown's Body.*
2. Greil Marcus, *Mystery Train*, 3rd rev. ed. (New York: Plume, 1990), 122.

CHAPTER 2: "ONE BY ONE"

1. Hopper's *Morning Sun* had just been completed in 1952 and had recently been shown in New York; the final lines of "One by One" might even be a direct reference to it. While Converse's letters of the time do not directly mention which galleries and museums she was frequenting, they do suggest that she was a cultural omnivore as far as the New York scene was concerned, regularly attending concerts, plays, readings, operas, lectures, and exhibitions. She likely would have seen Hopper's most recent work. Given her contemporaneous

attempts at oil painting, some of them realistic depictions of disconnected individuals, Hopper was likely an artist not only with whom she was familiar, but also whom she sought to emulate.

2. Molly Drake (1915–1993). The eponymous first complete album of Drake's music was released in 2011 by Dan Dzula and David Herman, the producers of *How Sad, How Lovely*. Although Drake is mostly known as the mother of her more famous son, Nick, her music stands alone, and shares many of the qualities found in Converse's guitar songs. It is beautiful, poetic, and haunting, and her recordings have that same tactile, intimate feeling of music being made by a person in a room. Drake and Converse, composing across the Atlantic from each other at virtually the same time, are spiritual sisters, and Drake, too, is worthy of greater study and wider recognition. But that's for another book.

3. For a thorough overview of existentialism in art during this time, see Louis Menand's *The Free World: Art and Thought in the Cold War* (New York: Farrar, Straus and Giroux, 2021), Chapter 3, "Freedom and Nothingness." "In the United States," Menand writes, "existentialism was taken to have something to do with avant-garde literature and painting, with jazz, with questions of meaning and value, with the possibility or impossibility of religious faith, with the mores of private life" (p. 91).

4. In her own annotation to the song's lyrics, Converse noted for posterity, "Yes, the moon is down, but hand in hand in the dark makes a passage possible." CC, "Musicks (Volumes I and II)," FC.

5. "Walkin' After Midnight," an easier-to-swallow take on the same image, was also written in 1954 by songwriters Alan Block and Don Hecht. It became a hit in 1957 when Pasty Cline made it her signature.

CHAPTER 3: A GHOST

1. Geeshie Wiley's "Last Kind Words Blues," from 1930, is one of the most haunting records ever made, and only one of two known to feature Wiley's vocals (her guitar is heard on at least two others). Little is known about Wiley, including whether she may have sung other songs using another name. For more, read John Jeremiah Sullivan's essay "The Ballad of Geeshie and Elvie" in *The New York Times Magazine* (April 13, 2014) and Greil Marcus's *The Old, Weird America* (New York: Picador, 1997).

CHAPTER 4: PHIL

1. Phil C. to author, email, May 17, 2011.

INTERLUDE: GENRES

1. Arguably as important, if less commercially successful, were Fiddlin' John Carson's recordings for the Okeh label, made the year before. One record he made, with "The Little Old Log Cabin in the Lane" on one side, and "The Old Hen Cackled and the Rooster's Going to Crow" on the other, sold out its initial pressing of five hundred copies, impressing upon record executive Ralph Peer the idea that there was a market for such music. Barry Mazor, *Ralph Peer and the Making of Popular Roots Music* (Chicago: Chicago Review Press, 2014), 54–55.

2. For a thorough exegesis on the origins of the term "hillbilly music," see Archie Green's informative "Hillbilly Music: Source & Symbol," *The Journal of American Folklore*, July–Sept. 1965.

3. When I was discussing this with music historian, composer, and musician Allen Lowe, he made the astute point that many musicians, especially if they came from poor, rural areas, may have been happy to have recording contracts at all. How their music got marketed was perhaps of less importance to them than the money it brought in. Allen Lowe to author, telephone interview, May 25, 2022.

4. As Amanda Petrusich wrote in "Mickey Guyton Takes on the Overwhelming Whiteness of Country Music," her June 14, 2021, *New Yorker* profile of Black country music star Mickey Guyton, "Perhaps country music isn't simply reflecting the reality of what it means to be white and American; perhaps it is actively (and repeatedly) inventing it."

5. Arguments around the absurdity and randomness behind definitions of various genres went mainstream in 2019 with the controversy surrounding the classification of Lil Nas X's "Old Town Road," the boundary-crossing hip-hop/country song that was disqualified for inclusion on *Billboard*'s Hot Country charts for not being country enough.

6. As Louis Menand writes in *The Free World: Art and Thought in the Cold War*, 310–20: "Most musicians are much more eclectic than their fans. If he had nothing else to do, [Elvis] Presley sang gospel . . . Muddy Waters sang 'Red Sails in the Sunset.' Robert Johnson sang 'Yes Sir, That's My Baby.' James Brown liked Sinatra and disliked the blues. Leadbelly was a Gene Autry fan . . . Race had a lot to do with the music business in the United States. It had much less to do with the music."

7. Big Bill Broonzy was recorded saying a version of this on the Smithsonian Folkways album *Trouble in Mind* (in his spoken introduction to the song "This Train"). The disputed origin of the saying is discussed here: fretboardjournal.com/features/bob-shane-big-bill-broonzy -louis-armstrong-and-horses-and-best-correction-ever/.

8. Stekert continued: "Even though almost all of us were from European origins a few or many generations back, none of us sang songs from the group from which our parents came. If anyone specialized in songs in a 'foreign' language they sang in a niche, a group devoted to that culture or language. (It is pretty well established that after the second generation or so, children of immigrants were often embarrassed when their parents or grandparents spoke in the original language. Second generation kids almost never learned the original language.) Since most of the folksinging groups I hung out with were around that genera- tion, we did not speak other languages and therefore could not sing in them or understand the cultural significance of the songs—so we did not sing them. Of course these folkies, like me, didn't understand the culture of most of the groups who sang the songs we sang (i.e., sailor, cowboy, lumberman, coal miner, Southern Mountains, etc.), but we knew what we thought was their life. Actually these 'understandings' were . . . our stereotypes of cul- tures (in these cases a positive white stereotype).

"Most of the singers in Greenwich Village at that time were suburban or urban kids whose families or cultures in school had developed a kind of new white culture where the offspring of mostly middle-class families found a 'home.' This new white culture had no background that these suburban kids could find; they usually identified with the British Isles since they could speak the language and observed that British speakers with British accents often were treated better than foreign speakers or foreign accented folks." Ellen Stekert to author, email, May 12, 2022.

9. Stekert is referring to Baez's paternal Mexican heritage. Baez's mother was Scottish. Phil Davison, "Obituary: Joan Bridge Baez, Anti-War Activist," *The Scotsman*, April 25, 2013.

10. Ethel Raim to author, telephone interview, Jan. 15, 2021.

11. In a 2019 essay discussing the phenomenon of Lil Nas X, Jon Caramanica takes the music industry notion of genre to task: "Take 'Look What God Gave Her,' the new single by Thomas Rhett, perhaps the ur-country gentleman of the last few years. It's a soft soul song with a faint disco undertow, nothing country about it beyond the perceived affiliation of the performer." *The New York Times*, April 11, 2019.

12. "I once heard a record producer remark about Janis Ian, 'Her music isn't folk, it isn't rock, it isn't country—who the hell am I supposed to sell it to?'" Dave Van Ronk and Elijah Wald, *The Mayor of MacDougal Street* (Cambridge, MA: Da Capo Press, 2005), 196.

13. Allen Lowe told me he thinks the beginning of today's relaxed attitudes toward genre really began to manifest in the 1980s and '90s, with people like Marc Ribot and John Zorn (and, although he is too modest to say it, Lowe himself), many of whom were working in the downtown NYC music scene at places like the old Knitting Factory. Allen Lowe to author, telephone interview, May 25, 2022. For a deep, deep plunge into the fascinating and murky waters of American vernacular music, see Lowe's two-volume set (with an accompanying *thirty* CDs) *"Turn Me Loose White Man," Or: Appropriating Culture: How to Listen to American Music, 1900–1960* (Schaumburg, IL: Constant Sorrow Press, 2020), 196.

14. Kelefa Sanneh, "The Education of a Part-time Punk," *The New Yorker*, Sept. 6, 2021. For further reading, see Sanneh's *Major Labels* (New York: Penguin Press, 2021), an entire book addressing the history of genre in popular music that explores in a more thorough way some of the topics only touched upon here.

CHAPTER 6: THE FILING CABINET

1. Converse numbered and coded her "transparencies" (what we today call slides) with letters and numbers. The code's first position was for quality. "A=Good B=Fair C=Poor." CC, Numerical Index of Transparencies with Descriptions, FC.

CHAPTER 7: WE HAVE NEVER SEEN HER LIKE

1. Eugene Merril Deitch was born in Chicago on August 8, 1924. His family moved to Los Angeles when he was still an infant, and he grew up in the Somerset Apartments in Hollywood, near Beverly Hills. He was an enterprising youth, one whose passion for amateur newspapers led to his self-publishing the *Somerset Scandals,* a gelatin newspaper printed with a hectograph and slipped under the doors of his family's neighbors. He later transformed it into something similar, called the *Hollywood Star News.*

   As a young man, Deitch collected rare 78s of early jazz recordings and proudly considered himself a "moldy fig," a pejorative then in currency among jazz aficionados to describe someone whose tastes were decidedly behind the times. To Deitch, nothing would ever surpass the recordings made by pioneers like King Oliver, Freddie Keppard, and Bix Beiderbecke, artists now considered giants in the jazz canon, but whose music was then considered hopelessly old-fashioned. While Deitch's purist tastes may have deprived him of the pleasures being offered by contemporary innovators like Charlie Parker, Miles Davis, and Dizzy Gillespie, his steadfast devotion to music that was decidedly out of style to the point of derision is an argument for the idea that he heard artistic brilliance where others did not.

The young Deitch ventured beyond the edges of his Hollywood neighborhood in search of shellac pay dirt. At one record store in particular, the owner told him about a mountainous stock of unsellable recordings that he kept stashed behind a curtain at the back of the shop. The owner didn't want to melt them down (a common practice of the day) and was instead simply waiting for the time when "that sort of music" came back into style. Trembling with anticipation, Deitch followed the man to a musty back room and found, to his ecstatic delight, treasures untold. "It was like finding the Taj Mahal," Deitch said to me. (For a terrific guided tour through this particular world of obsessive eccentrics, read Amanda Petrusich's book *Do Not Sell at Any Price*.)

Deitch was also something of a jokester, delighting in using the telephone to make prank calls to strangers. "Do you have Prince Albert [tobacco] in a can?" he would call and ask a pharmacist. Upon receiving a response in the affirmative, he would cry, "Well, for Chrissakes, let him out!" and then quickly hang up, collapsing in giggles. As a young man, he became the art director for the jazz magazine *The Record Changer*, before embarking on a career creating animated films for United Productions of America (UPA), Paramount, Metro-Goldwyn-Mayer (MGM), and 20th Century Fox. Gene Deitch to author, in-person interview, Aug. 12, 2013.

2. Gene Deitch, "The Mystery and Magic of Connie Converse," www.genedeitch.com. The website went away sometime after Deitch's death in 2020.

3. Arthur William Bernal was born in Oakland, CA, on September 12, 1913, the son of a Mexican immigrant father and an Irish mother. His parents split when Bernal was a teenager, and he would be raised by his mother in a small apartment above a café where she worked. Barbara Bernal to author, email, March 30, 2017.

4. She died in 2021.

5. Barbara Bernal to author, email, March 31, 2017. Though Barbara and I exchanged dozens of emails, she was adamant about our not speaking on the phone. "PLEASE, never call me!" she responded when I suggested a call—a reaction that may have been due to what Juana Culhane, the widow of her husband's former colleague, described to me as "a bad tone to her voice. When she got excited, she kind of squeaked," Culhane said, and remembered that Barbara took speech lessons to mitigate the issue. Juana Culhane to author, telephone interview, May 31, 2017.

6. Barbara Bernal to author, email, March 30, 2017.

7. Juana Culhane to author, telephone interview, May 31, 2017.

8. Barbara Bernal to author, email, July 2, 2011.

9. Gene Deitch, "The Mystery and Magic of Connie Converse," www.genedeitch.com.

10. Barbara Bernal to author, email, July 2, 2011.

11. Dick Weissman to author, telephone interview, Nov. 11, 2020.

12. Gene Deitch to author, in-person interview, Aug. 12, 2013.

13. Ellen Stekert to author, telephone interview, Nov. 19, 2020.

14. Victoria Bernal to author, email, July 12, 2015, and Bernal to author, email, July 2, 2011.

15. Thanks to the help of Andrea Kannes and Betsy and Ryan Maxwell.

16. Gene Deitch to author, in-person interview, Aug. 12, 2013.

17. Bernal started out as a writer for sci-fi and fantasy magazines, alongside contemporaries Robert E. Howard and L. Ron Hubbard. G. W. Thomas, "A. W. Bernal: The Man Who Was Two Men," *Darkworlds Quarterly*, July 16, 2020.

18. Barbara Bernal to author, email, March 30, 2017.

19. Hooker's biographer, Charles Shaar Murray, makes no mention of this in his terrific book *Boogie Man* (New York: St. Martin's Press, 2000), which should not stop anyone from reading it and learning more about Hooker and the primal music he made.

20. Kim Deitch, Gene's son, to author, email, Aug. 15, 2011.

21. Gene Deitch to author, in-person interview, Aug. 12, 2013.

22. Lindsay Bernal to author, in-person interview, Sept. 28, 2015.

23. Gene Deitch, "Bill Bernal," www.genedeitchcredits.com, undated.

24. Juana Culhane to author, telephone interview, May 31, 2017.

25. They would divorce ten years later, in 1964. Gene Deitch to author, in-person interview, Aug. 12, 2013.

26. Gene Deitch to author, in-person interview, Aug. 12, 2013.

27. Kim Deitch, "Part 6: Almost Adult," *The Comics Journal*, Aug. 11, 2011.

28. Gene Deitch to author, in-person interview, Aug. 12, 2013.

29. Julia Crippen to author, email, Aug. 9, 2017.

30. Terri Thal, the ex-wife of folk singer Dave Van Ronk, told me that "print shops were full of lefties in those days," so Converse's reasons for working at Academy may have been more than just taking a survival job. "A lot of Trotskyites worked in printshops." Terri Thal to author, telephone interview, Nov. 19, 2020.

31. David Garland to author, video interview, March 21, 2022.

32. Dr. Kelly Goedert to author, telephone interview, Aug. 2, 2017. Dr. Bob Hemmer also weighed in on the issue during a phone interview with me on July 31, 2017.

33. Gene Deitch to author, in-person interview, Aug. 12, 2013.

34. Gene Deitch to author, in-person interview, Aug. 12, 2013.

35. Barbara Bernal to author, email, July 2, 2011.

36. Gene Deitch to author, in-person interview, Aug. 12, 2013.

37. Barbara Bernal to author, email, July 15, 2011.

38. At least, no recordings of her performing it have come to light.

CHAPTER 8: CONVERSES

1. Converse and her brothers were visiting their parents during one of Tom's family's annual sojourns from Kentucky to the old Converse family homestead in New Hampshire. Tom's sharpest recollection from this visit was when Elizabeth (as she was always referred to, in his memory) corrected his pronunciation of the word *aunt*, telling him that an "ant" is something that crawls on the ground. She apparently did not succeed in instilling this view when she became an aunt herself; her own nephews called her "ant."

2. Tom C. to author, email, Feb. 13, 2016.

3. The full name of the publication—take a deep breath—is *The Converse Family and Allied Families: Some of the Ancestors and Descendants of Samuel Converse, Jr., of Thompson Parish, Killingly, Conn.; Major James Convers of Woburn, Mass.; Hon. Herman Allen, M.D., of Milton and Burlington, Vermont; Captain Jonathan Bixby, Sr., of Killingly, Conn., compiled and edited by Charles Allen Converse in Two Volumes* (hereafter *Some of the Ancestors and Descendants of Samuel Converse, Jr., ...*) (Boston: Eben Putnam, 1905). It was printed by the Salem Press in Salem, MA, and runs to 961 pages.

4. Ebenezer Converse (son of Robert, and Connie's great-great-grandfather) seems to have been the first to have his last name officially documented with the new spelling.

5. "Historical Sketch of Winchester," from *Some of the Ancestors and Descendants of Samuel Converse, Jr.,* ...

6. In addition to Edward Convers's duties as deacon, he worked as a ferryman and served as selectman beginning in 1635, when he became one of seven men chosen to receive a land grant from the newly elected representatives of the Great and General Court of Massachusetts Bay. Convers was entrusted to undertake the settlement of Charlestown Village. He and his men "were required to build houses for habitation within two years . . . [and] entrusted with the power to grant lands to other persons willing to build and live within the newly formed Village"; they also were to lay out the streets and maintain a civil and religious society. Edward Convers built the first house and mill in Charlestown, in 1640. Ibid.

7. Converse may even trace her rebellious streak all the way back to Edward, who, late in life, was arrested and jailed for civil disobedience in response to a letter from English king Charles II asserting "the King's supreme authority over the colonies, curtailing the liberties which [they] had hitherto enjoyed unmolested." Convers defiantly "denounced the letter as an embodiment of Popery." In 1663, he was summoned before a General Court sympathetic to his views, and acquitted. He died later that year.

8. Eaton's son, known as John the Planter, and John's wife, Martha (née Rowlandson), were the first Eatons to give birth to a child on American soil—another John Eaton, in 1646. From Evelyn E. Converse, "The Old Days," unpublished MS, Jan. 11, 1957, FC.

9. William G. Hill, *Family Record of Deacons James W. and Elisha S. Converse* (Boston: Alfred Mudge & Son, Printers, 1887), and Charles Allen Converse, *Some of the Ancestors and Descendants of Samuel Converse, Jr.,* . . . , 856.

10. The most complete discussion currently available on the subject can be found on the website www.converse-ancestry.org, maintained by members of the Converse family.

11. Military service was common in the Converse family. Edward Convers's son James (born in England in 1620; died 1715) became a lieutenant in the military, and his son (also named James) would become a major, remembered for "protecting the infant colonies from the repeated assaults of savages." As a reward for his services during King Philip's War, James was then put in charge of Massachusetts's entire military corps and served for ten years as a member of the General Court. In later years, he was thrice elected Speaker of the House of Representatives. Other Convers men—with old Yankee first names like Alpheus, Amasa, Chester, Pain, Asa, and Elijah—fought in every major military conflict in New England. Col. Thomas Convers was one of George Washington's men, wintering with him at Valley Forge, along with at least two other Convers men. Other officers of distinction in their ranks included Capt. Samuel and Col. James Convers (of the Fourth Worcester Company Regiment). Thomas Convers of Thompson and Goshen, Connecticut, also enlisted in the Old French War and, as a sergeant, participated in the capture of Quebec in September 1759. Elisha Convers, age seventeen, fought in the Battle of Bunker Hill. Also in the service during the War of Independence were Capt. Josiah Convers (known for his service in the French and Indian War) and Jude Convers, who served as a drummer in the army band. *Some of the Ancestors and Descendants of Samuel Converse, Jr.,* ...

12. "Converse, Charles Crozat" in *Appletons' Cyclopaedia of American Biography*, J. G. Wilson and J. Friske, ed. (New York: D. Appleton, 1900).

13. Mike Doolan to author, telephone interview, Jan. 10, 2017. Mike Doolan's grandfather was CC's uncle Henry.

14. "Another Old Home Owned by the Third Generation," Historical Society of Amherst, NH, Inc., newsletter 3, no. 3, Dec. 1968.

15. Robert Converse's first New Hampshire residence is recorded as being in Marlborough. Other Converses would settle in and around Lyme, NH, soon thereafter. Family lore also has it that the Amherst Converses were on close, personal terms with the future *New York Tribune* founder, presidential candidate, and historian Horace Greeley during his youth in nearby Meredith. Edith Neff to author, telephone interview, Dec. 8, 2015.

16. The other siblings were Charlotte (known as Eva), Sarah, and Robert. New Hampshire State Hospital was known for severe overcrowding ("History of Psychiatric Hospitals," Paul Shagoury, Director of Psychology, NHH, dhhs.nh.gov/sites/g/files/ehbemt476/files/documents/2021-11/nhh-history-shagoury.pdf), and Charles's death was also attributed, in part, to cerebral arteriosclerosis (New Hampshire, U.S., Death Records, 1650–1969).

17. Born 1856; died 1929. She was the daughter of William P. Conrey and Elizabeth McIntire, of New Hampshire.

18. Nellie's father had been killed in the war as well, and from a young age, she was left with the burden of having to help care for and support her family—"a hard life" that included taking in other people's laundry in order to "get the kids enough to eat and to keep them from nakedness," her son Ernest would later recall. Nellie married Luther Converse in 1877, at the age of twenty-one. Phil C. audio interview of Ernest C. and Evelyn C., tape reel, June 18, 1957 (hereafter "Phil C. 1957 audio interview of Ernest C. and Evelyn C."), FC.

19. He was officially reported to have starved to death in a Confederate prison, his demise occurring after peace had been declared. The prison was in Andersonville, Georgia. Phil C. 1957 audio interview of Ernest C. and Evelyn C., FC.

20. Tom Converse to author, email, Jan. 22, 2017.

21. Born August 20, 1883.

22. On June 18, 1957. The conversation took place at Phil and Jean's home in Ann Arbor and lasted for over two hours.

23. Luther was "economically less well-situated" than his brother, Robert, and received a lesser share of the family inheritance when their father died—owing mainly to the fact it was Robert who had housed and cared for him in his old age. Luther was permitted to raise his family on the property, but Robert owned it. Phil C. 1957 audio interview of Ernest C. and Evelyn C., FC.

24. According to Ernest, his father never traveled more than one hundred miles from where he was born his entire life—something Ernest recalled with clear, conservative pride. Phil C. 1957 audio interview of Ernest C. and Evelyn C., FC.

25. Phil C. 1957 audio interview of Ernest C. and Evelyn C., FC.

26. Born Nellie Grace in 1879. The other siblings were Florence ("Flossie," born 1893), Albert ("Bert," born 1887), Walter (born 1885), and Henry Thomas (Tom Converse's grandfather; born 1889). Tom Converse told me about Grace's epilepsy, email, Feb. 22, 2017.

27. The Old Home Place is described in a Historical Society of Amherst newsletter as "rather a large house. There are four sleeping rooms on the second floor and one on the first floor, together with a large kitchen, a dining room and a living room . . . it does still have two 'boilers' in the back room. One was a copper kettle and the other had an iron kettle . . . the iron kettle was used largely for heating water for hog killing." "Another Old Home Owned by the Third Generation."

28. Tom C. to author, email, March 1, 2017.

29. Walter became a farmhand and lumberman like his father. "Bert" tried college for a few months, but quickly found that "he didn't care much for study." He served in World War I, went to France, and was gased in the trenches. The lifelong respiratory difficulties that resulted from this did not inhibit his smoking an "ever-present cigarette." He married a woman named Eva Belle Richards and spent the rest of his life as a housepainter and carpenter. Phil C. 1957 audio interview of Ernest C. and Evelyn C., FC; and Tom C. to author, email, Feb. 22, 2017.

30. Tom C. to author, email, Feb. 22, 2017.

31. "She was a force of nature," Tom told me, "and I don't think there was much love lost between her and her siblings. There was a son or foster son of her husband Harry Richardson's who lived there off and on early in the marriage. Harry was older than Florence and died well before she did. As time passed and she got older, not many people would eat with her because she would let her dog, Tippy, lick the plates before she washed them (and sometimes she would forget to wash them and just put them in cabinet)." Ibid.

32. Tom C. to author, email, March 1, 2017.

33. CC to Phil C. and Jean C., letter, Oct. 28, 1951, FC.

34. CC to Jean C., letter, Dec. 4, 1950, FC. She signs the letter "Lavinia," a name that may have been inspired by her current reading of O'Neill's *Mourning Becomes Electra* (she refers to same in a January 7 letter), though it could also be a reference to Emily Dickinson's sister.

35. Members of her mother's family, the Eatons, were proud members of the Daughters of the American Revolution, though the relative who told me this asked not to be quoted by name.

CHAPTER 9: PEOPLE SAY

1. Ebenezer Converse, brother to Converse's great-grandfather Charles. Born August 15, 1805, married to Sabria Adams in 1829, drowned on September 4, 1842, at the age of thirty-seven.

2. Tom C. to author, email, Jan. 22, 2017.

3. Helen was the daughter of Ernest's uncle Robert and aunt Mary E. Noyes Converse. Family lore has Helen going to Boston for a few months, ostensibly to study music. A neighbor, Wilene Knight, told me that when Helen could no longer hide her pregnancy, "the minister stood behind her; the congregation did not," and that "she was ostracized by Amherst folk, not by Merrimack folk [the next town over]." Wilene Knight to author, in-person interview, Aug. 27, 2017.

4. Many pegged him to be the married minister of the local church, where Helen had been an organist. The other candidate for the father was Charlie Upham, a cousin who lived down the road, son of Jacob Upham and Sarah Fuller Converse Upham. Sarah Upham was Helen's father's sister, making Charles Upham Helen's first cousin. As Tom Converse opined, "Charlie would have been in his mid-40s then, perhaps in his mid-life crisis and casting a roving eye on his young cousin," who was "a tiny little woman, full of laughter and wit and musical talent." The Upham place (which last sold in 1792 and has been passed down in the family ever since) is just a few houses down from the Old Home Place. Tom C. to author, email, Feb. 22, 2017. Charles Upham married Eva V. Kelley, and she and Helen became best friends. They called each other every day for decades and saw each other almost as frequently. Wilene Knight told me that the two women "would go to the beach together in October and November and take a dip in the water." Whether they ever discussed the possible love triangle with Charlie that Tom Converse alleges is unknown. When Knight moved into the house next door to Helen's in 1955, Helen was sixty-seven

and quickly became known to Knight's children as "Aunt Helen." She made donuts for them and was a beloved presence. "I never heard her say a bad word about anybody," Knight said. Wilene Knight to author, in-person interview, Aug. 27, 2017.

5. "The genetics of the Converses were extraordinary," Knight recalled. "Also their intelligence." She remembered asking Alice Converse what she attributed their longevity to. "Squashes and potatoes, squashes and potatoes," came the reply, a reference to the well-maintained root cellar in the Old Home Place's basement. Wilene Knight to author, in-person interview, Aug. 27, 2017.

6. Phil C. to author, telephone interview, July 10, 2011.

7. Gene Deitch to author, in-person interview, Aug. 12, 2013.

8. Julia Bullock to author, video interview, April 1, 2021.

CHAPTER 10: EATONS, AND EVELYN AND ERNEST

1. Elizabeth Dunbar Day to author, email, Nov. 12, 2021.

2. CC to Phil C., letter, Oct. 17, 1951, FC. Some of those historic traits may have also included a belief in white supremacy. Emery's younger son, Converse's uncle Blythe, was described to me as blatantly racist by one family member who recalled him saying during a visit, "Someday the White House will be full of Negroes." Claire Eaton Motschman to author (with the help of her daughter, Lori Eaton Wood), email, May 12, 2022.

3. In 1708, John Eaton married Esther, daughter of Moses Swett. The next John Eaton, of Seabrook, born in 1749, was a tailor. He married Sarah French, and they settled in Pittsfield, New Hampshire, where they had eleven children. Their oldest child, Elisha Eaton (1774–1795), would become a farmer and marry Betsey Sherburne. That couple's one child, Elisha II (born 1794), was only four months old when his father, Elisha Sr., died. Elisha Jr. was raised by his grandparents and eventually inherited the family home. He married Betsey Brown, daughter of Ephraim Brown of Gilford, New Hampshire. They had ten children, including Connie Converse's maternal great-grandfather, Daniel Brown Eaton, born in Meredith on October 20, 1823. His siblings included Sarah Jane (died at age twenty-three), Miriam (married Isaiah C. Morrill of Gilford), Ruhamah G. (married Isaac Morrill), Emeline T. (married Calvin Rollins of Alton), John D. (settled in Salem, MA), Mary T. (married Henry McDuffee of Alton), Martin V. B. (lived in Moultonborough, NH), Joseph W. (lived in Salem, MA), and Laura A. (married William Downs of Salem).

   As a young man, D. B. Eaton attended public school in Gilford (now Laconia), and shoveled snow for ten hours a day during the winters, at a rate of $1.25 per day. "There was much more snow than nowadays," his son Emery recalled, noting that, at least one year, there was "still good sleighing" on May 1. Daniel Brown Eaton married Susan Lee Smith, daughter of Joseph Parsons Smith of Guilford (which is how the town's name is spelled in a contemporary citation of their marriage; "Guilford" may be "Gilford"). *Biographical Review: Containing Life Sketches of Leading Citizens of Strafford and Belknap Counties, New Hampshire,* vol. XXI (Boston: Biographical Review Publishing Company, 1897), 173. Eaton's wife died in 1876, and on October 12, 1882, he married Emily A. (Whidden) Corliss, daughter of Mark Whidden of Portsmouth, New Hampshire.

4. Evelyn C., "An Abridged Family History Featuring My Father, Daniel Emery Eaton," June 18, 1976. Courtesy of Phil C.

5. Daughter of Nancy Alcesta Goodnow (1829–1871) and Rev. Samuel P. Everett of Milford, NH (1826–1908). Ella was born May 31, 1858, in Rowe, MA. Because the town names Milford and Amherst were often used interchangeably, the Everetts would at least have been aware of the highly regarded Converses generations before the families became joined in marriage. Goodnow and Everett married in 1848 and gave birth to four other children besides Ella.

6. John Hopper to author, in-person interview, Feb. 23, 2022.

7. Ella attended Mount Holyoke from 1877 to 1881 and taught there through 1889. She and Eaton married on December 14, 1889. Mount Holyoke Female Seminary was originally chartered as a teaching seminary in 1836 and opened to students in 1837.

8. She was born on December 1, 1895. The other two siblings were boys: Everett Jewell, born 1890, and Blythe, born 1900.

9. Until 1908, the family lived right in the village, on Waukewan Street.

10. Reprinted by *The Meredith News*, July 28, 1988.

11. Converse and Eaton had some things in common, including a shared interest in the temperance movement and a passion for discipline. Phil C. 1957 audio interview of Ernest C. and Evelyn C., FC.

12. Phil C. 1957 audio interview of Ernest C. and Evelyn C., FC.

13. Phil C. and Jean C. to author, in-person interview, Sept. 8, 2011.

14. Everett T. Eaton to author, telephone interview, July 11, 2022.

15. Evelyn and her two brothers do not appear to have been particularly close. There's virtually no mention of these two uncles or their children in any of Converse's papers, though she did keep a photograph of one of her half cousins, Raymond Hill, in her album. Raymond was the stepson of Evelyn's brother Everett, and would grow up to fight in the Battle of the Bulge in World War II. According to his nephew Everett T. Eaton, Raymond was treated poorly as a child. He wasn't raised with his step-siblings; from the time he was twelve years old, Everett and his wife (Raymond's mother), Viviene, would drop Raymond off at a farm to work as a hand and leave him there. Viviene had a history of depression and mental illness. "She was harsh and tough, and not pleasant to anyone," Everett T. Eaton told me (Everett T. Eaton to author, telephone interview, June 30, 2022). Raymond's daughter Pam told me that it was Evelyn's brother Everett who did not want Raymond living in the house with them (Pamela Joyce to author, telephone interview, Aug. 11, 2022).

16. Phil C. 1957 audio interview of Ernest C. and Evelyn C., FC. She did well enough there to earn admission to Colby Academy in New London, New Hampshire, which her brother Everett J. Eaton also attended, and where she spent her last two years of high school, from 1912 to 1914.

17. As a young man, Ernest went to local public schools and dutifully performed chores at home. "Boys and girls both at that time had regular duties that did them no harm," he recalled—in contrast to today, when "there is no work for boys, and little for girls." Ernest remembered walking a mile and a half each way to the "little county district school," offering that he found this no great burden, as compared to the youth of today, "who require to be driven to and from school," and "there was only one other boy in [the entire] town who had been away to college." He also joined the ROTC. Ernest's younger brother, Henry, followed him to college, enrolling at the same school a year after Ernest graduated. "Dartmouth was a rich person's college. UNH was a poor family's school," Ernest recalled,

proudly. Henry majored in agriculture. In his college yearbook, Henry appears with the nickname "Conney." Though his grandson Tom doubted that Elizabeth would knowingly have adopted her uncle's nickname when she chose one for herself, it's interesting to note that she was not the first Connie Converse. Henry married in 1916 and moved to South Carolina to work as a dairyman, then to Beltsville, Maryland, in 1919, where he spent most of his adult life. Tom C. to author, email, Mar. 1, 2017; *The Granite*, yearbook, College of Agriculture and Mechanic Arts, New Hampshire College, 1910, Vol. II, p. 48; and Phil C. 1957 audio interview of Ernest C. and Evelyn C., FC.

18. From UNH Durham, in 1906, a bachelor of science. State of New Hampshire, *Biennial Report of the Adjutant-General of the State of New Hampshire*, October 1, 1906, to September 1, 1908.

19. He spent three years teaching math and science at Virginia Institute/Virginia Intermont College, a private college for women in Bristol, Virginia, in the Blue Ridge Mountains. He then went back to school for his bachelor of divinity, which he received from the Newton Theological Institution in 1912. His thesis was on "Jesus' Teachings on the Family, and Their Modern Application." "Rev. Converse Dies in Concord," *Manchester (NH) Union Leader,* June 1, 1965; "Fighter Leaves State," *Nashua Telegraph*, Feb. 16, 1948; and *The Newton Theological Institution Annual Catalog*, 1913–1914.

20. Phil C. 1957 audio interview of Ernest C. and Evelyn C., FC.

21. At the Freewill Baptist Church in Meredith Village, on Lang Street.

22. Though he admitted that he soon saw that she was "more than capable" of performing her duties. Phil C. 1957 audio interview of Ernest C. and Evelyn C., FC.

23. It's now known as Colby-Sawyer College. Colby Academy was, at the time, a secondary school.

24. The girlfriend was Freda Hopkins (actual spelling unknown). Phil C. 1957 audio interview of Ernest C. and Evelyn C., FC.

25. Ernest remembered an incident that fall, in Woodsville, NH, when "a group of us were swimming in Lake Winnipesaukee," and the two had felt some chemistry between them. Phil C. 1957 audio interview of Ernest C. and Evelyn C., FC.

26. "Alumnae Questionnaire," 1937, Mount Holyoke College, Alumni File on Evelyn Converse, Alumni Records (hereafter "Mount Holyoke Alumnae Questionnaire").

27. The twelve-year difference in their ages was nothing; Evelyn's great-great-grandfather Samuel P. Eaton married his bride, Mary Merrill, in 1778, when they were thirteen and eleven, respectively. New Hampshire, Marriage Records Index, 1637–1947.

28. Evelyn earned eight dollars per week. In the winter, when the cold and snow made the walk too difficult, she boarded at a local home for two dollars a week. Phil C. 1957 audio interview of Ernest C. and Evelyn C., FC.

29. She enrolled in 1915 and graduated four years later. Evelyn majored in history and religion, with a concentration in English literature. Ernest nursed hopes that she would stay only one year before agreeing to marry him and could then become his assistant, but she had other ideas, staying on to complete her degree. Phil C. 1957 audio interview of Ernest C. and Evelyn C., FC. Ernest temporarily "gave up hope" in their future together and continued to carry out his duties alone back in Meredith. He signed up for the draft in 1918, but unlike his brother, Albert, he was never called up. Evelyn kept close lifelong ties to her alma mater, maintaining relationships with classmates, many of whom called her by the nickname "Eat." "Mount Holyoke Alumnae Questionnaire."

30. The same year the Eighteenth Amendment went into effect, prohibiting the sale of alcohol in the United States. Her mother, Ella, had by then become corresponding secretary for the New Hampshire Woman's Christian Temperance Union, so the new law would have represented a signal moment for the family. Ella Eaton to Evelyn C., letter, Sept. 1924, FC.

31. "Mount Holyoke Alumnae Questionnaire."

32. He did not mention what those complications might be; there were no prohibitions against pastors taking wives. Phil C. 1957 audio interview of Ernest C. and Evelyn C., FC.

33. The ceremony was officiated by Ernest's close friend John Lewis. *New Hampshire, US, Marriage and Divorce Records, 1659–1947.*

34. They lived in a house in close proximity to Ernest's church. There, in Maine, they acquired one of the first radios in town and would often spend their evenings huddled around it with headphones. Phil C. 1957 audio interview of Ernest C. and Evelyn C., FC.

35. On the twenty-fifth, at the hospital in Bangor.

36. The Prohibition movement in America sprang from the religious revivalism of the early nineteenth century. By 1833, there were some 6,000 local temperance societies in the country, and Maine became the first state to pass prohibition laws. For more on the history of Prohibition, see Daniel Okrent's *Last Call: The Rise and Fall of Prohibition* (New York: Scribner, 2010), 30.

37. The post was educational superintendent. What was then known as the National Anti-Saloon League was formed in 1893 as a means of unifying regional temperance movements, with churches taking the lead in mustering support and soliciting donations for the cause. From 1893 to 1933, the Anti-Saloon League was a major force in American politics. Influencing the United States through lobbying and the printed word, it turned a moral crusade against the manufacture, sale, and consumption of alcohol into the Prohibition Amendment to the U.S. Constitution. Under the motto "The Saloon Must Go," the organization worked to unify public antialcohol sentiment, enforce existing temperance laws, and enact further antialcohol legislation. At first, the League appealed to local churches to carry its message to the people. Once they had established a loyal following, the League's leaders focused their efforts on getting individual politicians elected who supported the cause. The League was able to promote the temperance cause by publishing thousands of flyers, pamphlets, songs, stories, cartoons, dramas, magazines, and newspapers. From Anti-Saloon League Collection, Westerville Public Library, westervillelibrary.org/AntiSaloon.

38. Circumspect as ever, Ernest said only that he was "dissatisfied" and that Evelyn longed to return to New Hampshire "to be nearer her people." Phil C. 1957 audio interview of Ernest C. and Evelyn C., FC.

CHAPTER 11: SIS

1. Laconia was a then-bustling small city known for its lumber, grist, and textile mills. The baby weighed in at eight pounds, four ounces. Phil C. 1957 audio interview of Ernest C. and Evelyn C., FC.

2. Elizabeth Fuller Converse (1818–1875). The Converses and Fullers arrived in North America in the same year and may even have been on the same ship from England. From those Fullers came women's rights advocate Margaret Fuller of Massachusetts; other Fullers moved to New Hampshire, including Elizabeth Fuller, who married Charles Converse in 1843. It's hard to believe that Connie Converse was not proud to be named for someone with a direct familial relationship to Margaret Fuller.

3. CC, from TRIES folder, undated, FC.

4. Ernest got situated there first before sending for the rest of his young family, who stayed behind in Meredith, with Evelyn's parents, while Ernest took a room at the Concord YMCA, which served as his base while he looked for more permanent lodging. In addition to his new position with the Anti-Saloon League, he also found work as deacon of the local United Baptist Church. Phil C. 1957 audio interview of Ernest C. and Evelyn C., FC.

5. *Seventy-second Annual Report of the Receipts and Expenditures of the City of Concord for the Year Ending December 31, 1924*, 1925, Concord, NH, Archives.

6. Evelyn is listed as an alto in the choir, and Paul is listed as giving "The Robin's Sermon." Program, Pleasant Street Baptist Church, Concord, NH, April 17, 1927, FC, and "Baby's Own Book," FC.

7. Daniel Okrent, *Last Call: The Rise and Fall of Prohibition* (New York: Scribner, 2010), 30.

8. Evelyn C. to CC, letters, Nov. 28, 1928. "Elizabeth early showed a great fondness for books," Evelyn remembered. "Their stories and pictures. She loved 'Heidi' which was read to her in the winter of 1929, when she was 4½ years. To her Heidi seemed to be a real little girl, and she even mentioned her in her prayers." "Baby's Own Book," FC. A letter from Evelyn's mother to young Elizabeth in 1929 included drawings of the birds and squirrels outside her window, company Elizabeth would later catalogue herself in "Talkin' Like You." "Aren't you glad Hoover is going to be made President tomorrow!" Ella wrote, further evidence of the family's Republican views. "If I feel able, I want to go up to Mrs. Richardson's and hear his speech over the radio." Ella Eaton to CC, letter, Mar. 8, 1929, FC.

9. "She was reading nearly everything," Evelyn wrote. "It seemed to come to her all at once. By the following summer [1930] she was reading books like 'Black Beauty,' 'Dickens' Stories about Children,' 'Beautiful Joe,' etc." She attended the Cogswell School, on Broadway Street, for kindergarten, and South End Platoon School beginning in the first grade. Her 1929/30 school report card shows her enrollment on September 9, 1929, when she was five years old. In her first semester, she was marked as present sixty-four times and absent twenty-six; in the second semester, the figures are almost identical: sixty-six times present, twenty-four absent. In October and November of that year, she missed over six weeks of school due to illness. She received only As and Bs as follows: As in Health Habits, Hand Work, Music, Singing, Rhythms, Obedience, Originality, and Bs in English Expression, Promptness, Courtesy, Cooperation, Self-Control, Initiative, Concentration, Persever- ance, and Self-Dependence. "Baby's Own Book," FC.

10. "Elizabeth is just finishing sixth grade at the Conant School," Evelyn wrote in June 1936. "She is 11 now. She earned part of the bicycle which she had last month. She has been tak- ing piano lessons all winter and spring and has just begun violin lessons." "Baby's Own Book," FC.

11. Phil C., ed., "Connie's Guitar Songs," FC. Though Ernest and Evelyn admired Shakespeare, their literary tastes were decidedly conservative. Some years later, they visited Converse in New York City, and she recounted how they listened to "the 'Death of A Salesman' records and thought it was a very peculiar play. As Dad remarked dubiously, 'I suppose it's a good picture of a certain kind of life.'" CC to Phil C. and Jean C., letter, Nov. 28, 1954, FC.

12. What Ernest sarcastically referred to as his "theoretical salary" was $2,700 per year, though he claimed to have never actually received that figure, instead earning somewhere between $2,000 and $2,500 for his labors, part of which involved attending Anti-Saloon League

conferences in other cities. Phil C. 1957 audio interview of Ernest C. and Evelyn C., FC. A December 9, 1932, postcard from Washington, D.C., has him attending a conference there and makes mention of the fact that he'd stopped in Beltsville overnight to visit his brother Henry (Tom's grandfather) and his family. Ernest C. to CC, postcard, FC.

13. She held the position from 1931 to 1936. "Mount Holyoke Alumnae Questionnaire."
14. Phil C., ed., "Connie's Guitar Songs," FC.
15. "Addendum of some importance": CC to Phil C. and Jean C., May 3, 1957, FC.
16. Whether there was addiction in the family proper, and wherever and whatever that addiction may have been, Converse would come to take on the characteristics of the disease, the symptoms of which are often similar to those of the addict. Having myself grown up around active alcoholism, I'm well acquainted with how this plays out. Like a nasty engine that operates within the consciousness of the afflicted, the disease-mind feeds on a toxic stew of fuel composed of negativity, self-loathing, anger, worry, hopelessness, despair, fear, resentment, and judgment. Unrecovered addicts and their family members rarely know what it means to have peace of mind. Today, we talk about this as the "background noise" that those afflicted are constantly subject to, but in Converse's time, this sense of never really being at ease was not typically (or accurately) identified. And all of that negative self-talk can lead to behaviors that Converse began to show evidence of as she entered adolescence: overachieving perfectionism, isolation, low self-esteem, lack of self-care, secrecy, and becoming attached to unavailable and/or inappropriate people.
17. CC to Jean C., letter, Aug. 3, 1971, FC.
18. Ellen Stekert to author, telephone interview, Nov. 20, 2020.

CHAPTER 12: THE LIFE UNDER

1. Technically speaking, Converse's first known use of the nickname "Connie" didn't happen until college, a few years later. But still.
2. CC, from TRIES folder, undated, FC.
3. Dolly's mother had died when she was young, and she and her father and siblings began summering in Europe thereafter. In an unpublished memoir that Dolly wrote, and dedicated to Frannie, Concord is described at that time as being "rabidly Republican." Courtesy of Humphrey Morris.
4. U.S. Census, 1930.
5. Richard Mullavey to author, telephone interviews, Sept. 2017.
6. Jean Crowley to author, telephone interview, Oct. 6, 2017.
7. The topics of their writing included philosophical thoughts on the nature of sentimentality, Conan Doyle's writing (Flint's mother had spent time working in a British literary office where Doyle was a client), and gossip about their teachers. CC and Frances Flint, notebook, FC.
8. In what may be the earliest letter from Flint, she writes to Converse that she has enclosed "a highly sentimental little ditty" and asks for her friend's critical assessment of same, suggesting that there was a back-and-forth interchange of creative expression between the two girls. Frances Flint to CC, undated, FC.
9. Flint seems to have been the primary audience for Converse's early poems, contributing what is almost certainly the first extant peer feedback on the latter's verse: "Your language was better written for French Revolution days than 1939—it was a bit flowery, you must admit . . . Otherwise, palsy-walsy, it rates super-excellent! Dad says your literary style is

Notes

wonderful . . . The consensus of opinion (including that of myself, Dad, Ma, and the little birds who fly around our house every day and peek in . . .) . . . is that you are not well enough acquainted with your background. Paris, the texture of Spanish lace, crucifixes, inns, etc., all such things that you would have no occasion to know, which consequently you describe by means of cliches." Frances Flint to CC, letter, Dec. 23, 1939, FC.

10. Denison University Yearbook, 1943.

11. The two siblings seem to have had only one significant bit of correspondence during Paul's time at Denison. During the spring of Connie's junior year at Concord High, Paul began dating a woman named Margaret "Peg" Avey. In an envelope marked "Personal," he wrote to his sister about the courtship, to ask for her opinion. The letter has "Private" written and underlined at the top of the page. There is precious little revealed, other than the fact that he finds Avey to be "a Deep Thinker" and "fairly good-looking," so it's worth noting that Paul found it necessary to attempt to keep even this information private. From whom was he hiding it? Was the Converse household so strict that he feared that even news about his dating activities could be cause for parental rebuke? Paul C. to CC, letter, March 13, 1941, FC. Just before Thanksgiving of that year, Paul wrote again, this time to the entire family, with an update about his doings and studies, and he asked his father: "How do I go about to get my preacher's license . . . I think it would be a good thing to get it." Paul C. to Converse family, letter, Nov. 19, 1941, FC.

12. The Converse family took several lengthy family road trips as Elizabeth reached adolescence, further proof that her health improved as she matured. On a 1937 trip to Quebec, they brought with them her young cousin Eleanor. CC, photo album, undated, FC.

13. Edith Neff to author, telephone interview, Dec. 8, 2015.

14. Frances Flint to CC, letter, undated, FC. Converse may have taken Flint's words to heart. In 1940, she attended Camp Northfield, in Northfield, MA—a Baptist-run retreat—in what was likely her first extended time away from home (a photo preserved in one of her scrapbooks shows her there, though she never mentions it otherwise in her papers), FC.

15. *Syb*, 1942 Concord High School yearbook.

16. Converse earned the highest average on her entrance exams out of all her fellow candidates. The college's notification was dated May 23, 1942, and carried an award of full tuition for her freshman year (about six hundred dollars). The Scholarship Committee also reserved a place for Converse as a "table-waitress for luncheon and dinner, which gives a reduction of $125.00 for the year, and a place in one of the rooms on which there is a reduction of $50.00 a year, [with] a total possible deduction of $775.00 for the coming year." Helen MacM. Voorhees to CC, letter, May 23, 1942, FC. The scholarship prompted a congratulatory letter from New Hampshire senator (and former governor) Styles Bridges. Styles Bridges to CC, letter, June 5, 1942. Her family's ongoing relationship with the college may also have had something to do with Converse's acceptance. "As a very small girl I knew that I was going to Mt. Holyoke," Evelyn wrote at age eighty-nine, more than a decade after her daughter had disappeared, in a letter to the executive director of the college. "I have been thinking, as never before, what it has meant to me to have had a Mt. Holyoke mother!" she wrote, recalling Ella's attendance there. Evelyn C. to Carolyn M. Berkey, card, Jan. 30, 1985. In another card, addressed to the Mount Holyoke Alumni Association, Evelyn refers to the college itself as a "nurturing Mother." Evelyn C. to Mrs. Goodale, March 10, 1978, Mount Holyoke College Alumni Files.

17. Mount Holyoke College Alumni Files.
18. The distinction came with a year's subscription to *Reader's Digest.*
19. Frances Flint to CC, April 16, 1942.
20. Frances Flint to CC, letter, July 10, 1942, FC.
21. For example, Flint mentions recently seeing the film *Juke Girl,* with Ann Sheridan, "who continues to appeal to me with her throaty protestations and full, sexy beauty." There is nothing particularly telling about this description but for the social context in which it was written: *Sexy* may or may not have been an adjective that one woman would use to describe another in 1942. Certainly, it was not a word that would have been permitted in the Converse household. Converse's side of the correspondence, unhappily, does not survive.
22. It's a small thing, but I note Flint's use of the word *laden* here, also found in the title of A. E. Housman's poem "With Rue My Heart Is Laden," which Converse would later set to music—in what was likely her first serious composition.
23. The correspondence is not all mystery and insinuations. At one point, Flint writes at length on the subject of war and politics, espousing tartly, "I agree with you perfectly that the closer the nose, the greater the stink—as far as the U.S. is concerned. I think the government is rotten, the spirit wrong, the people selfish and the military authorities all nitwits." She goes on to write, "The solution to a world of comparative peace in the future is the extermination of the Germans and the Japs," Frances Flint to CC, letter, July 27, 1942, FC.
24. Frances Flint to CC, letter, July 27, 1942, FC.
25. CC to Clinton Fink, letter, March 31, 1971, FC.
26. Chris Rodley, ed., *Lynch on Lynch* (New York: Farrar, Straus and Giroux, 2005).

CHAPTER 13: MOUNT HOLYOKE

1. She lived in room 50 of Brigham her freshman year, and on the third floor of Abbey Hall, in room 304, her sophomore year, *Mount Holyoke Bulletin,* 1942–1943.
2. CC, *Pegasus* 23, no. 1, May 1943, FC.
3. During her freshman year, she is also listed as being class song leader and a member of the Blackstick Club—a literary society whose members were chosen for their writing and literary prowess, and who met to write together and workshop one another's pieces (per Mount Holyoke Archives). By the end of her second semester, she was on the Board of Editors for *Pegasus,* to which she contributed the essay detailing her early impressions of the college. Published in the May 1943 issue, the piece features clear, inspired prose about the experience of getting to know classmates. Converse did not declare a major upon entering Mount Holyoke, but class records indicate that her fields of concentration were French and philosophy. She may well have studied with the brilliant European philosophy professor, scholar, and virtuoso pianist Rachel Bespaloff, then on faculty, who was remembered by one of Converse's classmates as "the most incredible teacher. She was tough, and she was hard . . . You took a deep breath before you went into the classroom. She stretched our minds [and] challenged us continually." Renee Scialom Cary, quoted in Christopher E. G. Benfey and Karen Remmler, eds., *Artists, Intellectuals, and World War II: The Pontigny Encounters at Mount Holyoke College, 1942–1944* (Amherst: University of Massachusetts Press, 2006), 270. Bespaloff would die by suicide five years later, leaving behind a note that said she was "too fatigued to carry on." "The Legacy of Rachel Bespaloff, Writer and Teacher," audio,

Roundtable Discussion, Weissman Center for Leadership, Mount Holyoke College, mtholyoke.edu/courses/mackmann/webaudio2/wcl/pontigny/bespaloff.html.

4. Her activities during the summer after her freshman year, in 1943, are unknown. That summer, Mount Holyoke became a hotbed of intellectual and artistic discourse when it hosted "the Pontigny Sessions"—a sort of Chautauqua conference that included heavies like Wallace Stevens, Marc Chagall, Marianne Moore, Robert Motherwell, and Louise Bourgeoise. There's no evidence that Converse attended any of them. Benfey and Remmler, eds., *Artists, Intellectuals, and World War II* ...

5. CC, from TRIES folder, undated, FC.

6. Barbara C. to author, telephone interview, July 14, 2018.

7. Edith was born on December 5, 1920. Edith Neff to author, telephone interview, Feb. 6, 2013.

8. Barbara C. to author, telephone interview, July 14, 2018.

9. Edith Neff to author, telephone interview, Oct. 17, 2015.

10. "The Irene Glascock Poetry Contest ... How the Judges Voted," April 1944, and clipping from unknown newspaper, April 9, 1944, Mount Holyoke College Archives. Eleven years later, a young Sylvia Plath would win the award. Converse also received the Sarah Williston scholastic honor that year.

11. The others were called "The Beggar and His Cat," "They Tell Us the Commuter Shall Have Wings," "The Misbegotten," "Old Gentleman Returning from a Funeral," "Critique of Pure Religion," and "Ask Me Who Made the World." Mount Holyoke College Archives.

12. A letter in her Mount Holyoke student file, written by Robert Francis [likely one of the judges], cites her work as among the finest of that year's crop.

13. Polly Spofford, one of her closest Mount Holyoke friends, decided to drop out of college that spring as well, at the end of her junior year. Spofford left so that she could marry and start a family. Temple Spofford to author, email, Aug. 6, 2016.

CHAPTER 14: FANTASTIC CITY

1. Vassar College Alumni Archives.

2. Benfey, and Remmler, eds., *Artists, Intellectuals, and World War II* ... Recruiting agents from army and navy intelligence were also visiting the campus looking for help with code cracking. Converse was likely aware of this, possibly a reminder to her of the larger world churning beyond the secluded walls of the college.

3. Benfey, and Remmler, eds., *Artists, Intellectuals, and World War II* ...

4. In an unpublished memoir addressed to Frannie Flint, her mother, Dolly, wrote, "The future is so full of horror that you and [Flint's brother] Bob declare you will never have children." Dorothea Flint, unpublished MS, courtesy of Humphrey Morris.

5. Adelaide Aime to author, telephone interview, March 30, 2020.

6. "Report on a Bridge Built over Troubled Waters (and other metaphors)," May 2, 1971, CC to the Committee for Sponsorship of Independent Scholars and Educators, FC.

7. Michael R. Anderson to author, video interview, Sept. 10, 2022. Anderson is director of the International Relations and Global Studies program at UT-Austin; his 2009 dissertation, "Pacific Dreams: The Institute of Pacific Relations and the Struggle for the Mind of Asia," was of great help to me in understanding this milieu.

8. Jan Morris, *Manhattan '45* (New York: Oxford University Press, 1986), 7.

9. Louis Menand to author, telephone interview, May 26, 2022.
10. Some of the best political journalists in the world wrote for their two main publications (the other was *Pacific Affairs,* edited by Owen Lattimore). The IPR had offices stationed all over the world, and was supported by both the Rockefeller Foundation and the Carnegie Endowment for International Peace. Its New York City office, where Converse worked, housed both the American Council of the IPR as well as the larger IPR umbrella organization. In addition to Michael R. Anderson's *Pacific Dreams: The Institute of Pacific Relations and the Struggle for the Mind of Asia* (University of Texas at Austin, August 2009), see also Paul F. Hooper, ed., *Remembering the Institute of Pacific Relations: The Memoirs of William L. Holland* (Tokyo: Ryukei Shyosha, 1995). This was also where she met her friend Edythe ("Edie") Banks, who had begun working there as a stenographer in 1944 and continued on until 1946, when she and her husband, author Richard Banks, moved to Paris. IPR employment records, June 1950, Columbia University Libraries Archival Collections. Converse would stay with the Bankses when she visited Paris in the summer of 1971.
11. Though she refers to the novel several times in her diary and her letters, no trace of it seems to have survived.
12. Thompson was born on April 8, 1924. She died in 1994.
13. Edwin Bock to author, email, April 9, 2022.
14. Inaugurated in 1943, the division was plagued early on by widespread rumors that it was a haven for lesbians and for sexually immoral women, which may have led to the kinds of attacks that Thompson experienced, an incident Bock remembered her describing as "a resisted attempt, not a successful one." On Thompson's WAC application, she listed her occupation as "civilian writer/reporter." U.S. National Archives.
15. O'Neill set part of his early play *Bread and Butter* in a studio based on the one he stayed in there. Arthur and Barbara Gelb, *O'Neill: Life with Monte Cristo* (Guilford, CT: Applause Books, 2002), 421. The play itself can be found alongside much more satisfying O'Neill efforts in the Library of America's definitive three-volume set of his *Complete Plays,* 1988.
16. Soyer (1899–1987) built his reputation on his empathetic renderings of everyday working people, artists, and the down-and-out.
17. They grew up around Daniels Hill, in Metuchen, NJ.
18. Jonathan Barkhorn to author, email, Feb. 9, 2022.
19. Barbara (Ming)'s son, John Aime, described his mother to me as "incredibly thoughtful— someone you would go to with your problems. She always had the right touch—there was a lightness to her personality. She was a big reader, very close to her sisters." John Aime to author, telephone interview, April 4, 2020.
20. After Yale, Aime served in the war and then went on to have a successful career as an airline executive. He married Barbara "Ming" Eby in 1950.
21. Adelaide Aime to author, telephone interview, May 20, 2022.
22. Adelaide Aime to author, telephone interview, March 30, 2020.
23. Anonymous to author, telephone interview, Feb. 14, 2022. This echoes something that the poet Edward Field told me about lefties in New York City back then. He related a comment made by a friend of his, a former member of the Young Communists League: "It was great because [lefties] screwed like rabbits." Edward Field to author, telephone interview, May 27, 2022.
24. John Aime to author, telephone interview, April 4, 2020.
25. CC, from TRIES folder, undated, FC.

26. Howard Fishman, "Connie Converse's Time Has Come," *The New Yorker*, Nov. 21, 2016.
27. Edwin Bock to author, emails, Feb./March 2022.

CHAPTER 15: A DEATH IN THE WOODS

1. The only other letter Converse kept from this time was written to her by someone named John, with a return address of 1612 Yale Station in New Haven. It's entirely unremarkable but for the fact he notes at the end that he's on his way to the post office "to see if you've written me . . ." "John" to CC, letter, Aug. 7, 1942. No other letters from him appear in Converse's effects, nor is there any last name attached to this one.
2. She performed piano recitals there of works by Bach and Scarlatti and graduated with honors. She lived in Strong House, room 404. Vassar College Alumni Records.
3. Flint left Concord to look for work in New York City on September 5, 1945. On October 3, she began working at the ARI. Dorothea Flint, unpublished MS, courtesy of Humphrey Morris.
4. Mrs. Leonard W. Cronkhite, dean of the Radcliffe graduate school, described Flint as "a happy, normal girl." Friends said that "she dated often," though she was not known to have a steady boyfriend. She was also recorded as manifesting "considerable strain and anxiety" and being "in a state of depression" as a student at Radcliffe. *Daily Boston Globe*, Nov. 28, 1947.
5. Margarita Silva-Santiago. The two lived together in Eliot Hall. Subsequent mentions of Flint's roommate refer to Silva-Santiago.
6. Dr. James H. Townsend.
7. The play ran in Boston from November 3 to 15.
8. In *The New York Times* alone, there were 439 items relating to suicide in 1947.
9. On November 5, 1947. He was fifty-eight at the time.
10. He asked that neither he nor his store be named. "Our business is difficult enough right now," he said.
11. Wayland retired police chief Robert Irving was familiar with the historical case. "I found it strange that a person, especially a woman, would shoot themselves with a rifle," he wrote me. "In my career, I remember cases of men shooting themselves with shotguns but never a woman . . . Most women do not choose this method of suicide." When I asked him about the difficulty of the actual act, he wrote, "A lot depends on the length of the rifle and the length of her arms . . . I attended two suicides by shotgun in my career, both by men. One we believe sat on the side of his bed, put, shotgun butt on floor and barrel under chin and reached down and pulled the trigger. The other was lying down on his garage floor and was able to reach the trigger with the barrel against his head. I would consider it possible for Frances to do this, but I find it unusual. My theory is that she was contemplating suicide, decided the method to be self-inflicted gunshot but was only able to purchase a rifle and not a handgun . . . Perhaps the awkwardness in firing the rifle resulted in the fact the bullet did not immediately kill her." Robert Irving to author, email, April 4, 2022.
12. Flint's first cousin Carol Paradise recounted to her sister-in-law Jeanne Paradise that "in his late 20s Bob became 'head of the family,' a responsibility he seemed to take very seriously. Bob was ambitious for Frannie and pressured her to take on more than she could handle . . ." Jeanne Paradise to author, email, April 2, 2017.
13. Other than Phil's recollection of his sister getting her back up about the Concord community's reaction to Flint's end, there is no record of how Converse processed her friend's

death: no mention in her sometime diary and never a single reference in any of the many dozens of her letters in the years and decades that followed.

14. Nelle Chilton, who became part of Converse's social circle when she moved to Ann Arbor in the 1960s, told me a similar thing. "Connie always said that people had a right to take their own life." Nelle Chilton to author, telephone interview, Feb. 6, 2013.

15. Phil C. to author, in-person interview, Sept. 8, 2011.

CHAPTER 16: THE TAKING AND THE KEEPING

1. "I'm writing this so that I can say I've corresponded with you this year," Converse wrote to him there in May of 1947. "Otherwise it would be a total loss . . . We're both going to have to write two-volume autobiographies and exchange autographed copies. You'll have to start at the age of thirteen [his age when she left for college]." CC to Phil C., letter, May 7, 1947, FC.

2. No evidence of Converse living in New Jersey, or with a roommate, has surfaced.

3. Dr. Michael Kahn to author, in-person interview, Apr. 8, 2016.

4. According to the AIPR's internal documents, the staff began holding internal meetings about how to respond to such allegations primarily brought by one of its own members, a businessman named Alfred Kohlberg. Kohlberg saw an opportunity to increase his wealth by wrapping the interests of his business dealings up in jingoistic warnings about the dangers of free trade and how it threatened American interests. When his views were not embraced by his colleagues in the AIPR, he turned on them and reported their activities as suspect. The AIPR was formally investigated by the Senate Internal Security Subcommittee (SISS), aka the McCarran Committee. East Carolina University Libraries, the Cold War and Internal Security Collection (CWIS): SISS.

5. "The office routine has been getting me down for the last two years," she wrote to Phil (CC to Phil C., May 7, 1947, FC). He told me he had no idea where she took the car for those three weeks.

6. Now the Christian Civic League.

7. Daniel Okrent, author of *Last Call: The Rise and Fall of Prohibition*, detailed the ways that liquor laws changed after Prohibition was repealed. New Hampshire was the only place where alcohol could be sold by the state only. Okrent suggested that Ernest Converse's efforts must have played a part in getting such strict regulations passed. Daniel Okrent to author, telephone interview, Aug. 14, 2022.

8. Paul's residence there was recorded on September 5, 1947. He arrived by steamer from Southampton, England, and took an apartment at 152 Madison Avenue while studying for his degree at Yale Divinity School, New York, U.S., Arriving Passenger and Crew Lists (including Castle Garden and Ellis Island), 1820–1957.

9. Conley Chang began working at AIPR in February 1949. The Ohio-born Conley was a recent graduate of the University of Chicago, where she had met her soon-to-be husband, Kuo-ho Chang, then a law student. Kuo-ho and Irene Conley Chang papers, courtesy of Rita Chang.

10. As an interpreter. He was fluent in Mandarin, English, and French. His grandfather had been a Presbyterian minister in Hangzhou. Rita Chang to author, telephone interview, March 30, 2017.

11. Rita Chang to author, in-person interview, Aug. 9, 2017.

12. Waldemar Hille, ed., *The People's Songbook* (New York: Boni and Gaer, 1948). This compendium of American topical tunes was devoted mainly to songs about work, traveling, unions, and protest. It had a foreword by ethnomusicologist Alan Lomax and included traditionals like "Go Down Moses" and "John Henry" and contemporary additions to the canon like "Strange Fruit" along with some of Woody Guthrie's compositions.

13. CC, from TRIES folder, undated, FC.

14. Nadya Chang to author, email, June 16, 2017.

15. Where the nickname "Connie" came from—whether Converse chose it at Mount Holyoke or whether it was bestowed upon her—is unknown. It was not, as Gene Deitch would later erroneously say, because she was from Connecticut (!).

16. Kuo-ho Chang, private diary, July 24, 1949, courtesy of Rita Chang.

17. Kuo-ho Chang, private diary, July 28, 1949, courtesy of Rita Chang.

18. Chang later told me that, after reading through much of her father's diary from that year, she could say that "Johnny was dating women, and seemingly looking for the right woman that year." Rita Chang to author, email, Sept. 18, 2017.

19. Kuo-ho Chang, private diary, July 24, 1949, courtesy of Rita Chang.

20. Clifton Johnson, *What They Say in New England* (Boston: Lee and Shepard, 1896), 190.

21. No last names are included in her account, either, and no one I talked to knew friends of hers by these names. My hunch is that one of them was either a colleague at the AIPR or an old schoolmate from Mount Holyoke and that the other was that person's partner, but really it's anyone's guess.

22. A graduate of Sarah Lawrence College, Carolyn also worked at the AIPR during Converse's time there, albeit briefly. Kizer's biographer, Marian Janssen, wrote to me: "Carolyn and her parents were very close, and Ben was one of the top men in the IPR. When in NYC, [Carolyn's mother] Mabel shared an apartment with Carolyn—and knew her friends. Carolyn was in contact with most of her parents' friends and vice versa. Ben and Mabel, left-liberals, also were forefighters of culture in Republican Spokane. Ben was on all kinds of cultural committees, got artists to come and perform in Spokane, fought for black and Jewish artists, etc. The Kizers knew the Roosevelts, [historian and critic] Lewis Mumford, [poet] Vachel Lindsay, [economist] Harold Laski, [painter] Mark Tobey, [painter] Morris Graves, etc. Everyone who was anybody would go and see them in Spokane, and the Kizers were only too glad to have artists and politicians visit them." Marian Janssen to author, email, May 14, 2020.

23. Lilienthal's daughters, Andrea and Sukey, helped me to confirm the details and timeline of this visit in a series of emails in February and March, 2018.

24. CC, "Notes on a Journey," unpublished MS, undated, FC.

25. "The journey took 26 days," she wrote of her trip. "Cost me $260; traveled 4600 miles by car in 12 days, including stopovers; and 12 days by Greyhound, including all stopovers but the Palo Alto interim. Saw a good bit of the country." From "Notes on a Journey," unpublished MS, undated, FC.

CHAPTER 17: SHE EMERGES

1. Gay Talese to author, in-person interview, June 2, 2016. Kuo-ho Chang's October 28, 1949, diary entry reads, "Went to Connie's house warming party with Irene. All the IPR girls turned out. What a noisy, disorderly + high spirited group. Never knew girls to be that way before. Sang + danced like mad, most of them. Connie, Helen, Irene + myself were the

quietest in the group. Sure thing, after 11 p.m. somebody complained about the noise."
Kuo-ho and Irene Conley Chang papers, courtesy of Rita Chang.

2. In the 1950 Census, Converse is listed as living at this address. Kuo-ho Chang's October 28, 1949, diary entry reads, "Went to Connie's house warming party with Irene. All the IPR girls turned out. What a noisy, disorderly + high spirited group. Never knew girls to be that way before. Sang + danced like mad, most of them. Connie, Helen, Irene + myself were the quietest in the group. Sure thing, after 11 p.m. somebody complained about the noise."

3. On her 1972 résumé, she notes 1950 as being her last year working for *Far Eastern Survey*. "Elizabeth E. Converse Biographical Information (8/72)," typewritten résumé, FC. By that July, the AIPR was in a financial crisis, and an internal document prepared by the secretary of the organization lists a number of potential scenarios for cutting its budget, including terminating Converse. Although her name would continue to appear on the payroll until March 1951, it's likely her services were either bought out wholesale at this point or else diminished to almost nothing. Columbia University Archives. Her last published work for *Far Eastern Survey* came in the February 7, 1951, issue—an essay titled "Pilot Development Projects in India."

4. Jack Gordon, *Fifties Jazz Talk: An Oral Retrospective* (Lanham, MD: Scarecrow Press, 2004), and "New York Songlines: Grove Street," nysonglines.com/grove.htm.

5. CC, Reel 6, Part One, Nov. 30, 1954 (but recorded almost surely several days before that), FC.

6. CC, TRIES, May 3, 1950, FC.

7. "[T]he easy atmosphere of Washington Square, where nobody raised their eyebrows at free love, divorce, or remarriage, where rents were low . . ." Barbara Ozieblo, *Susan Glaspell: A Critical Biography* (Chapel Hill: University of North Carolina Press, 2000), 53.

8. *The Ballad of Greenwich Village,* documentary, directed by Karen Kramer (2005).

9. Penny Jones to author, telephone interview, May 26, 2022.

10. Edward Field to author, telephone interview, May 27, 2022.

11. "Elizabeth E. Converse Biographical Information (8/72)," FC.

12. Michael R. Anderson to author, email, Sept. 13, 2022.

13. Converse wrote to Jean about the novel "which I aim to complete by 1975. Whatever you do, don't stop writing for months at a time as I have done." Phil wrote to her, "Glad to receive news of your writing projects, despite its condescending vagueness . . . Although you refuse to categorize, I suppose what you are working on is a novel, an epic or a dramatic tetralogy." CC to Jean C., Jan. 7, 1951, and Phil C. to CC, letter, "spring 1951," FC.

14. Grouped in a file she labeled "TRIES," the entries are mainly reflections on people, places, and things, some small glimpses into her interior life and state of mind at the time, mentions of what she was reading or had seen at the theater or cinema, at least one full-length book review, and sometimes sentences or paragraphs bulleted with hashtags that appear to be musings she either wanted to record for posterity or else to return to at a later date. These last are mostly undated, making it impossible to know whether they precede or follow the longer, dated entries that run from late 1949 into about halfway through the following year. The fact that she makes mention of the 1948 Nauru riots by Chinese laborers in the phosphate mines of that island nation would seem to suggest that the undated, hashtagged entries begin before the later, more formal entries. She also references the "Noach Levinson archives" in the hashtagged entries; this reference to John Hersey's novel *The Wall* perhaps

suggesting that these were a separate concern from her more formal diary, written concurrently or when the muse struck. The Levinson archives were the basis for the Hersey novel, which she records reading in May 1950.

15. "Flapdragons" also appears in Shakespeare's *Love's Labour's Lost* as a reference to a drinking game in which players snatch raisins out of burning brandy and eat them while they are still burning. More recently it's been used as slang for both the condition of a woman having a venereal disease and for extra-loose vagina lips. www.urbandictionary.com.

16. A monthly journal published by the Book and Magazine Guild, Local 18, United Office and Professional Workers of America, CIO, one of the unions whose leaders were brought before the Senate Internal Security Subcommittee (SISS) for Hearings on Subversive Influence in the Educational Process. There were roughly one hundred CIO and AFL trade union leaders. Eddie Meskin was the organizer of Local 18 of the Book and Magazine Guild, which lasted from 1946 to 1952. From *Subversive Influence in the Educational Process: Hearings Before the Subcommittee to Investigate the Administration of the Internal Security Act and Other Internal Security Laws of the Committee on the Judiciary,* Eighty-fourth Congress 1952, 1st Sess., Part 1.

17. Lawrence Kaelter Rosinger researched and wrote for the journal and for a number of other publications, including *Pacific Affairs, The New Republic,* and the aforementioned *Saturday Review of Literature.* Rosinger was also the author of important books on China and India. He and Converse remained in touch well into the 1960s, after each of them had moved to Michigan.

18. And Mankoff would know. He once gave an interview in which he said he'd submitted some five hundred cartoons over the course of two years before he had his first one published. *The Washington Post,* Nov. 5, 2004. Mankoff's fellow longtime cartoonist Sam Gross looked at a sampling of Converse's collaborations with Rosinger and told me, "The drawing is very good, but it's not *funny.* For the cartoons to work, the drawing itself has to be funny, in some way." Sam Gross to author, telephone interview, May 20, 2022; and Bob Mankoff to author, email, May 6, 2022.

19. It's entirely likely that she made earlier songwriting attempts—Edith Neff told me that her cousin was "always making up songs, always writing poems"—but 1949 is the year Converse gives for her first formal composition.

20. She also writes of reading Faulkner, who "seems to deal heavily in futility and the painful pilgrimage toward an almost ridiculous goal," but whom she finds "brilliant" and "deep," having dipped into a number of his stories and his 1930 novel *As I Lay Dying.* In December she reports, "I went down to Washington to the UOPWA-CIO [United Office and Professional Workers of America—Congress of Industrial Organizations] trial . . . Phil was in town the week before Christmas and I still like him very much. How nice to have a friend in the family. (Paul is an acquaintance.)" CC, from TRIES folder, undated, FC.

21. Anatole Broyard, *Kafka Was the Rage: A Greenwich Village Memoir* (New York: Carol Southern Books/Random House, 1993), 80.

22. Converse was said by so many to have known everything about everything, so, though it may seem far-fetched, I will nevertheless posit the following: When she went about choosing this set of lyrics, she was aware of Barber's music, admired it, and may even have consciously chosen to align herself with this cutting-edge American composer by composing her own setting for the same poem at roughly the same age he'd been when he wrote his. Call me crazy.

23. In many of Converse's guitar songs, I hear echoes of the Carter family. "The Carters had a way of giving voice to . . . unspoken dread. What they cut down into those early recordings (in songs such as 'Will You Miss Me When I'm Gone?') was the sound of a single person facing down the desolate emptiness of uncaring time, a distant, ghostly cry from the darkest hollows: *Don't forget me. I mattered.*" Mark Zwonitzer with Charles Hirshberg, *Will You Miss Me When I'm Gone?* (New York: Simon & Schuster, 2002), 102.

INTERLUDE: DIZZY FROM THE SPELL

1. Michael R. Anderson to author, video interview, Sept. 10, 2022.
2. CC, from TRIES folder, undated, FC.

CHAPTER 18: MUSICKS

1. CC, "Musicks (Volumes I and II)," FC.
2. Phil C., ed., "Connie's Guitar Songs," FC.
3. Based on the hymn "When the Chariot Comes." Other possibilities: In tarot, the number six brings opposites together; in numerology, it brings justice and represents an ideal; in the Bible, it is man and his weakness.
4. For a taste of NYC commuting in that era, watch D. A. Pennebaker's short *Daybreak Express*, shot in 1953.
5. Hsing had by then met and begun dating his future wife, Lily, according to Rita Chang.
6. One of them was Deb Chapman, whom—with her husband—Converse describes as "the happiest, best adjusted, and luckiest couple I've laid eyes on . . .," CC, TRIES, Feb. 5, 1950, FC. They had two children at the time, Mike and Chris. Mike was six, born in 1944. Chris would die the following year, from meningitis. Deb Chapman to CC, letter, "c.1951," FC. The other was Pauline "Polly" Fawcett Spofford (1925–2008), oldest child of Arthur "Spig" Fawcett and Mary Phelps Fawcett. Spofford left Mount Holyoke after three years, in 1944, to marry her longtime sweetheart, William "Bill" Spofford Jr. By age twenty-five, she had delivered five sons, including a set of triplets. What followed was a sixty-year journey crisscrossing the country, balancing a life in which she partnered with her husband in training clergy, parenting her children, and playing an active role in the League of Women Voters, which remained a passion until she died. From "Obituary," *The Oregonian*, Oct. 12, 2008.
7. Owen Lattimore was another of the political heavy hitters alongside of whom she worked. He was Rosinger's co-editor, adviser to Chiang Kai-shek in 1941, and former director of the U.S. Office of War Information for Pacific operations.
8. Born in Chicago (1891–1976). At age forty, Salisbury was described in a newspaper account as "a quiet, studious young man; [he is said to be only thirty-seven here] who looks more like a movie star than a diplomat," and "tall, bespectacled and handsome." *Nassau Daily Review*, Oct. 27, 1931. Salisbury led a fascinating life; his archive is housed at the Hoover Institution at Stanford University.
9. Betty Bouallegue—who would later make Salisbury the godfather of her child Rafet Laurence Bouallegue—to author, telephone interview, Feb. 12, 2017.
10. Where "he brought hundreds of coolies over to the Western Front to dig trenches," according to his friend Sir Laurence Martin. Laurence Martin to author, email, June 12, 2017.
11. Laurence Martin to author, email, June 2, 2017.

12. Back in the States, he rose to the level of acting chief of the Division of Southwest Pacific Affairs before taking the top post at *Far Eastern Survey* a year before Converse's arrival there.

13. A sample entry: "Another weekend with Larry S., whose crochets seem to grow as the swift seasons roll; no cog he, but a marble rolling around loose in the engine. I wonder if there is any distinction between his inner and outer thoughts . . . He seems to have built himself a whole world just to sleep in." (Salisbury was no longer working for the AIPR by this point, which does not seem to have affected Converse's relationship with him.) Her theatergoing at the time included performances of *The Member of the Wedding* and *The Cocktail Hour*. For reading, she'd absorbed Hersey and Seán O'Casey (a favorite), along with Ilya Ehrenburg's *The Storm*. For films, she was enthusiastic about *The Bicycle Thief, The Hasty Heart, Fame Is the Spur,* and *Woman of Dolwyn*; less so about *Adam's Rib* (save for one scene, she wrote) and *All the King's Men*. Other entries from this time indicate that Converse was playing the field, at one point taking a drive to New Jersey with a nameless businessman and wishing he had more to offer in the way of conversation.

14. CC, from TRIES folder, undated, FC.

15. Maggie Berkvist to author, telephone interview, May 27, 2022.

16. This charge can be found in "Pacific Affairs Through War and Peace," University of British Columbia, pacificaffairs.ubc.ca/about-us/our-history/our-secret-history/.

17. CC, from TRIES folder, May 3, 1950, FC.

18. CC, from TRIES folder, undated, FC.

19. CC, from TRIES folder, undated, FC. Hiss was also president of the Carnegie Endowment for International Peace. After two highly publicized trials, he would be convicted of perjury and sentenced to prison. According to Robert Heinold, the son of *Outdoor Life* writer George Heinold (whom Converse would later edit), Salisbury was a staunch supporter of Hiss's, often encouraging him to "keep up the good fight" and "stay strong." Robert Heinold to author, telephone interview, June 25, 2019. Lawrence Rosinger would not be called until 1953, and when he was, he invoked the Fifth Amendment, refusing to acknowledge knowing Hiss. His unwillingness to name names destroyed his career, and he moved with his family to Detroit, where he took a job managing one of his brother-in-law's hardware stores. Rosinger later taught English at Henry Ford Community College. Bill Rosinger to author, email, May 12, 2022.

20. CC to Phil C., letter, Oct. 17, 1951, FC.

21. CC, "The Beggar and His Cat: An Interlude," FC.

22. *4'33"*, Works Index, www.johncage.org.

23. See again Louis Menand's *The Free World: Art and Thought in the Cold War* and its chapter "The Emancipation of Dissonance."

24. Phil and Jean had met at Denison, when they were both students there. The seriousness of their relationship was evidenced by his plans to bring her with him to meet the Converses for Christmas in New England, likely at their parsonage in Florida, MA. CC to Jean C., letter, Jan. 7, 1951, FC.

25. "Spike—Converse, Paul—License to Preach," July 29, 1951, Judson Memorial Church Archive, Fales Library and Special Collections, NYU Libraries. Paul had been granted a "License to Preach" by Judson Church, also known as a Lay Minister's License. Ordination is not necessary for a person granted a Minister's License to render acceptable service in public preaching, teaching, or other ministry skills. A Licensed Minister often fills the gap within a traditional church by relieving the workload of the Senior Minister. What's

interesting here is that Paul received this license from his fellow Denison alum Robert W. Spike (1923–1966), a theologian, social activist, and civil rights leader who worked closely with (and was greatly admired by) Martin Luther King Jr. Davis W. Houck and David E. Dixon, eds., *Rhetoric, Religion and the Civil Rights Movement, 1954–1965* (Waco, TX: Baylor University Press, 2006), 668. Spike was murdered at Ohio State University in 1966, found beaten to death and naked but for a green raincoat. *Springfield News-Sun* (OH), Oct. 18, 1966.

26. Hyla Clark Stuntz, born October 31, 1920, in Lahore, India (now Pakistan). Hyla's parents were Methodist missionaries Clyde Bronson Stuntz and Florence Watters. She attended Smith College, Union Theological Seminary in New York City, and Columbia University and traveled with her parents for their work. By September 29, 1949, she was listed as living at 150 Fifth Avenue in Manhattan (at the corner of Forty-second Street), and the following year she was living with her uncle (also a pastor) at the United Methodist Church at West Fourth Street in the Village. She married Paul on October 27, 1951, at Washington Square Methodist Church, with her uncle performing the ceremony, assisted by Ernest. "Hyla Stuntz Wed to Paul Converse," *The New York Times,* Oct. 28, 1951.

27. Phil C., ed., "Connie's Guitar Songs," FC.

28. Phil also mentions in the letter that they have been playing and singing her "Down This Road" and "The Moon Has No Heart." Phil C. and Jean C. to CC, letter, Aug. 1951, FC.

29. Phil C. to CC, letter, dated "summer 1952?" by CC, FC. Converse went to Battle Creek to visit Phil and Jean that summer, the first of many trips to Michigan that decade.

30. Phil C. to CC, "Thanksgiving," 1952, FC.

31. Phil C. to CC, Jan. 1952, FC.

32. CC to Phil C. and Jean C., Oct. 28, 1951, FC.

33. Linda Duffy to author, telephone interview, Feb. 16, 2022, and email, March 14, 2022.

34. Her final letter of 1951 to Phil and Jean is written from "Grave St." and signed "Cassandra." CC to Phil C. and Jean C., letter, Dec. 12, 1951, FC.

CHAPTER 19: A FAMILY VISIT

1. CC to Phil C. and Jean C., letter, Oct. 17, 1951, FC.

2. "Mother, Dad, Paul, Hyla at Grove St.—1/27/52–33 min—carols and conversation— Woodville, x-mas, 1952," tape reel, FC.

3. In a notch just south of Cannon Mountain, reachable by hiking trails.

4. A three-LP compendium of early blues, hillbilly, string band, and gospel music that served as a lightning rod for the folk and blues revivals to come.

5. As Amanda Petrusich writes in *Do Not Sell at Any Price,* "At the very least, the *Anthology* contextualized—if not accelerated—the folk revival of the 1950s and '60s, coaching new fans about the genre's recorded precedents. The songs Smith included may have only been twenty to twenty-five years old, but they were hardly accessible (or even known) to noncollectors in 1952." *Do Not Sell at Any Price* (New York: Scribner, 2014), 142.

6. Dave Van Ronk and Elijah Wald, *The Mayor of MacDougal Street* (Cambridge, MA: Da Capo Press, 2005), 47.

7. Happy Traum to author, email, Nov. 17, 2020.

8. Ellen Stekert to author, telephone interview, Nov. 19, 2020.

9. Ibid.

10. Van Ronk and Wald, *The Mayor of MacDougal Street,* 42.

11. Bruce C. to author, telephone interview, May 29, 2014.

12. After Francis James Child, who published anthologies of them, with his commentaries, in the late nineteenth century.

13. Sometimes called "traditional" or "old-time" music. As my favorite explanation goes (heard delivered from the stage at a bluegrass festival), there are subtle differences between new country music, old country music, and old-time music. New country music has three major themes: cheating, being rowdy, and trucks. Old country music has three major themes: being away from home, missing a significant other, and trains. Old-time music's three major themes are: going home and finding out that everyone you know and love is dead, going home to make *sure* that everyone you know and love is dead, and going home dead.

14. *Aeschylus I, Orestia*, trans. Richard Lattimore (Chicago: University of Chicago Press, 1953), 71.

15. The *North Adams Transcript* made mentions of the comings and goings of its local population and their families. Every time Ernest and Evelyn hosted family there, it was noted in the paper.

16. CC to Phil C., letter, Dec. 1, 1952. Paul and Hyla were now living at 237 Thompson Street, at the Judson Student House, less than a ten-minute walk from Converse's apartment (CC, Numerical Index of Transparencies with Descriptions, FC), and may have given tapes of Converse's songs to listen to at home. On Christmas Day 1952, Converse recorded Evelyn, Paul, and Hyla taking turns reading. There is stifled girlish giggling throughout. Does the laughter arise from the events of the story, or at their delight at the expert recitation (or at Evelyn's cartoonish New Hampshire accent)? Converse takes over the recitation at the nineteen-minute mark, her voice decidedly less playful and stentorian than her mother's. "Is it a blackbird or a starling?" comes a question in the story at the 20:00 mark, bringing to mind "Honeybee." Paul begins reading at 27:57. Hyla reads last. The giggling is revealed to be coming from Converse—a feminine, coquettish sound that doesn't seem at all in keeping with her character. A "Christmas Song for Peter" ("Mary, Take My Hand") comes in at 59:35. The camaraderie, especially between Converse and Hyla, may be what made Converse feel comfortable joining them on a vacation to Tupper Lake, in upstate New York, the following summer, where the couple had rented a cabin, and to eventually consider living with them in New York City. Tupper Lake was some three hundred miles north of Manhattan—a not-insignificant distance for a weekend jaunt, especially when speed limits were slower. CC to Paul C. and Hyla C., letter, July 16, 1953, FC.

CHAPTER 20: FREE TO BE FREE

1. On East Twenty-second Street near Madison Square Park. Phil wrote about her "taking an offset job" in a letter. (Phil C. to CC, "Dear Frank," Feb. 1952?, FC.) In it, he also offered his extensive feedback (most of it negative) on a story she'd sent him, the title, subject, and contents of which are lost. Converse's résumé, completed in 1972, has her beginning the Academy Photo Offset job in January 1953. During her first year there, she "assisted the Production Manager of the company, and became familiar with the general operations of the shop," according to her boss, N. M. Turkel, in a letter of recommendation he wrote for her ("To Whom It May Concern," Jan. 27, 1961, FC). (Converse also kept her hand in as a writer on Far Eastern relations; in November, a two-part study written with Emily C. Keeffe called "The Japanese Leaders Program of the Department of the Army" was the result of a "special one-year assignment" as operational researcher for the Institute of International Education, and was published in the *News Bulletin of the Institute for International*

Education. "Elizabeth E. Converse Biographical Information [8/72]," FC.) In addition to its printing services, Academy also published books, including a number of titles by artist, scholar, and thinker Saul Raskin, who illustrated his own work and seems to have used Academy as a kind of vanity press. A public listing for the company advertised the services offered as "offset printing, mimeographing, stuff, fold and mail service." Converse's job there came to include proofreading, operating the shop's Fotosetter Correction Device, touching up Fotosetter galleys, working closely with the shop's art director to coordinate typography deadlines, and becoming "a skilled Varitypist," according to Turkel's January 1961 letter.

2. CC to Phil C. and Jean C., letter, April 13, 1953, FC.
3. Though she later listed her professional work in 1951 as consisting of jobs as a freelance editor, there is no record of what this work led to, if any.
4. "In photo-offset printing, typed page proofs and illustrative material were pasted onto sheets of paper with painstaking attention paid to the layout's composition. This layout was photographed and a printing plate was created from the negative by a chemical process. That printing plate was then inked and pressed to a rubber cylinder; the rubber cylinder in turn was rolled over reams of paper, with the still-wet ink, thus 'offsetting' text and images onto the paper sheets." "To Make a Book" (ca. 1960), *Stanford University Press Blog,* stanfordpress.typepad.com/blog/2014/11/to-make-a-book-circa-1960.html.
5. Ron Gordon to author, telephone interview, May 10, 2022.
6. CC to Phil C. and Jean C., letter, April 13, 1953, FC.
7. "Love in the Afternoon," unpublished music MS. Received for copyright on June 16, 1953, Library of Congress.
8. CC, from TRIES folder, undated, FC.
9. CC, "Thunder Mountain," unpublished music MS, received for copyright by the Library of Congress on September 30, 1953.
10. Ishii's Disney career was interrupted when he was swept up in the mass incarceration of Japanese Americans during the war. Upon his release from a camp, and following his marriage to the Shanghai-born Ada Suffiad, the couple moved to New York City in 1949, where Ishii reunited with his old pal Kuo-ho Chang. Naka Ishii to author, telephone interview, March 31, 2020.
11. Naka Ishii to author, telephone interview, March 31, 2020.
12. CC, "Musicks (Volumes I and II)," FC.
13. Another mystery: At the time of the song's writing, in 1951, Dick Van Dyke was not yet a household name. Converse's name-checking him here makes no sense. When I contacted the actor via his friend and colleague Eric Bradley and sent along the song, I was told that Van Dyke listened to it, read the lyrics I'd supplied, and drew a complete blank. Converse was either incorrect in her dating of the composition or else . . . what?
14. A type of song called *Moritat* ("morality tale") or *Küchenlied* ("kitchen song"), similar to murder ballads and popular in Germany, especially in the late nineteenth century, were sung by traveling musicians. A good example is the one that the German film actor Bruno S. performs in Herzog's *Stroszek.*
15. The song even contains a reference to a Daisy Chain, a famous tradition at Mount Holyoke's sister school (and Frances Flint's alma mater), Vassar College.
16. Ellen Stekert to author, telephone interview, Sept. 30, 2021.

CHAPTER 21: BLOOM BY NIGHT

1. He arrived on April 11, 1954. CC, PHOTOS II, FC.
2. Andrew J. Cherlin, *The Marriage-Go-Round* (New York: Knopf, 2009), 70.
3. Mary McCarthy, "Greenwich Village at Night," *New York Post,* Feb. 20, 1950.
4. Anne Bernays and Justin Kaplan, *Back Then: Two Lives in 1950s New York* (New York: William Morrow, 2002), 115.
5. Barbara Smaller to author, email, May 28, 2022.
6. In what may have been a typical evening, Kuo-ho Chang recorded in his 1954 diary that he and Irene were invited to the Ishiis' for dinner and that Bill and Barbara Bernal were there, too. Chang wrote, "Let myself go after a few drinks + a good meal. Played on uke and guitar like mad." Kuo-ho Chang, diary, Sept. 17, 1954, Kuo-ho and Irene Conley Chang papers, private archive.
7. Bernal had first encountered Deitch in Los Angeles in 1946—at the Marine Terrace Garden Apartments—when Deitch posted a notice in *The Record Exchange* magazine indicating that he was looking for a rare Jelly Roll Morton 78 rpm recording of "Smokehouse Blues." Bernal sent him a postcard saying that he had the record, and the two arranged to meet. Gene Deitch to author, in-person interview, Aug. 12, 2013. They became fast friends and began co-hosting listening sessions at which attendees were asked to contribute fifty cents each to various political causes as the cost of admission.
8. Kim Deitch, "Part 6: Almost Adult," *The Comics Journal,* Aug. 11, 2011.
9. Gene Deitch to author, in-person interview, Aug. 12, 2013.
10. (Né Ira Stadlen, 1924–2010.) Swift was known for supplying voices on *The Howdy Doody Show, Underdog,* and *Tom and Jerry* —all franchises that Deitch was also actively involved with.
11. When I played these recordings for Allen Swift's widow, Lenore Stadlen, in 2017, she told me it was not his voice we were listening to. "Allen did not have sustained tones like that," she told me. Lenore Stadlen to author, in-person interview, Feb. 20, 2017.
12. Even Phil was hip to this cultural trend. "I am as much a folk as you are," he'd written to her from his army post in early 1951. "Probably more so. The army's just the place to pick up that pleasant peasant feeling." Phil C. to CC, letter, Feb. 27, 1951, FC.
13. Fred Crippen met Bernal when the two men were living in Detroit, and Bernal then helped him land a job in New York, much as Deitch had done for Bernal. Julia Crippen and Fred Crippen to author, telephone interview, July 29, 2017.
14. "Fortune's Child" was one of a handful of guitar songs Converse later formally arranged for piano and voice.
15. In her diary, Converse alludes with familiarity to: Thomas Wolfe, Milton, Faulkner, Shakespeare, Marlowe, Foucault, Bacon, Mailer, Jonson, Shaw, Chaucer, Dante, Ilya Ehrenburg, Dumas, Tennyson, and Proust.
16. When recording the song again for Phil and Jean in 1956, she wrote them:

> I am much interested in your latching on to Here Is the Door. To the best of my recollection I've never played this for anyone, although I wrote it two or three years ago; and I can't exactly explain why I haven't, except that I never quite finished it to my satisfaction. I had another verse in the middle there starting:
> *I'll tell her this:*
> *If we fear to be forsaken,*

> *Have we not mistaken*
> *The taking and the keeping*

But I could never wind it off right, and I had more in the middle leading from the idea of mere death to the idea of murder; and in general I just couldn't make it go. So when I put it on your tape I just lopped off what I couldn't make go. Maybe it's all for the best.

CC to Phil C. and Jean C., letter, Nov. 4, 1956, FC.

17. There is some confusion as to the exact dates and sequence of Deitch's recordings, as many of them were dubbed in later years onto cassette and then minidisc, in seemingly random order, and some of his original seven-inch reels were lost in a flood. Deitch told me he did not recall what he recorded when, though the complete reel from May 29, 1954, is clearly marked and annotated. Gene Deitch to author, in-person interview, Aug. 12, 2013.

18. Artist Cliff Roberts and his wife. Deitch had met Roberts when the latter attended one of Deitch's record-listening sessions in Detroit, when both men were living there, and they became fast friends. As Deitch's now-defunct website had it, when he got the call to move to New York City and work for UPA, it wasn't long before he convinced the company to send for Roberts as well.

19. Barbara Bernal to author, email, July 2, 2011.

20. Barbara Bernal to Gene Deitch, email, Feb. 10, 2009, in which she forwarded thoughts she'd relayed to *San Francisco Gate* writer Delfin Vigil.

21. Mary Halvorson to author, telephone interview, May 6, 2021.

22. Like Deitch, Swift (Stadlen) lost touch with Converse after she left New York, according to his widow, Lenore. Deitch did record two different versions of "How Sad, How Lovely" (the first without a bridge), three different takes of "One by One," and a couple of experiments with the kind of overdubbing Converse had been trying at home for the two-part vocals on "We Lived Alone" and "Down This Road."

23. Gene Deitch to author, in-person interview, Aug. 12, 2013.

24. The anthology reel is the one Phil digitized when he embarked on his "Connie's Guitar Songs" project.

25. In a later project in which she listed all of her completed compositions (including songs that exist in name only, like "Dark River" and "Long Have I Wandered"), "When Lilacs Last" is indicated as having four discrete parts, each with its own line entry. Using Whitman's original poem as a guide, Deitch's recording is probably a section of what she later called "When Lilacs Last (3)." Like a number of these unknown songs, no other recordings or sheet music for "Lilacs" has surfaced.

26. "A puppet can render opinions on people and things that a human commentator would not feel free to utter," Cronkite wrote later. "I was and I am proud of it." Walter Cronkite, *A Reporter's Life* (New York: Knopf, 1996), 343.

27. Cronkite had already distinguished himself as the anchor of CBS's coverage of the Democratic and Republican National Conventions in 1952 and as the host of the popular program *You Are There*, which offered reenacted historical events in the guise of actual news broadcasts. He would go on to have one of the twentieth century's most distinguished careers in broadcast journalism. See Cronkite, *A Reporter's Life*.

28. The first color TVs would be introduced by RCA later that year.

29. Richard Wirth, "CBS and New York's Grand Central Terminal," ProVideo Coalition, Aug. 10, 2018.

30. Jemal Creary, CBS account coordinator, to author, emails, Feb.–May 2022.

31. Phil and Jean were abroad in France and missed the broadcast. There's no evidence that Ernest and Evelyn, or Paul and Hyla, saw it, either.

32. Kim Deitch, "Part 6: Almost Adult," *The Comics Journal*, Aug. 11, 2011.

33. Terri Thal to author, telephone interview, Nov. 19, 2020.

34. Kim Deitch to author, telephone interview, Oct. 16, 2021.

CHAPTER 22: NOTHING ELSE WOULD DO

1. Phil enrolled at the University of Michigan to get another master's, this time in sociology. The couple rented a small student-type apartment at 1030 East Huron Street, adjacent to the main campus. Peter C. to author, email, Feb. 25, 2020.

2. What made it a pilgrimage, by Converse's lights, is unclear, though Phil would often tell me about his sister's fondness for going to the farthermost points of land. She and Brogan visited the Georgian Bay and the eastern shore of Lake Huron on the trip. CC, PHOTOS, FC.

3. Jean C. to author, telephone interview, Feb. 17, 2017.

4. CC, PHOTOS II, undated, FC. Ernest and Evelyn's new home was at 27 South Spring Street, a block away from their first Concord home.

5. This was something Phil mentioned to me on several occasions. In one email, he went so far as to call Maude's influence "evil." Phil C. to author, email, July 31, 2012.

6. The original poem, "Deux escargots s'en vont pour un enterrement," is a bit of absurdist whimsy: In autumn, two snails depart for the funeral of a dead leaf, but by the time they arrive, it is already spring and all the leaves are blooming again. Taking the advice of the sun above, they get drunk and stagger home.

7. CC to Phil C. and Jean C., letter, Nov. 28, 1954, FC.

8. CC, "Musicks (Volumes I and II)," FC.

9. CC to Phil C. and Jean C., letter, Dec. 15, 1954, FC.

10. The Weill opera was *The Tsar Has His Photograph Taken*.

11. CC to Phil C., letter, Nov. 13, 1954 (in French; translated by Susan Oetgen), FC.

12. The tape begins with what sounds like furniture being moved, and then the Converse family can be heard entering. At no point in the hour-long recording is any mention made of the tape machine running, so unless Converse told her family before their arrival that she would be recording, she did so in secret. The tape is muffled and, at times, difficult to make out, further advancing the idea that the machine was hidden or at least out of sight. Reel 6, Part One, Nov. 30, 1954 (but recorded almost surely several days before that), FC.

13. Omitted from Converse's transcription for Phil and Jean is her mother's question as to whether the opera is written for an orchestra (to which she answers "a small ensemble") as well as the information that the opera has two acts.

14. Paul, Hyla, and P. Bruce went to Concord for the holiday without her. CC to Phil C. and Jean C., letter, Dec. 15, 1954, FC.

15. CC to Phil C. and Jean C., letter, Oct. 12, 1956, FC.

16. CC to Phil C. and Jean C., letter, Jan. 3, 1955, FC.

17. Ibid.

18. CC to Phil C. and Jean C., letter, Jan. 31, 1955, FC.

19. Howard Pollack to author, email, May 22, 2022. Pollack is the author of *Marc Blitzstein*, published by Oxford University Press.

20. "My 3-nights-out-a-week quota system is finally beginning to work. A retyping of the libretto for Act I is being delayed while I go through some hesitations about rearranging the sequence of scenes, which also affects Act II somewhat. But soon, soon." CC to Phil C. and Jean C., letter, Jan. 31, 1955, FC.

21. CC to Phil C. and Jean C., letter, Jan. 3, 1955, FC.

22. I would bet my shirt that Converse was eyeing a debut for the project with the Punch Opera Company, a now long-defunct group based in Greenwich Village that championed new opera and up-and-coming talent (it later became part of New York City Opera). Maude volunteered for them, and in 1952 they staged Vaughan Williams's folk opera *Hugh the Drover.* "Punch Opera Bows July 1," *The New York Times,* June 2, 1952. Brogan listed her volunteer work for the group as lasting from 1953–1956 on her 1971 résumé, located in the Martha Baird Rockefeller Fund for Music Records Collection, Rockefeller Archive Center.

23. One of them reads "1954(?)," though it's clear from her January 3, 1955, letter to Phil and Jean that these sessions had not happened yet.

24. Judith Raskin (1928–1984) had just won the Marian Anderson Award for the second time (in 1953), and would come to be considered one of the greatest lyric sopranos of the twentieth century. "Judith Raskin, Soprano Acclaimed for Musicianship," *The New York Times,* Dec. 22, 1984.

25. Lisa Raskin to author, email, May 28, 2022.

26. Converse disappeared a week after turning fifty; it's unknown whether she lived to see fifty-one.

27. CC, "Lyrics for Tapes," FC.

28. CC to Phil C. and Jean C., letter, Feb. 5, 1955, FC.

CHAPTER 23: HARLEM

1. Barss and Chris Ishii had been stationed in China together during World War II, and both had remained in Asia for some time after the war's end. Barss also assisted with the publication of the magazine *Asia Calling.* Taiya Barss to author, telephone interview, Aug. 3, 2016.

2. William Barss to CC, letter, April 19, 1975 [*sic,* actually 1955], FC.

3. Like many alcoholics, Barss seems to have had a complicated relationship with his children. "I didn't like him that much," Taiya Barss told me. "We were not close. I don't think he was happy being married and a father. He should have been free to go and live his life . . . But he was generous with his talent, showed me proportions, how to draw a face, and let me use whatever paints I wanted to as a kid," she said. Taiya Barss to author, telephone interview, Aug. 3, 2016.

4. Taiya Barss to author, telephone interview, Oct. 8, 2019.

5. Caroll Spinney to author, telephone interview, Sept. 4, 2016.

6. Taiya Barss to author, telephone interview, Aug. 4, 2016.

7. He mentions borrowing her "records" from the Ishiis. It must be assumed he meant tapes. William Barss to CC, letter, April 19, 1975 [*sic,* actually 1955], FC.

8. William Barss to CC, letter, undated ("Back at the Ranch"), FC.

9. William Barss to CC, letter, July 17, 1955, FC.

10. William Barss to CC, letter, Aug. 2, 1955, FC.

11. CC to Phil C. and Jean C., July 18, 1955, FC.

12. Sara, born that December. Peter, Taiya, and Christopher were fourteen, twelve, and two, respectively. A fifth child, Andrew, would be born in 1960.

13. William Barss to CC, letter, Sept. 13, 1955, FC.

14. Barss also knew Amy Schaeffer, a friend of Converse's, so it's possible the two kept up with each other through her. Barss and his wife, Currie, divorced in 1975.

15. Phil, who told me he'd never heard anything about Barss or any significant other in his sister's life, does not seem to have registered this.

16. CC to Phil C. and Jean C., letter, June 22, 1955, FC.

17. CC to Phil C. and Jean C., letter, July 18, 1955, FC.

18. For an affecting remembrance of the scene's early days, see Lee Haring's essay "Rapid Transportation," collected in *The Individual and Tradition: Folkloristic Perspectives*, eds. Ray Cashman, Tom Mould, and Pravina Shukla (Bloomington: Indiana University Press, 2011).

19. John Wilcock, "Music Makers Quit the Square (But Only for the Wintertime)," *The Village Voice*, Oct. 26, 1955.

20. CC to Phil C. and Jean C., letter, July 18, 1955, FC. Bruce Converse told me that it was always his impression that the arrangement was made for financial reasons. As for the racial implications of moving to that neighborhood, he remembers his parents at that time as being "liberal types," both of them involved in the local Democratic Party and both early supporters of the burgeoning civil rights movement. (Bruce C. to author, telephone interview, May 29, 2014.) As evidence of Converse's depleted finances at the time, in a September 19, 1955, letter to Phil and Jean, she asks, with embarrassment, whether she might borrow nine dollars from them (about a hundred dollars in 2022, adjusted for inflation). FC.

21. Jack Elliot recalled hearing Davis on the corner of "about 135th Street in Harlem," *Jack Takes The Floor*, Topic Records, 1958.

22. Elizabeth C. Roberts to author, email, July 10, 2013.

23. When I told Luther's cousin Tim Converse about this, Tim was taken aback. "That's really weird," he told me. Tim Converse to author, video interview, Aug. 13, 2021.

24. Elizabeth C. Roberts to author, Facebook and text messages, July 2013.

25. Her parents fought "a lot," Leslie told me. When Paul became terminally ill, one of her friends told her, "When your father dies, turn on the heat." Leslie C. to author, in-person interview, Jan. 18, 2017.

26. As Harlem scholar John T. Reddick pointed out, that subway stop was typically used by City College students. There was also a movie theater nearby. John T. Reddick to author, email, Aug. 26, 2022.

27. John T. Reddick to author, telephone interview, Aug. 26, 2022; and Jonathan Gill to author, video interview, Aug. 28, 2022.

28. His lover was a colleague at the Student Christian Movement of NYC. He'd been secretly seeing her for months before the family's move to Harlem and was having rendezvous at her apartment, much to the consternation of her then-roommate, Judy Speyer, who later told Hyla that Paul was there "constantly," that the two were deeply involved long before he came on staff at SCM, and that it was her roommate who'd gotten him a job there. Hyla C. to CC, letter, Sept. 3, 1963, FC. Hyla disclosed the details to Converse years later, after she and Paul had separated, telling her about Paul's mistress, "to whom he professed his wholehearted love from 1955–1959 and his hatred and disgust for me." Hyla C. to CC, letter, Dec. 7, 1963, FC.

29. The "Granados: Rondalla Aragonesa," "Chanty," and "Little Suite," respectively.
30. CC to Phil C. and Jean C., letter, Sept. 19, 1955, FC.
31. CC to Phil C. and Jean C., letter, Oct. 6, 1955, FC.
32. CC to Phil C. and Jean C., letter, Dec. 4, 1955, FC.
33. CC to Phil C. and Jean C., letter, Jan. 7, 1957, FC.
34. Bruce C. to author, telephone interview, May 29, 2014.
35. As relayed to me by Luther Converse's ex-wife, who heard the story from him. Barbara C. to author, telephone interview, July 14, 2018.
36. CC, tape boxes and reels, FC.
37. Tellingly, in his audio letter to her that October 1956, Phil gushes to his sister that he'd been playing through "Vanity of Vanities," along with another new piano song of hers she called "The Eliot Bit," and that they were "just the very best things you've ever done" (Phil C. to CC, audio reel, Oct. 1956).
38. "So much of it I find so moving," she wrote to him. "Your paces all so appropriate whether light or stately; and I do so love the quality of your voice." CC to Phil C. and Jean C., letter, Jan. 1, 1957, FC. A week later she writes: "I am simply creamed with delight everytime I hear the way you say 'I will squint at the moon and be peaceful because I am dead'—which is also a small example of how you have turned up delights that I was not before aware of even in poems I knew fairly well . . ." CC to Phil C., letter, Jan. 7, 1957, FC.
39. Phil C. to CC, Reel 50, Side One, "Phil in praise of Musicks," Oct. 1956, FC.
40. Ibid. Phil and Jean also talk about the French songs she has sent them, and ask for clarification of some of the words. It's unclear whether these are unknown Converse originals, though that seems to be case.
41. "I saw ERNANI the other night at the Met. Sometimes I think that Verdi is definitely the all-time opera champeen." Of Stravinsky and Orff, she found the former "moderately interesting" and the latter "a catastrophe," but noted: "Better a few turkeys than an opera season composed of sure-fire time-tested Bohemes and Carmens." CC to Phil C. and Jean C., letter, Oct. 17, 1956, FC.
42. CC to Phil C. and Jean C., letter, Jan. 25, 1957, FC.
43. CC to Phil C. and Jean C., letter, Oct. 12, 1956, FC. Eight months later, in a note postmarked June 27, 1957, and addressed to "Connie Converse," Seeger thanks her for her "contribution to legal defense funds." Although the handwritten note reads perfunctorily, it is significant for the fact that Converse and Seeger were on familiar enough terms for him to address her by her first name and for the fact that Converse, despite her always precarious financial situation, had felt strongly enough about the cause to make a donation. In footage taken from an interview provided to me by Ryan Maxwell, Phil stated unequivocally that Seeger was familiar with his sister's music, and that he had once tried calling Seeger to talk with him about it but Seeger's wife, Toshi, would not give him the phone. Phil C. to Betsy and Ryan Maxwell, March, 2011. The letter from Seeger comes from the FC.
44. CC to Phil C. and Jean C., letter, Nov. 29, 1956. "Recuerdo" was a setting for Edna St. Vincent Millay's poem, and is lost. "I warn you now that the style of the accompaniment is rather remote from Eliot ['The Eliot Bit'] or Tombstone ['Vanity of Vanities'], being closer to Fantastic City [from 'The Prodigal Nephew']. Also it's harder to play than Eliot or Tombstone . . . ," she wrote to Phil and Jean on November 4, 1956, FC. No recordings or sheet music for "Recuerdo" are extant, and she is also referring here to something she titled

"The Eliot Bit," a setting she'd composed for seven lines from T. S. Eliot's poem "La Figlia che Piange." CC to Phil C. and Jean C., letter, Dec. 1, 1956, FC.

45. Linsley was a songwriter in his own right and would go on to write tunes for Buddy Holly and Don McLean.

46. CC to Phil C. and Jean C., letter, Dec. 11, 1956, FC.

47. She also mentions current international politics including the fact that Russia is due for a "whaling," and that China should be admitted to the United Nations.

48. CC to Phil C., letter, Jan. 7, 1957, FC.

49. CC to Phil C. and Jean C., Jan. 11, 1957, FC.

50. CC to Phil C. and Jean C., letter, Feb. 6, 1957, FC.

51. Jonathan Gill to author, telephone interview, Aug. 28, 2022. For more, see Gill's superb *Harlem: The Four Hundred Year History from Dutch Village to Capital of Black America* (New York: Grove Atlantic, 2012).

52. "... Each time I send out an MS [*sic*] I have a little nightmare about how it will sound when *you* play it, and this arises not from lack of confidence in your reading ability but from ditto in my ability as a notational amateur or tyro," she wrote to Phil on January 25, 1957, FC.

53. Phil C. to author, email, Aug. 9, 2011.

54. Phil C. to author, email, May 19, 2011.

55. Dickinson: "I'm nobody! Who are you? Are you—nobody—too?" Dickinson also spent a short time at Mount Holyoke, in 1847.

56. CC to Phil C. and Jean C., letter, Feb. 13, 1957, FC.

57. The quatrain is known as "Westron Wynde" and dates back to at least the sixteenth century. It's also been set to music also by Stravinsky and the Limeliters (among others) and was quoted in Virginia Woolf's *The Waves* and Hemingway's *A Farewell to Arms*. Allen Ginsberg once called it "maybe the greatest poem in the English language" (and even connected it to Jimmie Rodgers's "Waiting for a Train"). "Western Wind" and "A Thousand Miles Away from Home," Allen Ginsberg Project, Nov. 23, 2015.

58. CC to Phil C. and Jean C., letter, Jan. 18, 1957, FC.

59. "Western Wind" and "A Thousand Miles Away from Home," Allen Ginsberg Project, Nov. 23, 2015.

60. John T. Reddick to author, telephone interview, Aug. 26, 2022.

61. CC to Phil C. and Jean C., Jan. 25, 1957, FC.

62. CC to Phil C., letter, Jan. 18, 1957, FC.

63. CC to Phil C., letter, Feb. 16, 1957, FC.

64. CC to Phil C. and Jean C., letter, undated, FC.

65. At one point, the couple went together to Paul's psychologist, who deemed the possibility of divorce unlikely, mainly because of what he determined to be "the real possibility ... that complete personality collapse or suicide may be possibilities." Hyla C. to CC, letter, March 11, 1961, FC.

66. Born June 7, 1956. CC, PHOTOS II, undated, FC. In her 1963 affidavit for her divorce suit against Paul, Hyla wrote that he "had refused to have sexual relations with me since 1957" and refers to her eventually moving out, with the children, because of cruelty and assault. Hyla C. to CC, letter, March 17, 1963, FC.

67. Hyla C. to CC, letter, Feb. 22, 1963, FC.

68. "Hyla has had to take a part-time editing job to help pay the bills because Paul will not work," Converse wrote to Phil and Jean on June 4, 1957. "Hyla seems cheerful about it and

I have suppressed my feeling of outrage." Two months later, she wrote to Phil and Jean about coming home late one night to find Paul "wearing half an undershirt. I don't believe he has really changed in two weeks, but somehow it seemed that he was more feeble and dazed and small—until I realized that I was unconsciously comparing brothers, may the gods forgive me." CC to Phil C. and Jean C., letter, Aug. 11, 1957, FC.

69. Hyla told Converse that Paul had then left her and the kids alone, without access to transportation, telephone, or hot water. "I could not drive and so we were stuck until he came for us ... I had come for a week and was most embarrassed to be left imposing on my sister for two months." Hyla C. to CC, letter, Dec. 7, 1963, FC. Converse's correspondence with Phil and Jean during this time became both more urgent and detailed as the situation continued—one she deemed "beyond my understanding."

70. In one letter, Converse details a late-night conversation initiated by Paul that lasted for a couple of hours. "I offer him the bare little seedling gospel of knowing-and-being-known [a reference to her intimate letter to Phil about relationships from the previous month], but we have gone into that before and I do not get any new feeling that he knows what I am talking about." CC to Phil C. and Jean C., letter, Feb. 6, 1957, FC.

71. CC to Phil C. and Jean C., letter, Feb. 28, 1957, postscript dated March 4, FC.

72. CC to Phil C. and Jean C., letter, June 4, 1957, FC.

73. CC to Phil C. and Jean C., letter, June 8, 1957, FC.

74. During the visit, Converse's father proposed hiring her to ghostwrite a 2,500-word essay for him for a *Reader's Digest* competition. The essay was to be about former New Hampshire governor John Winant, who'd died by suicide in the same year as Frannie Flint's death. "As a dutiful and curious-minded daughter[,] I will see what if anything can be done. I fear that Dad has some mistaken notions about how many non–New Hampshire people retain any interest in the late Mr. Winant." CC to Phil C. and Jean C., letter, June 8, 1957, FC, and CC to Phil C. and Jean C., letter, June 8, 1957, FC.

75. On June 27, she wrote to Phil and Jean to let them know that she'd booked a flight to Detroit, leaving New York City at eleven P.M. on Friday, July 26, and arriving after midnight on the twenty-seventh. She tells them to "keep in mind that this is my gin-and-quinine year, the silver anniversary of the year I discovered that people are people." CC to Phil C. and Jean C., letter, June 27, 1957, FC.

76. Michael Harburg to author, email, Oct. 19, 2020.

77. CC to Phil C. and Jean C., letter, July 14, 1957, FC.

78. The mutual friends were "the Rosens," though Warren did not recall anything more about them when I spoke to her.

79. She also wrote about the songs, "If you decide you can't use them, I'd appreciate having the copies back—I *HATE* to copy music." CC to Annette Warren, letter, July 11, 1957, FC.

80. Converse could have had been dipping into the sometimes misogynistic fiction and drama of August Strindberg and Knut Hamsun—two Scandinavians whose characters sometimes become obsessed by jealousy and questions of paternity. Both writers feature plot points in their work that use the odd color of a child's eyes as evidence of its mother's infidelity. Converse's characters in the song, a witch and a wizard, give birth to an elf who is really the devil, and who has lavender eyes.

81. She offered to make recordings of her versions of "Playboy" and "Roving Woman" and send them to me; sadly, this never happened.

82. Annette Warren to author, telephone interviews, Aug. 1, 2014, and May 3, 2016.

83. CC to Phil C. and Jean C., letter, Aug. 19, 1957, FC. Loesser's publishing company was called Frank Music Corp., now owned by Paul McCartney's MPL Communications. No correspondence or demos related to Converse survive in the company's archives.

84. "You have my permission to sing this song in non-recorded commercial appearances for one year, starting from the date of this letter, and during this period I will not give similar permission to any other professional singer to sing this song . . . If you should want to record it—and I hope the occasion arises!—let me know and we will make some arrangement about it." CC to Elly Stone, letter, July 24, 1959. A year later, Converse wrote, "You offered me $50.00, but I hope the lower fee will help you get a good arrangement of the music," adding that she "shall be delighted to come and view your new penthouse sometime next month, if you get around to it." CC to Elly Stone, letter, Aug. 28, 1960, FC.

85. At the end of December, Converse wrote again to Stone: "I gather you . . . weren't able to use my song, 'How Sad, How Lovely' this fall. Well, maybe someday!! I'm writing now chiefly to tell you that I'm migrating to Michigan for a while . . . I will have a sort of unofficial agent operating for me (in emergencies) here in N.Y.C. His name is . . . Cliff Roberts, 180 Riverside Drive." CC to Elly Stone, letter, Dec. 29, 1960, FC. On the bottom of the carbon copy of the letter kept in Converse's filing cabinet is a note in her hand: "2/61 No reply rec'd. No payment either."

86. Elly Stone to author, telephone interview, Oct. 29, 2014.

87. CC, "A Thousand Shapes and Shades," unpublished MS, registered for copyright with the Library of Congress, Oct. 16, 1957.

88. CC to Phil C. and Jean C., letter, Aug. 11, 1957, FC.

89. When the three took a trip to Grand Bend and East Huron, Ontario. CC, PHOTOS II, undated, FC.

90. CC to Phil C. and Jean C., letter, Aug. 11, 1957, FC.

91. Peter Converse was born on December 3, 1957.

92. Letter, quoted in Blair McClendon, "Radical Acts: The Many Visions of Lorraine Hansberry," *The New Yorker*, updated Jan. 24, 2022.

93. The outfit's headquarters were in White Plains, New York. She was paid seventy-five dollars for "Recorded Voice and Guitar Performances of 'The Twelve Days of Christmas.'" Invoice, FC. No copies of the recording have surfaced.

94. Roland Barthes, *A Lover's Discourse: Fragments*, trans. Richard Howard (New York: Hill & Wang, 1978), 222.

95. Goddard also noted that "you can see all through Converse's variations little subtle alterations to the Happy Birthday theme, with different rhythmic profiles and grooves mapped onto it. The second variation is especially revealing because it employs the inverted form of the theme. And a final unusual element is the length of each variation; Classical sets will always contain a minimum of five or six variations, so to have only three long variations is quite unique." Bruce C. to author, telephone interview, May 29, 2014.

96. Paul was "mentally ill," Hyla wrote to Converse. Trying to accommodate his demands led to a nervous breakdown for her, as it had for his former girlfriend in college. Hyla C. to CC, letter, Nov. 17, 1963, FC. After Hyla moved out, Paul fled to Europe for the summer, "hardly remembering to say goodbye to the children. He overdrew our joint checking account before he left, leaving me with no money at all." Hyla C. to CC, letter, Dec. 7, 1963, FC. By the following April, in 1964, Converse, Phil, and Jean all advised Hyla to take measures to protect herself, with Converse going so far in a wee-hour letter to suggest

arranging professional surveillance of Paul. CC to Hyla C., letter, April 27, 1964, FC. Then, in a May 1964 letter to Converse, Jean, Phil, and Hyla's sister and brother-in-law, Hyla refers to Paul as a "sodomist" and despairs at the options available to her via the courts, which were heavily biased toward men in divorce cases, no matter how bad their behavior. FC.

97. Hyla C. to CC, letter, March 31, 1963, FC. Hyla wrote to Converse that Paul had been physically violent with her, and that police had been called. Hyla C. to CC, letter, Nov. 20, 1962, FC. On Feb. 28, 1959, the family moved to Ridgefield Park, New Jersey. Bruce C. to author, telephone interview, May 29, 2014. They eventually settled into a home at 24 Highland Place. Hyla C. to CC, letter, Feb. 6, 1963, FC. Paul was unreasonable and dangerous to the last; when Hyla finally began divorce proceedings, she confided to Converse her fear that he might rape her as a means of discrediting her case against him. All this information comes from Hyla's letters to Converse, including Hyla C. to CC, letter, Sept. 3, 1963, and Hyla C. to CC, letter, March 5, 1963, FC.

98. Evelyn expressed disapproval of Hyla for not being a more conventional wife. Hyla C. to CC, letter, Feb. 22, 1963, FC.

99. Peter C. to author, telephone interview, Jan. 4, 2014.

CHAPTER 24: CASSANDRA

1. Phil C. to author, email, May 19, 2011.

2. I was not in contact with the Maxwells in 2011 when they were working on a Converse-related project of their own. It wasn't until much later, after the release of *Connie's Piano Songs*, that I learned about Phil's having shared this music with them during their visit to his house.

3. Video footage of the Maxwells' spring 2011 Ann Arbor visit was provided to me by Ryan Maxwell in 2022.

4. For a good discussion of Woolf's immersion into the world of Cassandra, see Yopie Prins's chapter "Otototoi: Virginia Woolf and the 'Naked Cry' of Cassandra," in *Agamemnon in Performance*, eds. Fiona McIntosh, Pantelis Michelakis, Edith Hall, and Oliver Taplin (New York: Oxford University Press, 2004).

5. Joseph Shragge to author, email, Feb. 14, 2022.

6. Emily Pillinger, *Cassandra and the Poetics of Prophesy in Greek and Latin Literature* (Cambridge, UK: Cambridge University Press, 2019), "Introduction."

7. There's also the chance that the title was taken from the novel *Age of Noon* by Henrietta Weigel. Published by Dutton in 1947, the book deals with illicit romance, suicide, and love between women. In Nona Balakian's discussion of the book's leading character, she is described as being "starved for affection, [but] incapable of love or lasting friendship; for she expects everything of others and can give only a counterfeit reflection of herself in return." *New York Times*, Nov. 30, 1947.

8. In the annals of outsider artists whose work was not appreciated in their day, Converse has good company with regard to her habits. Vincent van Gogh "gorged on alcohol, coffee and tobacco to heighten or numb his senses . . . stopped bathing, [and] let his teeth rot." Russell Shorto, "The Woman Who Made Van Gogh," *The New York Times Magazine*, April 14, 2021.

9. James Harrison Monaco to author, telephone interview, Oct. 21, 2021.

10. Phil told me that the manuscript must have gotten lost at some point. The lyrics come from Converse's typed libretto for the entire cycle (see Appendix B).

11. Rachel Kitzinger to author, email, May 21, 2022. Kitzinger is professor emeritus at Vassar College.
12. CC to Mary Critchell, letter, Nov. 10, 1963, FC. (See Appendix B).

CHAPTER 25: "CONNIE CONVERSE SINGS"

1. Cooper was an amateur musician himself and can be heard on a tape recording Converse made on January 4, 1959, at the home of Bill Bernal. On an out-of-tune guitar, Cooper drunkenly performs the songs "Venezuela" and "Delia's Gone" for a crowd of revelers.
2. "She was delightful," Cooper told me. "A plain, simple woman" who transformed when she began performing. Peter Cooper to author, telephone interview, March 1, 2017.
3. Peter Cooper to author, telephone interviews, March 1 and June 6, 2017.
4. Located on Fifth Avenue and West Fifty-seventh Street, the studio was known mostly for commercial advertising work and was run by brothers Hal and Carl Lustig.
5. Peter Cooper to author, telephone interview, June 6, 2017. The tape box bears the inscription "Connie Converse Sings," but Cooper couldn't verify that this was a working title for a potential commercial release.
6. Laurence Salisbury to CC, letter, April 16, 1962, FC.
7. Converse was paid a flat fee of $250 for the composition. Bill Bernal to CC, letter, June 13, 1960, FC.
8. Laurence Salisbury to CC, letter, Feb. 19, 1960, FC. He also wrote, "I recongratulate you on the affluence union membership will bring you. I also hope Ann Arbor will render your soul flexuous." A few weeks later, he wrote to ask for Converse's help in assisting "an 18-year-old Puerto Rican here [who] is trying to market cartoons . . . How about sending me three or four gags that you cartooned and failed to sell? I'll see that he shares profits." Laurence Salisbury to CC, letter, March 23, 1960, FC. As the date of their next rendezvous approached, he wrote again to give her detailed instructions about the train and bus schedule from New York City to Guilford. "I hope you will come in your work clothes. Do not waste time by returning to your apartment to gild the lily." Laurence Salisbury to CC, letter, April 18, 1960, FC.
9. Heinold was born in Madison, Connecticut, on January 14, 1912, and lived there for most of his life before moving to Killingworth for his final six years. He was an editor at *Outdoor Life* magazine until retiring. He also wrote stories published in *Yankee Magazine* and *Reader's Digest.* George Heinold papers, Archives & Special Collections, University of Connecticut Libraries. Converse edited his piece on bone fishing, one that would be published by *The Saturday Evening Post.* George Heinold to CC, letter, Jan. 19, 1958, FC.
10. Laurence Salisbury to CC, letter, Feb. 14, 1956, FC.
11. "May I hire you as a critic to the extent that you will accept a roundtrip ticket, NY to New Haven, in August so that you can read the manuscript here and help me?" Salisbury wrote to her on June 16, 1957 (FC).
12. Laurence Salisbury to CC, letter, Oct. 24, 1957, FC.
13. Laurence Salisbury to CC, letter, Nov. 19, 1959, FC.
14. As Sir Laurence Martin wrote to me (and as I would go and see for myself), Salisbury's home in Guilford was "a very interesting if small one on the river bank designed for him by a student of [architect Walter] Gropious [*sic*]." Laurence Martin to author, email, June 5, 2017.
15. Salisbury was "sometimes depressed," Martin wrote, and may have been anorexic. Laurence Martin to author, email, April 12, 2017.

16. They also made Salisbury the godfather to their son, Rafet.
17. Betty Bouallegue to author, email, Feb. 15, 2017.
18. She also recalled that Salisbury was a kind of patron to a young blind girl pianist in Paris at the time. Betty Bouallegue to author, email, April 6, 2017.
19. ASCAP to CC, letter, Sept. 6, 1960, FC.
20. He eventually gave up on the recording's ever surfacing and was shocked to learn, over a half century later, that Converse had retained a 7½-inch dub tape of the master all along and that it had remained intact.
21. Daughter of playwright, screenwriter, and actor Daniel Reed (1892–1978).
22. Dick Weissman to author, telephone interview, Nov. 11, 2020.
23. Ellen Stekert to author, telephone interview, Nov. 19, 2020.
24. Terri Thal to author, telephone interview, Nov. 18, 2020.
25. The actor James Karen and their son, Reed.
26. James Karen remembered the visit, and described Converse to me as "a pleasant, rangy" woman. James Karen to author, telephone interview, Nov. 25, 2013. The handwriting on the back of the tape box includes: "Converse songs" and "w/Connie guitar."
27. The original run of *The Fantasticks* ran for forty-two consecutive years, a record.
28. Betty Bouallegue to author, telephone interviews, Feb. 11 and 14, 2017.
29. Marcia Barrabee to author, email, Oct. 9, 2011.
30. "A pleasant single-story, three bedroom ranch at 2564 Easy Street . . . in a subdivision in the southeast side of Ann Arbor." Peter C. to author, email, April 2, 2016.
31. "I looked in my diary of my Club, The Fifth Peg, that became Folk City, 58–59, where I listed visitors, before the club was stolen from me," he wrote me, "but couldn't locate her name." Izzy Young to author, email, July 18, 2011.
32. Edith Neff to author, telephone interview, Oct. 17, 2015.
33. It could not, however, save her from her own demons: Arbus died by suicide in 1971.
34. CC to Edie Banks, letter, May 8, 1960, FC.
35. In September 1959, her friend Edie Banks had written her, "I hope you can see your way clear to getting a little green travel document and beating your way to Paris before your plan and my plan for 1961 go into operation . . . and sleep on our living room couch without the borscht or the N.Y. heat getting in the way"—which suggests that Converse may have been planning at least a respite from New York for some time. Edie Banks to CC, letter, Sept. 7, 1959, FC.
36. Phil C. to author, telephone interview, Jan. 31, 2013.
37. Phil C. to author, email, July 22, 2012.
38. A Renault Dauphine, according to Peter Converse. As Pete astutely pointed out to me, that's a small car and it would seem well-nigh impossible for Converse to pack into it with them for this ride. Besides Phil, Jean (who was pregnant), and toddler Pete (and all of their luggage from a year abroad), Converse would also have all of *her* belongings for her relocation to Ann Arbor. So, either Bruce's memory is incorrect, or else they tied a bunch of things to the roof for the drive or rented a trailer. Peter C. to author, email, Feb. 18, 2020.
39. Bruce C. to author, telephone interview, May 29, 2014.
40. On October 14, 1960, Kennedy spoke at the University of Michigan in Ann Arbor on a campaign stop. In a brief speech, he floated the idea of what would become the Peace Corps. It would be officially established by executive order on March 1, 1961. peacecorps.gov/about /history/founding-moment/.

41. E. B. White, *Here Is New York*, collected in *Essays of E. B. White* (New York: Harper Colophon, 1979), 118.

42. The exact month that Dylan first arrived in New York is a matter of some dispute; he told different writers and biographers different things, especially early in his career. Howard Sounes's *Down the Highway: The Life of Bob Dylan* (New York: Grove, 2011, p. 78) has Dylan arriving in Manhattan on January 24, 1961, with Fred Underhill and Dave Berger.

43. Ellen Stekert to author, telephone interview, Nov. 20, 2020.

CHAPTER 26: THE NEAREST STAR

1. Alan Glenn, "The Times, They Were A-Changin'," University of Michigan Alumni Association, alumni.umich.edu/michigan-alum/the-times-they-were-a-changin.

2. Phil C. to author, telephone interview, Feb. 20, 2013.

3. "Elizabeth E. Converse Biographical Information (8/72)," FC. Author Florence Kraut, who also volunteered for Women Strike for Peace in the early 1960s, recognized Converse from photos I sent her from those days. "It was quite a time," she told me. "We were very Left, and there were people in town who didn't like what we were up to. Once, while we were handing out leaflets on the street, we were approached by some angry Right-wingers. We just did what we were trained to do, which was just to sit down. Another time, some of us infiltrated a meeting of the John Birch Society, pretending we were interested in their views. We wanted to see what they were up to. It was a little scary"(Florence Kraut to author, telephone interview, Oct. 1, 2022). Women Strike for Peace "burst upon the American political scene on November 1, 1961, when an estimated fifty thousand women in over 60 cities across the United States walked out of their kitchens and off their jobs in a one-day women's strike for peace." (From *Feminist Studies* 8, no. 3 [Autumn, 1982], 493–520.) The Ann Arbor chapter's informational pamphlet described the group as "a do-it-yourself movement, depending on individual women who move *freely* in and out of our activities as their interest, concerns, energies, time, permit . . . We are unique in our non-structured, chosen, fiercely guarded lack of organization and yet we accomplish a great deal, learn even more, inspire each other . . . No one must wait for orders from headquarters—there aren't any headquarters." (From Amy Swerdlow, *Women Strike for Peace: Traditional Motherhood and Radical Politics in the 1960s* [London: University of Chicago Press, 1993], 70.)

4. "Our basement was like the underground railroad to Canada," her son, David, told me. David Barrabee to author, telephone interview, Sept. 3, 2020.

5. Marcia Barrabee to author, telephone interview, Feb. 21, 2013.

6. Phil C. to author, telephone interview, Jan. 31, 2013.

7. Marcia Barrabee to author, email, Sept. 18, 2011.

8. Hyla C. to CC, letter, Aug. 29, 1961, FC.

9. The list of other performers in the series included Richard Dyer-Bennet, Josh White, and Martha Schlamme. Program for Susan Reed Concert at Kaufmann Concert Hall, Nov. 11, 1961, FC.

10. Mostly chestnuts like "Michie Banjo," "Greensleeves," and "He Moved Through the Fair." Program for Susan Reed Concert at Kaufmann Concert Hall, Nov. 11, 1961, FC.

11. Reed performed the following Converse originals: "Sun, Go Down," "Lullaby for P. Bruce," "There Is a Vine," "Trouble," "Honeybee," "I Have Considered the Lilies," "Fortune's Child," and "Playboy of the Western World." Program for Susan Reed Concert at Kaufmann Concert Hall.

12. Ruth Karen to CC, letter, Nov. 14, 1961, FC.

13. A postscript written in longhand at the top of the typed page notes "My daughter Vicky loves 'Ballad of Cowboy Slim.' And have you heard Joan Baez?" Bill Bernal to CC, letter, Sept. 28, 1963, FC.

14. Sarah Thompson to CC, letter, Sept. 25, 1963, FC.

15. Reed wrote of finding a good male singer to accompany her and said that the two of them made demos of "Sun, Go Down" and "There Is a Vine," which she hoped to shop around to people, including Harold Leventhal. She sent the tape to Converse, who preserved it. Leventhal was, if not the top "folk" manager, then certainly one of the most influential, representing Pete Seeger; the Weavers; Peter, Paul and Mary; et al. If Converse's music was in his ears, it had reached the highest echelons of the business. Susan Reed to CC, letter, March 6, 1964, FC. Converse replied, and included her feedback on her demos. She found "Sun, Go Down" to be "just dandy," but says of "There Is a Vine" that it "seems in this instance to be done too slow and . . . it comes out sort of over-enriched . . . a faster tempo would be more to my taste." She closes by asking whether Reed has a score for "We Lived Alone." CC to Susan Reed, letter, March 15, 1964, FC.

16. Maude Brogan to CC, letter, June 6, 1961, FC.

17. The project may have to do with a book on statistics given to her by Phil and Jean in 1957. "I may be forced to buy textbooks in Statistics 101–2 and 201–2 and sweat a little," she wrote to them upon receiving it. "I thank you heartily, both for the book and the implicit confidence in my central nervous system." CC to Phil C. and Jean C., letter, Feb. 1, 1957, FC.

18. Professor Susan A. Nolan, Ph.D., of Seton Hall University, went on to explain: "If several characteristics of a song were tagged (and it was computerized, as Converse seemed to be trying to do), you could automatically find songs that fit certain categories. You could choose, say, three characteristics and find the songs that had those characteristics in common. It could be really interesting if it showed connections across different types of music . . . If she had stuck around long enough, she may have moved her tagging project to something resembling an algorithm." Susan Nolan to author, email, May 23, 2022.

19. In Walter Isaacson's biography *Leonardo da Vinci*, he notes that the artist "pursued his scientific inquiries not just to serve his art but out of a joyful instinct to fathom the profound beauties of creation . . . His curiosity was pure, personal, and delightfully obsessive" (New York: Simon and Schuster, 2017), 2.

20. Phil C. to author, telephone interview, Jan. 31, 2013. He did suggest that she use IBM cards. Note written on study, dated Feb. 1961, FC.

21. She drew illustrations for them and made a little eight-page booklet with an allegory for Pete. She was "very informal" with them, "affectionate, never strict, supportive, loving." Peter C. to author, telephone interview, Jan. 4, 2014.

22. In Virgil's *Aenid*, Dido flees her home to escape her violent, domineering brother. She helps found the city of Carthage, and eventually kills herself. And in Dante's *Divine Comedy*, Dido is condemned to hell for her lustful promiscuity.

23. Sophie Blackall to author, email, May 22, 2020.

24. Hyla C. to CC, letter, Dec. 7, 1963, FC.

25. Hyla C. to CC, letter, June 27, 1961, FC.

26. Bruce C. to author, email, May 9, 2016. In late 1966, Converse created a "fantasy-full Christmas mobile" for them. Hyla C. to CC, letter, Jan. 1, 1967, FC. In March 1967, she sent

him thirteen dollars (not an insignificant amount for her) for his thirteenth birthday, and he mentions how much he appreciates having her violin. Bruce C. to CC, letter, March 1967, FC.

27. Leslie C. to author, in-person interview, Jan. 18, 2017.

28. Hyla C. to CC, letter, March 31, 1963, FC. According to Bruce C., that August, Hyla took a bus to Washington, D.C., for the March on Washington for Jobs and Freedom and was on the Mall to hear Martin Luther King Jr.'s "I Have a Dream" speech. Family lore has it that Converse met her there, but there's no evidence to support this. Hyla and the boys also visited Ann Arbor, where they stayed with Converse and Phil and Jean. Hyla C. to CC, letter, April 8, 1964, FC. Hyla eventually moved south with the kids to pursue her Ph.D. Bruce C. to author, telephone interview, May 29, 2014. Converse visited them there at least once, in 1965. Hyla C. to CC, letter, Jan. 12, 1966, FC. Hyla died in 1990.

29. He also mentions Shelby Flint's hit song "Angel on My Shoulder," which "sounds as if it had been written by you!" He suggests that it "might help pave the way . . . If one person does it, then that proves it can be done." Bill Bernal to CC, letter, March 3, 1961, FC.

30. There's no way of knowing whether she'd brought her Crestwood recording machine with her from New York City, or if she used whatever machine Phil used to make his own recordings. Given that this is the one and only tape that's surfaced from her time in Ann Arbor, my hunch is that it was the latter.

31. Maude Brogan to CC, letter, June 6, 1961, FC.

32. Amy Schaeffer to CC, letter, Feb. 17, 1961, FC. Amy Lyon Schaeffer (1918–1976) was a reporter specializing in food writing for *The New York Times* in the 1930s, and who went on to be the news and feature editor for the Chinese branch of the Voice of America. It's likely that she and Converse met as neighbors in the Village, when Schaeffer lived on Bedford Street and then on Morton, maybe through Bill Barss, who also knew Schaeffer.

33. Like Brogan, Gerhard never married or had kids. Her nephew told me that she never had a male partner of any kind. Gerhard's niece Katy Carter told me, "Virgie was a great conversationalist. In the 60s I was a Sister of St. Joseph and Virgie and I had lots of conversations about chastity and how to live life without a partner. She had lots of men friends but not romantic partners." Katy Carter to author, email, May 22, 2020.

34. Lisa Raskin to author, email, May 27, 2022.

35. Both Thompson and Brogan did have relationships with men when they were young. Thompson had dated Edwin Bock, and Brogan's premarital affair with an unidentified man had caused her to be consumed by religious guilt, as per the story related to me by Jean Converse.

36. Amy Schaeffer to CC, letter, March 9, 1961, FC.

37. "Anthony" to CC, letter, March 18, 1961, FC.

38. Anonymous to author, telephone interview, Feb. 29, 2020.

39. "Anthony" to CC, letter, March 18, 1961, FC.

40. "Anthony" to CC, letter, May 19, 1961, FC.

41. "Anthony" to CC, letter, undated, likely Aug. 1961, FC.

42. Ed Pierry to CC, letter, Aug. 24, 1961, FC.

43. Stranger still would be the last-known communication from her former co-workers that October. Anthony and Pierry together sent her an illustrated greeting card. On the front is a cartoon drawing of a frazzled-looking man with a noose around his neck, one that has frayed and broken off from the hook it was tied to far above his head. By the panicked

expression on the caricature's face, and the position of his splayed legs, it would seem that he is in free fall. Inside the card are the printed words "How are things . . . Otherwise?" Greeting card, FC.

44. Schaeffer sent Converse suggestions and advice for getting her manuscript into the hands of agents and publishers: "I hope you are enjoying your sabbatical," she wrote, "and that it will continue forever if it enables you to do what you really want to do." Amy Schaeffer to CC, letter, Aug. 10, 1961, FC.

45. Darcy Coyle was the editor. Barss wrote to Converse, "Send the MSS to Coyle without haste. I am quite sure she [*sic*] will do everything possible for you." Later in the letter, Barss writes of staying with Amy Schaeffer in her new Central Park West apartment and laments that he is "so sorry that we shall never see Amy and 71 Bedford St. together again." Bill Barss to CC, letter, Oct. 14, 1961, FC. Coyle's stepdaughter Rebecca was unaware of any papers or manuscript archive that Coyle left behind at his death. Rebecca Coyle to author, telephone interview, Feb. 10, 2022.

46. CC to Ellen Joy Hammer, letter, Jan. 12, 1963, FC. Converse and Ellen Joy Hammer (1921–2001) probably became friends when Hammer was studying at Columbia University in the 1940s, where she specialized in international affairs with an emphasis on Asia. In the 1950s, she became one of the first American scholars of Vietnamese history, publishing the pioneering books *The Struggle for Indochina* and *A Death in November*. Hammer was a close friend and colleague to Prince Nguyen Phuc Buu Hoi (1915–1972), a Vietnamese diplomat, scientist, and cancer researcher, and her correspondence with Converse reveals all three of them to be on close terms.

47. Laurence Salisbury to CC, letter, Aug. 7, no year, but probably 1962, FC.

48. Pearl S. Buck's 1931 novel about life in a Chinese village became a bestseller, won the Pulitzer, and was influential in Buck's becoming the first American woman to be awarded the Nobel Prize for Literature. Laurence Salisbury to CC, Aug. 24, no year, but probably 1962, FC.

49. Laurence Salisbury to CC, letter, Aug. 18, 1963, FC.

50. CC to Ellen Joy Hammer, letter, Jan. 12, 1963, FC.

51. Ibid.

52. Boulding (1910–1993) and his wife, Elise Boulding (1920–2010), were central to the Ann Arbor scene at that time, and both were also devoted Quakers. These quotes come from Kenneth Boulding's *New York Times* obituary, March 20, 1993.

53. The Center's director, Robert Hefner, told me that he'd helped coin the term *conflict resolution* in 1954, when he was a graduate student, as an alternative to *peace*, which had Communist, lefty connotations. Robert Hefner to author, telephone interview, Aug. 28, 2020.

54. "Conversations with History: Kenneth Boulding," March 1987, University of California Television, posted June 12, 2008. youtube.com/watch?v=cLjhaaP9bP8&t=707s.

55. "An Editorial," *The Journal of Conflict Resolution* 1, no. 1, March 1957.

56. Riley Trumbull to author, telephone interview, March 16, 2018.

57. Bruce Weber, "Elise Boulding, Peace Scholar, Dies at 89," *The New York Times*, July 1, 2010.

58. "I'm getting more and more intrigued by the theoretical tools of economics and what they're good for and where they tend to fall apart," she wrote to him. CC to Ken Boulding, letter, July 8, 1963, FC.

59. "While his formal academic training was in mathematics, his writing was also eloquent and innovative when it focused on metatheoretical ideas and philosophy. His research spanned

scientific disciplines through pioneering work applying mathematical models to biology and the social sciences." S. Kopelman, "Tit for Tat and Beyond: The Legendary Work of Anatol Rapoport," *Negotiation and Conflict Management Research (NCMR)* 13, no. 1 (2020): 60–84.

60. Researcher, professor, and author Shirli Kopelman told me that Converse's approach was unusual for that time because it was meta-theoretical. And Rapoport's son Anthony, an accomplished musician and activist in his own right, pointed out that Converse, "by focusing on conflict *definition*, rather than conflict resolution, showed a keen understanding of the potential and limitations of systemization." I spoke to Kopelman and Rapoport together on a video call on September 15, 2022.

61. CC, "Modular Dialog: A Game of Ideas," draft for comment, Oct. 1962, unpublished MS, FC.

62. CC to Kenneth Boulding, letter, Oct. 5, 1962, FC.

63. Peter Critchell wrote to me: "It makes total sense that my mother would have sought to help Connie Converse, once she learned of her and her aims. My mother was very plugged in to university and other intellectual circles in Ann Arbor, including through the First Presbyterian Church, which was a congregating place for them given the national prominence of some of the pastors. She and my father met and married in Japan, during the Occupation—my father being a Captain working in MacArthur's staff in Tokyo whereas my mother had a civilian rank of Colonel (!) and was responsible for promoting democratic education/ideals among Japanese women in Kagoshima. She grew up in Atlanta and had a masters in Guidance from Columbia Teachers College. My father, originally from New York City, was a writer (won an O'Henry award for a story on WWII published in *The Atlantic* and wrote a lauded history of the 101st airborne) and later a PR exec at Ford Motor. [He] died in 1957 and my mother held numerous jobs. She also reached out on numerous occasions to help people where she thought she could. Marina Oswald was in Ann Arbor after the Kennedy assassination, and my mother was one of the number of people who tried to support her. But beyond this, I found numerous instances in her papers of help she provided editing manuscripts for friends who were either publishing or hopeful of publishing and it was completely within her wheelhouse to try and help someone like Connie through whatever contacts she had. Honestly, in many such cases, I think her eagerness and willingness to help, may have exceeded her ability to do so. I should note that, given the prominence of the UofM music department, she would certainly have drawn on those people to try and help." Peter Critchell to author, email, April 8, 2022.

64. CC to Mary Critchell, letter, Nov. 10, 1963, FC.

65. "Elizabeth E. Converse Biographical Information (8/72)," FC.

66. Phil C. to Betsy and Ryan Maxwell, in-person interview, April 2011.

67. Dee Wernette, then a grad student who knew and worked with Converse at the Center, had a different perspective: "*JCR* (and [the] CRCR) was . . . something of a step-child both of the university and of the academic departments within it. So I seriously doubt there was much if any competition for her ME position—given the low status of peace/conflict studies in [that] . . . era, who was eager to get on that bandwagon? Especially since the dominant mindset/ideology in the social sciences at that time (and still I'd suggest) was/is to be value-neutral!" Dee Wernette to author, email, Sept. 15, 2020.

Converse was still keeping her hand in as a freelance editor, but that may have been only as a favor to Salisbury. As late as March 1965, he was still sending her manuscripts for her editing suggestions, and she was still making them. Laurence Salisbury to CC, letters, March 6 and 20, 1965, FC. Her long relationship with Salisbury seems to come to an end with a short note from him that November detailing his Thanksgiving plans. Laurence Salisbury to CC, letter, Nov. 23, 1965, FC.

68. Robert Hefner to author, telephone interview, May 10, 2018.

69. Riley Trumbull to author, telephone interview, March 16, 2018.

70. Riley Trumbull to author, email, March 30, 2018.

71. When Trumbull first moved to Ann Arbor, in 1960, she was known as Caroline Cohen. Riley Trumbull to author, telephone interview, March 16, 2018.

72. Riley Trumbull to author, telephone interview, Sept. 24, 2020.

73. Robert Hefner to Prof. Frank Rhodes, letter, May 22, 1972, Bentley Historical Library, University of Michigan, Ann Arbor (hereafter cited as "Bentley Library") and Robert Hefner to author, telephone interview, Aug. 28, 2020.

74. Robert Hefner to author, telephone interview, May 10, 2018.

75. Riley Trumbull to author, telephone interview, April 5, 2018.

76. John Tropman to author, video interview, March 23, 2022.

77. Jerry Hinkle to author, telephone interview, July 16, 2020.

78. Riley Trumbull to author, telephone interview, March 16, 2018.

79. Edith Neff to author, telephone interview, Oct. 18, 2015.

80. John Tropman to author, interview, March 23, 2022.

81. The teach-in was formed by a group calling itself the Faculty Committee to Stop the War in Vietnam, headed up by Bill Gamson. "The First U of M Teach In, from Resistance and Revolution," history.com/news/anti-war-movements-throughout-american-history.

82. Renowned psychologist Herbert Kelman (1927–2022) told me that the purpose of the conference was "to make use of all of the available academic expertise and intellectual firepower" and focus it on the conflict in Vietnam. "Elizabeth played a big role in the planning of that conference," he told me. Herbert Kelman to author, telephone interview, May 19, 2020. In 1966, he, Converse, and Edward L. Vandenberg edited a publication about the conference called *Alternative Perspectives in Vietnam: Report on an International Conference* (Ithaca, NY: Inter-University Committee for Debate on Foreign Policy, 1966).

83. If stretched a bit thin. The year before, Salisbury wrote, "You imply you are overworking. This is a great mistake, unless it accelerates your progress toward ease and security. Are you doing any writing of your own?" In a postscript, he writes, "I congratulate you on your becoming Man. Ed. of the quarterly and agree that congenial (and adequately paid) work reduces or eliminates value of degrees." Laurence Salisbury to CC, letter, March 25, 1964, FC.

84. On Monday, May 31, 1965, at Concord Hospital. Hyla C. to CC, letter, July 9, 1965, FC; and "Rev. Converse Dies in Concord," *Manchester* (NH) *Times Union,* June 1, 1965. Ernest had been in ill health since at least 1963. Evelyn C. to Marion Dunbar, letter, Sept. 19, 1963, FC.

CHAPTER 27: MARKETS OF THE MIND

1. Claire Eaton Motschman to author (with the help of her daughter, Lori Eaton Wood), email, May 12, 2022.

2. If it seems fair to assume that Converse received something in the way of an inheritance that helped with her move, think again. Although Ernest left her a sizable sum in his will

($19,895.52 or about $177K in 2022 money), she immediately transferred that money back to Evelyn. New Hampshire Merrimack County Probate Records, 1660–1973.

3. Ken Burns couldn't recall the Converse family. Ric Burns did not reply to a query. Author emails, Sept. 25, 2020 (Ken) and May 6, 2022 (Ric).

4. He'd gotten Converse's Michigan address from Ada Ishii. Peter Cooper to CC, letter, June 2, 1966, FC.

5. Peter Cooper to author, telephone interview, June 6, 2017.

6. CC to Peter Cooper, letter, June 7, 1966, FC.

7. Via his colleague Allan Dennis, a director of commercials. Allan Dennis to CC, letter, Aug. 16, 1967, FC.

8. She paid five dollars for a building permit to reserve a two-hour block of time (from seven to nine P.M.). "*Connie's Song* paper," Aug. 21, 1967, FC.

9. The arrangement was by radio and television commercial composer Jimmie Fagas (1924–1982).

10. CC to Allan Dennis, Aug. 28, 1967, FC.

11. Dan Dzula to author, email, Feb. 5, 2022.

12. Marcia Barrabee to author, telephone interview, Sept. 18, 2011.

13. Phil C. to author, telephone interview, Feb. 20, 2013.

14. Ruth Zweifler to author, telephone interview, Aug. 23, 2014.

15. Riley Trumbull said that the keyed-up sexual energy also played out in the workplace at the CRCR in ways that would today be cited for harassment. Riley Trumbull to author, telephone interview, Sept. 24, 2020.

16. Lisa Williams to author, email, March 24, 2014.

17. Dr. Michael Kahn to author, in-person interview, April 8, 2016.

18. Riley Trumbull to author, telephone interviews, March 16, 2018, and Sept. 24, 2020.

19. William P. Barth (1923–2002). Trumbull remembers him telling her that he left his childhood home in rural Missouri on foot when he was eight years old, "sleeping in doorways and trying everything from shoeshine boy to 'bagman' from one gambling den to another, and as a look-out for speakeasies until some business owner unofficially adopted him, got him into school and on to college and the military. His tales always reminded me of that movie *The Champ* with Wallace Beery and Jackie Cooper." Riley Trumbull to author, email, Nov. 24, 2021.

20. Riley Trumbull to author, email, May 6, 2022.

21. Riley Trumbull to author, telephone interview, Sept. 24, 2020.

22. Marcia Barrabee to author, telephone interview, Sept. 18, 2011.

23. As far back as 1957, Converse was talking about her nicotine addiction. A throat infection and its prescribed treatment then had revealed the extent of it: "Ay, it's been more than three long days since I last lit a fag, and I'm drawing up a list of dreadful withdrawal symptoms . . . overeating, drowsiness, inability to concentrate, vertigo, everything tastes lousy. I couldn't do a single creative or intellectual thing this weekend or today," she wrote to Phil C. and Jean C. on Jan. 1, 1957, FC.

24. Riley Trumbull to author, telephone interview, March 16, 2018. Mary "Jill" Ault told me that although she "didn't think of Elizabeth as a drinker," after Converse had left the Center but before it closed, Ault had "found a couple of bottles in the back of her filing cabinet." Mary "Jill" Ault to author, telephone interview, Mar. 20, 2018.

25. Nelle Chilton to author, telephone interview, Feb. 7, 2013.

26. Marcia Barrabee to author, telephone interview, Feb. 21, 2013.

27. Peter C. to author, telephone interview, Jan. 4, 2014.
28. Converse wrote at least one check to Discount Records, on Nov. 17, 1970.

CHAPTER 28: REASONS

1. Riley Trumbull to author, telephone interview, Sept. 24, 2020.
2. "Elizabeth E. Converse Biographical Information (8/72)," FC.
3. CC to Clinton Fink, letter, March 31, 1974, FC.
4. Robert Hefner to author, telephone interview, Aug. 28, 2020.
5. Evelyn C. to CC, letter, Aug. 21, 1968, FC.
6. Phil C. to author, in-person interview, Sept. 9, 2011.
7. A quote Phil never seemed to tire of repeating.
8. Elizabeth Converse, "The War of All Against All: A Review of *The Journal of Conflict Resolution*, 1957–1968," *The Journal of Conflict Resolution* 12, no. 4 (Dec. 1, 1968): 532.
9. Robert Hefner to author, telephone interview, Aug. 28, 2020. As Charles C. McClelland, editor of *Journal of the International Studies Association*, had written in a 1963 letter to the CRCR's director, Robert Angell, "The most common complaint about the JCR is that 'it is hard to read and understand,'" and he suggests that the publication consider including an aid for interpreting its articles. Charles McClelland to Robert Angell, letter, May 13, 1963, CRCR collection, Bentley Library.
10. Kenneth E. Boulding, "Preface to a Special Issue," *The Journal of Conflict Resolution* 12, no. 4 (Dec. 1, 1968): 409–11.
11. Ivan Bojanic to author, interview, Dec. 17, 2021. Bojanic later wrote to me: "To me, as a business and social researcher who spends his days looking for common threads across disparate themes and trends, what she decided to try—and pulled off—was nothing short of staggering." Ivan Bojanic to author, email, May 25, 2022.
12. Part of the lead-up to a "City Seminar on Unintended Racism in Ann Arbor," which Converse helped organize. "Elizabeth E. Converse Biographical Information (8/72)," FC.
13. Robert Hovey to author, telephone interview, March 25, 2019.
14. CC, letter to the editor, *The Ann Arbor News*, Sept. 17, 1963, FC.
15. Raymond Chauncey to author, telephone interview, July 17, 2018.
16. "Group Asks 10 Police-Conduct Steps," *The Ann Arbor News*, May 22, 1969, aadl.org/node /84082.
17. Raymond Chauncey to author, telephone interview, July 17, 2018.
18. Peggy McIntosh to author, email, April 9, 2022. McIntosh (b. 1934) founded the National SEED Project on Inclusive Curriculum (Seeking Educational Equity and Diversity), and is the senior research scientist of the Wellesley Centers for Women. McIntosh was so impressed by Converse's memo, she offered to go through it with me line by line, seminar-style, to study Converse's thinking and approach for our mutual edification.
19. Robin DiAngelo to author, email, April 19, 2022.
20. CC, typescript to Peter Meyers, provided to author, and email, March 4, 2019.
21. Vicki Peters to author, email, May 26, 2022.
22. CC to Peter Meyers, May 31, 1969, courtesy of Peter Meyers. In the wee hours of Thursday, June 5, 1969, Phil drove his sister the fifty-odd miles to Toledo, Ohio, to meet the westbound train that Evelyn and Helen had boarded in Boston. Evelyn C., "Notes on a Grand Tour: May 30–July 7, 1969," unpublished MS, FC.
23. Evelyn C., "Notes on a Grand Tour: May 30–July 7, 1969," unpublished MS, FC.

24. Jean C. to author, in-person interview, Sept. 8, 2011.
25. Marcia Barrabee to author, telephone interview, Sept. 18, 2011.
26. Edith Neff to author, telephone interviews, Oct. 17 and 18, 2015.
27. The two corresponded by mail with some frequency. Most of Converse's letters to her mother do not survive, but many of Evelyn's do, and are mainly concerned with her own domestic preoccupations and finances. A good example was one in which she sent along a local newspaper clipping with a photo. The article described a "historical pageant" that Evelyn had written for the ninetieth anniversary of the Concord Missionary Society and noted that the United Baptist Church in Concord was "packed" for the occasion. "Concord Missionary Society Celebrates Its 90th Birthday," *New Hampshire Baptist News,* November 1963, FC.
28. "Mother Converse was portrayed as a monster," Converse's Ann Arbor friend Rose Wilson told me, "though she didn't seem that way to me." Rose Wilson to author, telephone interview, Feb. 15, 2013.
29. Evelyn C., "Notes on a Grand Tour: May 30–July 7, 1969," unpublished MS, FC.
30. Converse presumably typed the forty-six-page, single-spaced document to allow Evelyn to copy off and distribute to friends and family. The title would seem to reference Converse's account of her 1949 adventure, "Notes on a Journey."
31. Edith Neff to author, telephone interviews, Oct. 17 and 18, 2015.

CHAPTER 29: THE HARD TUG OF THE EARTH

1. William Porter (1918–1999) was a noted journalism professor at the University of Michigan and served on the editorial board of the *Journal of Conflict Resolution.* news.umich.edu /retired-journalism-prof-william-porter-died-at-age-80/.
2. CC to Clinton Fink, letter, March 31, 1971, FC.
3. Riley Trumbull to author, telephone interview, Sept. 24, 2020.
4. The Center recognized her value, and the fact that she was grossly underpaid. In the summer of 1969, Converse's pay increased to $900 per month gross, of which she took home $542.60 net, giving her an annual net salary of $6,511.20 (or $48,555.83 in 2022 money, adjusted for inflation). As she would later write: "Thanks to the Center's efforts—I was zoomed from non academic to academic status and from $7900 to $10,800 . . . a statistical rarity among women in the labor market. I think it's only two or three percent . . . who make over $10,000 a year." CC, "Report on a Bridge Built over Troubled Water (and other metaphors)," May 2, 1971, FC; and "Elizabeth E. Converse Biographical Information (8/72)," FC. Her new co-editor was Clinton Fink.
5. Jean C. to Evelyn C., Sept. 15, 1974, courtesy of Peter C. In April 1970, Converse went to an internal medicine appointment at Ann Arbor's University Hospital; this was followed by a series of diagnostic tests and blood work a few weeks later. CC, medical bills, FC.
6. CC to Clinton Fink, letter, March 31, 1971, FC.
7. Clinton Fink to author, telephone interview, Aug. 23, 2013.
8. Ibid.
9. Tim C. to author, telephone interview, March 27, 2013. He was not the only one to whom she offered her services as a piano teacher. Marcia Barrabee tried to get her son, David, to take lessons from Converse, too, but after only one or two sessions, Converse told Barrabee that her son seemed too resistant to the idea and that she didn't think it wise to force the issue. David Barrabee recalled Converse as heavyset, quiet, and patient, and told me she reminded him "of an old farm girl." David Barrabee to author, email, Sept. 3, 2020.

10. Tim C. to author, telephone interview, March 27, 2013.
11. Tim C. to author, video interview, Aug. 13, 2021.
12. The party was held in James Hall, at Evelyn's church, United Baptist, on the corner of South Street and Fayette Street, from four to seven P.M. Phil told me that although he and Jean were officially listed as co-hosts, his sister had done all the heavy lifting. Phil C. to author, in-person interview, Sept. 8, 2011.
13. Helen Isaacson to author, telephone interview, Feb. 10, 2013.
14. CC to Robert Hefner, unsent draft of letter, March 5, 1971, FC. The English History project is something else that Phil threw out.
15. She kept the typewritten draft, but drew a line through it and scrawled "obsolete" in the upper-right-hand corner.
16. She requested that the leave begin on June 1, 1971. She added that she would like to take the vacation due her for the month prior to that, May 1–31. "I may require hospitalization and surgery within four or five months, but the whole problem is so life-process-connected that a rest in time may save a large incapacitation and expense." CC to Robert Hefner, "final version," March 5, 1971, FC.
17. An obscure reference.
18. "... and I remain fascinated by my half-born project on English foreign and domestic conflict; and I want to set down on paper something about my FEDD idea ... These things constitute a real agenda." CC to Clinton Fink, letter, March 31, 1971, FC.
19. Marcia Barrabee to author, telephone interview, Feb. 21, 2013.
20. CC to Clinton Fink, letter, March 31, 1971, FC.
21. "I don't mean to take full credit for it, but I am the one who initiated the whole thing," Barrabee wrote to me. Marcia Barrabee to author, emails, Feb. 5 and 6, 2013.
22. The sum, $1,800, would be a little over $12,000 today, adjusted for inflation.
23. The letter was presented on April 29, 1971. More than three dozen people contributed, FC.
24. Evelyn C. to CC, letter, May 5, 1971, FC.
25. CC, "Report on a Bridge Built over Troubled Water (and other metaphors)," May 2, 1971, FC.
26. Ibid.
27. CC, passport, FC.
28. She sold the car for $550 (about $3,800 in 2022 money, adjusted for inflation). CC, checkbook register, FC.

CHAPTER 30: THE WORLD AND TIME AND SPACE

1. There does seem to be indication that she visited Hyla and the kids once in the '60s when they were still living in New Jersey, but no details about that trip (including whether she ventured into the city while she was there) have surfaced.
2. CC to Ann Arbor friends, letter, June 6, 1971, FC.
3. CC to Phil C. and Jean C., letter, June 6, 1971, FC.
4. She spent the first night in Sussex Gardens, and wrote of her plans for the rest of the week, which included stays on Praed Street and two nights in Norfolk Square. CC to Phil C. and Jean C., letter, June 6, 1971, FC.
5. CC to Phil C. and Jean C., letter, June 9, 1971, FC. The production had opened in 1952.
6. CC to "Dear People," letter, June 13, 1971, FC.
7. "It must be at least 12 x 15, since it accommodates—without over much crowding—a twin-size bed, a sofa, a sort of coffee table with an old marble top that is just the right height to

type on when you're sitting on the sofa . . . another old table . . . two small chests of drawers, a small bookcase, a straight chair, and a row of kitchen cupboards containing a washbasin and counter space and a hotplate . . . the room is on the first floor (i.e. up one flight) and overlooks the street . . . It is in the Brook Green neighborhood of the Borough of Kensington." She also mentions "this is certainly the longest letter I've written to anybody in at least a decade," which would include the entirety of her time in Ann Arbor—a telling detail. CC to "Dear People," letter, June 20, 1971.

8. CC to Torry Harburg, letter, June 25, 1971, FC.

9. Madeleine Pincott to author, in-person interview, Oct. 18, 2018.

10. Phil C. to author, email, July 10, 2011.

11. CC to Torry Harburg, letter, Oct. 23, 1971, FC.

12. There she stayed with her old friends Edie and Richard Banks, whom she hadn't seen since 1959 in New York. CC, various letters, FC.

13. Converse is referring here to the Winged Victory of Samothrace (also known as the Nike of Samothrace), displayed at the top of the main staircase of the Louvre since 1884.

14. CC to "Dear People," letter, July 21, 1971, FC.

15. CC to Vicki Vandenberg, letter, July 30, 1971, FC.

16. Robert Hefner to author, telephone interview, Aug. 28, 2020. The Black Action Movement (BAM) was formed to promote greater diversity on campus at the University of Michigan and better treatment and higher enrollment of minorities. In early 1970, the group (which included both students and faculty) went on strike because of what it perceived to be the university's lackluster response to its demands. The strike disrupted classes and generated unfavorable press for the school. (Emily Barton, "Birth of the Black Action Movement," *Michigan Daily*, Dec. 1, 2006.) Hefner offered that the university's decision to shut down the CRCR was at least in part a punishment for the Center's support for BAM.

17. A. J. A. Symons, "The Quest for Corvo," *New York Review of Books* (2001), 242.

18. CC to Jean C., letter, Aug. 3, 1971, FC.

19. CC to Vicki Vandenberg and Torry Harburg, letter, Oct. 23, 1971, FC.

20. Ibid.

21. The woman in question was Faith Abbey, who, in 2022, was amused to hear about this encounter but had no recall of it. Faith Abbey to author, telephone interview, May 12, 2022.

22. Mary Shurman was Jean Converse's student when the latter taught senior English at Belleville High School, in Belleville, Michigan. Shurman attended Belleville High from 1955 to 1959. Later, she and her husband became friends with Jean and Phil. They moved to London in 1960, and when Converse's trip was planned, Jean connected the two of them. Mary Shurman to author, emails, April 2017.

23. Converse wrote of the visit: "Had a Reel [*sic*] Old English Family Christmas in Highgate . . . absolutely comparable to anything I have ever observed at an American Family Christmas. At the end of the day, I was dazed, glassy-eyed." CC to Converse family, letter, Jan. 5, 1972, FC.

24. "I remember the children and much excitement and making paper chains with Connie. I do remember she said she was doing 'some writing' but, as I recall nothing specific was mentioned to me. What she did late at night in her room is unknown. Connie's mood was soft, receptive but restrained." Mary Shurman to author, email, March 25, 2017.

25. She would arrive in Detroit on January 20, and gave instructions to Phil and Jean for picking her up there. CC to Converse family, letter, Jan. 5, 1972, FC.

26. For $800.56 in June. CC, Ann Arbor Bank, checkbook register, FC.

27. Jean had spruced up the attic for her the previous summer, before the family left for a trip to Brazil. Jean C. to CC, letter, July 17, 1971, FC.

28. CC to Dean Frank H. T. Rhodes, June 1, 1972, Center for Research on Conflict Resolution, University of Michigan records: 1952–1972, Bentley Library.

29. Converse's replacement as managing editor, Bruce Russett, told me that he had no communication with her at all. Bruce Russett to author, email, Sept. 5, 2020.

30. Robert Hefner to author, telephone interview, Aug. 28, 2020.

31. Phil C. to author, in-person interview, Sept. 8, 2011.

32. "It wasn't that she wouldn't be able to find a job to support herself financially, but rather that such jobs wouldn't meet her other needs. She, like virtually all of us, was a product of her time, background, and social position. And for bright and sensitive types, as I remember her being, that may have led to a personal-spiritual dead end." Dee Wernette to author, email, Sept. 15, 2020.

33. Dee Wernette to author, email, Sept. 10, 2020.

34. Jean C. to Evelyn C., letter, Sept. 15, 1974, courtesy of Peter Converse.

35. On April 16, she paid one hundred dollars for rent from March 21 to May 29.

36. "Elizabeth E. Converse Biographical Information (8/72)," FC.

37. Kostman had gone on to move to New York City, where his experiences as a professional locksmith led him to write the autobiographical book *Keys to the City* (New York: Penguin, 1999).

38. Joel Kostman to author, email, March 27, 2013.

39. "I met Marcia in 1969, at the end of my freshman year at U of M. I knew Lisa, her daughter, who was a high school student in Ann Arbor, through a mutual friend who lived in my dorm. She and I became pals, and she invited me to her house for dinner. Marcia became a kind of surrogate mom for me, and I spent more than a few hours hanging out there." He described Marcia to me endearingly as "a kooky woman." The two continued their friendship after Lisa graduated and moved away in 1972. Joel Kostman to author, email, Jan. 12, 2017.

40. Joel Kostman to author, email, Jan. 12, 2017.

41. Helen Isaacson to author, telephone interview, Feb. 10, 2013.

42. "I think I spent perhaps two or three nights over a period of several months with her at Marcia's and . . . another night at someone else's house, perhaps her brother's." Joel Kostman to author, email, Aug. 13, 2013.

43. Peter Meyers to author, telephone interview, March 14, 2019.

44. Riley Trumbull to author, telephone interview, May 10, 2018.

CHAPTER 31: OUT AND OUT

1. "My grandma's sweet and sour cabbage and tomato soup, or a good thick pea soup with ham and potatoes and carrots, or cold soups like beet borscht with boiled potatoes and spinach soup with hard-boiled eggs in the summer. I'd leave rye bread or pumpernickel hunks to go with them. She loved them all. 'They will put hair on your chest,' she used to say." Marcia Barrabee to author, telephone interview, Nov. 23, 2013.

2. Marcia Barrabee told me that Schensted "worked seventeen-hour days and walked everywhere" and "wouldn't take a car or a bus. She believed that the emissions were ruining the atmosphere. Irene would walk the six miles from her house to class in terrible weather." Marcia Barrabee to author, telephone interview, Feb. 21, 2013.

3. Schensted also told me that Converse "had interesting theories about how organizations behave" and referenced her "Modular Dialog" strategy game. Irene Schensted to author, telephone interview, April 29, 2014.

4. Robert Pirsig, *Zen and the Art of Motorcycle Maintenance* (New York: William Morrow, 1974), 356.

5. John Martin, publisher of Black Sparrow Press.

6. Peter C. to author, email, April 2, 2016.

7. Tim C. to author, telephone interview, March 27, 2013.

8. Tim did not describe his parents as alcoholics, per se. He said that his father, Phil, drank three cans of Stroh's beer every night, and told me how a friend of his had once described his mother, Jean, as a "two-fisted Chardonnay drinker." Both his parents and his aunt Connie enjoyed drinking, he told me, and on the rare occasion when there would be an argument, it was generally fueled by alcohol. Tim C. to author, video interview, Aug. 13, 2021.

9. Tim C. to author, telephone interview, March 27, 2013.

10. Ibid.

11. Peter C. to author, telephone interview, July 15, 2015.

12. Peter C. to author, telephone interview, Jan. 4, 2014.

13. Marcia Barrabee to author, telephone interview, Sept. 19, 2011.

14. A small apartment there would have represented one of the least expensive living situations in town. From there, "she could walk everywhere downtown," Trumbull said. (Riley Trumbull to author, email, May 5, 2018.) Within a two-minute walk were the post office, Keaton's Rec Hall, Midway Lunch, Easley's Barber Shop, Whitman's Pool Hall, DeLong's BBQ, and the Colored Welfare League. The Ann Arbor Community Center was a block away, at 625 North Main Street and the Dunbar Community Center was on North Fourth Street.

15. Initially, she paid $22 weekly, but beginning in April 1973, she paid a monthly rent of $94.20; the next month, $97.34—and it continues like that: $94.20 and then $97.34. A peculiar landlady, no doubt, but it represented some good savings; she'd previously been paying $145 to a "Mr. Maeder" for her place on Oakland Avenue, before moving into Phil and Jean's attic. She had this new address printed on her checks, which seems to indicate that she planned to stay for a while.

16. Peter Converse quoted this line to me over the phone on July 15, 2015. He wouldn't share the complete letter with me because it painted his parents in an unflattering light— his mother's comments about Connie in particular, which he called "uncharacteristically intemperate."

17. Converse paid a total of $132.84 (or almost $900 in 2022) to the Bell Tower Hotel on January 2, 1973.

18. John Tropman to author, interview, March 23, 2022. Peter Di Lorenzi told me the same thing, in a February 26, 2022, email, and others mentioned this misconception to me as well.

19. And Alan Nelson, who remembered Converse and Phil visiting him and his late wife, Marjorie, in the fifties, told me that he always assumed that they were married. Alan Nelson to author, telephone interview, May 5, 2016.

20. Riley Trumbull to author, telephone interview, March 24, 2018.

21. Phil C. to author, telephone interview, Feb. 20, 2013.

22. The first one was created by Denis Detzel and Robert Lewis, students at Northwestern University, who'd been inspired by the book *Deschooling Society* by Ivan Illich. David C. Brake,

"The Case for Decentralized Connected Learning (Part 2: The Learning Exchange)," lrngo.com/blog/2017/01/14/the-case-for-decentralized-connected-learning-part-2-the -learning-exchange/.

23. CC, draft text for Fall 1973 brochure, courtesy of Ed Vandenberg.

24. For a good overview of origins and purposes of the Learning Exchange, see Gregory Douglas Squires's thesis "The Learning Exchange: An Experiment in Alternative Education," Michigan State University, 1974, d.lib.msu.edu/etd/13552/datastream/OBJ/view.

25. Converse and her cohorts applied for nonprofit status, incorporating as "The Learning Exchange of the Huron Valley."

26. Sally Ryan to author, email, April 8, 2022.

27. Sally Ryan to author, telephone interview, March 30, 2022.

28. Nelson Keyes to George McWhorter, letter, Aug. 16, 1973, FC.

29. Elise Isaacson to author, email, July 23, 2018. Saint Christopher was dropped from the Roman Catholic calendar in 1969. britannica.com/biography/Saint-Christopher.

30. catholic.org/saints/saint.php?saint_id=98.

31. "The Movable Feast of Ms. Ex-Saint Philomena," typescript, CC to Ed and Vicki Vandenberg, courtesy of Edward Vandenberg.

32. The group included Harburg and his wife, Torry; Burgess; Converse; a man associated with the Del Rio Bar named Bill Voight; and a few others. ("Special Meeting #3 Re: Purchase of Del Rio Building, Feb. 17, 1974, Notes by Connie," FC.) From the few surviving documents related to this initiative, it's hard to know exactly what role Converse saw for herself once it got established, but she does seem to have put some effort into the idea that one of the new businesses would be a record store and another a community music venue, both of which she appears to have had a vested interest in. A version of the plan eventually succeeded, but Converse had withdrawn her involvement and left Ann Arbor by then. Ernie Harburg to author, telephone interview, May 5, 2018.

33. Ernie Harburg, *Liberty, Equality, Consensus and All That Jazz at the Del Rio Bar* (Ann Arbor: Huron River Press, 2009), 9. The Del Rio has been described as "a combination bohemian sanctuary and bold socioeconomic experiment," annarborchronicle.com/2009/11/10 /column-remembering-the-del-rio-bar/index.html.

34. From "Ann Arbor's Downtown," undated, unpublished typescript, FC. Although Burgess's and Harburg's names are on the document, the ideas, illustrations, and syntax are all Converse's. Harburg confirmed for me my hunch that it was indeed her handiwork. Ernie Harburg to author, May 26, 2022.

35. Jean C., letter, "To Connie and Torry," April 16 and 17, 1974, FC.

36. CC to Jean C. and Torry, letter, April 1974, Monday P.M., FC.

37. Ernie Harburg to author, telephone interview, May 19, 2022.

38. Jean C. to author, in-person interview, Sept. 8, 2011. But Jean's father sent more than that; in a letter she wrote that April, Jean writes that she "acted as a damper and literally talked him DOWN to the $1000 he sent." Jean C. to CC and Tory Harburg, April 16 and 17, 1974, FC.

39. Clinton Fink to author, telephone interview, Aug. 23, 2013.

40. "There were a lot of people back then who objected to using synthetic products to cover up their natural scent," Hefner told me. "I'm sure, at the Center, no one would have minded." But Berenice Carroll was "a persnickety person—very tight and particular." Leslie Hefner to author, telephone interview, Aug. 28, 2020.

41. Riley Trumbull to author, telephone interview, March 16, 2018.

42. Ellen Stekert to author, telephone interview, July 15, 2021.

43. Riley Trumbull to author, email, March 30, 2018.

44. Before I'd first contacted her, Trumbull told radio host David Garland in an on-air interview that the phone call had occurred later, in 1975. But she told me that she'd since realized that this was impossible given the timeline of her divorce from Bill Barth.

45. Riley Trumbull to author, telephone interview, Sept. 24, 2020.

46. Tim C. to author, telephone interview, March 27, 2013.

47. In a 1974 letter to Evelyn, Jean Converse wrote that Converse's doctor had indicated that surgery would be required "if menopause did not come first." Jean C. to Evelyn C., letter, Sept. 16, 1974, courtesy of Peter Converse.

CHAPTER 32: THE DISAPPEARANCE

1. Helen Isaacson to author, telephone interview, Feb. 10, 2013.

2. Tim C. to author, telephone interview, March 27, 2013.

3. Jean C. to author, in-person interview, Sept. 8, 2011.

4. Phil C. to author, in-person interview, Sept. 8, 2011.

5. Peter C. to author, email, April 27, 2016.

6. Ibid.

7. Phil C. to Andrea Kannes, 2010 interview, courtesy of Andrea Kannes.

8. Tim C. to author, video interview, Aug. 13, 2021. He made three statements about this: "I think I was up north with my parents, but I'm not sure"; "I feel like I have a memory of her packing up her car, but I don't think I did"; and "I assume that I was on the trip [with my parents], but I don't know for sure."

9. Phil C. to Andrea Kannes, 2010 interview, courtesy of Andrea Kannes.

10. As this book neared publication, I reached out more than once to Pete and Tim to clarify this and other discrepancies. Neither of them responded to these queries.

11. Peter C. to author, telephone interview, Jan. 4, 2014.

12. CC to Marcia Barrabee, letter, Aug. 1974, courtesy of Marcia Barrabee, email, Aug. 3, 2013.

13. Marcia Barrabee to author, telephone interview, Feb. 23, 2013.

14. CC to Vicki Vandenberg, letter, Aug. 1974, courtesy of Edward Vandenberg.

15. CC to Edward Vandenberg letter, Aug. 2, 1974, courtesy of Edward Vandenberg.

16. CC to Helen Isaacson, letter postmarked "11 August 1974 Ann Arbor." Courtesy of Helen Isaacson. The union Converse had belonged to was the International Typographical Union (ITU). Ron Gordon told me "the union was extremely important in New York City. They controlled everything, and you had to be a member to get a job. It was probably run by the mafia." Ron Gordon to author, telephone interview, May 22, 2022.

17. He did not think it anything momentous at the time, he told me. Tim C. to author, telephone interview, March 27, 2013.

18. CC to Nancy Williams, letter, Aug. 1974, courtesy of Phil C.

19. Rose Wilson to author, telephone interview, Feb. 15, 2013.

20. CC to Evelyn C., letter, Aug. 10, 1974, courtesy of Peter Converse.

21. This note to her mother seems to suggest just how rattled Converse was. She could not keep her narrative together. If she was going to get in touch after getting settled, why would she be telling her mother goodbye? The inconsistency might be evidence that she was ambivalent about exactly what it was she was about to do.

22. "If I'm Long Unheard From" is handwritten, and seems to have been an afterthought.

CHAPTER 33: PAST RECALL

1. When I interviewed private detective Manuel Gomez of Black Ops Private Investigators and told him the story that Phil had told to me, to Dzula, and to others about his conversation with the detective he'd spoken to, Gomez scoffed. "That's bullshit," he said. "That's what we're hired to do. We find people. And when we find them, we record where they are, take a picture, and show it to the client. There's no law anywhere that prevents us from doing that." Gomez holds Counterterrorism and Homeland Security certifications and has worked for the U.S. Department of State. When I asked for his professional opinion about Phil's story, he told me: "It makes him suspicious. To me, it sounds like a cover-up. Even if this person *had* told him some crazy story like that, from what you're telling me, this was not a dumb guy. He was a college professor. He would have gone to someone else, gotten a second opinion, a third opinion. Anybody would do that." Manuel Gomez to author, telephone interview, May 26, 2022.

   When I brought the matter up to Wayland, MA, retired police chief Robert Irving, who'd helped me think about Frannie Flint's death, he wrote to me: "I can think of no law that would prevent [the detective] from telling her brother if he located her. Ethically, if the private detective felt it would not be in Connie's interest or that he could be putting her in danger, I suppose he might not divulge it, but he could certainly inform the brother that she was alive and how she was doing. Also curious that apparently neither her brother nor any other family member reported her missing to authorities. Sure, any adult can leave and not tell anyone if they want, but if the brother felt she was suicidal and a danger to herself, I would think that the least a family member would do is file a report to see if she could be found and potentially helped." Robert Irving to author, email, May 26, 2022.

2. Phil C. and Jean C. to Andrea Kannes, 2010 interview, courtesy of Andrea Kannes. Converse's premium payments with Detroit Automobile Inter-Insurance Exchange appear to be for a policy for high-risk drivers.

3. Phil C. to Bellevue Hospital, letter, Sept. 6, 1974, FC.

4. Helen Isaacson to author, telephone interview, Feb. 10, 2013.

5. Joel Isaacson to author, telephone interview, Feb. 10, 2013.

6. Jean C. to Evelyn C., letter, Sept. 15, 1974, courtesy of Peter Converse.

7. Jean C. to author, in-person interview, Sept. 8, 2011.

8. Everett T. Eaton (b. 1958) to author, telephone interview, June 30, 2022.

9. Evelyn C. to Marion Dunbar, letter, July 1977, courtesy of Elizabeth Dunbar Day. Evelyn eventually moved from her home to an assisted-living facility in Concord called Oddfellows in October 1989, before spending her final year or so near Phil and Jean, at the University Convalescent Hospital in Menlo Park, California. She died on September 7, 1991.

10. Claire Eaton Motschman (with the help of Lori Eaton Wood) to author, email, May 12, 2022.

11. Hyla had gotten a goodbye letter, too, though it has not surfaced.

12. Bruce C. to author, telephone interview, May 29, 2014.

13. Ibid.

14. Phil became director of the Center for Advanced Study in the Behavioral Sciences in Stanford, California, a job he would keep until 1994. Philip E. Converse papers, Bentley Library.

15. Bruce C. to author, telephone interview, May 29, 2014.

16. David Barrabee to author, telephone interview, Sept. 3, 2020.

17. Tom C. to author, email, Feb. 13, 2016.

18. Tom C. to author, email, Feb. 22, 2017.

19. Barbara C. to author, telephone interview, July 14, 2018.

20. Peter C. to author, email, Jan. 4, 2014.

21. During the time when he dabbled with music in his early adulthood, Tim wrote "ten or twelve songs" and briefly considered a music career. Tim C. to author, telephone interview, March 27, 2013. He still plays piano from time to time, and was a generous benefactor of the premiere production of *A Star Has Burnt My Eye.*

22. Peter C. to author, email, Jan. 4, 2014.

23. CC, check boxes 1968–73, FC.

24. A sampling of the subscriptions Converse paid for beginning in 1968 until she left for England include: *Ramparts, New York Review of Books, Scientific American, The New Yorker,* and *I. F. Stone's Bi-Weekly.* She held Stone's publication in high enough esteem to archive them in her filing cabinet; Phil later threw them out during his consolidation.

25. The Del Rio Bar, where she was said to hang out frequently, did not take checks. Ernie Harburg, *Liberty, Equality, Consensus and All That Jazz at the Del Rio Bar,* 2nd ed. (CreateSpace Independent Publishing Platform: 2009).

AFTERWORD

1. Peter Guralnick puts this idea more eloquently, and might as well be talking about Connie Converse in his discussion of the 1960s "discovery" of Robert Johnson: "The point is that [he] never went away. We may congratulate ourselves on our perspicacity in finding our way to the music—but in fact the music has always had the power to find its way to us . . . This is the thing I think we have to keep straight. Art is always there to be found. It's up to us to open our eyes and ears. Even now there is some contemporary Robert Johnson, some painter, some poet, some unacknowledged novelist, performance artist, musician, waiting to be discovered, and if we are fortunate enough to make that discovery, we are uplifted by it. But our presence in the room makes not the slightest difference to the vitality of the work.

"Art is a mystery. Where does it come from? It arrives unbidden, out of nowhere; it shows up when we least expect it. If it is too calculated a bid for greatness, most likely it will reveal its seams. It is not the product of a finishing school or a creative writing program; it springs full-blown from the head of Zeus." *Looking to Get Lost* (New York: Little, Brown & Co., 2020), 10, 12.

POSTSCRIPT: THE FALL OF A LEAF

1. Deitch had been living in Prague since the late 1950s, and there were any number of tracks featuring Czech ensembles performing songs from the "Trad Jazz" repertoire—music mostly first created in, or inspired by, the era just before swing (and big band and bebop). Garland, known for exploring the reaches of alternative, non-mainstream music on his show, had little appetite for most of what he heard, giving them each a polite listen before forgetting them entirely. David Garland to author, interview, March 21, 2022.

2. Kim Deitch told me that it was actually his brother Seth who, one day sometime in the 1990s, said to him something like, "Hey, remember that singer Connie Converse? Wonder whatever happened to those recordings of her singing at our house?" This then led to one

of them asking their father about it, and to Deitch locating the tapes after having not thought about her for many years. Kim Deitch to author, in-person interview, Aug. 21, 2022.

3. David Garland told this story from the stage at the *Connie's Piano Songs* CD release show at Le Poisson Rouge in New York City on February 17, 2014.

4. At the time, Dzula and his brother Mark had a band called the Magic Caravan, a multimedia alt-vaudeville outfit that included guerrilla puppet shows, skits, narrative slide presentations, and 16 mm cartoons. The ensemble had succeeded in hitching its wagon to the Bindlestiff Family Cirkus, a bigger, more successful concern that had just taken up residence at a venue the Bindles were calling the Palace of Variety (at the now-demolished Chashama Theater in Times Square). The Magic Caravan was gigging there, and over winter break, Dzula was commuting back and forth from his parents' house in New Jersey for the shows. Dan Dzula to author, in-person interview, Aug. 13, 2016.

5. *Spinning on Air* broadcast, WNYC radio, Jan. 9, 2004.

6. Before podcasts and archiving became commonplace, streams of shows like Garland's were typically hosted on a radio program's website for a short window of time and then disappeared forever. Dzula remembers that he wanted to make sure to grab this one. Dan Dzula to author, in-person interview, Aug. 13, 2016.

7. The Magic Caravan, always a bit too large and unwieldy to be sustainable, was reconfigured into an educational kids' outfit called Jukebox Radio. One of the band's members, Alexis Krauss, would go on to help form the pop band Sleigh Bells; another, Elle Varner, has had success as a solo artist. Dan Dzula to author, email, June 15, 2022.

8. Dan Dzula to author, telephone interview, Jan. 8, 2015.

9. Dzula told me that placement in brick-and-mortar stores was limited to specialty outlets on the coasts and in Chicago. Dan Dzula to author, in-person interview, Aug. 13, 2016.

INDEX